The CHRISTIAN *Bed & Breakfast* COOKBOOK

The CHRISTIAN *Bed & Breakfast* COOKBOOK

Edited by
Rebecca Germany

BARBOUR
PUBLISHING, INC.
Uhrichsville, Ohio

Front cover illustration compliments of Cliffside Inn
in Newport, Rhode Island.

ISBN 1-55748-950-5

Published by Barbour Publishing, Inc., P.O. Box 719, Uhrichsville, Ohio 44683 http://www.barbourbooks.com

Printed in the United States of America.

Table of Contents

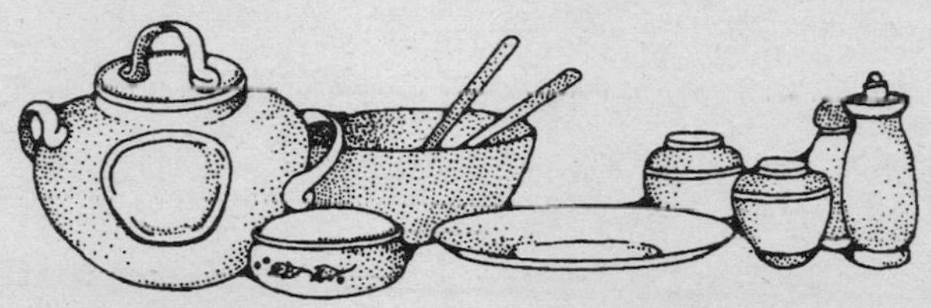

Joy
in the Morning

General Breakfast Dishes

"My voice shalt thou hear in the morning, O Lord; in the morning will I direct my prayer unto thee, and will look up."
Psalm 5:3

Grimmon House Bed and Breakfast

John and Myrna Grimmon
1610 15 Avenue
PO Box 1268
Didsbury, Alberta, CANADA
T0M 0W0
(403) 335-8353; FAX (403) 335-3640

Often our young guests preceed their parents downstairs in the morning. To ensure quiet for other guests and provide parents time to enjoy their wake-up coffee, children are invited to gather at the kitchen table to participate in this fun-for-all breakfast craft. This craft allows me to continue with breakfast preparation and the children are supervised. One nine-year-old guest writes she had "the bestest time ever." What more could we ask for?

A Breakfast Portrait

- 1 tablespoon milk for each color desired
- 4-5 drops food coloring of any color
- Bread slices

Combine milk and food coloring in very small containers. With a cotton swab or small brush, each child is encouraged to paint a face onto the piece of bread. When completed, toast the bread on a medium setting. Each child is encouraged to present this "portrait" to the person it represents. Great fun and laughter when dad eats off his left ear.

Breakfast in a Cookie

1/2 cup canola oil
1/2 cup unsweetened applesauce
1/2 cup brown sugar
1/4 cup egg substitute
1 tablespoon vanilla extract
1 tablespoon orange juice
1 tablespoon lemon juice
1/2 cup oat bran
1/2 cup 7-grain cereal
1/2 cup all-purpose flour
1/2 cup whole wheat pastry flour
1 teaspoon baking soda
1/2 teaspoon salt
1 teaspoon ground cinnamon
1 teaspoon ground allspice
1/2 teaspoon ground cloves
3 cups old-fashioned oats
1 cup golden raisins
Optional: 1/4 cup unsweetened coconut and/or 1/4 cup chopped walnuts (these items do add significant fat to the recipe)

Preheat oven to 350°. In a large mixing bowl, beat together with electric mixer oil, applesauce, and brown sugar. Add egg substitute, vanilla, and juices, then beat again. Sift together oat bran, 7-grain cereal, flours, baking soda, salt, and spices. Mix these ingredients with the wet mixture. Stir in oats. Fold in raisins (and other optional ingredients if you wish). Place dough on ungreased cookie sheets by the tablespoonful. Bake 15 minutes or until golden. Remove cookies from the sheet immediately and cool. Yield: 3 dozen large cookies.

The Manor at Taylor's Store B&B Country Inn

Lee and MaryLynn Tucker
Route 1, Box 533
Smith Mountain Lake, VA 24184
(540) 721-3951; (800) 722-9984;
FAX (540) 721-5243

We serve our full breakfast in the formal dining room between 8:30 and 10:00 since most of our guests are on holiday and want a more leisurely start to their day than they are used to. However, we also have guests who are very early risers and head out to go fishing, hiking, or just exploring. We set up an early coffee pot for them in the guest kitchen and leave them a nice plate of fresh fruit, a can of juice, and a couple of these delicious "Breakfast in a Cookies". Makes you feel like a kid to eat such a delicious treat for breakfast, and they are so tasty, you'd never suspect they're good for you, too!

Cliffside Inn Bed and Breakfast

2 Seaview Avenue
Newport, RI 02840
(401) 847-1811

Nestled upon a quiet neighborhood street just steps away from the historic Cliff Walk, the Cliffside Inn displays the grandure of a Victorian manor with the warmth and comfort of a home. A full breakfast, consisting of homemade muffins, granola, fresh fruit, and a hot entree, such as Eggs Benedict or whipped cream topped French toast, is served each morning in the spacious parlor. Victorian teas is served from 4:30 to 5:30 P.M.; A morning coffee and juice service is available from 7:00 to 9:00 A.M. There are thirteen guest rooms, each uniquely decorated in period Victorian antiques blended with luxurious Laura Ashley linens and drapes.

Cliffside Inn's Granola Recipe

4 1/2 cups rolled oats (not cereal)
3 cups sunflower seeds
3 cups raw chopped almonds
1 cup safflower oil
1/2 cup malt syrup extract
1/2 cup maple syrup
1 tablespoon vanilla
1 1/2 tablespoons ground cinnamon
1/2 teaspoon almond extract
pinch of ground cloves

Preheat oven to 325°. Mix dry ingredients in a large bowl, heat rest of ingredients. Mix liquid with dry ingredients and stir well. Bake in two 9x13 pans for 25-30 minutes until golden brown. Stir a few times while baking to ensure even browning. Let cool and store in covered container. Enjoy!

Hill Farm Inn Low-Fat Granola

1 cup raw rolled oats
1/3 cup chopped walnuts
1/3 cup raw wheat germ
1/3 cup unhulled sesame seeds
1/3 cup sunflower seeds
1/3 cup shredded coconut
1/3 cup chopped banana chips
1/4 cup brown sugar

Place oats and nuts in large, heavy skillet (we use cast iron); place over medium-low heat and roast for five minutes, stirring often. Add wheat germ, sesame seeds, sunflower seeds, coconut and banana chips. Continue to stir and dry roast for ten more minutes. Add brown sugar — stir and roast two more minutes. Cool; store in airtight container.

Hill Farm Inn

George and Joanne Hardy
RR 2, Box 2015
Arlington, VT 05250
(802) 375-2269; (800) 882-2545;
FAX (802) 375-9918

This recipe has been a favorite for many years. It is much lower in fat than most granola recipes because it is dry roasted in a pan on top of the stove and there is no added oil. If fat content is a really serious concern, it would be possible to reduce the amount of coconut, or even omit it. Of course, it is always possible to adjust the sweetness by adding more or less brown sugar to taste.

The Seal Beach Inn and Gardens

Marjorie Bettenhuasen
212 5th Street
Seal Beach, CA 90740
(310) 493-2416; (800) HIDE-AWAY; FAX (310) 799-0483
As of 2/1/97, the new area code will be (562)

Elegant, historic Southern California inn, one block from ocean beach in a charming, prestigious, seaside town next to Long Beach. Lush gardens, lovely estate appearance. Exquisite rooms and suites. Pool, library, and kitchens available. Complimentary full breakfast and social hour served with genuine warmth and attention. Short walk to restaurants, shops, and beach pier. Three freeways close by. Easy drive to major Los Angeles attractions and business centers.

Inn-Made Granola

8 cups regular (old-fashioned) rolled oats
1 1/2 cups wheat germ
1/2 cup coconut
1 cup chopped dried fruit
1 cup sliced almonds
1 1/2 cups brown sugar, firmly packed
1 1/2 cups unprocessed bran
1 cup raisins
1 cup dried bananas
1 cup sunflower seeds
3/4 cup vegetable oil
1 1/4 cups honey
3 teaspoon vanilla

Combine oats, wheat germ, coconut, fruit, almonds, brown sugar, bran, raisins, bananas and seeds in a large mixing bowl. Set aside. Heat oil, honey and vanilla and combine thoroughly with first mixture. Place on large cookie sheet. Bake at 350° for 30-40 minutes, checking at 10-minute increments until nicely browned. Stir granola as it cooks to break up mixture. Yields 16 servings.

Briar Rose Granola

Blend together in a large bowl:

6 cups regular rolled oats (NOT instant or quick oats)
1 cup coconut
1/2 cup raw sunflower seeds
3/4 cup pecan or walnut pieces
3/4 cup raw cashew pieces
1/6 cup sesame seeds

Mix until well combined:

1/2 cup canola oil
1/2 cup honey
1/3 cup warm water
1 1/2 teaspoon vanilla

Pour over the dry ingredients.

Mix ingredients together, stir until well coated. Spread in a thin layer on two cookie sheets. Bake on a middle rack, at 325°, until golden brown. Check after 15 minutes and stir browned edges to center. Push center to edges. Repeat checking and stirring at 5-minute intervals. Cool thoroughly when browned to taste. Add 1 cup raisins (or to taste).

The last few minutes of baking and stirring are very important to getting just the desired crispness and golden color. Lock the kitchen door if you must, but checking the granola at least every 5 minutes during the last 15 minutes of baking is a MUST. Set the timer!

In addition to the ingredients listed, you can experiment with a variety of dried fruits and berries to match your palate, and add variety.

Briar Rose Bed and Breakfast

Margaret and Bob Weisenbach
2151 Arapahoe Avenue
Boulder, CO 80302
(303) 442-3007; FAX (303) 786-8440

The Briar Rose Granola goes back as far as the history of the Briar Rose. The original recipe was introduced by Emily Hunter in 1981, just after she opened the Inn. Since that time, some small modifications have been made, but the recipe remains virtually the same. The granola is a favorite of guests, and we proudly give away many copies of the recipe to guests who ask. The smell of freshly baking granola fills the house, and draws guests to the kitchen whether it's afternoon or evening. They can't wait until breakfast to give it a try.

Real Boulderites eat their granola sprinkled over yogurt, and topped with fresh berries. Many of our guests have never tried granola this way and are wonderfully surprised at the luscious combination of sweet and tart flavors. We also serve a lot of granola in bowls with milk and fruit.

Bed and Breakfast at The Pines

Richard and Donna Hodge
327 Ardussi Street
Frankenmuth, MI 48734
(517) 652-9019

The source of the original recipe was A Taste of the Country *magazine and was submitted by Wilma Beller of Hamilton, Ohio. (I have never met Wilma but believe she should receive credit.) I have added the nutmeg and cinnamon as well as the almond extract. All additions are enjoyed by our guests. The low amount of oil makes the granola truly healthy and nutritious as well as delicious. We serve it with milk or yogurt plus fruit as guests desire. The granola has become a staple and favorite item served at the Bed and Breakfast at The Pines.*

The Pines Granola

Pour 4 cups old-fashioned oatmeal into large roasting pan (9x13). Heat oats in 350° oven for 5 minutes. Remove from oven, stir, heat 5 minutes more.

Heat together:

1/3 cup honey
1/4 cup oil

Remove from heat and cool, then add:

1 teaspoon vanilla extract
1 teaspoon almond extract

Combine together:

1 cup chopped nuts (pecans are good)
3/4 cup bran cereal
1 cup flaked coconut

Add to heated oats and mix thoroughly. Pour honey-oil mixture over oat mixture. Mix thoroughly.

Add:

1 teaspoon cinnamon
1 teaspoon nutmeg

Return to oven, bake at 350° for 20 to 25 minutes, stirring about every 5 minutes for even browning.

Remove from oven and add:

1 cup raisins
1 cup chopped dates

Mix thoroughly. Cool and store in an airtight container. Makes about 8 cups of finished granola. Our granola is excellent served with milk or yogurt and fruit, for breakfast or snack!

Michigan Baked Oatmeal

2 cups old-fashioned oats
4 cups milk
1/2 teaspoon almond flavoring
1/4 cup brown sugar
1/2 cup sliced almonds
1/2 cup dried cherries
1 large apple, grated, unpeeled

Preheat oven to 400°. Coat a 3-quart baking pan with cooking spray. In a large mixing bowl, combine all the ingredients, except the almonds. Transfer to the baking dish. Sprinkle the almonds on top. Bake uncovered for 45 minutes. Serve hot. Makes 6-8 servings.

The Parish House Inn

Mrs. Chris Mason
103 S. Huron Street
Ypsilanti, MI 48197
(313) 480-4800; (800) 480-4866;
FAX (313) 480-7472

This is usually served with a quiche, since they can bake at the same time. The dried cherries are a Michigan product and I use as many local products as possible. This very unusual recipe always causes a discussion among the guests, and is very popular with repeat guests. The consistency is more like a pudding than the traditional "gooey" oatmeal. It would make a nice better dish baked in a pretty casserole.

Millstone Inn

Paul and Patricia Collins
PO Box 949
Cashiers, NC 28717
(704) 743-2737; (888) 645-5786;
FAX (704) 743-0208

This is an old favorite at the inn and is requested more than any other dish, ever, in the summer! We get requests for the recipe everytime we serve it.

Our inn was selected by Country Inns *magazine as one of the best twelve inns. Millstone Inn has breathtaking views of the Nantahala forest. The exposed beams are complemented by the carefully selected antiques and artwork. Our guests enjoy a gourmet breakfast in our glass-enclosed dining room overlooking Whiteside Mountain.*

Baked Apple Oatmeal

4 cups milk
1/2 cup brown sugar
2 tablespoons butter
1/2 teaspoon cinnamon
2 cups old-fashioned oats
2 cups chopped apples
1 cup raisins
1 cup chopped nuts

Preheat oven to 350°. Bring milk, sugar, butter, salt, and cinnamon to boil in a heavy pot. Add the remaining ingredients and bake uncovered for 30-35 minutes in buttered casserole dish.

Serve with banana or strawberry and accompany with cream and honey (on the side) so the guest can adjust its consistency and sweetness.

Baked Peach Oatmeal

1 cup oil
2 cups sugar
4 eggs, beaten
6 cups oatmeal
2 teaspoons baking powder
2 teaspoons salt
2 cups milk
2 teaspoons vanilla
1 can (or 6 cups) either: peaches, pears, plums, or cherries, diced or sliced, fresh, or canned.

In large mixing bowl, combine oil, sugar and eggs. Add oatmeal, baking powder, salt, milk, vanilla. Add fruit and mix gently. Pour into prepared pan. Bake at 350° for 30-35 minutes.

Three Hills Inn

Doug and Charlene Fike
PO Box 9, Route 220
Warm Springs, VA 24484
(540) 839-5381; (888) 23-HILLS;
FAX (540) 539-5199

This recipe is great for company. This is one of our most popular. Even those who don't normally like oatmeal like this!

Our inn is a casually elegant retreat in a beautifully restored historic manor. Spectacular mountain views, acres of woods and trails — serenity at its best! We have missionary backgrounds and speak fluent Spanish. From a romantic getaway to an executive retreat (meeting/conference facility), our inn is the perfect choice for the discriminating traveler.

Annie's Bed and Breakfast

Anne and Lawrence Stuart
2117 Sheridan Drive
Madison, WI 53704
(608) 244-2224; FAX (608) 242-9611

This is a recipe much beloved by my guests. I've had requests for it from as far away as Germany and Australia! I serve it as a main course, along with a plate of fragrant bacon, sausages, and English muffins topped with sharp cheddar cheese. Our eight children were raised on good Wisconsin dishes such as this!

Cranberry-Apple Breakfast Pudding

4 cups skim milk in big, microwave-proof, bowl
1/2 cup brown sugar
1/2 teaspoon salt
2 tablespoons butter

Heat this until very hot, but not boiling, about 5 minutes on high heat.

Add in order:
1/2 box golden seedless raisins
2 cups uncooked old-fashioned oatmeal
4 to 5 large red delicious apples, cored, sliced thin, not peeled
1 cup fresh cranberries (or may used dried). If fresh, cut in half, and shake in a small bag with 1/4 cup brown sugar
1 cup chopped nuts, either pecans, walnuts, or almonds

Mix well. Put into buttered stoneware bowl and bake in preheated oven at 350° for thirty minutes.

Stir to integrate fruit throughout. Serve in bowl with dollop of caramel sauce or/and sweetened sour cream and cinnamon.

This will serve 8-12, depending long they've been enjoying the fire and the Sunday morning papers and coffee!

Homemade Muesli Breakfast Cereal

1 cup quick rolled oats
1/2 cup apple juice
2-8 ounce cans crushed pineapple, in juice
1 cup 100% bran cereal
1/4 cup oat bran
1 cup raisins
1/4 cup each optional ingredients (chopped apricots, dates, chopped prunes, coconut, raisins, and/or nuts)

Combine all ingredients in airtight container and refrigerate overnight. Serve with milk or plain yogurt.

Behm's Bed and Breakfast

Bob and Nancy Behm
166 Waugh Avenue
Wilmington, PA 16142
(412) 946-8641; (800) 932-3315

Muesli was introduced to me in Scotland when served by my son and his wife. They topped it with kefir, which they made from their own goat's milk. Yogurt comes close, but many of our guests choose to eat it plain.

Madam Dyer's Bed and Breakfast

Linda and Larry Brown
1720 Post Office Street
Galveston, TX 77550
(409) 765-5692

This is my most requested recipe. Our guests love it. We use this as a "starter" before the main breakfast course. I place a small amount of flavored liquid cream (French vanilla) in the bottom of small individual pedestal dishes and spoon a portion on top. Sometimes I serve this in pretty china teacups with saucers.

Granola Pudding

3 cups Kellogg's lowfat granola cereal
1 egg, slightly beaten (or 2 egg whites for non-fat cooking)
1 1/2 cups milk (or use skim milk)
1 tablespoon sugar

Spray casserole dish with cooking spray. Place the cups of granola cereal into casserole dish. (1 quart or 1 1/2 quart works great). In small bowl mix together egg, milk, and sugar. Pour over the cereal in casserole dish. Bake at 350 degrees approximately 20-25 minutes, until set but not dry. Let stand 10 minutes. Serve warm. Serves 6-8.

This dish can be assembled the night before and baked in the morning.

Baked Apples

4 medium cooking apples, peeled and cut into 8 slices
1/2 cup brown sugar
1/4 cup maple syrup
1 cup water
2 teaspoons Minute Tapioca
1/8 teaspoon cinnamon
raisins (optional)

Combine all ingredients except apples and simmer for five minutes. Combine apples and syrup mixture in baking dish and bake at 400° for 45 minutes.

Apple Pancakes

1 medium apple, cored and chopped
1 1/3 cups milk
1 egg
1/2 teaspoon cinnamon
2 cups baking mix

In blender, puree the apple, milk, egg and cinnamon; add baking mix. Fry on a hot, lightly oiled griddle. Served with Apple Syrup.

Apple Syrup

1 cup sugar
2 tablespoons cornstarch
2 cups apple juice
2 tablespoons lemon juice
1/4 cup butter

Mix sugar and cornstarch in a saucepan, add juices. Cook, stirring constantly, until mixture thickens and boils. Boil and stir 1 minute. Remove from heat; blend in butter.

Hospitality Plus

Charles and Joan Budai
7722 Anne Circle
Anchorage, AK 99504
(907) 333-9504

Hospitality Plus specializes in serving "theme" breakfasts. Here is the menu and recipes for our famous apple breakfast. Serve with apple juice (of course) and pork/apple breakfast sausage.

Diamond District Bed and Breakfast Inn

Sandra and Jerry Cavon
142 Ocean Street
Lynn, MA 01902
(617) 599-4470; (800) 666-3076;
FAX (617) 595-2200

We serve home-cooked, plentiful breakfasts and make vegetarian and low fat options available at our gracious 1911 inn. We feature a grand staircase winding up the three floors, a spacious fireplace living room with ocean view, finished in Mexican mahogany, French doors leading to an adjacent large veranda that overlooks the gardens and ocean.

My mother sent me this recipe from a newspaper and I adapted to all made from scratch.

Breakfast Pizza

Dough:
- 1 package yeast (active dry)
- 1 cup warm water (105° to 115°)
- 1 teaspoon salt
- 2 teaspoons olive oil
- 2 1/2 to 3 1/2 cups flour

Toppings:
- 1 pound bulk sausage
- 1 cup shredded potatoes
- 1 cup grated sharp cheddar cheese
- 5 eggs
- 1 small onion, minced
- 1/4 cup milk
- dash Habenero pepper
- salt and pepper
- sun-dried tomatoes

Make pizza dough by first combining flour, oil, and salt. Knead 2 minutes then add water and yeast. Knead 2 minutes more. Put into PAM sprayed bowl. Cover and put in refrigerator overnight. Roll into individual rounds and place in 4 1/2 inch tart pan. Sauté sausage and onions, drain on towel. Add to dough in pan. Arrange potatoes first, salt and pepper, then sausage and onion, tomatoes, and cheese. Beat eggs and milk. Pour over dough. Bake at 375° for 30 minutes.

Guests love individual pizzas. I change ingredients with fresh vegetables or no sausage. You can add feta cheese also. Good to eat on the go.

Easy Breakfast Pizza

1 pound pork sausage
1 package refrigerated crescent rolls
1 cup shredded cheddar cheese, or
 Monterey Jack cheese
5 eggs
1/2 teaspoon pepper
2 teaspoons grated Parmesan cheese

Cook crumbled sausage until browned. Drain fat. Roll out crescent rolls until flat, on bottom of 12 inch ungreased pan. Spoon sausage over crust. Top with shredded cheese. In a bowl beat eggs, milk, a little salt and pepper. Pour over cheese and sprinkle with Parmesan cheese. Bake at 350° for 30 minutes.

Alpine Lodge

Dr. and Mrs. David Livingston
5310 Morgantown Road
Bowling Green, KY 42101
(502) 843-4846; (888) 444-3791
or 6293

We serve a typical southern breakfast of eggs, sausage, biscuits, gravy, fried apples, grits, coffee cake, coffee, and orange juice. The breakfast pizza is nice for an occasional change of pace.

Our Alpine Lodge is a spacious, Swiss chalet-style home that has over 6,000 square feet and is located on eleven and a half acres. The furnishings are mostly antiques.

We are retired musicians who can often be persuaded to play something for our guests' pleasure.

Riverside Bed and Breakfast

Lynn and Nancy Perey
2231 Thiel Road
Laurel, MT 59044
(406) 628-7890; (800) 768-1580

I serve this family-style to my guests. That way the heartier eaters can take as much as they want. I also serve fruit and muffins as accompanying dishes. It is a fantastic breakfast

We are on a main route to skiing and Yellowstone National Park. Guests can fly fish the Yellowstone from our backyard, soak away stress in the hot tub, llinger and llook at the lloveable llamas, take a spin on our bicycle built for two, and enjoy a peaceful sleep and a friendly visit.

Easy Breakfast Pizza

1 pound sausage, browned
1 package crescent rolls
5 eggs, or equal substitute
1/4 cup milk
12 ounces frozen hash browns, thawed
1 cup cheddar cheese, shredded

Unroll crescent rolls and press in 9x13 inch pan. Spoon sausage over crust, sprinkle hash browns, sprinkle cheese over hash browns. Beat together eggs and milk, pour over top. Bake at 375° for 25-30 minutes, until bottom crust is browned and center set. Serve with salsa. Serves 8-10. Reheats well for leftovers.

Daissy's Burrito

4 large size potatoes
8 slices of smoked bacon
1/2 pound cheddar cheese, shredded
4 flour tortillas (7-8 inch size)
1 teaspoon curry powder (or cumin)
salt, pepper to taste
chives
medium hot sauce, add some water if too thick

Boil potatoes with skin. Drain and dry. Fry bacon, when crisp, place on paper towels. Cut boiled potatoes in small pieces and fry in bacon grease. Add salt, pepper and curry.

When ready to serve: Fill half of tortilla with potatoes and bacon pieces, some cheese, chives and sauce. Fold in half, cover with more cheese, top with more sauce and chives. Place in microwave oven for about 1/2 minute to melt cheese. Do this in the same plate you will use to the table. Makes 4 servings.

Bella Vista Place Bed and Breakfast

Daissy P. Owen
2 Bella Vista Place
Iowa City, IA 52245
(319) 338-4129

I always try to offer unusual gourmet breakfasts to complement my international decor. Knowing how popular Mexican food is, I decided to add my own special burrito to my breakfast repertoire. I just borrowed the Mexican name, because it has the flour tortilla, but the filling changes with my mood so that I won't get bored cooking it often. I usually serve this popular dish with fruit, juice and some sweet bread, coffee or tea.

La Hacienda Grande

Shoshana Zimmerman
21 Baros Lane
Bernalillo, NM 87004
(800) 353-1887; FAX (505) 867-4621
Internet:http//www.viva.com/nm/lahaci.html LAG@swep.com

Here are some of our very popular recipes. If you want to try something that is a little different with a hint of the southwest, do the complete breakfast. Or change the sauce to something else, and add fruit and breads from your region. Either way, the Cheese Strata will be a hit.

Ever wonder what to do with all those crusts from the ends of your bread? The Cheese Strata makes wonderful use of the crusts, and we have never had leftovers even when we have made twice as much as needed.

Cheese Strata

3 cups bread crusts in small pieces (cover the bottom of a 9x13 pan)
6 eggs
3 cups of half and half
1 1/2 teaspoon Dijon mustard
3 cups shredded cheddar cheese
Optional: 2 cups diced turkey ham, drained sausage or bacon

Spread crusts on an oiled pan. Cover with 2 cups of cheese. (If adding meat, spread out crusts, add meat and then cheese.) Mix eggs, half and half and mustard, and pour over. Top with remaining cheese. Bake at 350° for about 45 minutes. Top with Southwest Sauce. Serves 6-8.

Southwest Sauce

1 cup sour cream
1/3 cup salsa (picante is good)
1 tablespoon chopped cilantro

Mix the above ingredients. Serve atop the cheese strata and with a cilantro sprig. Excellent with orange and avocado slices, or mango, banana and kiwi garnish. Good with any bread, but especially with green chili-cheese bread.

Green Chili-Cheese Bread

1 teaspoon yeast or 1 packet
3 cups bread machine flour
2/3 cups green chili (mild to hot depending on preference)
1 cup shredded cheese
1 cup water (add teaspoon at a time, more if too dry)

Mix together in bread machine and enjoy upon completion.

Smoked Turkey Puffs

1/2 pound smoked turkey breast
1/2 pound shredded cheddar cheese
12 eggs
1 cup milk
1/4 teaspoon garlic salt
sour cream
Tabasco sauce

Spray individual bowls with PAM, or other shortening spray. Make two layers with pieces of smoked turkey, and handfuls of cheddar cheese. In blender add eggs, milk, garlic, dash of Tabasco. Blend and pour over turkey and cheese. Top with a heaping tablespoon of sour cream, and fresh grated pepper.

Bake at 350° for 45 minutes to an hour, until golden brown. Serve topped with edible flowers. Great accompanied with blueberry muffins.

Hardy House Bed and Breakfast

Carla and Mike Wagner
605 Brownell, PO Box 156
Georgetown, CO 80444
(503) 569-3388; (800) 490-4802

The Hardy House with its late 19th century charm invites guests to relax in the parlor by the potbellied stove, sleep under feather comforters, and enjoy a candlelight breakfast. Georgetown is only 55 minutes from Denver and the airport. Surrounded by mountains, it boasts unique shopping, wonderful restaurants, and close proximity to seven ski areas.

Historic Benvenue Manor B&B

Margo Hogan
160 Manor Drive
Zelienople, PA 16063
(412) 452-1710

Benvenue, *the original name of our 1816 stone manor home, means a "Good Welcome." Our guests enjoy a spectacular view, relax by the open fire, feast on a gourmet breakfast, and soak up the gracious hospitality. We prepare a high tea at 3:00 P.M. on Tuesday and Thursday afternoons and Saturday by special arrangement. We also enjoy hosting birthday parties and showers for guests. We are just 35 minutes from downtown Pittsburgh.*

Country Breakfast Pie

1 pound breakfast sausage, any flavor
1-9 inch pie shell
1 1/2 cups Monterey Jack cheese
1/4 cup chopped green pepper
1/4 cup red bell pepper
1/2 chopped onion
4 slightly beaten eggs
1 cup light cream

Cook sausage until done. Crumble and drain on paper towel. Prepare pie shell. Mix cheese, and sausage. Sprinkle in pie shell. Lightly beat the eggs. Combine remaining ingredients and add to egg mixture. Pour in shell. Bake 375° for 45 minutes: Cool 10 minutes and serve. Serves 6-8.

Part of this recipe can be done the night before. Prepare pie shell, brown sausage and drain. Shred the cheese, chop the vegetables, store these in Zip-Loc bags. In the morning, place all in the pie shell, mix eggs and cream and bake.

Susan's Sunrise Surprise

1 cup diced ham
3/4 cup shredded Swiss cheese
3/4 cup shredded cheddar cheese
2/3 cup diced onion
1/2 package (5 oz.) frozen spinach
1 cup milk
1 1/4 cup firmly packed Bisquick
4 eggs
1/4 teaspoon salt
1/4 teaspoon pepper

Thaw spinach and drain all moisture. Mix spinach, ham, cheeses, and onion. Sprinkle evenly in a lightly greased quiche pan. Combine milk, Bisquick, eggs, salt, and pepper in a mixing bowl. Beat for 1 minute at high speed. Pour evenly over ham and cheese mixture. Microwave on high, uncovered, for 17 minutes. Let stand for 5 minutes before serving. Cut in eight pie-shaped pieces and serve.

I prepare the first ham, cheeses, onion, and spinach the day before. Cover with clear plastic wrap and refrigerate in quiche pan overnight. This saves time and mess in the morning.

Seascape Bed and Breakfast

Susan Meyer
20009 Breton
Spring Lake, MI 49456
(616) 842-8409

New guests always ask for this recipe and guests who have enjoyed it here before frequently ask to have me make it during their visit. Served on a clear glass plate with fresh baked muffin and fresh fruit bowl.

Peters Creek Bed and Breakfast

Bob and Lucy Moody
22626 Chambers Lane
Chugiak, AK 99567
(907) 688-3465; (800) 405-3465;
FAX (907) 688-3466

Long-time Alaskans, Bob and Lucy wish to make each guest's stay a pleasure! Bob is an experienced fisherman and currently captain of a commercial fishing vessel. Lucy is a watercolor artist, ceramist, pianist, and all-around crafter. Their home is located on 2.5 acres of wooded terrain on the north shore of Peter's Creek. The spacious, large custom home was designed with physically challenged in mind and furnished with antiques. Lucy's full Alaskan breakfast might well include these favorite crepes. "I serve these with warmed syrup, homemade and sugar-free."

Lucy's Fast and Easy Crepes

1 - 8 or 16 ounce frozen strawberries
crepes, homemade or store bought
(can be made with egg substitute for lower fat and cholestrol)
1 lowfat strawberry yogurt
powdered sugar

Place each crepe on cookie sheet, place several strawberries with a little yogurt sauce in center — gently fold or roll up. Place tablespoon or two of yogurt on top, then top with sliced strawberries. Sprinkle with powdered sugar. Warm in microwave about 50 seconds or bake in warm oven about 5-10 minutes until sugar melts.

Ham and Orange Cream Crepes

10 orange crepes
10 slices Danish ham, sliced thin
1 package cream cheese
3 tablespoons honey mustard
3 tablespoons orange rind
3 teaspoons orange flavored extract
orange marmalade
fresh or canned cranberry sauce (must use whole berry sauce)
orange slice garnish

Make traditional crepe batter, adding orange rind and orange flavored extract. Cook crepes and set aside. Mix together cream cheese and honey mustard. Make cranberry/orange marmalade using fresh or canned cranberry sauce and orange marmalade. Mix together. In morning, spread cream cheese mixture on each crepe, add slice of ham and roll up. Bake at 325° for 15 minutes. Top with marmalade and garnish with orange slice twist. Can be made ahead.

Willows Inn

Carolyn, Kerry, and Elven Boggio
224 S. Platt Ave., PO Box 886
Red Lodge, MT 59068
(406) 446-3913

Home-baked pastries are just one of the specialties at Willows Inn. Nestled beneath the majestic Beartooth Mountains in a quaint historic town, is this delightful turn-of-the-century Victorian, complete with picket fence and porch swing, awaits you. A light and airy atmosphere with warm, cheerful decor greets the happy wanderer. Five charming guest rooms are in the main inn, while two delightfully nostalgic cottages with kitchen and laundry are also available.

The Tudor Rose

Jon and Terre Terrell
PO Box 89
Salida, CO 81201
(709) 539-2002; (800) 379-0889;
FAX (719) 530-0345

We serve a hot breakfast to our guests twice each morning, once at 8:00 and once at 9:00. Because much of this meal can be prepared the night before, the morning "rush" is less stressful. When the egg and potato crepes are served on white dishes with the colorful garnishes and accented with the cherry crepes as a side dish in our charming formal dining room, the results are nothing short of "ooos and aaahhs."

In the B&B, I like to take a few shortcuts when I can to save time. I usually make my crepes the day before and layer parchment paper or waxed paper between the cooled crepes, wrap in plastic and refrigerate. I warm them in the microwave until slightly warm, then fill. These crepes can also be frozen for later use.

Seasoned Eggs and Potato Crepes

with Béarnaise Sauce

Crepes:

- 1 cup sifted all-purpose flour
- 1 1/2 cups milk
- 2 eggs
- 1 tablespoon salad oil

In bowl, combine all ingredients and 1/4 teaspoon salt; beat until smooth. Lightly grease a 6-inch skillet or crepe pan; heat. Remove from heat; spoon in about 2 tablespoons batter. Spread batter evenly. Return to heat; brown on one side for one minute then turn over and cook the other side until lightly browned. Grease pan lightly for each crepe. Makes about 12 crepes.

Filling:

- 8 eggs
- salt and pepper to taste
- 1/8 teaspoon Mrs. Dash garlic and herb seasoning
- 1/2 teaspoon parsley flakes
- 1/4 cup milk
- 1 1/2 to 2 cups diced, cooked potatoes

Beat all ingredients (except potatoes) together with wire whisk until well blended. Add diced cooked potatoes. Cook over medium heat in skillet until desired doneness.

Spoon mixture onto crepes then fold sides of crepes to make a roll, seamside down. Makes 4 servings of 12 crepes each.

Béarnaise Sauce

2 shallots, very finely chopped
1 teaspoon tarragon
2 tablespoons chopped parsley
3 egg yolks
3/4 pound unsalted butter, clarified
salt and freshly ground pepper

Place shallots, tarragon, vinegar and parsley in stainless steel bowl. Place bowl on stove top over low heat. Cook until vinegar evaporates. Remove from heat and let cool. Add egg yolks and mix well with whisk. Place bowl over saucepan containing hot water. Add clarified butter, drop by drop, mixing constantly with whisk. When sauce begins to thicken, continue to add butter but in a thin stream. Mix constantly with whisk. Season sauce well and serve.

Shortcut: A package of Knoll's Béarnaise Sauce works just as well. This also can be made the day before and refrigerated. If it is too thick the next day, you can add a little bit of water to thin, as you warm it.

Presentation: For this dish I use an orange slice which is then cut with a cookie cutter to remove the rind. On top of that I place a fanned half strawberry both of which are set on the rim of the dish. Sprinkle parsley flakes all over the plate before putting on the fruit and crepes. Top with Béarnaise Sauce spooned over the crepes and all over the plate for decor. Serve with cherry-filled crepes on the side. Enjoy!

Mt. Sopris Inn

Barbara Fasching
Box 126
Carbondale, CO 81623
(970) 963-2209; (800) 437-8675;
FAX (970) 963-8975
E-mail: mtsoprisin@compuserv.com

At Mt. Sopris Inn, country elegance surrounds the visitor who appreciates our extraordinary property. Central to Aspen, Redstone, and Glenwood Springs, the Inn offers 15 private rooms and baths professionally decorated. All rooms have king or queen beds, TV, telephone, and include full breakfast, some have fireplaces, Jacuzzis, and steam baths. Guests use swimming pool, whirlpool, pool table, library, great rooms, and seven-foot grand piano.

Mt. Sopris Inn Spinach Crepes

16 - 7 inch crepes
2 cups medium white sauce
2 teaspoons chicken bouillon, or 2 cubes
1/2 cup onions, chopped, sautéed in butter
1 1/2 cups shredded cheddar cheese
10 ounces thawed frozen, drained spinach
10 slices bacon, cooked crisp, torn

Add chicken bouillon to white sauce. Butter 9x13 inch pan. Layer center of each crepe with a few sautéed onions, most of the cheese and bacon, and spinach. Fold sides of crepe over filling. Spread a little sauce in baking pan, placing crepes seam-side down. Cover with sauce, leaving a little sauce to drizzle over crepes after baking. Sprinkle with remaining cheese and chopped bacon. Bake 350° for 25-30 minutes. Serves 8.

Tips for serving: Sliced ripe olives, mushrooms, sour cream, salsa, a strawberry sliver, a sprig of parsley could be served with the crepes. A slice of crisp bacon and a ramekin of chilled fresh fruit and a columbine or pansy complete an attractive plate. The columbine is Colorado's state flower, so we try to use them when available.

Libby's Fruit Soufflé

4 extra large eggs, separated
2-3 tablespoons lemon juice
1/2 teaspoon grated lemon rind
1/2 - 1 cup fruit (use either rhubarb, strawberries, raspberries, prune plums, or pineapple, partially stewed with sugar to sweeten and soften if necessary. Red fruits will color soufflé a little)
1 tablespoon butter
1 tablespoon icing sugar

Preheat oven to 400°. Beat egg whites until stiff but not dry. Whisk egg yolk until pale yellow and add lemon juice, grated rind and 1/2 of the fruit. Gently fold in egg whites. Melt butter in large nonstick frying pan, spoon in soufflé, and cook for 6-8 minutes in oven. Score across center with knife, spread remaining fruit on one half and fold over. Sift icing sugar on top. Slice in pie wedges. Serves 2.

Pauper's Perch Bed and Breakfast

Libby Jutras
225 Armond Way
Salt Springs Island, British Columbia, CANADA V8K 2B6
(604) 653-2030; FAX (604) 653-2045

Because the Gulf Islands on the West Coast have Canada's warmest climate I often serve the four-course breakfast on the sun deck overlooking our vast panoramic view in the morning sunshine. I like to decorate all my breakfast dishes with edible flowers on a patch of endive from my garden. I serve this soufflé as a main course with lamb sausages, crab or smoked salmon, all Salt Spring Island specialties.

Sand Dollar Inn
Bed and Breakfast

Bob and Carolyn Della Pietra
50 Rachel Carson Lane
Wells Beach, ME 04090
(207) 646-2346

Breakfast was always a time of gathering and sharing in our household. This feeling and special time has continued with our "extended" family here at our B&B stories are exchanged, strangers become friends, and love is the nurturing ingredient.

Friendship Hash

4 medium Russet potatoes, boiled and cubed
1 small onion, chopped
4 sausage links, crumbled
2 teaspoons garlic granules
teaspoon parsley
1/4 teaspoon salt
3 tablespoons olive oil
1/4 teaspoon cracked black pepper
4 eggs
1 cup mild cheddar cheese sauce
nutmeg

Cheese Sauce

3/4 stick unsalted butter
4 tablespoons Wondra Flour
2 cups milk
6 slices of cheese
Melt butter, add flour, stir in milk and then cheese until thick.

Sauté onion and sausage in oil until tender. Add potatoes and sauté until heated through, add parsley, salt, pepper, and garlic. Heat and stir. Keep warm. Poach eggs. Place one egg over 1/2 cup of potato mixture. Top with Cheese Sauce and sprinkle with nutmeg and parsley sprigs. Serves 4. Optional: Serve with baked tomato slice and wedge of orange. Toasted Italian bread completes this dish.

Sausage Pastry

1 can refrigerator crescent rolls
1 pound hot sausage
8 ounces cream cheese
1 teaspoon dry mustard
1/2 teaspoon dill

Brown sausage and drain well. Mix with cream cheese, mustard and dill. Remove crescent rolls from can and place flat on a sheet of wax paper, use your fingers to connect the pieces so that you end up with a rectangle. Spread sausage mixture on flattened crescent rolls. Lift the end of the wax paper and roll up and off into a small presprayed loaf pan. Place in refrigerator overnight. Remove and slice, place pieces in a pan, bake at 350° for 20 minutes or until golden brown.

This may be prepared, sliced, and put in the freezer for use later.

Ridgeway House Bed and Breakfast

Becky and "Sony" Taylor
28 Ridgeway
Eureka Springs, AR 72632
(501) 253-6618; (800) 477-6618;
FAX (501) 253-2499 (call first)

A very dear friend passed this luscious recipe on to us. All of our guests want this recipe!

We treat all of our guests like VIPs! Sumptuous breakfasts, luxurious rooms, antiques, desserts, quiet street within walking distance of eight churches, five-minute walk to historic downtown, trolley one block. Porches, decks, private Jacuzzi suites for anniversaries/honeymoons.

Canaan Land Farm Bed and Breakfast

Theo and Fred Bee
4355 Lexington Road
Harrodsburg, KY 40330
(606) 734-3984

This is a recipe from my mother, now 88 years old. She has made these sausage biscuits all my life. They can be baked ahead and frozen, then reheated for guests. Most of our guests have never had them before. Everyone thinks they are delicious!

Sausage Biscuits

1 pound whole hog sausage
1 batch *Mother's Biscuit Dough*

Dough:
- 2 cups flour
- 4 teaspoons baking powder
- 1 teaspoon salt
- 4 tablespoons shortening
- 1 egg
- 2/3 cup milk

Preheat oven to 400°. Sift together flour, baking powder and salt. With the side of a spoon, cut in shortening. Beat egg and milk; add to dry ingredients.

Divide dough into 2 bowls. Turn out first half of dough onto a floured board and roll to 1/2 inch thick, in rectangle shape. Spread dough with raw sausage (1/2 pound), roll up lengthwise, jelly roll style. Cut into 1/2 inch slices and place on ungreased cookie sheet. Repeat with second bowl of dough and rest of sausage. Bake for 15 minutes.

Ashley Inn Welsh Rarebit

2 tablespoons butter
3 tablespoons flour
1 cup milk
1 cup beer
3-4 cups shredded orange cheese
2 teaspoons prepared mustard
Worcestershire sauce to taste
sliced tomatoes
cooked bacon
toast

Melt butter in saucepan, stir in flour. Gradually whisk in milk and beer, allow to thicken. Stir in cheese until melted. Add mustard and Worcestershire sauce. Quantities can be adjusted to suit individual tastes. Beer and Worcestershire sauce are essential to the rarebit flavor. Cut toast in triangles, alternate toast, slice tomato and bacon, overlapping. Pour rarebit over all. Serves approximately 10.

Ashley Inn Bed and Breakfast

Sally and Bud Allen
201 Ashley Avenue
Charleston, SC 29403
(803) 723-1848; FAX (803) 768-1230

In our stately 1835 inn, guests can sleep in . . . until the aroma of freshly brewed coffee and sizzling bacon lures them to the piazza for breakfast overlooking a beautiful Charleston garden. Guests rave over our low-country creations such as savory sausage soufflé with fluffy zucchini and cheddar biscuits, crunchy French toast (yes, crunchy) with hazelnut peach syrup, southern style grits casserole with white cream gravy, or our special Welsh rarebit. . . To pamper guests even further we've added afternoon tea with sumptuous home-baked goods and evening sherry. Our warm hospitality and professional service is unmatched.

Courthouse Square Bed and Breakfast

Les and Bess Aho
210 E. Polk Street
Crandon, WI 54520
(715) 478-2549

Breakfast is served in courses at Courthouse Square, and when this main entree is presented on brightly colored Fiestaware with a garnish of edible fresh nastarium or a scented geranium leaf, it elicits "ooh and aahs," and upon finishing, guests invariably request the recipe.

Strawberry Blintz

Filling:

- 8 ounces cream cheese
- 15 ounces ricotta cheese
- 2 egg yolks
- 1 tablespoon sugar
- 1/2 teaspoon almond extract

Blintz:

- 1/2 cup butter, softened
- 1/3 cup sugar
- 5 eggs, plus the whites from the filling
- 1 cup all-purpose flour
- 2 teaspoons baking powder
- 1 1/2 cups vanilla yogurt
- 1/2 cup orange juice
- 1/2 teaspoon vanilla

Preheat oven to 350°. To make the filling, beat cream cheese until smooth, add ricotta, egg yolks, sugar and almond extract. Mix thoroughly and set aside.

To prepare the blintz, in a small bowl, combine flour with baking powder and set aside. In a second bowl, blend yogurt, orange juice, and vanilla then set aside. In another bowl, cream butter and sugar, add the eggs and egg whites and beat until well mixed. Add the flour mix and yogurt mixture alternately to the egg mixture. Pour half of batter into a 9x13 inch greased glass baking dish. Gently add filling, spreading over batter base. Top with remaining batter gently covering filling to sides of dish. Bake for 45-50 minutes until golden brown.

To serve: Cut into eight servings. Place serving on plate, cover with fresh strawberries (sugared if desired), and garnish with a dollop of whipped cream.

Baked Cheese Blintz

Filling:
- 1 pound cottage cheese, drained
- 1-8 ounce cream cheese, softened
- 2 egg yolks
- 1 tablespoon sugar
- 1 teaspoon vanilla

Batter:
- 1 1/2 cups sour cream
- 1/2 cup orange juice
- 6 eggs
- 1/4 cup butter, melted
- 1 cup flour
- 1/3 cup sugar
- 2 teaspoons baking powder
- 1/2 teaspoon cinnamon

Filling: Mix all ingredients with electric mixer or food processor until combined. Set aside.

Batter: Gradually add all ingredients in order given in mixer or blender. Grease 8 to 10 8 ounce ramekins. Add enough batter to each ramekin to cover bottom. Divide filling among ramekins gently spreading over the top of batter. Pour the rest of the batter evenly over the filling. Cover, refrigerate overnight. Bake in 375° oven for 30 minutes or until golden brown.

We garnish the top of each cheese blintz with a dollop of sour cream and fruit preserves, a few fresh raspberries, blueberries, and a sprig of fresh mint.

The Gingerbread Mansion Inn

Ken Torbert
400 Berding Street, PO Box 40
Ferndale, CA 95536
(707) 786-4000; (800) 952-4136;
FAX (707) 786-4381

Nestled between the giant redwoods and the rugged Pacific Coast is one of California's best-kept secrets: the Victorian village of Ferndale. A state historic landmark and listed on the National Historic Register, Ferndale is a community frozen in time with Victorian homes and shops relatively unchanged since their construction in the mid-to-late 1800s. One of Ferndale's most well-known homes is the Gingerbread Mansion Inn. Decorated with antiques, the eleven, romantic guest rooms offer private baths, some with old-fashioned clawfoot tubs, and fireplaces. Also included is a full breakfast, high tea, four parlors, and formal English gardens.

McKay House

Alma Anne and Joseph Parker
306 E. Delta Street
Jefferson, TX 75657
(903) 665-7322; (800) 468-2627
(9:00 A.M. - 5:00 P.M. only)
FAX (903) 665-8551

"One of the 10 most romantic inns in America." boasts Vacation Magazine *and American Bed & Breakfast Association rated it "outstanding." And what could be more romantic than finding Victorian nightgowns and sleep shirts to wear in the privacy of your antique-filled bedroom. Sip a fireside cup of coffee or cool lemonade on the porch while listening to the chords of music from the old Packard pump organ. After the gentleman's breakfast, a McKay classic served in period dress, you can take a garden stroll to refresh the soul.*

Blintz Soufflé

Filling:
- 16 ounces small-curd cottage cheese
- 2 egg yolks
- 1 tablespoon sugar
- 1 teaspoon vanilla
- 8 ounces cream cheese, softened

Batter:
- 1 1/2 cups sour cream
- 1/2 cup orange juice
- 6 eggs
- 1/4 cup butter or margarine, softened
- 1 cup flour
- 1/3 cup sugar
- 2 teaspoons baking powder
- 1/2 teaspoon cinnamon (optional)

Grease a 9x13 inch pan. In a small bowl, beat all the filling ingredients until well blended, set aside. Spoon flour into measuring cup and level off. In blender container place all the batter ingredients; cover and blend until smooth. Scrape sides often. Pour half the batter into prepared pan. Drop filling by teaspoonfuls over batter; spread evenly (filling will mix slightly with batter). Pour remaining batter over filling. Cover, refrigerate at least 2 hours or overnight.

Preheat oven to 350° and bake, uncovered, for 50-60 minutes or until puffed and light golden brown. Serve topped with fresh fruit. An alternate topping is sour cream and apricot preserves. Serves 8.

Special Creamed Chipped Beef

- 4 tablespoons butter
- 4 tablespoons flour
- 1/2 teaspoon freshly ground pepper
- 2 cups milk
- 2/3 cup sour cream
- 1/2 cup dry white wine
- 1/2 teaspoon Worcestershire Sauce
- 8 ounces chipped dried beef
- 1 cup sliced fresh mushrooms
- 1/2 cup freshly grated Parmesan cheese

Melt butter in saucepan. Add flour and pepper. Stir and cook for 1-2 minutes. Slowly add milk and cook, stirring constantly until well thickened. Add Worcestershire Sauce, cheese and wine. Stir and cook until thick and just beginning to boil. Add beef and mushrooms and heat until hot throughout. Add sour cream and heat just until hot. DO NOT BOIL. Serve over homemade waffles.

Bedford Inn

Alan and Cindy Schumucker
805 Stockton Avenue
Cape May, NJ 08204
(609) 884-4158; FAX (609) 884-0533

This recipe is an unusually good twist on an old-fashioned breakfast favorite. Even guests who profess not to like creamed chipped beef usually end up raving about it. Garnished with fresh parsley and a big beautiful strawberry, sliced partly through, it presents an attractive breakfast entree and leaves them with a special memory of breakfast at Bedford Inn.

The Daly Inn

Sue and Gene Clinesmith
1125 H Street
Eureka, CA 95501
(707) 445-3638; (800) 321-9656;
FAX (707) 444-3636

This exquisite Colonial Revival mansion, built in 1905, has four fireplaces, lovely Victorian gardens, a third floor "Christmas Ballroom" and is completely furnished with turn-of-the-century antiques. We are known for our wonderful breakfasts and making our guests feel at home in a quiet, romantic atmosphere.

My grandmother, who came from Germany, made this recipe every Sunday morning. It is one of my favorite childhood memories.

Noodle Kugel

1 package wide egg noodles
1 stick butter, melted
2 cups sour cream
1 cup sugar
1/2 cup milk
4 eggs
1 teaspoon vanilla
1 cup raisins
1 tablespoon cinnamon and sugar

Cook noodles (al dente), melt butter in 9x13 inch pan. Toss noodles in melted butter. Mix sour cream, sugar, milk, eggs and vanilla; pour over noodles. Sprinkle raisins and cinnamon and sugar over mixture. Bake at 350° for one hour. Can be served warm or cold.

Pain Perdu

4 eggs
1/3 cup super-fine sugar
3/4 teaspoon nutmeg
1 quart half and half
1 1/2 teaspoon vanilla
1 tablespoon lemon peel, grated
16 slices (1 inch thick) sourdough baguette

Beat together first six ingredients and pour over the sliced baguettes. Let stand for 5 minutes then turn pieces over. Cover and refrigerate overnight.

Cook in a skillet, over medium heat, in a mixture of butter and vegetable oil, until brown (about 5 minutes per side). Serve with fresh blackberries, whipped cream, and maple syrup. Makes 8 servings.

Mendocino Village Inn

Kathleen and Bill Erwin
44860 Main Street PO Box 626
Mendocino, CA 95460
(707) 937-0246; (800) 882-7029
Email: Mendolnn@aol.com
URL: http://www.mcn.org/cbc/bussect/villageinn/mendolnn.html

This is the breakfast everyone wants the recipe for. We serve it with real whipped cream and fresh seasonal berries. We garnish the plate with edible flowers (roses, nasturtiums, etc.) and powdered sugar. We suggest trying it for dessert!

Sweet Sunrise

Deluxe Breakfast Fruits

"Every good gift and every perfect gift is from above, and cometh down from the Father of lights, with whom is no variableness, neither shadow of turning."

James 1:17

Hill View Acres Bed and Breakfast

Jim and Dawn Graham
7320 Old Town Road
East Fultonham, OH 43735
(614) 849-2728

This is an original recipe created by Dawn, and a favorite with our guests. It is served with fresh fruit cup or juice, scrambled eggs, hot flaky biscuits, jams and jellies. Guests' comments are "it's like having dessert for breakfast," and "it's delicious!"

Crispy Apple-Sausage Bake

5 cups sliced apples
1 cup firmly packed brown sugar
1 tablespoon lemon juice
1/3 cup flour
2/3 cup quick oats
1/2 cup chopped nuts
1/3 cup margarine
1 pound sausage links, browned

Combine apples, 1/2 cup brown sugar, lemon juice and 1/3 cup oats. Mix lightly. Place in greased 3-quart baking dish. In separate bowl, combine remaining 1/2 cup brown sugar and flour, cut in margarine until well blended. Stir in rest of oats and nuts. Spoon over apples. Bake in 350° oven for 45 minutes. Lay browned sausages on top of apples and bake 10 minutes more.

Apple Breakfast Sandwiches

- 1/3 cup firmly packed brown sugar
- 2 tablespoons all-purpose flour
- 1/2 teaspoon ground cinnamon
- 1 tablespoon butter or margarine, melted
- 1 - 10 ounce can refrigerator buttermilk biscuits
- 1 cup (4 ounces) shredded sharp cheddar cheese
- 2 apples, peeled, cored and chopped, microwave 2 minutes

Combine first four ingredients in a small bowl; set aside. Separate biscuits and press each into 3-inch circle. Place on lightly greased baking sheet; sprinkle with cheese, and top with apples. Sprinkle with sugar mixture and bake at 350° for 15 minutes, or until golden.

Applegate Inn Bed and Breakfast

Emil and Judy Milkey
163 Hemlock Street
PO Box 567
Dillsboro, NC 28725
(704) 586-2397

The "Gateway" to country charm, relaxation, and southern hospitality at its best. Situated in the village of Dillsboro, we are located on Scott's Creek, a footbridge from the Great Smoky Mountain Depot and Dillsboro's 50 unique shops. A quaint country home — families and seniors appreciate our one level. Private baths and queen beds, and efficiencies with kitchen facilities.

We serve these on a pretty plate as part of our full country breakfast. We include these on a day we serve eggs, grits, and homemade biscuits. We try to have something with apples everyday for our guests.

Let us make you the apple of our eye! Proverbs 3:24, 26.

BevLen Haus

Bev and Len deGeus
809 N. Sanders Street
Ridgecrest, CA 93555
(619) 375-1988; (800) 375-1989;
FAX (619) 446-3220

At BevLen Haus we serve Danish Apple Pastry warmed for breakfast as a side dish. It is always well received, and has been a favorite of guests since we first opened.

Danish Apple Pastry

Pastry:
- 3 cups flour
- 1/2 teaspoon salt
- 1 cup Crisco
- 1 egg yolk (save egg white)
- 1/2 cup milk

Filling:
- 6 cups thin-sliced, peeled tart apples
- 3/4 cup white sugar
- 1/4 cup butter, melted
- 2 tablespoons flour
- 1 teaspoon cinnamon
- 2 tablespoons lemon juice
- 2 teaspoons lemon zest

Glaze:
- 1 egg white, beaten lightly
- 1/2 cup confectioners' sugar
- 2-3 teaspoons water

Combine flour and salt; cut in shortening until mixture resembles coarse crumbs. Add egg yolk and milk, stir well. Roll half of dough to 15x10 inch. Transfer dough to same size pan. Set aside.

Mix all filling ingredients, spoon over pastry. Roll second half of pastry to fit pan; place over filling, sealing edges. Paint with some of beaten egg white. Bake 35 minutes at 375° or until golden brown.

Mix glaze. Drizzle over warm pastry.

Baked Apples

Mixture for one apple:

1 tablespoon brown sugar
1 teaspoon butter
1/4 teaspoon cinnamon
Vermont maple syrup (optional)
fresh mint leaves (optional)

Heat oven to 375°. Core apples and remove 1 inch of skin around middle of each apple to prevent them from splitting. Place apples upright in baking dish. Fill center of each apple with above mixture. Pour water (1/4 inch deep) into baking dish. Bake about 30-40 minutes or until apples are tender when pierced with a fork. Time will vary with variety and size of apple. You may spoon pan juices over apples during baking.

For presentation, place each apple in a serving dish. Pour equal portions of pan juices in the center of each apple. Drizzle a teaspoon of warm maple syrup over apples and place a sprig of fresh mint leaves in the middle of the apple to resemble the apple leaves.

The Maple Leaf Inn

Gary and Janet Robison
PO Box 273
Barnard, VT 05031
(802) 234-5342;
(800) 51-MAPLE

My husband Gary and I are partners in our personal and professional lives together. Our dream became a reality as we planned for and built The Maple Leaf Inn. As innkeepers we share responsibilities and have found our comfortable niches in handling our daily routines. Although Gary feels somewhat intimidated in the kitchen, he is a tremendous help to me in the mornings when we are organizing breakfast for our guests. One morning when I was pressed for time, I asked Gary to prepare the Baked Apples for me as I walked him through the recipe. They turned out great and he was happily surprised with the results. Now the Baked Apples have become his specialty and I beam with pride as guests rave about his efforts.

Ashton Country House

Dorie and Vince DiStefano
1205 Middlebrook Avenue
Staunton, VA 24401
(540) 885-7819; (800) 296-7819

This is a great dish served warm, and during breakfast, it makes your home smell wonderful! Also, this is a wonderful dessert topped with a scoop of vanilla ice cream, or whipped cream. Served at room temperature it is equally delicious. An easy way to add a home baked item to your menu and aroma to your house.

Baked Breakfast Apples

6 apples
1/4 cup granola
1/4 cup golden raisins
1/2 cup brown sugar
1/2 cup orange juice
1/4 teaspoon allspice or cinnamon
2 tablespoon butter

Core apples and place in baking dish. In a small saucepan combine orange juice, butter, brown sugar, and allspice. Bring to a boil. Pour over apples that are stuffed with granola and raisins. Baste halfway through baking. Serve warm from oven. Bake at 350° for 35-40 minutes.

Blizzard Fruit

3 can pineapple chunks
2 bananas
1/2 cup shredded coconut
2-3 tablespoons Cool Whip

Drain pineapple. Mix with sliced bananas coconut and Cool Whip. Serve in individual glasses (i.e., sherbet) topped with strawberry or maraschino cherry. Serve on Lenox china to make for an elegant breakfast.

Farmstead Bed and Breakfast

Meb and John Lippincott
379 Goodwin Road
Eliot, ME 03903
(207) 439-5033; (207) 748-3145

Blizzard Fruit came into being while I was serving in the air force. When I started to do all the cooking here at The Farmstead I got the recipe from Meb. I use it on Sunday mornings to accompany Cheese and Sausage Strata and or Cheese and Mushroom Strata. This menu allowed me to serve 12-16 people alone between 8:00-9:00 A.M. and finish in time to get to the Eliot United Methodist Church where I teach adult Sunday school at 9:30. It has turned out to be very popular among both our first time and return guests.

Kenmore Farms Bed and Breakfast

Dorothy and Bernie Keene
1050 Bloomfield Road
Bardstown, KY 40004
(502) 348-8023; (800) 831-6159;
FAX (508) 348-0617

In preparing the menu for our bed and breakfast, we relied on family and local recipes. We wanted to build our reputation around our warm, comfortable home and our full country breakfast. For many years Banana Croquettes have been a favorite dish at family reunions and potluck dinners in the Bardstown area. We serve them as part of one of our breakfast menus, and guests exclaim over them. As most of our guests have never heard of this dish, it must be unique to our area. The dressing is an original homemade recipe of Bernie Keene's mother. It has many uses such as toppings for fruit and fresh green salads. It is also good on cooked green vegetables (kale, spinach, or broccoli).

Banana Croquettes and Dressing

2 eggs, beaten well
1 cup sugar
1 cup vinegar (white)
3/4 teaspoon salt
3/4 teaspoon celery seed

Mix first four ingredients together until well blended. Cook and stir constantly over medium high heat, until slightly thickened. Put into sterilized jar, and add celery seed. Stir. Cover and refrigerate. Keeps up to three weeks.

Cut bananas into 3-4 pieces. Roll in dressing then roll in chopped skinless peanuts. Can be used for breakfast, lunch, or dinner.

The dressing is good on salads, such as the following: fresh spinach, romaine lettuce, mandarin oranges, sliced red onion rings, and sliced almond.

Banana Split Supreme

2 bananas, sliced lengthwise
8 ounce container strawberry yogurt
1 can whipped cream (optional)
1/2 cup granola
1 cup sliced strawberries
sliced kiwi for garnish (optional)

Slice bananas and place in banana split boat. Combine yogurt and strawberries. Spoon 1/4 cup of yogurt mixture on each of the banana slices. Garnish with additional strawberries. Top with granola, whipped cream, and kiwi. Serves 4.

Cameron's Crag

Glen and Kay Cameron
Box 295
Branson, MO 65615
(417) 335-8134

Located high on a bluff overlooking Lake Taneycomo and the valley, three miles south of Branson, guests enjoy a spectacular view from a new spacious, detached, private suite with whirlpool tub, kitchen, living, and bedroom area. Two-room suite with indoor hot tub and private bath. A third room has a great view of the lake and a private hot tub on the deck. All rooms have king-size beds, hot tubs, private entrances, TVs, VCRs, and a video library.

Oak Haven Bed and Breakfast

Alan and Brenda Smith
4975N. Hurricane Road (400 E)
Franklin, IN 46131
(317) 535-9491

My grandmother always used the peanuts on the "logs," however when I started serving it as our fruit for breakfast, I added the granola. Guests enjoy knowing they are sampling an "old family recipe," which I gladly share with them.

Grandmother's Banana Logs

1/2 cup sugar
1 egg
2 tablespoons flour
2 cups milk
1 teaspoon vanilla
1/8 teaspoon salt
6-8 bananas

Optional:
1/2 cup peanuts, chopped
1/2 cup granola, any type

Mix together sugar and beaten egg. Add the flour to sugar mixture and combine with milk in saucepan. Using medium to low heat, cook until just starts to bubble up. Stir constantly to keep mixture from burning. Remove from heat, put in bowl and add vanilla and salt. Cover and put in refrigerator until cold. Cut bananas into thirds (such as a "log"), dip in cold custardlike mixture until coated, and roll in peanuts for a dessert, granola for breakfast.

Serve bananas in the log shape or cut into slices, with peanuts and/or granola in separate dishes for guests to use choice of toppings.

Berry Parfait

1 cup granola with nuts
1/2 cup fat-free sour cream
1/2 cup fat-free yogurt (flavored or plain)
1 cup fresh or frozen berries

Place 1/8 cup granola in each of 4 stemmed glasses. Mix together the sour cream and yogurt, adding some sugar or artificial sweetener to taste. Save out about 1/2 cup of sour cream mixture. Divide balance evenly in glasses. Top with berries, a dab of sour cream, and sprinkle last of granola over the top. Serves 4.

McGillivray's Log Home Bed and Breakfast

Evelyn R. MGillivray
88680 Evers Road
Elmira, OR 97437-9733
(541) 935-3564

With an abundance of marion berries, this is a great cereal/fruit first course at breakfast. I freeze extra berries for winter use. They "hold up" when thawed. I like to put the stemmed glassware on a small serving plate, with a lace doily beneath the glass.

I often alternate a fresh fruit with a cooked fruit when guests stay more than one day. A stay in a log home relates to cooking from scratch. While guests have this fruit and cereal first course, I proceed with the cooked hearty part of the meal. I enjoy seeing guests relax in this quiet, wooded atmosphere.

Pikes Peak Paradise

Priscilla Arthur
236 Pinecrest Road
Woodland Park, CO 80863
(719) 687-6656; (800) 728-8282;
FAX (719) 687-9008

This is a favorite fruit serving of our guests and since we are a southern mansion it is an appropriate offering. This recipe comes from Martin's (Martin Meier, one of the owners) grandmother, a southern lady who baked it in the oven for 45 minutes. I add a maraschino cherry and serve warm.

Baked Grapefruit

1/2 grapefruit (per person)
1 teaspoon brown sugar
1 teaspoon butter
sprinkle cinnamon

Cut the grapefruit in half with sharp knife in sawtooth pattern. Section and cut around to loosen bite-size sections. Sprinkle cut surface with cinnamon and brown sugar. Dot with butter and bake in microwave-proof glass serving dish for three minutes, full power in microwave.

Broiled or Microwaved Grapefruit

Bechtel Mansion Inn

Charles and Mariam Bechtel
with Ruth Spangler
400 West King Street
East Berlin, PA 17316
(717) 259-7760; (800) 331-1108
Internet: uhl: www.net.com/bechtel.html

This recipe has been used for the past year to serve a single fresh fruit to guests, when we have one to three couples. It is delightful because so many different single, or combined toppings can be used, during different seasons of the year. This recipe can be made to look very simple or more formal by using different serving dishes and garnishments. It is always a guest pleaser.

- 2 grapefruits
- 4 tablespoons brown sugar (one for each half)
- 1 tablespoon butter
- topping of your choice (suggestions below)

Use grapefruit that is at room temperature. If using grapefruit directly from refrigerator, allow extra broiling/microwave cooking time. Cut grapefruits into halves. With sharp paring knife, section halves by cutting along the membrane that forms the triangular-shaped pieces. Generously sprinkle brown sugar on tops. Dot with butter. Set on cookie sheet and place under the broiler until sugar is caramelized and the grapefruit is warm, approximately 2-3 minutes for broiling, 2 minutes for microwave preparation.

Toppings:

- Fresh strawberry
- Fresh raspberry
- Lemon curd
- Slivered almond slices, lightly toasted.
- One half teaspoon of your favorite jam, jelly, or marmalade.
- Robertson's Golden Three Fruits Marmalade (consists of oranges, lemons, and grapefruits).
- Maraschino cherry, with 1/2 teaspoon of maraschino cherry juice per half grapefruit.

The Bridgewater House Bed and Breakfast

Steve and Katherine Mistilis
7015 Raleigh LaGrange Road
Cordova, TN 38018
(Memphis Area)
(901) 384-0080; FAX (901) 384-0080

A Greek Revival home converted from a schoolhouse that is over 100 years old, this lovely, elegant dwelling is filled with remembrances of travels, antiques, family heirlooms, and Oriental rugs. The Bridgewater House has original hardwood floors cut from trees on the property, enormous rooms, high ceilings, leaded-glass windows, and deep hand-marbelized moldings. There are two very spacious bedrooms with private baths. A certified chef and a food and beverage director serve a full gourmet breakfast and pamper guests with refreshments upon arriving.

Grand Marnier Grapefruit au Meringue

1 each grapefruit
2 teaspoons Grand Marnier liqueur
2 each egg whites
2 teaspoons sugar
Optional: 1 teaspoon orange zest can be added with the Grand Manier or other liquors substituted as well as making a simple syrup and adding the liquor for a sweeter variety.
Syrup: water, brown sugar, orange zest, liqueur

Cut grapefruit in half and section. Evenly drizzle Grand Marnier liqueur sauce over grapefruit. Whip egg whites until frothy. Add sugar a teaspoon at a time and whip until stiff. Top each grapefruit with an even portion of meringue. Bake in 350° oven until browned evenly. Serve immediately with grapefruit spoons.

Kiwi-Peanut Butter Parfait

1 cup chunky peanut butter
1 cup nonfat vanilla yogurt
1/4 cup honey
1/4 cup apples chopped and cooked, or apple sauce
1/2 cup granola
10 kiwi, peeled

Topping:
1/2 cup nonfat vanilla yogurt
1/2 teaspoon brown sugar

Mix together peanut butter, yogurt, honey and apples. Slice 1/3 kiwi into the bottom of a parfait glass. Add 1 tablespoon of the peanut butter mixture and sprinkle on granola. Layer kiwi, peanut butter mixture and granola until parfait glass is full. I allow one kiwi per person. Mix topping and pour over the layers. Serves 10.

All Seasons River Inn

Kathy and Jeff Falconer
PO Box 788
Leavenworth, WA 98826
(509) 548-1425; (800) 254-0555

Limited in the winter to very few fresh fruits, I came up with a way to serve kiwi, which always seems to be available. It may not sound too exciting, but trust me. My guests love it. On a return, one guest was very disappointed this dish was not served. I brewed her up my special recipe. She was delighted!

Windward House

Sandy and Owen Miller
24 Jackson Street
Cape May, NJ 08204
(609) 884-3368; FAX (609) 884-0533

Great for summer breakfast or brunch especially when fresh peaches are in season. A nice variation on breakfast fruit dishes which can become humdrum. My guests give this dish rave reviews.

"Sandy's homemade breakfasts have become legend," says County Lines.

Poached Peaches
with White Cheese Mousse

Peaches:

- 3 cups water
- 1 1/2 cups sugar
- 1/3 cup lemon juice
- 1 tablespoon vanilla
- 6 medium peaches, halved, pits removed

In large bowl, microwave first four ingredients on high for ten minutes. Stir until sugar dissolves. Add peach halves to syrup. Microwave for four minutes. Refrigerate, covered.

Mousse:

- 1/2 cup part skim ricotta
- 1/4 cup Neufchatel cheese
- 3 tablespoons confectioners' sugar
- 1 1/2 teaspoon lemon rind
- 1/2 teaspoon vanilla

Beat together until smooth. Refrigerate until serving time. To serve, place peach half on serving plate, cut side up. Place a spoonful of mousse on top and garnish with mint.

Hamilton Peach Melba

12 whole peaches (24 halves), canned may be used
1 tablespoon brown sugar
1/4 cup raspberry jam

Topping:
1 cup sour cream
3 tablespoons brown sugar
1 teaspoon vanilla

Place peaches round side down in baking dish, sprinkle lightly with brown sugar, place small amount of raspberry jam in center of each peach half. Place in oven at 350° until peaches are soft and glazed, about 12 minutes — depending on ripeness of peaches. Can also be placed in microwave for 8-10 minutes on high.

Before serving, pour melted raspberry syrup over all and add a dollop of topping. Place a mint garnish on top. Serves 12.

Hamilton House Inn

Bud and Anne Benz
15 Mercer Avenue
Spring Lake, NJ 07762
(908) 449-8282; (908) 449-0206

While having Peach Melba at one of our favorite restaurants, Anne decided to adapt a version for breakfast for our guests. It is so popular that we have it often. We receive requests for this recipe from our guests. It is easy to make which is great for a busy morning at the Inn and the fresh peaches are especially good in season.

Commencement Bay Bed and Breakfast

Sharon and Bill Kaufman
3312 N. Union Avenue
Tacoma, WA 98407
(206) 752-8175; FAX (206) 759-4025
Email: greatviews@aol.com

This dish is not only delicious but it also has a beautiful presentation. It is one my guests often request over and over again. It is also quite versatile and can be easily adapted to available fresh fruit. Maury Island Farms produces wonderful fruit products. I use their Red Raspberry Ecstasy and their Blackberry Delight in place of the fruit puree. I can't improve on perfection! In case you can't find theirs, I've included a basic recipe. No matter how you serve them, your guests or family will love them!

Peach Melba Dutch Babies

6 tablespoons margarine
2 peaches, peeled and sliced
6 eggs
1 1/2 cups milk
1 cup flour
2 tablespoons sugar
1 teaspoon vanilla extract
1/2 teaspoon salt
1/2 teaspoon cinnamon
1 cup raspberry puree

Melt margarine in a 9x13 inch baking dish, or four individual au gratin dishes. Set peaches aside. Whirl remaining ingredients in blender until well mixed. Pour batter into baking dish or au gratin dishes and bake in preheated oven at 425° until puffed and golden, about 20-25 minutes. Remove from oven and quickly place peach slices on top. Drizzle raspberry puree on top and serve immediately. Garnish with a few fresh raspberries.

Raspberry Puree

1 cup fresh or frozen raspberries
1 tablespoon sugar, or to taste

In a small microwave-safe bowl, place raspberries and sugar. Cover and microwave on high about 2 minutes, or until mixture boils. Strain through fine sieve to remove seeds. Cool.

Poached Pears
with Raspberry Sauce

4 Bartlett or other green pears, halved, cored
orange juice
1 stick cinnamon
raspberry sauce

Place cored pear halves, cut side up, in bottom of a Dutch oven. Add enough orange juice to cover. Add cinnamon stick. Bring to boil over medium heat, cover pan, reduce heat to simmer and cook 10 minutes, or until tender, yet still firm. Remove pan from heat. Cool pears in liquid. Refrigerate in juice until chilled. Will keep up to one week. Make sauce just before serving.

Raspberry Sauce

1 cup fresh or frozen raspberries
1/3 cup confectioners' sugar
1/4 cup orange juice, or to taste

Place raspberries in a blender, along with sugar and juice. Process until smooth. Strain and discard seeds.

To serve, place each pear half on a dessert plate. Cut in half from large end toward stem end, being careful not to cut all they way through. Slices should be about 1/4 inch thick. Spread into a fan shape. Drizzle raspberry sauce across center of each pear half. Garnish with a mint leaf, if desired. Serves 8.

The Homeplace Bed and Breakfast

Peggy and Frank Dearien
5901 Sardis Road
Charlotte, NC 28270
(704) 365-1936; FAX (704) 366-2729

Restored 1902 country Victorian with wraparound porch and tin roof is nestled among two and one-half wooded acres. Secluded "cottage style" gardens with a gazebo, brick walkways, and a 1930s log barn further enhance this nostalgic oasis in southeast Charlotte. Opened in 1984, the Homeplace is a "reflection of the true bed and breakfast."

Experienced innkeepers offer a full breakfast. This is one of our specialties — a favorite of all guests. Wonderful presentation on crystal plates with decorative china plate underneath. It is an impressive fruit introduction to breakfast.

Maple Hedge Bed and Breakfast Inn

Joan and Dick Debrine
355 Main Street, Route 12
Charleston, NH 03603
(603) 826-5237 (voice and FAX);
(800) 9-MAPLE-9

I serve a three-course breakfast at Maple Hedge, and fresh fruit is always a part of the menu. In New England in the summer there is always an abundance of locally grown berries and melons, but winter does present something of a challenge. My guests thoroughly enjoy these pears, which may be baked the night before and just slightly reheated the next morning, to take off the chill. They make and elegant presentation with some of the "sauce" drizzled around the plate.

Spicy Sweet Baked Pears

pears, one per serving, halved, cored, stems removed
brown sugar
margarine
2 tablespoons orange juice
ginger
nutmeg

Select ovenproof pan large enough to hold desired amount of pears, without overlapping. Cover bottom of pan with brown sugar. Place pears cut side down on brown sugar. Dot with margarine and sprinkle with juice and ginger. Bake at 350° for 20 minutes, or until browned. Serve cut side up; fill cavity with topping and sprinkle with nutmeg. Two halves per serving.

Topping:
1 cup cottage cheese
1/3 cup sour cream
1/4 cup powdered sugar

Place topping ingredients, except for nutmeg, in blender and process until smooth.

Baked Pears 'n Sauce

4 fresh ripe pears (Anjou, Bosc, or Comice)
2 tablespoons butter
4 tablespoon honey
4 teaspoons grated lemon rind
4 tablespoons fresh lemon juice
2 tablespoons water
2 tablespoon slivered almonds

Yogurt almondine topping:
Sweeten plain yogurt with powdered sugar and almond extract to taste.

Rinse, halve, and core unpeeled pears. Place cut side up in well-buttered baking dish. Fill pear halves with the butter and honey. Sprinkle with lemon rind. Combine lemon juice and water. Pour over pears. Bake at 350° about 20 minutes until pears are tender. Top with yogurt almondine and slivered almonds. Serve while warm.

The Franklin Victorian Bed and Breakfast

Lloyd and Jane Larson
220 E. Franklin Street
Sparta, WI 54656
(608) 269-3894; (800) 845-8767

We serve lovely three-course breakfasts and always have a fruit course. These pears can be served before the main course or after it, as a dessert. Our guests love it.

Carriage Way Bed and Breakfast

Bill and Diane Johnson
70 Cuna Street
St. Augustine, FL 32084
(904) 829-2467; (800) 908-9832;
FAX (904) 826-1461

Built in 1833, our Victorian home is located in the heart of the historic district amid unique and charming shops, museums, and historic sites. The atmosphere is leisurely and casual, in keeping with the general attitude and feeling of Old St. Augustine. All guest rooms have a private bath with a clawfoot tub or shower. Rooms are furnished with antiques and reproductions including brass, canopy, or four poster beds. A full home-baked breakfast is served.

Pineapple Breakfast Bake

2 eggs
2 sticks butter
1 cup sugar
2 - 20 ounce cans chunk pineapple
5-6 cups cubed French bread (crusts removed)

Drain pineapple. Melt butter. Beat eggs. Add sugar to eggs and add to butter. Mix well. Put bread cubes in 9x13 inch greased baking dish. Place pineapple in egg mixture and pour over the bread cubes. Bake at 350° for 45 minutes.

I serve this with Eggs Benedict. The pineapple compliments the Canadian bacon.

Pineapple Whipped Cream Fruit Dressing and Dip

1 cup pineapple juice
2 eggs
1 cup sugar
1 1/2 teaspoons lemon juice
1 teaspoon flour
1/2 pint whipped cream (unsweetened)

In saucepan, beat the eggs and the sugar, add pineapple juice and lemon juice. Gradually add flour while stirring with wire whisk. Cook over medium heat until thick and lightly boiling. Set aside to cool or overnight in refrigerator. Whip cream until stiff. Mix well with pineapple mixture (when cooled) until well blended. Refrigerate and serve as sauce for cut up fruit or as dip for fruit. 16-20 servings.

The Honor Mansion

Cathi Fowler
14891 Grove Street
Healdsburg, CA 95448
(707) 433-4277; (800) 544-4667;
FAX (707) 431-7173

We serve this in the bottom of a compote glass with sliced and chopped fruit on top. It is very refreshing and not too sweet. It really dresses up fruit. You can also pipe it into large hollow-centered strawberries for a side fruit.

Bakketop Hus Bed and Breakfast

Dennis and Judy Nims
RR2, Box 187A
Fergus Falls, MN 56537
(218) 739-2915; (800) 739-2915

Raspberries have always been a favorite summertime fruit. As children we always had our own patch and would eat them off the vines.

When we opened our bed and breakfast, we found our guests also enjoyed them, so we developed this recipe as a way to delight our guests with fresh raspberries served in compote dishes prior to the main meal.

Breakfast is served overlooking the crystal clear lake as the sun glistens on the water. You may see a squirrel go by, hear loons calling to each other, or hear song birds as you sip your morning coffee and plan you day's activities. This may include picking up a box of fresh raspberries at a local farmers market!

Raspberry Delight

3 tablespoons tapioca
1 cup water
1/2 cup sugar
1 6 ounce can frozen orange juice, undiluted
1 1/2 cup water
1 box frozen raspberries
1 tablespoon lemon juice
1 can mandarin oranges

Mix first three ingredients, and let set 5 minutes. Then cook until it thickens. Mix remaining ingredients into cooked mixture. Add additional fruit as desired: bananas, kiwi, peaches, etc.

Serve in sherbet dishes on doilied plate. Garnish with fresh raspberry and mint leaf.

Strawberry and Yogurt Sundae

2 ounces Neufchatel cheese (low-fat cream cheese)
1 cup vanilla yogurt
1 tablespoon sugar
1/8 teaspoon vanilla
1 cup fresh strawberries
1/4 cup granola

Soften Neufchatel cheese slightly. In a medium bowl, combine Neufchatel cheese, sugar, vanilla. Gradually add vanilla yogurt, stirring to remove any lumps. Refrigerate. Wash and slice strawberries; sweeten to taste. To assemble: Divide the yogurt mixture among 4 pretty sherbet dishes. Top with fresh berries and sprinkle 1 tablespoon granola over the berries. Serve at once.

North Shore Inn of Holland

Beverly and Kurt Van Genderen
686 North Shore Drive
Holland, MI 49424
(616) 394-9050; FAX (616) 392-1389

The three-course gourmet breakfast at the North Shore Inn always includes dessert. Even guests who say they don't like yogurt enjoy this combination. It is a good ending to a heavy meal or pancakes or French toast. In late summer I use blueberries instead of strawberries, since blueberries are one of this area's agricultural specialties.

Brookhaven Manor

Ralph Stutzman
Nancy Forbes, manager
128 W. Mistletoe
San Antonio, TX 78212
(210) 733-3939; (800) 851-3666;
FAX (210) 733-3884

This fruit sundae is great with a bagel and cream cheese, or a large muffin, for a breakfast tray. We are small enough that we can cater the breakfasts to meet our guests' needs. We serve a full sit-down breakfast at 9:00 A.M., but if our guests have to leave early for business meeting, or a convention, we prepare a tray for them.

Anyday Breakfast Sundae

Grape Nuts cereal or granola
yogurt, any flavor (I coordinate it with one or two kinds of fruit — strawberries, bananas, blueberries, peaches, and kiwi!)
Cool Whip topping

In individual parfait glass or fruit dish, layer 2 tablespoons Grape Nuts or granola; 2 tablespoons yogurt, fresh fruit, repeat. Top with dollop of Cool Whip and a cherry.

Fruit Breakfast Parfaits

1 cup old-fashioned oatmeal, uncooked
2 - 8 ounce containers vanilla yogurt
1 - 8 ounce can crushed pineapple, with juice
2 tablespoons sliced almonds, chopped walnuts or pecans
2 cups blueberries or sliced strawberries, fresh or frozen

In medium bowl with a lid, combine the oats, yogurt, pineapple, and nuts; mix well. Cover and refrigerate overnight or up to one week. To serve, layer the fruit and the oat mixture in 4 parfait glasses. Garnish with additional fruit. Serve chilled. Serves 4.

Carousel Inn

Jim and Kathy Hughes
712 10th Street
Galveston, TX 77550
(409) 762-2166

In addition to Jim's fresh-baked pastries, we serve a variety of fruit dishes. This recipe, served in sparkling parfait glasses makes an appealing addition to an already beautifully set table, and it is very popular with our guests.

Hill Top Country Inn

Chuck and Becky Derrow
1733 County Road 28
Auburn, IN 46706
(219) 281-2298

The morning glory of our inn's winter breakfast table is this delightful warm dish of fruit. The bright colors provide the perfect touch to an often used embroidered tablecloth and flowered dishes. Most of the fruit in this recipe comes from our fruit trees and is frozen during the summer season for use throughout the year. The recipe was originally printed in Country Woman *magazine.*

Hot Fruit Compote

1 - 20 ounce can pineapple chunks
1 - 16 ounce can peach slices
1 - 16 ounce can pear pieces
1 - 16 ounce can apricot halves
1 jar maraschino cherries

Orange Sauce

1/3 cup sugar
2 tablespoons cornstarch
1/4 teaspoon salt
1/2 cup light corn syrup
1 cup orange juice, fresh
2 tablespoons orange rind

Drain fruit, arrange in a 9x13 inch baking dish with cherries in hollows. Set aside. Combine orange sauce ingredients in pan, heat to a boil. Remove from heat, pour sauce over fruit. Bake at 350° for 30 minutes. Makes 12 servings.

Serve in stemmed glasses on matching glass plates with a muffin and fresh strawberry jam.

Frozen Fruit Cups

1 12 ounce frozen orange juice, thawed
1/3 cup frozen lemonade concentrate, thawed
2 quarts sliced strawberries
2 - 20 ounce cans pineapple tidbits or chunks, drained, reserving liquid
2 small cans mandarin oranges, drained, reserving liquid
4 kiwi, peeled and cut up
5-6 bananas, sliced
2-3 cups of other fresh fruit such as pears, blueberries, peaches, nectarines, raspberries

Combine thawed frozen juices with juice from pineapple and oranges. Add fruit to the juices and mix well. Divide into 25-30 plastic cups, set on trays and freeze. When frozen, place in plastic bags to store longer. Let thaw in individual serving dishes about 30-45 minutes before breakfast time.

Parkview Bed and Breakfast

Tom and Donna Hofmann
211 North Park St.
Reedsburg, WI 53959
(608) 524-4333
Email: parkview@tes.itis.com

This has been a great time-saver in breakfast preparation. This recipe is prepared ahead of time and is ready to thaw and serve to a few or many people. Be creative in the fruit that you use. The guests at Parkview have really enjoyed this as the fruit course in our breakfast that features a full breakfast.

the secret Bed and Breakfast Lodge

Diann and Carl Cruickshank
Route 1, Box 82
Leeburg, AL 35983-9732
(205) 523-3825; FAX (205) 523-3825
Web site: http://www.bbonline.com/~bbonline/al/the secret

A special place, the secret, come, enjoy, discover why. Dining is just one of the many "secrets" awaiting your discovery. Located at the foothills of the Lookout Mountain Parkway, guests dine around a 10' dining table which hosts an 8' lazy susan (a great conversation starter in the mornings).

Although a complete country breakfast is served, we are always looking for quick and easy fruit dishes as accompaniments. This is one of our favorites, especially during the winter months. A variation is to slice bananas, sprinkle with walnuts and drizzle with honey. Simple and delicious.

Fruit Delight

1 cup raisins
3 bananas
sprinkle of sugar
1 1/2 cups orange juice (more if desired)
optional: garnish with a slice of orange or sprinkle of coconut

Place 1 cup of raisins in a container. Pour 1 1/2 cups of orange juice over the raisins. Cover overnight. 30 minutes before breakfast slice 3 bananas. Add more juice, if desired.

Garnish with slices of fresh oranges around rim of bowl. (May be eaten.) Top with sprinkles of coconut. Makes a beautiful display in a glass bowl. Colorful. Tasty. Quick. Easy. Impressive! Enjoy!

Fruit in a Flower

1 cup per serving mixed fruit
1 sprig lemon verbena or mint
1 tulip, per serving

Mix several kinds of fruit. Remove pistils and stamens from tulips. Place tulips in clear glass sherbet cups and fill with fruit. Garnish with sprig of mint of lemon verbana. We have been told that the Dutch settlers use the tulip as a symbol of the Father, Son and Holy Spirit. We have used this throughout the house as decoration.

Zephyr Glen Bed and Breakfast

Noreen and Gil McGurl
205 Dester Road
Scottsdale, PA 15683
(412) 887-6577; FAX, call first, (412) 887-6177

This is very easy but makes your guests feel very special. When breakfast begins with a fruit cup as pretty as the tulip cup, it doesn't matter what else you serve — they are so enchanted by the presentation! We just love surprising our guests. We have many other interesting ideas but this is everyone's favorite.

Village Green Inn

Diane and Don Crosby
40 Main Street
Falmouth, MA 02540
(508) 548-5621; (800) 237-1119;
FAX (508) 457-5051

Our gracious, old, 1804 Colonial-Victorian is ideally located on Falmouth's historic village green. Guests enjoy 19th-century charm and warm hospitality amidst elegant surroundings. Four lovely guest rooms and one romantic suite all have private baths and unique fireplaces (two are working). A full gourmet breakfast is served featuring delicious house specialties.

This recipe gives our guests the feeling that they are eating dessert for breakfast and is also refreshing during a warm season. It sets the mood for the main entree along with freshly baked pastry.

Fresh Fruit Medley

2 cups strawberry halves
1 cup grapes
1 banana
1/4 cup slivered almonds
3 cups whipped topping
1/2 cup sour cream
1 cantaloupe

Lightly toast almonds. Slice banana into bite-size pieces. Combine these with strawberries and grapes. Mix 2 cups whipped topping with sour cream. Fold this into fruit mixture. Cut cantaloupe into six slices and remove skin. Place generous amount of fruit mixture on each piece. Top with remaining topping.

Make sure all ingredients are fresh and chilled. Serve immediately. Garnish with almonds if desired.

Red, White, and Blue Parfait

pecans, finely chopped
fresh strawberries, sliced lengthwise
cream cheese
whipped topping
sugar
fresh blueberries

Combine cream cheese, whipped topping and sugar in food processor, set aside. In each parfait glass layer in order: pecans, fresh strawberries, cream cheese mixture, fresh blueberries, cream cheese mixture. Repeat second, third and fourth layer, top with a dollop of whipped topping and a strawberry half on top! Beautiful, easy and very festive.

Simply Southern Bed and Breakfast

Carl and Georgia Buckner
211 North Tennessee Boulevard
Murfreesboro, TN 37130
(615) 896-4988
Web site: http://www.bbonline.com/tn/simply southern/

Here at Simply Southern, every day is an occasion to celebrate. Our table is always set with a holiday theme or with the season of the year in mind. Some of our favorite times are when we celebrate the patriotic holidays. Red, white, and blue prevails on our menu as well as our table.

One of our hobbies is collection kaleidoscopes and other optical novelties. Kaleidoscopes are perfect for our inn as one of the definitions, according to Webster, is — a series of some of constantly changing phases and events. Guests will find some of our optical devices on the table every day. Our guests seem to really enjoy them and they have turned out to be a great ice breaker.

Magnolia House

Joyce and Patrick Kenard
101 East Hackberry
Fredericksburg, TX 78624
(210) 977-0306; (800) 880-4374;
FAX (210) 997-0766

We serve a full, sit-down breakfast each morning at 8:30 A.M. in the formal dining room and breakfast room. Each breakfast begins with a freshly baked muffin, orange juice, fresh fruit cup which can be topped with our famous fruit dip. The buffet table changes every day, including a combination of waffles, French toast or crepes and an egg entree. Everything is prepared from scratch and served on antique china and silver.

Some guests have used this dip as a topping for their muffins or stirred into their coffee. One gentleman was caught cleaning out the bowl with his finger!

Fruit Dip

1 cup whipping cream
1 cup light brown sugar
1 cup sour cream
4 teaspoons Kahlua
1 teaspoon vanilla

Whisk all together. We start each breakfast with a fresh fruit cup topped off with this tasty sauce. One guest asked for a straw!

Country Mixin's

Breakfast Casseroles

"And all that believed were together, and had all things in common; . . . breaking bread from house to house, did eat their meat with gladness and singleness of heart, Praising God, and having favour with all the people. And the Lord added to the church daily such as should be saved."

Acts 2:44, 46-47

Littleton's Maplewood Manor Bed and Breakfast

Helen and Alan Burtchell
PO Box 1165, 120 College St.
Littleton, NC 27850
(919) 586-4682

We serve a full breakfast to our guests either in the formal dining room or the screened porch, on warm mornings. With the good morning casserole, I can make it the night before, refrigerate overnight, then pop it in the oven to cook in the morning. When I have breakfast at different times, for the early risers, or the late, it is hot and ready. It also gives me time to chat with my guests, and I do not have to rush. All in all it makes for a very pleasant morning. But the topper is it tastes great!

Maplewood's Good Morning Casserole

1 pound of sausage, any flavor, cooked and drained. Squeeze out all fat.
4 eggs or egg substitute
2 cups regular milk, or 2%
1 regular can of mushroom soup
1 cup cheddar cheese, grated
1- 5 1/2-6 ounce box of seasoned croutons

Spray a 9x9 inch or 9x13 inch glass baking dish. Line bottom with croutons. Add sausage to cover bottom. Beat eggs, milk together in bowl. Add rest of ingredients. Mix well. Pour over sausage. Bake at 350° for 1 hour. Serves 6-8.

This is great for making the night before. Just put all ingredients together, cover, and put in refrigerator.

You may want to add mushrooms, or assorted small cut vegetables. This will give you a different taste. But still great!

Sausage-Mushroom Breakfast Casserole

2 1/4 cups seasoned croutons
1 1/2 pounds bulk pork sausage
4 eggs, beaten
2 1/4 cups milk
1 - 10 1/4 ounce can cream of mushroom soup, undiluted
1 - 4 ounce can sliced mushrooms, drained
3/4 teaspoon dry mustard
2 cups (8 ounces) shredded cheddar cheese
cherry tomato halves (optional)
parsley sprigs (optional)

Spread croutons in a lightly greased (I use Pam) 13x9x2 inch baking dish; set aside. Cook sausage until browned, stirring to crumble; drain well. Sprinkle sausage over croutons. Combine eggs, milk, soup, mushrooms, and mustard; mix well, and pour over sausage. Cover and refrigerate at least 8 hours or overnight.

Remove from refrigerator; let stand 30 minutes. Bake uncovered at 325° for 50-55 minutes. Sprinkle cheese over top; bake an additional 5 minutes or until cheese melts. Garnish with tomatoes and parsley, if desired. Serves 8-10.

Anderson House Inn

Jim and Susan Hildebrand
201 E. Main Street
Heber Springs, AR 72543-3116
(501) 362-5266; (800) 264-5279;
FAX (501) 362-2326
Internet site: http://www.bbonline.com/ar/anderson

We have a country inn in the bed and breakfast tradition. Guests enjoy a wonderful lodging alternative in a beautiful Ozark foothills setting. We are convenient to Greens Ferry Lake and Little Red River fishing and water sports. Trophy trout fishing is available. We feature handmade quilts, antiques, and a southern flavor. Our great room has a large screen TV for guests to enjoy.

The Cedars Bed and Breakfast

Carol, Jim, and Brona Malecha
616 Jamestown Road
Williamsburg, VA 23185
(757) 229-3591; (800) 296-3591

When we bought The Cedars B&B in October, 1993, we truly began a new life. Having been bankers for 20-plus years in Chicago, we not only changed our lifestyle but moved to a totally different part of the country. Drawn by the history of the area, we soon felt immersed in the 18th century and the "South." We were quickly introduced to GRITS — something very foreign to the Yankee pallet. To prove that we had assimilated into our new culture, we decided that we had to have at least a token grits entree! In an old file left by a previous owner, we found a yellowing, handwritten recipe that married the plain grits to cheese and bacon. After several tries with the proportions, we settle don the following concoction. We hope you enjoy it as much as our guests do and that it gives you a "taste of the South!"

Grits Breakfast Casserole

2 1/4 cups grits and 9 cups water (Approximate. Brands of grits vary slightly.)
3 cups shredded Cheddar cheese
2 cups bacon bits (or to taste)
3 eggs
1/2 cups butter
3/4 cup milk

Cook grits as directed. While hot, add cheese and bacon. Let cool. Add eggs, butter, and milk. Pour into greased 9x13 inch baking dish. Refrigerate overnight. Bake in preheated 350° oven for 50-60 minutes, until bubbly.

Serves 12-16. If smaller amount is needed, the recipe can be divided by thirds.

Cheese Grits Supreme

1 cup grits
1/2 cup butter (softened)
1 roll (6 ounce) bacon cheese
3 eggs
2/3 cup milk
1/2 cup cheddar cheese, grated

Cook grits. Add butter and bacon cheese to hot grits and mix well. Cool. Beat eggs with milk and stir into grits. Pour in greased 2 quart casserole dish. Top with grated cheese. Bake 45 minutes at 325°. Garnish with bacon curls.

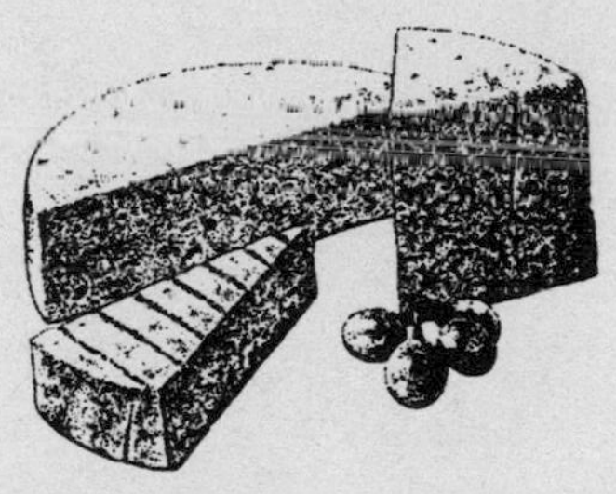

Trail's End

Joan G. Ramey
5931 Highway 56
Owensboro, KY 42301
(502) 77-5590; FAX (502) 771-4723

I use my own garden club's cookbook for almost everything. My garlic cheese grits are done also with my own seasonings.

This recipe is well received by the variety of guests who come to our riding stables, tennis schools, and two bed and breakfast locations. Our "Barn Cottage" sits next to our riding stables near Rockport, Indiana, while our "Red House" is adjacent to our indoor tennis club where Ramey tennis school camps are held in season. We offer a little something for everyone.

The Quilt House Bed and Breakfast

Miriam and Hans Graetzer
PO Box 339
Estes Park, CO 80517
(907) 586-0427

A beautiful view can be enjoyed from every window of our sturdy mountain home. It is just a 15-minute walk to downtown Estes Park and only four miles from the entrance of Rocky Mountain National Park. There are three bedrooms upstairs for guests plus a lounge where guests can read, look at the mountains, and have a cup of coffee or tea. A guest house beside the main house has a kitchenette. We gladly help with information concerning hiking trails, car drives, wildlife viewing, shopping, etc.

Yorkshire Casserole

1 pound pork sausage
4 large eggs
1 cup flour
1 cup milk

In a skillet, brown sausage on medium heat, stirring to break up the meat. When all red color is gone, drain off oil and discard (you can do this part the night before and then refrigerate.) An hour before serving time, place the sausage in a greased 7x11 inch pan. In blender or Mixmaster, add the eggs and beat until foamy; add the flour and milk and mix thoroughly. Bake in preheated 350° oven for 40-45 minutes. Cut in squares. Serves 8.

This is lovely served with fruit juice, a fruit cup, assorted breads and a hot beverage of choice. Fresh apple slices make a pretty edible garnish.

Hash Brown Casserole

1 pound bag hash browns
1 cup sour cream
1 cup shredded cheddar cheese
1 can cream of mushroom soup
1/4 cup finely diced onion
salt and pepper to taste

Mix all together in large bowl. Bake in 9x13 inch pan at 350° for 30-40 minutes. I top with paprika and parsley for color, before I bake. Serves 10-12.

Margie's Inn on the Bay

Margie L. Vorhies
120 Forrest Road
Sequim, WA 98382
(360) 683-7011 (voice and FAX);
(800) 730-7011

We have Sequim's only waterfront bed and breakfast. It is a contemporary ranch-style home with 180 feet on the water. Guests enjoy a terrific view of the water from our hot tub. Five well-appointed bedrooms with private baths. A large sitting room with VCR and movies. Two Persian cats and a talking parrot are also residents. Close to the marina, fishing, Dungeness National Wildlife Refuge and Spit, Olympic Game Farm, hiking, biking, Hurricane Ridge, gift shops, and much more.

Magnolia House Bed and Breakfast

Kim and John Trudo
315 George Street
New Bern, NC 28562
(919) 633-9488 (voice and FAX);
(800) 601-948

We serve a full breakfast at guests' convenience. Guests may choose to have it served under the magnolia tree for which the inn is named.

Located two doors from Tryon Place, once home to the Royal Governor of North Carolina, guests find Magnolia House to be centrally located in the heart of the historic district. Magnolia House is furnished with local estate antiques and family pieces, and it features three uniquely decorated guest rooms, each with private bath.

Kim's Hash Brown Bake

4 cups frozen, shredded potatoes
1/2 cup butter or margarine, melted
2 cups diced ham
1 small onion, diced
1 clove garlic, minced
2 cups shredded cheddar cheese
1 cup milk
1/2 cup Parmesan cheese
8 eggs
salt and pepper to taste

Thaw potatoes between paper towels to remove excess moisture. Press potatoes into bottom of greased 9x13 inch pan, drizzle with butter and sprinkle with Parmesan cheese. Bake at 425° for 25 minutes. Cool on wire rack 10 minutes. Add onion, ham, cheddar cheese, over potatoes. Combine eggs, milk, garlic, salt and pepper, stirring well; pour over ham mixture. Bake at 350° for 30 minutes, or until set. Let stand for 10 minutes before serving. Yield 8-10 servings.

A dollop of sour cream can top each serving for extra tang.

NOTE: Hash Brown Bake may be assembled, omitting the egg mixture, and refrigerated overnight. Let stand at room temperaturc 30 minutes. Add egg mixture; pour over ham mixture. Bake as above.

Breakfast Supreme

1 pound pork sausage, cooked
1 small onion, sautéed
2 cups milk
9 eggs
1 - 4 ounce can mushrooms
1 - 7 ounce can diced green chilies
1 pound grated cheddar cheese
1 loaf white bread

Line 9x13 inch pan with bread (crusts trimmed). Sprinkle on cooked sausage, sautéed onion, drained mushrooms, green chilies. Mix eggs and milk; pour over bread and toppings, top with shredded cheese and refrigerate overnight. Bake at 375°, uncovered, for 45 minutes. Let stand 10 minutes before serving. (Can be halved and cooked in a 9x9 inch pan). Serves 9

Serve with fresh fruit, home fried potatoes, and rolls.

Locust Hill Bed and Breakfast

Bill and Beverly Beard
1185 Mooresville Pike
Columbia, TN 38401
(615) 388-8531; (800) 577-8264

Our delicious gourmet breakfasts feature country ham, featherlight biscuits, and homemade jams enjoyed in the dining room or sunroom.

We have a beautifully restored, 1840 antebellum home, decorated with family antiques. Our guests pamper themselves with morning coffee in their room and evening refreshments at the fireside. They can enjoy the fireplaces and relax in the library, flower gardens, or on the three porches.

Mountain View Bed and Breakfast

Brenda and Cecil Dunn
28050 County Road P
Dolores, CO 81323
(970) 882-7861; (800) 228-4592

People who visit us enjoy being served something "Southwest" so we try to serve this about every two to three days, so folks have some at least once during their stay. Almost anything can go in the casserole, but I use variations of the above recipe. Guests love it served with salsa.

Brenda's Southwest Casserole

- 6-8 four tortillas (to cover bottom and sides of 9x12 pan)
- 4-5 cups cheese mixture of cheddar, colby, Parmesan, cottage cheese
- 2-3 cups broccoli
- 8-10 slices ham
- 1/2 cup mushrooms
- 1/2 cup onions
- 16 eggs
- 1 cup milk
- lemon pepper to taste

Melt stick of margarine in 9x12 inch pan (or any size needed). Layer tortillas to cover bottom and up sides. Sprinkle 1 cup grated cheese over tortillas. Layer broccoli, ham, mushrooms, and onions to cover pan; sprinkle with lemon pepper. Mix in separate bowl 16 eggs, milk, 4 cups grated cheese mixture, salt; pour over ham and vegetables. Bake at 350° 45 minutes, or until knife inserted into middle comes out clean. Allow to sit 15-20 minutes so that pieces will cut more evenly. Serve with

Do Ahead Sausage-Egg Casserole

8 slices white bread, cubed
2 cups shredded cheddar cheese
1 1/2 pounds bulk sausage
4 eggs
2 1/4 cups milk
1/4 teaspoon dry mustard
1 can cream of mushroom soup
1/2 cup milk

Place bread in bottom of greased 9x13 inch pan, top with cheese. Brown sausage, drain and put on top of cheese. Beat eggs with 2 1/4 cups milk and mustard. Pour over all. Cover and refrigerate overnight. To bake, dilute soup with 1/2 cup milk and pour over casserole. Bake uncovered at 300° for 1 1/2 hours, or until set. Let stand about 10 minutes before cutting and serving.

Fresh sliced, mixed fruits or berries, and light textured muffins go well with this entree.

Whispering Waters Bed and Breakfast

Lana and Ray Feldman
HCR 5, Box 125B
Priest Lake, ID 83856
(208) 443-3229

The wonderful aroma coming from this dish as it bakes fills the house, and guests are more than ready to eat by the time it is placed before them.

Casa de Angeles

Marilynn and Bill Milligan
5115 Twin Acres Drive
Bee Cave, TX 78736
(512) 263-7378

We built our dream home on a creek bank among old oaks, where wildflowers and native grasses abound, where people can escape. Many of the people who stay with us here in the Texas Hill Country like and expect something a little on the spicy side. We developed this dish to satisfy those needs, and besides, it is a easy, complete meal in itself. Serve it with fresh fruit and homemade muffins.

Casa de Angeles Hill Country Casserole

In an 8x8 inch greased square casserole dish, layer the following:

2 3/4 cup frozen hash brown potatoes
3/4 cup grated jalapeno Monterey Jack cheese
1 cup diced Canadian Bacon
1/4 cup chopped green onion

Mix and pour over the above:
4 eggs, beaten
12 ounce can skim evaporated milk
1 tablespoon parsley or cilantro
1/4 teaspoon pepper
1/8 teaspoon salt
dash of chili powder or red pepper

Cover and refrigerate overnight. Bake uncovered at 350° for one hour. Let stand 5 minutes. Cut into squares and serve. Garnish with salsa, cheese wedge, and parsley. Serves 4-6.

Breakfast Casserole

- 1 pound fresh sausage, browned slightly, crumbled
- 6 eggs
- 2 cups milk
- 6 slices bread, cubed
- 1 teaspoon salt
- 1/2 teaspoon dry mustard
- 1/8 teaspoon pepper
- 1 cup grated cheddar cheese

Beat eggs well; add bread cubes, milk, salt, pepper, and mustard. Add sausage and cheese last. Pour into greased 9x9 inch baking dish. Bake for 45 minutes at 350°, or until set. Serve with or without sausage gravy. This may be prepared at night to be baked the following morning. If chilled, it will need a little longer to bake. Serves 9.

I prefer canned fresh sausage using the top, grease layer of a pint jar for the gravy and the rest of the meat for the casserole If you cover with lid while baking, it will rise nice and fluffy.

The Shepherd and Ewe Bed and Breakfast

Twila and Robert Risser
11205 Country Club Road
Waynesboro, PA 17268
(717) 762-8525; (888) 937-4393;
FAX (717) 762-5880

Our inn is renowned for its rich shepherding heritage, The Shepherd and Ewe extends that same nurturing tradition to its guests who are invited to unwind in one of four guest rooms or the spacious master suite. Filled with Victoriana and lovingly restored and collected antiques, each room is clean and inviting. A full country breakfast with homemade breads, muffins, and other delights may easily include this casserole. Located high atop lush acres of rolling farmland, the B&B is a short drive to Gettysburg and Mercersburg, PA, Sharpsburg, MD, fine restaurants, state parks, hiking trails, art galleries, and antique shops.

Buckmaster Inn Bed and Breakfast

Sam and Grace Husselman
Lincoln Hill Road, Box 118
Shrewsbury, VT 05738
(802) 492-3485

Our guests rave about this breakfast. They really enjoy it and ask for the recipe. I use Vermont cheddar cheese.

The Buckmaster Inn (1801) was an early stagecoach stop in Shrewsbury. Standing on a knoll overlooking a picturesque barn scene and rolling hills, the Inn is situated in the Green Mountains.

Cheddar Cheese-Egg Casserole

4-6 slices bread (crusts removed)
1/2 pound cheddar cheese grated
a pinch of onion powder
a pinch of garlic powder
4 eggs
2 1/4 cups milk
Variations: green pepper, sausage

Butter 9x13 inch casserole dish, place bread slices in pan. Place grated cheese over bread. Sprinkle onion, garlic powders over cheese. Beat eggs until well blended, add milk and beat a little longer. Pour over cheese and bread. Bake at 350° for 45 minutes. Serve immediately. Serves 6.

Place above on serving dish (cut 6 pieces). I serve with a sprig of parsley and home fried potatoes, or potato cake and toast cut in triangle pieces.

Federal Crest Egg Casserole

6 eggs
9 bread slices, buttered
1 cup shredded cheddar cheese
1/2 cup crumbled, precooked bacon or sausage
1 1/2 cups milk
1/4 teaspoon salt
1/4 teaspoon pepper

Prepare 5-6 individual casserole dishes (ramekins), by spraying lightly with PAM cooking spray. Mix in one bowl: crumbled bread pieces, bacon crumbs, salt, pepper and cheese. In another bowl beat eggs lightly and add milk. Mix both bowls together and fill casseroles 3/4 full. Refrigerate overnight. Cook at 350° for 20-25 minutes or until bubbly and golden. Inserted knife should come out clean. Garnish with parsley.

Federal Crest Inn Bed and Breakfast

Ann and Phil Ripley
1101 Federal Street
Lynchburg, VA 24504
(804) 845-6155; (800) 818-6155;
FAX (804) 845-1445

This casserole works grand for large or small groups and allows for the cook to place them in the oven at different times for various breakfast seatings. We serve baked apples and biscuits with the egg dish, which is preceded with our "Message Muffins," (sort of like fortune cookies), and fresh fruit and juice. Hearty breakfast or brunch!

Butternut Farm

Don Reid
1654 Main Street
Glastonbury, CT 06033
(860) 633-7197; FAX (860) 659-1758

Overnight accommodations at Butternut Farm are in rooms furnished in keeping with the Colonial period. A full breakfast with fresh eggs, milk, cheese, and homemade jams is served in the original kitchen or intimate breakfast room. I discovered this recipe while looking for a way to use excess eggs during our chickens' heavy laying season.

Dorothy's Brunch Egg Casserole

Make white sauce using:

2 tablespoons melted margarine
2 tablespoons flour
2 cups milk

1 cup shredded cheddar cheese
1/2 to 1 cup crumbled, cooked bacon
1 dozen eggs
butter
1/2 to 1/4 cup mushrooms, cooked
1/4 cup chopped onion
salt and pepper to taste

Combine flour and a small portion of the milk, removing all lumbs. Pour in a saucepan with butter and remaining milk. Cook on a medium heat until it thickens and bubbles. Add cheddar cheese to white sauce, stirring to melt. Optional: add as much of a cup of crumbled cooked bacon as desired.

Beat a dozen standard, shelled, raw eggs and sauté in butter, scrambling only until "set," no more than half done. Add cooked mushrooms and onions. Transfer eggs mixture to 12x7x2 inch glass baking dish; top with buttered crumbs and paprika, or just use seasoned salt. Bake at 350° for about 30 minutes.

If freezing this dish, let thaw for a few hours before baking.

Potato and Egg Casserole

8 medium potatoes
4 slices ham or bacon
12 eggs
1/4 teaspoon paprika
1/4 teaspoon black pepper
salt
1/4 cup finely chopped parsley
1 cup finely chopped onion
1/2 cup sour cream

Peel potatoes. Parboil potatoes for 20 minutes. Drain and cool. Cut into 1/8 inch slices. Cook onion in 2 tablespoons oil. Remove onion with slotted spoon. Add potatoes and sauté until browned. Return potato slices to a skillet, arranging so they lie flat. Make 2 to 3 layers, sprinkling each with parsley and onion. Put eggs, salt, pepper, paprika, and sour cream into bowl; beat with electric mixer. Pour egg mixture over potatoes; sprinkle with chopped ham or bacon. Cook over low heat for approximately 15 minutes, until eggs are "set." Remove from heat and cut into 12 servings.

Christmas Inn

Lynn Durfee
232 W. Main Street
Aspen, CO 81611
(970) 925-3822; (800) 625-5581;
FAX (970) 925-3328

Serve with spicy salsa and dribble with finely shredded cheddar cheese. This is a great hearty breakfast with lots of carbohydrates for the strenuous outdoor activities, such as skiing, hiking, rafting, or mountain biking!

Dairy Hollow House: Country Inn

Ned Shank and Crescent Dragonwagon
515 Spring Street
Eureka Springs, AR 72632
(501) 253-7444; (800) 562-8650;
FAX (501) 253-7223

Layered casseroles, usually called "stratas," of eggs, bread, and cheese in various permutations are served for breakfast, at inns all over the country. Ours is truly special, thanks to Ned, who came up with the idea of using our own fabulous skillet-sizzled buttermilk cornbread for the bread. Our strata's enchanting name is courtesy of Marion Cunningham's Breakfast Book. *Serve with fresh fruit, hashbrowns.*

"There's nothing like waking up to a breakfast at a B&B — particularly a breakfast at Arkansas' Dairy Hollow House." — Southern Living *magazine.*

Featherbed Eggs

leftover, crumbled cornbread (a couple of slices will do)
1 1/2 cups grated, extra sharp cheddar cheese
6 eggs
1 1/2 cups milk
Tabasco, Pickapeppa sauce
salt and fresh-ground black pepper
seasoning salt, such as BellMystika

Preheat oven to 375°. Spray 6 - 3 1/2 inch ramekins or custard cups with PAM cooking spray. Place ramekins on a baking sheet. Place a few tablespoons of coarsely crumbled cornbread into the bottom of each ramekin. Divide cheddar cheese among the ramekins, sprinkling over the cornbread crumbs. Beat together eggs and milk, seasoning to taste with Tabasco, etc. Pour egg mixture over cornbread in ramekins. Bake 20-25 minutes, or until golden and puffed. Serves 6.

Farmer's Strata

1 pound sliced bacon cut into 1/2 inch pieces
2 cups chopped, fully cooked ham
1 small onion, chopped
10 slices white bread, cubed
1 cup cubed, cooked potatoes
3 cups shredded cheddar cheese
8 eggs
3 cups milk
1 tablespoon Worcestershire sauce
1 teaspoon dry mustard
salt and pepper

In a skillet, cook bacon until crisp, add ham and onion; cook until onion is tender, drain. In a greased 13x9x2 inch pan layer 1/2 the bread cubes, potatoes, and cheese. Top with all of bacon mixture. Repeat layers of bread, potatoes and cheese. In a bowl beat eggs, milk, Worcestershire sauce, mustard, salt and pepper. Pour over all, cover, chill overnight. Remove from refrigerator let stand 30 minutes before baking. Bake uncovered at 325° for 65-70 minutes. Yield 12-16 servings.

The Farmer's Strata can be made with or without the potatoes, and sausage can be used instead of ham. This recipe goes well with the atmosphere of the Plum Bear Ranch, which is located in farm and ranch country.

Plum Bear Ranch

Wendy and Rory Lynch
PO Box 241
29461 County Road 21
Springfield, CO 81073
(719) 523-4344; FAX (719) 523-4324

The recipe for the Farmer's Strata came from a magazine called Taste of Home, *I like it so much I decided to make it for my guests and have had very good reviews ever since. I feel the Farmer's Strata goes so well in this area because most of this country is farm and ranch land. The ingredients in the recipe use many of the products that are farmed and/or raised in this area. There are many wheat, pig, and vegetable farmers in southern Colorado, so I thought this recipe represents this area well.*

Rest and Repast Bed and Breakfast Reservations

Box 126
Pine Grove Mills, PA 16868
(814) 238-1484
FAX (814) 238-9890
Web site: http://iul.com/business/bnbinpa

This particular host has been with Rest and Repast since 1991. She has a restored 1850s farmhome out in the country that is a bird lover's dream come true. Her prized asparagus beds provide her in the spring with ample bounty to share with her guests. This is a recipe she has found is both easy to prepare the night before and that guests enjoy and ask for again and again. Please call us for more information on her or any of our 60-plus inns that we represent.

Our many selections include scenic farms, estates, private apartments, cottages and lodges, as well as a variety of contemporary homes in all of central Pennsylvania and selected inns statewide. Several sites appropriate for small wedding receptions, family reunions, and corporate retreats.

Asparagus-Cheese Strata

from Just Country Bed and Breakfast

- 1 - 1 1/2 pounds fresh asparagus, cut into 2 inch pieces
- 3 tablespoons butter or oleo, melted
- 1 loaf (1 pound) sliced bread, crusts removed
- 3/4 cup shredded cheddar cheese, divided
- 2 cups cubed fully cooked ham
- 6 eggs
- 3 cups milk
- 2 teaspoons dried minced onion
- 1/2 teaspoon salt
- 1/4 teaspoon dry mustard

In a saucepan, cover asparagus with water; cover and cook until just tender but still firm. Drain and set aside. Lightly brush butter over one side of bread slices. Place half of the bread, buttered side up, in a greased 13x9x2 inch baking dish. Sprinkle with 1/2 cup cheese. Layer with asparagus and ham. Cover with remaining bread, buttered side up. In a bowl, lightly beat eggs; and milk, onion, salt, and mustard; pour over bread. Cover and refrigerate overnight. Bake, uncovered at 350° for 50 minutes. Sprinkle with the remaining cheese. Return to oven for 10 minutes longer or until cheese is melted and a knife inserted near the center comes out clean. Yield: 10-12 servings.

Scofield House Egg and Sausage Strata

- 2 pounds bulk pork sausage
- 8 ounces sour cream
- 6 whole English muffins (sour dough, whole wheat, plain)
- 1 pound grated Monterey Jack cheese
- 6 extra large eggs
- 2 1/2 cups milk (2% or skim)
- 1 can condensed cream of mushroom soup
- 1 cup finely grated green pepper (optional)

Brown and drain pork sausage. Mix soup and sour cream together. Crumble muffins and line a greased 9x13 inch baking pan. Mix eggs and milk together in a separate bowl. Layer in pan 1/2 sausage, 1/2 grated cheese, 1/2 soup mixture onto crumbled muffins. Repeat layers ending with soup mixture, then smooth with spatula. Pour milk and egg mixture over all (poke with sharp knife to help absorb milk mixture). Wrap with plastic and foil and refrigerate overnight. Next day, bake uncovered at 300° for 1 hour. "Rest" on rack for 5 minutes. Cut into squares and serve. Serves 10-12. Reheats and freezes well.

The Scofield House Bed and Breakfast

Bill and Fran Cecil
908 Michigan Street
Sturgeon Bay, WI 54235-1849
(414) 743-7727 (voice or FAX);
(888) 463-0204

The Scofield House B&B established 1987, believes in the promotion of the "true bed and breakfast experience" — providing guests with lovely accommodations, warm hospitality and great food. In the true Victorian tradition, breakfast is served in the dining room and parlor, with tables set with fine china, silver and crystal. At breakfast the fine art of conversation, a Victorian avocation, is practiced and encouraged.

Very rich, very delicious — our Egg and Sausage Strata is a big favorite of our guests.

Greenfield Inn

Barbara and Vic Mangini
Box 400
Greenfield, NH 03047
(603) 547-6327; (800) 678-9144;
FAX (603) 547-2418

Barbara and I have been extraordinarily fortunate to have enjoyed Bob Hope and his wonderful wife, Dolores, as personal friends for over 31 years. Bob and I met first to market one of his road movies. From the minute we met there was a chemical reaction, i.e., we kidded each other and like each other from the start. Dolores, too. They came to our inn several times in our ten years here. Bob said he loved Barbara's "Egg Strata" so we named it for him. The Hopes and our 5,000 repeat guests come back, they say, because ". . . your inn, Barbara, is wonderfully Victorian, romantic, clean, and best of all comfortable. Your breakfasts are a party with Vic and his Bob Hope style humor."

Egg Strata Bob Hope Style

4 cups cubed firm white bread (8 slices of Pepperidge Farm)
2 cups shredded sharp cheddar cheese
8 to 12 ounces diced ham or sautéed sausage or cooked, crumbled bacon
10 eggs, lightly beaten
4 cups milk
1 tablespoon dry mustard
1 tablespoon onion powder
fresh ground pepper
salt to taste (I don't use any)

Generously butter 9x13 inch glass baking dish. Arrange bread cubes on bottom. Sprinkle with meat, then with cheese. Beat together milk, eggs, mustard, onion powder, salt, and pepper. Before baking, sprinkle with paprika. Preheat then bake at 300° for 1 hour. Makes 12 servings. Suggestion: Make it the night before and refrigerate.

On the Sunny Side

Egg Dishes

"Turn us again, O God of hosts, and cause thy face to shine; and we shall be saved."

Psalm 80:7

Duke and Duchess Bed and Breakfast

Doris Marsh
151 Duke of Gloucester Street
Annapolis, MD 21401
(410) 268-6323

We have a beautifully renovated 1850 home located in the historic district of Annapolis. Just a short walk to the US Naval Academy, City Dock, restaurants, and shops. Furnished tastefully with antiques and artwork, guests can relax and enjoy an atmosphere of cozy elegance. The B&B offers clean, comfortable accommodations with modern conveniences, including central air-conditioning. A full, complimentary breakfast is served.

Simply Fancy Eggs in Pastry

8 pastry puff shells
8 extra large eggs
2-3 (1/4 inch) slices ham, diced
1/3-1/2 pound jalapeno Havarti cheese, grated
1/2 cup milk
salt and pepper to taste
1 tablespoon butter

Prepare pastry puffs according to package directions. In large mixing bowl, combine eggs, ham, cheese, milk, salt and pepper; beat lightly. In large skillet melt butter. Over high heat scramble egg mixture. Fill pastry puffs. Serves 4-8.

Serve either one or two per person or all on a platter for buffet-style. Serve with sausages or bacon strips and tomato slices (to dress up), and a sprig of parsley.

Elegant Egg Bake
with Lingonberry Sauce

1 cup milk
6 eggs
1 cup flour
1 cup low-fat cottage cheese
1 cup shredded Monterey Jack cheese

Preheat oven to 350°. Grease 8x11 inch baking dish and cover bottom with shredded cheese. Mix milk, eggs, flour and cottage cheese; pour into pan. Bake for 45 minutes. Remove promptly and serve piping hot.

Babette's Inn

Jim and Alicia Johnson
308 S. Tyler Street
Tyler, MN 56178
(507) 537-1632

I serve these fluffy eggs in large squares with a dollop of sour cream and a beautiful drizzle of deep red Scandinavian lingonberry sauce or raspberry sauce. The fruit and Jack cheese combination are a gourmet treat at Babette's table, where they rate a four-star rating from restaurant critics and the "Reader's Favorite" award in the Minneapolis Tribune.

DeLevan House

Mary M. DePumpo
188 DeLevan Avenue
Corning, NY 14830
(607) 962-2347

I started my B&B, because my husband was in the hospital for six years and one month. I had to keep the house going and pay taxes, because everyone wanted to buy my house. I started to look in cookbooks for recipes. People really liked this one. And also, Stuffed French Toast and Morning Pizza.

Eggs Florentine

1/2 pound cooked spinach
4 poached eggs
3 tablespoons butter
2 tablespoons chopped onion
1 recipe Mornay sauce

Heat butter in skillet. Add onions and cook until tender. Add spinach and toss until mixed. Place in a baking dish. Slip eggs into hollow made in mixture. Cover with Mornay sauce and bake at 350° for 10 minutes, or until eggs are set.

Eggs Mornay

4 tablespoons butter
4 tablespoons flour
2 cups milk
1 teaspoon salt
1/2 teaspoon dry mustard
1/8 teaspoon pepper
dash hot pepper
1/4 cup Parmesan cheese
1 egg yolk
2 tablespoons cream
8 eggs

Melt butter over medium heat. Add flour, stirring constantly. Slowly add milk using a wire whisk to blend. Continue stirring until thickened, then add seasonings. Sprinkle in Parmesan cheese very slowly while continuing to whisk until smooth. Stir in egg yolk and cream and remove from heat. Pour a small amount of sauce in the bottoms of 4 one-cup ramekins. Break two eggs into each ramekin, then top with additional sauce. Bake at 400° for 15 minutes.

H.C. Richard Bed and Breakfast

Jackie Williams
PO Box 2606
Jackson, WY 83001
(307) 733-6704; FAX (307) 733-0930

One and one-half blocks from the center of town, Homer and Eliza Richards' granddaughter Jackie is the hostess of a charming bed and breakfast. Amenities included in every room: private baths, goosedown comforters, tea service, telephones, and cable TV. Gourmet breakfasts. Guests may take afternoon tea in the sitting room in front of a glowing fire. Many of the beautiful antiques were Homer and Eliza's and guests can feel the warmth of their presence and the love that they shared just relaxing amidst their treasured belongings.

Historic Brock House Bed and Breakfast

Margie and Jim Martin
1400 Webster Road
Summersville, WV 26651
(304) 872-4887 (voice and FAX)

Historic Brock House has hosted travelers for over 100 years. Daniel and Melvina Brook built the large Queen Anne farmhouse for their family and for guests in Summersville when the county court was in session. Melvina Brook provided meals for lodging guests preparing food grown on their farm. We at Brock House, today, carry on the southern Appalachian hospitality and tradition of serving homemade breads and muffins, freshly ground and brewed coffee, and a variety of deliciously brewed teas.

Baked eggs with a basil sauce is one of the Brock House favorite entrees and is served with lightly sautéed, cider marinated ham slices. We often serve steaming hot, pie-shaped scones and always West Virginia-made jellies and preserves. In late summer entrees feature our own grown tomatoes cut into slices along with garnishes of our own herbs, or nasturtium blossoms.

Baked Eggs
with Brock House Sauce

3 tablespoons margarine
1/8 teaspoon pepper
1/4 teaspoon salt (optional)
2 eggs
1/2 teaspoon fresh chopped basil
2 tablespoons all-purpose flour
1/2 teaspoon dried basil
1 cup skim milk
1/4 cup freshly grated Parmesan cheese

Melt margarine in small saucepan. Stir in flour, pepper and dried basil. Add milk and stir over medium heat until bubbly. Stir for 1 minute more. Spray two 8 ounce baking dishes with nonstick spray. Spoon about 2 tablespoons of sauce into baking dishes. Break each egg over the sauce into the two dishes and spoon remaining sauce over eggs. Bake at 350° for 18-20 minutes. Sprinkle cheese over hot sauce and let stand until it melts, several seconds. Garnish with chopped basil and serve immediately with Canadian bacon or ham slices, fresh tomato slices, homemade raisin biscuits. Serves 2.

Eggs Benedict Caledonia

Ingredients per serving:
2 eggs
1 quality split English muffin
2 slices Canadian bacon or ham
3 tablespoons lemon juice
butter or margarine
1 package Hollandaise Sauce mix
garnish of choice

Toast or broil muffin halves and spread with butter. Top with slices of Canadian bacon or ham. Poach eggs 3 1/2 minutes in cups sprayed with vegetable oil. With whites set and yolks liquid, place inverted eggs upon the waiting muffins. Decoratively smother with Hollandaise Sauce and top with a twisted sliver of lemon. Garnish aside with fresh parsley and any house specialty such as homemade applesauce . . . and proudly present.

The Hollandaise Sauce is the key to great Eggs Benedict and after trying a variety of recipes and mixes, Phil suggests the French Knorr packaged sauce but replace milk with three tablespoons of lemon juice. Unlike anything else, he says, it's foolproof, mixes well, refrigerates, and is ready whenever you turn up the heat. A turn-on anytime for guests . . . and with practice, great fun for the host.

Caledonia Farm Bed and Breakfast—1812

Phil Irwin
47 Dearing Road
Flint Hill, VA 22627
(540) 675-3693 (voice and FAX);
(800) BNB-1812

Eggs Benedict are among the many morning specialties at Caledonia Farm Bed and Breakfast near Washington, VA. Retired international broadcaster Phil Irwin has fine-tuned a rather basic recipe into an offering guaranteed to produce rave reviews. Timing and practice are critical. Phil relies on a microwave oven to keep his food perfectly hot, but a conventional oven will do as well.

Augusta Ayre Bed and Breakfast

Maynard Krum
201 West Second Street
Augusta, KY 41002
(606) 756-3228

I'm not a morning person by nature so I like recipes that don't require a lot of "morning of" preparation. However, I still want something that is special and is substantial. This breakfast fits the bill perfectly. An hour before breakfast I put coffee outside the guest rooms. I then have plenty of time to cube the fruit, bake a batch of muffins, set the table, and assemble the entree. This recipe is also ideal for those occasions when guests want breakfast at different times.

Eggs Benedict
with Fruit Kabobs

2 English muffins
4 slices ham
4 eggs
Cheese Sauce
Fruit Sauce
assorted fresh fruit (melon, banana, strawberries, etc.)

Beat each egg and microwave approximately two minutes for two eggs. Toast muffins and grill ham (25 seconds per side). Assemble: muffin, ham, egg, top with Cheese Sauce. Garnish with paprika. Serves 2.

Cheese Sauce

1 can cheddar cheese soup mixed with 1/3 can milk.

Fruit Sauce

1 can sweetened condensed milk combined with 1/3 cup water, and 1/3 cup orange juice concentrate. Chill overnight.

Fruit Kabobs

Place cubed fruit on bamboo skewers. Serve Fruit Sauce separately.

A gravy boat makes and ideal container for the fruit sauce. This is a fairly quick and easy recipe, but it looks elegant. This is a perfect dish for those times when guests want to eat at different times. Danish, muffins, juice, coffee and/or tea round out your breakfast.

Eggs Benedict Cannonboro

2 packets Knorr Hollandaise Mix
10 ounce package frozen spinach, drained
dash Tabasco sauce
1/4 cup Parmesan cheese
1/4 cup vinegar
6 English muffins
12 eggs
2 beefsteak tomatoes, sliced

To Hollandaise sauce add spinach, dash of Tabasco sauce and Parmesan cheese. Keep warm. Boil water 2-3 quarts in medium saucepan; add vinegar and keep at boiling point. Add eggs; poach for 2 minutes. Toast English muffins. Poach each egg to medium. Place sliced tomato on toasted muffin; top with poached egg and garnish with dollop of Hollandaise Sauce. Serves 12.

Cannonboro Inn Bed and Breakfast

Sally and Bud Allen
184 Ashley Avenue
Charleston, SC 29403
(803) 723-8572; FAX (803) 768-1230

This 1853 historic home offers six beautifully decorated bedrooms with antique four poster and canopied beds. A place to be pampered, where guests sleep in until the aroma of sizzling sausage and home baked biscuits lures them to a full breakfast on the columned piazza overlooking a low country garden and fountain. After breakfast, guests may tour nearby historic sites on complimentary bicycles and return to more pampering with afternoon sherry, tea, and sumptuous home baked goods. Our private baths, off-street parking, color TV, and air-conditioning along with that very special southern hospitality, says this is what Charleston is all about!

Grey Whale Inn

Colette and John Bailey
615 N. Main Street
Fort Bragg, CA 95437
(707) 964-0640; (800) 382-7244;
FAX (707) 964-4408
Email: gwhale@mcn.org

At the Grey Whale Inn, our buffet breakfast is served in a cozy room and available to the guests from 7:30 to 10:00 A.M. The Eggs Rellenos casserole is colorful and tasty, and peppers of all colors are available in the California markets year-round. We keep the dish on an electric warmer tray where it stays hot and fragrant. The Salsa has a great flavor that we vary, dependent upon the fresh ingredients available. We fill one of the expectations of our guests by providing a generous, tantalizing breakfast.

Eggs Rellenos

3 green bell peppers
3 red bell peppers
(or acombination of red, green, yellow to equal six peppers)
3/4 pound sharp cheddar cheese, grated
3/4 Monterey Jack cheese, grated
6 large eggs
9 egg whites
1 quart cottage cheese
1 pint sour cream
8 ounces cream cheese
1 1/2 teaspoon seasoning salt
1/2 teaspoon white pepper
1/4 cup flour
1 teaspoon baking powder

Batter: Process cottage cheese and cream cheese in food processor until smooth. Add seasonings, flour, baking powder, and sour cream and blend 15 seconds more. Beat eggs and egg whites together in large bowl, add the cottage cheese mix and beat well.

Slice the peppers into 1/4 inch slices. Grease two 9½ x 13½ inch baking dishes. Layer half the pepper slices with half of the two grated cheeses. Pour half of batter over, then make second layer of pepper slices and cheeses, and the rest of the batter. Bake at 350° for 50 minutes, or until done. Serves 24-30 people. Serve with fresh Salsa on the side.

Salsa

I buy Home Style Mild La Mexicana Salsa, 64 ounce container at the grocery refrigerator section. Before serving, add to the serving bowl at least a couple of the following fresh vegetables:

- diced tomato, preferably Roman
- sliced green onion, or diced sweet onion
- diced Pasilla chili
- minced parsley, either common or cilantro
- a splash of fresh lime juice

The salsa takes on a whole new dimension. This valuable tip was given to me by Ruth Bowman, assistant innkeeper.

Rhodes House Bed and Breakfast

Marlene and Frank Sipes
PO Box 7
West Baden Springs, IN 47469
(812) 936-7378

Relax in homey luxury of our 1890s Victorian home filled with beautiful carved wood and stained glass. Rock on one of the wraparound porches and enjoy the peaceful view of the town park or the famed, historic West Baden domed hotel. Enjoy Hoosier hospitality with a home-grown, home-cooked breakfast of your choice.

We serve this recipe with a cool fruit compote and corn muffins, and all the fixin's on the side, for summer. When cool breezes blow we use a warm fruit compote. This is fun as all can participate by building their own versions. This is a casual, user friendly breakfast for all ages.

Eggs Mexicalli

6-8 eggs, room temperature
1/3 cup half and half
fresh ground pepper, to taste
options to egg mixture: 1-2 tablespoons chopped green onion, green pepper
crisp crumbled bacon
mushrooms
4-6 tortilla rounds
Monterey Jack or mozzarella cheese

Soft scramble eggs, half and half, and pepper. Add any of the options you choose. When eggs are set (not dry) spoon over tortilla (warmed) and place on cookie sheet. Shake finely shredded Monterey Jack or mozzarella cheese. Place in oven just long enough to melt cheese. Serve with chopped pepper, green onion, tomato, sour cream and/or salsa of choice, on the side.

John's Salsa Eggs

5 eggs
2 - 5 inch slices salami, chopped
2 - 2 inch slices pepperoni, chopped
1 tablespoon favorite salsa
1/4 cup shredded "co-jack" (cheddar and Monterey Jack) cheese
1 teaspoon chopped chives
1 teaspoon parsley
Dash of salt and pepper

In a large bowl, beat eggs with salami and pepperoni. Mix in salsa, then cheese. Beat in chives, parsley and salt and pepper. Cook in a non-stick frying pan over medium heat, stirring occasionally to scramble. Serve hot topped with a dollop of salsa. Makes 2 servings.

Village Park Bed and Breakfast

John Hewett
60 W. Park Street
Fruitport, MI 49415-9668
(616) 865-6289; (800) 469-1118

Innkeeper John Hewett might serve up these eggs on mornings when he has breakfast duty. He cuts the fresh chives and parsley from the herb garden.

Health conscious visitors in the late 1800s came to visit a hotel with mineral baths that once stood just across the street from the B&B, where the village park is now. The Hewetts try to run a "heart smart" B&B with nutritious food and an exercise room, sauna and hot tub open to guests. Overlooking Spring Lake and in the "fruit belt," their B&B attracts many active guests who enjoy swimming, sailing, boating, golfing, cross-country skiing, and biking.

The Seymour House

Tom and Gwen Paton
1248 Blue Star Highway
South Haven, MI 49090
(616) 227-3918 (voice and FAX)

Since we are transplants from Colorado where the southwest influence is very strong, Eggs Santa Fe and our presentation has special meaning to us. We serve Eggs Santa Fe with salsa, a dollop of sour cream and sliced black olives with 2 slices of thick bacon and wheat toast. This colorful entree might be presented on clear dishes, silverware with rust colored handles, blue denim plate mats, napkins and handmade pottery cowboy hat napkin rings for an extra western touch.

Eggs Santa Fe

10 eggs
1/2 cup all-purpose flour
1 teaspoon baking powder
1/8 teaspoon salt
4 cups (16 ounces) shredded Monterey Jack cheese
2 cups (16 ounces) cottage cheese
1/4 cup butter or margarine, melted
2 cans (4 ounces each) chopped green chilies

In a large bowl, beat eggs. Combine flour, baking powder and salt, stir into eggs. Add cheeses, butter and chilies. Pour into a greased 9x13 inch pan or two 9 inch pans. Bake uncovered at 350° for 40 minutes, or until knife inserted in center comes out clean. Let stand 5 minutes before cutting. Serves 12.

Green Chili Egg Bake

12 eggs
1 small can chopped green chilies
1 pint cottage cheese
1 cup grated cheddar, colby, or mozzarella cheese
1 cup flour
1/2 cup melted butter
season to taste

Mix together and pour into Texas muffin pans. Bake 50-55 minutes. Serve with salsa on side and top with white cheese sauce.

White Cheese Sauce

3 cups milk
3 tablespoons butter
1/2 cup flour
1 cup grated mozzarella cheese
seasoning

Heat 2 cups milk and butter, bring to boil. Add flour, shaken with 1 cup milk. Stir constantly until thickens. Stir in cheese and dash of salt.

Light Cheddar Cheese Sauce

Same as above, only add cheddar instead of mozzarella cheese.

Amberwood Beach Inn

Jan and George Davies
N7136 Highway 42
(Lakeshore Drive)
Algoma, WI 54201
(414) 487-3471

Waterfront luxury, private baths, decks open to Lake Michigan. Whirlpool, hot tub, sauna. Sleep to the sound of waves, awake to the sunrise over the water. Walk or picnic or relax on your private deck opening to our 300-foot private beach. Very romantic, secluded getaway. The ultimate in privacy and luxury.

Cowslip's Belle Bed and Breakfast

Jon and Carmen Reinhardt
159 N. Main Street
Ashland, OR 97520
(541) 488-2901; (800) 888-6819;
FAX (541) 482-6138

Teddy bears, chocolate truffles, cozy down comforters, and scrumptious breakfasts are some of our specialties. Our home is a delightful 1913 Craftsman bungalow and carriage house in the heart of Ashland's historic district. A nationally recognized award-winner, featured in McCall's *as one of the "Most Charming Inns in America,"* Country Accents *magazine, "Northwest Best Places," "The Best Places to Kiss in the Pacific Northwest," and "Weekends for Two in the Pacific Northwest — 50 Romantic Getaways."*

Chili Cheese Egg Puff

10 eggs
1/2 cup flour
1 teaspoon baking powder
1/2 teaspoon salt
2 cups cottage cheese
4 cups shredded Monterey Jack cheese
1/2 cup butter
1 large can (7 ounces) diced green chilies
salsa
sour cream

Beat eggs until lemon colored. Add flour, baking powder, salt, cottage cheese, Jack cheese, and butter. Mix until smooth, add chilies, stir. Pour mixture into buttered 9x13 inch glass baking pan. Bake in preheated 350° oven for about 40 minutes or until firm and top is slightly browned. Slice into eight serving portions and serve with salsa and sour cream on the side.

Butterfield Puffed Eggs Surprise

2 packages Pepperidge Farm Puffed Pastry Shells (bake 10, follow instructions)
1 dozen eggs, beaten
1/4 cup shredded Monterey Jack cheese
1/4 cup chopped ham
2 tablespoons chopped scallions
5 large mushrooms sliced and sautéed
Cheese Sauce

Scramble eggs until wet and soft, fold in cheese, ham and scallions and put in prepared puffed pastry shell. Put back in oven for 5 minutes to crisp shell and finish cooking egg. Cover with Cheese Sauce. Sauté mushrooms for garnish. Serves 10.

Cheese Sauce

1/4 cup flour
1/4 cup butter
2 cups milk
1 cup Monterey Jack, or cheddar cheese, grated

Mix together flour and butter to make roux, blend in milk; cook until thickens, boil slowly. Add cheese, blend but do not boil.

Butterfield Bed and Breakfast

Mary Trimmins
Box 1115
Julian, CA 92036
(619) 765-2179; (800) 379-4262;
FAX (619) 765-1229

This dish is delicious for breakfast. It is light and flavorful. Serve with potatoes and fresh fruit. This makes a nice portion. It has become one of our signature dishes and the guests love the puff pastry. Other sauces can be used. For a brunch buffet place shells on a warming tray and put the sauce on the side.

Arrowhead Windermere Manor

Judee and Paul Evers
PO Box 2177
Lake Arrowhead, CA 92352
(909) 336-3292; (800) 429-BLUE

Formerly the Bluebell House, European-style house with Country English/Victorian decor provides a touch of England in a mountain setting. Enjoy a candlelit gourmet breakfast, served on china and crystal in our morning room, with light classical music in the background. We request that our guests come, and be prepared to be pampered! Our guests never want to leave. Beverages and hors d'oeuvres are served between 5:00 P.M. and 6:00 P.M.

The Perfect Egg Dish

Ingredients per serving:
- 1 crepe
- 1 tablespoon cheddar cheese
- Canadian bacon, chopped
- 1 egg
- 1 teaspoon heavy whipping cream
- salt and pepper

Crepes:
- 1/2 cup all-purpose flour
- 1 tablespoon sugar
- 1/2 teaspoon baking powder
- pinch of salt
- 1 large egg
- 1/2 cup milk
- 1 tablespoon unsalted butter, melted

To make crepes: Stir together flour, sugar, baking powder, and salt; in a separate bowl mix egg and milk. With a fork, quickly stir the egg mixture into the dry mixture. Melt 2 tablespoons of butter in a 5 inch crepe pan and pour it into the batter, then stir into the mix; heat the pan over moderate heat. Ladle in only enough to cover the bottom of the pan, swirling the pan to coat it quickly. Cook the crepe long enough until the edges turn golden; remove it quickly from the pan cooked side up on a kitchen towel. I usually cut pieces of waxed paper and stack the crepes on each piece, then freeze some ahead for future use.

To make Perfect Egg Dish: Spray muffin pans with vegetable oil. Place a crepe in a muffin pan cup, and create folds as it is layered around individual cup. Put a small amount of cheese in the bottom of the crepe flower (about 1 tablespoon). Add bacon on top of the cheese. Break an egg into a small cup then pour it over the bacon, sometimes I will break the yolk of the egg, they seem to cook better. Top each egg with a teaspoon of heavy whipping cream. Add salt and pepper. Cover muffin pan lightly with foil, so that the crepes do not burn. Bake at 400° for 15 minutes or until desired doneness is achieved.

I usually serve this on a beautiful china plate, garnished with Hollandaise Sauce, sliced oranges and a cilantro sprig for color. A sprinkling of paprika makes a pretty presentation.

Arrowhead Inn

Jerry, Barbara, and Cathy Ryan
106 Mason Road
Durham, NC 27712
(919) 477-8430 (voice and FAX);
(800) 528-2207

We feature Easter Sunrise Eggs whenever asparagus is available and good. Because we like colorful plates, we garnish with a spiced crab apple ring, or an orange slice and whole-berry cranberry sauce. Alongside we present cream-cheese coffee cake, blueberry muffins, cinnamon Bundt cake, or whatever treats we decide to make that day. It's a breakfast that guests love, and that we find satisfying to serve.

Easter Sunrise Eggs

1/3 cup onions, chopped
5 tablespoons butter
5 tablespoons flour
2 1/2 cups milk
3/4 cup sharp cheddar cheese
1 1/2 cups ham, chopped
7-8 hard boiled eggs
18-24 stalks fresh asparagus
toast or cornbread squares

Sauté onion in butter. Stir in flour. Add milk, stirring until thick. Stir in cheese until it melts. Add ham and sliced or chopped eggs, reserving a slice or two to top each serving. Boil asparagus for a minute or two. Place 3 asparagus spears on each piece of toast or cornbread. Spoon sauce over all. Serve immediately. Serves 6-8.

Poached Eggs in Maple Syrup

Ingredients per serving:

- 1 1/2 inch depth, maple syrup
- 2 farm fresh eggs
- 2 slices 12-grain bread

Pour maple syrup into a frying pan to a depth of 1 1/2 inches. Heat to just below simmering (bubbles forming in liquid but not breaking on surface). One at a time, carefully break eggs into a saucer. Slip one at a time gently into pan. Cook until eggs are set, 3 to 5 minutes. Remove eggs from pan and serve on toast with syrup poured over top.

Gregory's Guest House

Elizabeth and Paul Gregory
5373 Patricia Bay Highway
Victoria, British Columbia
CANADA V84 1S9
(604) 658-8404; FAX (604) 658-4604

Our home is an early 1900s restored, historic farmstead overlooking Beaver/Elk Lake and park. Ten minutes to downtown Victoria. Convenient to ferries, airport, and Burchart Gardens. Children of all ages enjoy our farm animals and unique hobby farm setting. The Little Garden Farm has four character guest rooms decorated with antiques and down quilts. Private bathrooms are available. Our library welcomes guests with fireplace and lake view. Lake activities include swimming, hiking, canoeing, and windsurfing. A full country breakfast is included.

The Doctor's Inn Bed and Breakfast

Marion and Beth Griffith
716 South Park Street
Asheboro, NC 27203
(910) 625-4916 or 4822

Our bed and breakfast was born out of the ashes of a tragic time in our life, the loss of our only son. Surrounded by a lot of love, we were encouraged to open a bed and breakfast in our home. Since cooking and entertaining had always been my favorite things, this idea brought a spark of life to my spirit. In the past ten years God has blessed us in many ways and restored our joy. We now have many friends from all over the world. This recipe came from a dear friend.

Baked Eggs in Maple Toast Cuplets

3 slices crisp bacon
6 small eggs
6 slices decrusted bread
2 tablespoons butter
2 tablespoons maple syrup

Butter 6 - 2 3/4 inch cups of a muffin tin. With a rolling pin lightly press out bread slices. Preheat oven to 400°. Melt together butter and maple syrup; brush this mixture on each slice of bread. Carefully press bread into muffin tin. Carefully break an egg into each cup. Sprinkle each egg with bacon, salt, and pepper. Cover with foil. Bake for 20 minutes.

Serve in a pretty silver or china dish. Place egg cuplets on a bed of fresh parsley!

Festive Egg Squares

1 pound sausage, cooked, drained
4 ounce mushrooms
1/2 cup chopped green onions
2 cups shredded mozzarella cheese
1 1/4 Bisquick
2 medium chopped tomatoes
12 eggs
1 cup milk or cream
1 1/2 teaspoon salt
1/2 teaspoon pepper
1/2 teaspoon oregano

Layer sausage, mushrooms, green onions, tomatoes and cheese in greased 13x9x2 inch baking dish. Beat together remaining ingredients and pour over layers. Bake at 350° for 30-40 minutes or until golden brown. Serves 12. May be prepared the night before.

Put a side dish of picante sauce on the table for anyone who want to spice up their lives a little. Serve with some wedges of watermelon or kiwi to give the plate some added color. I always have fresh homemade bread and a specialty butter.

Hideaway Inn Bed and Breakfast

Julia Baldridge
Route 1, Box 199
Hardy, AR 72542
(501) 966-4770

Modern B&B on 376 acres. Three guest rooms, queen beds and central air. TV/VCR in common area. Beautiful setting, picnic sites, and outdoor pool. Log cabin with two bedrooms, two baths, living/dining/kitchenette combo. Gourmet breakfast and evening snack served.

Night Swan Intercoastal Bed and Breakfast

Martha and Chuck Nighswonger
512 South Riverside Drive
New Smyrna Beach, FL 32168
(904) 423-4940; FAX (904) 427-2814

Guests come to our bed and breakfast to watch the pelicans, dolphins, sailboats, and yachts along the Atlantic Intracoastal Waterway from our beautiful front room, our wraparound porch, our 140-foot dock, or the individual guest rooms. Our spacious three-story home has kept its character and charm of 1906 in the historic district of New Smyrna Beach, with its central fireplace and its intricate natural wood in every room.

Egg and Cheese Bake

- 8 egg whites, or use egg subsitutute product
- 1 cup skim milk
- 2 teaspoons sugar
- 1 pound light Monterey Jack cheese, grated
- 4 ounces light cream cheese, cubed
- 16 ounces nonfat small curd cottage cheese
- 6 tablespoons margarine
- 1/2 cup all-purpose flour
- 1 teaspoon baking powder

Beat together eggs, milk, and sugar. Add the cheeses and margarine. Mix well, then add the flour and baking powder. Pour into a greased 9x13 inch glass baking dish (I use PAM cooking spray to grease pan). Bake in a 325° oven for 60 minutes or until knife inserted in the center comes out clean. This may be made ahead of time and refrigerated. If the pan goes from the refrigerator to oven, bake 75 minutes. Serves 12.

Wisconsin Cheese and Egg Bake

10 eggs
1 pound grated cheddar cheese
1 pound cottage cheese
1/2 cup flour
1 teaspoon baking powder
1/2 teaspoon salt
2 ounce jar diced pimientos

Beat eggs until light and fluffy. Add flour, baking powder and salt. Then add cheeses and pimiento. Pour into greased 9x13 inch baking dish. Bake in 325° oven for 35 minutes, or until set. Serves 8.

This dish can be made totally nonfat by substituting Eggbeaters and no-fat cheddar and cottage cheeses.

The Atrium Bed and Breakfast

Celia and Dick Stoltz
5572 Prill Road
Eau Claire, WI 54701
(715) 833-9045

Proudly featuring our home state product, this delectable dish is a natural, often requested by returning guests. We serve it with salsa, vegetable bagels, and homemade Wisconsin breakfast sausages. Our guests are then ready to explore the beautiful Wisconsin countryside, canoeing, birding, biking, antiquing, cross-country skiing, or snow shoeing. And you're always welcome to enjoy the gardens, creek and hiking paths on our 15 wooded acres.

Brackenridge House

Bennie and Sue Blansett
230 Madison
San Antonio, TX 78204
(210) 271-3442 (voice and FAX);
(800) 221-1412

My husband and I tasted this recipe for the first time when he was in graduate school in Boulder, CO, in 1972. A friend served it at a Easter brunch. Since then, I have made some changes. I like it because it is so hard to mess up. If you cook it a little too long or not quite long enough it really doesn't make that much difference. It can be doubled or tripled or cut in half. It looks great served in individual ramekins or in a huge casserole. Most of the work can be done ahead of time.

We always enjoyed entertaining, particularly with a Saturday or Sunday brunch. This recipe has always been a hit with our guests and our family. I have served it all over the world.

When we bought the Brackenridge House four years after my husband, Bennie, retired from his 35 year air force career, this was the first breakfast I cooked for our guests.

Eggs and Artichokes

2 packages (9 ounce each) frozen artichoke hearts, or 2 cans
1 bay leaf
2 cans condensed cream of chicken soup
1 tablespoon chopped onion
1/2 cup sherry
8 hard boiled eggs, quartered
8 slices Old English cheese (American will work)
2 cups diced cooked ham

Cook artichoke hearts as directed on package adding bay leaf during cooking, if desired. Drain. You can use canned artichokes and just drain them. Combine soup, onion, and sherry. Sometimes I add a small can of mushrooms. Mix well. Arrange artichoke hearts, eggs and ham in a 3 quart casserole dish. Add soup mixture. Top with slices of cheese. Bake in a hot oven at 400° for 25-30 minutes, or until cheese is lightly browned. Makes 8 servings.

Most of the time I leave meat out of my casserole dishes, since so many of my guests are vegetarians. This dish is just as good with the meat served on the side.

Scottish Eggs

1/2 pound ground meat
1/2 cup dried bread crumbs
1 egg
2 tablespoons minced onion
1 tablespoon chopped fresh parsley
1/4 teaspoon salt
1/2 teaspoon sage
1/4 teaspoon thyme
1/8 teaspoon pepper
4 eggs, hard boiled

Combine all ingredients except eggs. Form around peeled, hard boiled eggs. Bake at 350° in a covered casserole dish about 30 minutes, removing cover for last five minutes or until browned. Serve warm with Sweet Mustard Sauce.

Sweet Mustard Sauce

2 tablespoons Dijon mustard
1 tablespoon sugar
1 1/2 tablespoons vinegar
1/2 teaspoon salt
1 teaspoon chopped fresh dilll
1/3 cup canola oil

Stir together mustard, sugar vinegar, salt, and dill. Gradually blend in oil.

One of a Kind

Jack and Joyce Stufflebeem
314 W. State
Centerville, IA 52544
(515) 437-4540 (voice and FAX)

Scottish Eggs are a favorite of many of our regular customers, as well as our B&B guests. The original recipe (in a Weight Watchers cookbook) caught my eye because of my Scottish ancestry. We have modified the recipe and added mustard sauce, which we think adds just the right touch of tang and makes the serving really attractive.

We always include a small serving of fruit with each meal, as part of our overall plan to serve food that no only tastes good, but is good for you.

Most of the time, our guests are served in the dining room of this 1867 home, but once in a while our guests ask if they can eat in the big family kitchen. It's great to linger over coffee and get acquainted with each guest.

Abed and Breakfast at Spark's Hearth

Neoma and Herb Sparks
2515 S.W. 45th Street
Corvallis, OR 97333
(541) 757-7321; FAX (541) 753-4332

Part of the enjoyment of being a B&B family is working together, including creating new recipes. We want all of our dishes to be a bit unusual, attractive, and really tasty. Since we serve a full breakfast they should also be easy to make, and we need a variety of menus so many of the guests who stay several days can have something different every morning. To manage this we rely on some old standbys. But our favorites are those that our guests are unacquainted with . . . and eat every bite.

Sunny Baked Eggs fits all these criteria. It came from a recipe told to us several years ago. We hadn't tried it out because it seemed — at least the way we had written it — a bit complicated. Then one day one of us ran across it again which led to a new addition in our repertoire. Most important, our guests agree it's a keeper.

Sunny Baked Eggs

Ingredients per serving:

- 1 1/2 tablespoons minced ham
- 1 tablespoon minced fresh parsley
- 1 1/2 tablespoon brie cheese
- 2 eggs
- 1 tablespoon whipping cream
- dash of salt and pepper
- slice of fresh fruit

Individual servings are baked in ramekins. Place a pan large enough to hold the ramekins you are preparing, with about 1/2 inch of water, in the oven and preheat to 400°. Put the ham, parsley and brie cheese in the ramekins. Break two eggs into each ramekin, and top with cream. Place ramekins in the water bath and bake 20-25 minutes, or until the top is opaque and firm to touch. To serve, dust with salt and pepper, and garnish with fresh fruit.

Place the ramekin and garnish on an 8 inch plate to serve. This is an easy to prepare, foolproof recipe. Get it in the oven before the guests come to breakfast, and you have plenty of time to chat and see to their needs.

Oven Breakfast Omelet

8 eggs
1/2 cup milk
1/4 cup (scant) butter or oleo
1/2 cup cubed ham or cooked, crumbled bacon
6 slices American cheese
1 tablespoon chives or parsley
salt and pepper to taste

Preheat oven to 375°. In a medium sized bowl, beat eggs well. Add milk, salt and pepper. Stir in ham or cooked bacon and chives or parsley. Melt butter or oleo in 9 inch round cake pan in oven, while it is preheating. When melted, remove from oven and lay cheese slices in pan to cover bottom (will have to cut some slices to fit). Carefully pour egg mixture over cheese slices. Bake for 30 minutes. Serve immediately.

Old Brick Bed and Breakfast

Jerry and Caroline Lehman
2759 Old Highway 54
New London, IA 52645
(319) 367-5403

As owner of a small bed and breakfast, I am always interested in recipes "sized" to the number of guests we have. This easy dish bakes at the same temperature as my Sugarloaf Coffee Cake, requiring only one oven!

Cut in pie-shaped wedges, this omelet is pretty on the plate with a colorful fruit garnish. If served family-style, I like to bake the omelet in a crockery high-sided dish.

Old Yacht Club Inn

Nancy Donaldson, Sandy Hunt
431 Corona Del Mar Drive
Santa Barbara, CA 93103
(805) 962-1277; (800) 676-1676;
FAX (805) 962-3989

The inn at the beach! These 1912 California Craftsman and 1925 early California-style homes house nine individually decorated guest rooms furnished with antiques. Bicycles, beach chairs, and towels are included, and an evening social hour is provided. Gourmet dinner is available on Saturdays.

Santa Barbara Omelette

1 tomato, diced
4 tablespoon water
2 tablespoons butter
8 eggs
1 scallion, sliced
2 whole green chilies, cut into 8 slices
  or 2 tablespoons diced chilies
1/2 cup grated Monterey Jack cheese
1/2 cup grated cheddar cheese
sliced avocado
green chili salsa
lemon pepper
chervil

For our omelettes we use 2 eggs per person and we often make an omelette large enough to serve 4, in one pan. We use the large 12 inch Silverstone pans, and then slice the omelette into individual servings.

Break eggs into a bowl. Add water. Melt butter in pan over medium-low heat. Use wire whisk to beat eggs 1-2 minutes. Pour eggs into pan. Allow to harden on the bottom. Using a spatula, push cooked part to middle of pan and allow liquid to run around edges and cook through. Continue to do this until eggs are set but not hard. Be careful not to cook too high and brown the bottom. Place tomato, scallion, and green chilies on top of omelette. Cover with grated cheese. Fold omelette over. Season with lemon pepper and chervil. Cover and cook 4-5 minutes until cheese melts. Place avocado slices and a teaspoon of salsa on top. Slice into servings and serve at once.

Big Shrimp Omelet

6 eggs
1 tablespoon butter, melted
1 tablespoon finely chopped green onion
1 teaspoon finely chopped parsley
1/3 cup butter
1/4 pound peeled, cleaned, freshly boiled small shrimp
pepper
green onion, finely chopped
salt
garlic salt
American cheese (optional)

In a medium bowl beat the eggs thoroughly and add 1 tablespoon of melted butter and the onions. Add the parsley and mix lightly. In a warmed cast iron frying pan combine 1/3 cup of butter and the egg mixture. Increase the heat slightly and roll the mixture as it cooks. Roll mixture over, decrease the heat, and continue to cook. As the softness disappears, add the shrimp, pepper, another sprinkle of green onions, and season lightly with salt and garlic salt. If cheese is added, omit most of the garlic salt. Serve with home-grown, sliced tomatoes and freshly baked bread, rolls, and homemade jams. Serves 2.

Red Creek Inn, Vineyard, and Racing Stable

Karl and "Toni" Mertz
7416 Red Creek Road
Long Beach, MS 39560
(601) 452-3080; (800) 729-9670;
FAX (601) 452-4450

Karl moved to the Mississippi Gulf Coast as a third-grader. He was surprised at how large some Gulf shrimp are. Being a "little shrimp" himself, he began referring to the real thing as big shrimp. So, when his late mom would have (or make up) a special occasion to fix a shrimp omelet, she'd always ask Karl, and his sister Karen, "Do you little shrimps want a big shrimp omelet?" Karl's answer was always the same: "Better them than us!" Served with home fries, a "Big Shrimp Omelet" is still one of Dr. Karl Mertz's favorite treats and fondest memories, even at 6'3".

Rustic Mountain Lodge Bed and Breakfast

Mayvon Platt
Star Route, Box 49
Encampment, WY 82325
(307) 327-5539 (voice and FAX)

A peaceful mountain view, located on a working ranch with wholesome country atmosphere and lots of western hospitality. Guests enjoy daily fishing on a private pond, big game trophy hunts, cookouts, retreats, pack trips, photo safaries, youth programs, cattle drives, trail rides, hiking, rock hunting, numerous ranch activities, mountain biking and four wheeling trails, and survival workshops. Individuals, families, and groups welcome! A terrific atmosphere for workshops. Lodge and cabin rentals available. Reservations only. Private fishing cabins available May through September. Write for a complete brochure!

Country Vegetable Omelette

Velveeta Cheese
optional vegetables: peppers, potatoes, broccoli, tomatoes, onions, etc.
12 eggs
1/2 cup milk
1/2 cup crisp bacon, broken into pieces

Layer mild or hot Velveeta Cheese on 9x13 inch glass cooking ware. Dice your favorite vegetables. Mix eggs, milk, bacon; add vegetables. Pour into baking dish. Bake at 350° for about 40 minutes.

Serve with toast, juice, fruit, or my favorite buckwheat or blueberry pancakes.

Fluffy Omelet

2 eggs (sorry, egg substitutes will not work)
3/4 cup cream
1 tablespoon seasoned salt
butter

Separate egg whites from the yolks. Add seasoned salt and cream to the yolks. Beat yolks on medium until blended well. Beat the egg whites on high until stiff like a meringue. Then gently blend egg yolks with egg whites. Melt 1 teaspoon butter in each omelet pan. Cook on medium-low heat until firm and lightly brown. Flip over and cook other side until brown. Fold in half on plate and pour cheese sauce over center of omelet. Garnish with fresh parsley. Serves 2. Add one egg for each person serving.

Cholesterol-free variation: after whipping the whites, add seasoning and cream. Do not use egg yolks.

Easy, Creamy Cheese Sauce

3/4 cup cubed Velveeta cheese
1/4 cup cream

Place cheese and cream in a saucepan and melt, stirring often. Do not let the cheese at the bottom burn. You may have to add a little cream to obtain the smooth consistency you want.

The Old Northside Bed and Breakfast

Susan Berry
1340 N. Alabama Street
Indianapolis, IN 46202-2524
(317) 635-9123; (800) 635-9127 (reservations only); FAX (317) 635-9243

My home is a luxurious 1885 Victorian mansion in historic downtown, convenient to I-65, I-70, and city attractions. The city's finest example of Romanesque Revival architecture with an elegant European turn-of-the-century decor. Themed rooms with Jacuzzi tubs in private baths, two with fireplaces. Exercise room, conference room, and corporate services. A personal coffee service delivered to guests' rooms before the full gourmet breakfast. Complimentary snack and exceptional service.

Desoto at Prior's Bed and Breakfast

Dick and Mary Prior
1522 Desoto Street
St. Paul, MN 55101-3253
(612) 774-2695

The beauty of this recipe is that all of the preparation can be done ahead of time. Just a few minutes before serving, it can be assembled, cooked and served to any number of guests by adjusting ingredients to fit.

It was originally a casserole to serve 8, cooking for 30 minutes. But we kept refining the recipe until it works for any number with a short cooking time. If the guests arrive late for breakfast, most recipes won't keep, but since this is cooked after they arrive in the dining room, it is perfect. It's very attractive, and looks difficult to prepare. It's been a winner for us!

Fluffy Muffin Cup Omelets

2 strips bacon
2 teaspoons finely chopped celery
1 teaspoon finely chopped onion
1 teaspoon butter
2 large eggs
2 tablespoons milk
dash of salt and pepper
1/4 cup American cheese cut into 1/4 inch cubes
1 teaspoon seasoned bread crumbs
2 cubes American cheese, 1/4 inch

Fry bacon until crisp, paper towel dry; shape in muffin cups as lining. Beat eggs until fluffy. Add milk, salt and pepper. Sauté celery and onion in butter until clear. Add eggs, then cheese. Cook over medium heat stirring until eggs start to "set." Spoon into bacon lined muffin cups quickly. Sprinkle with crumbs and top with cheese cube. Bake at 400° until eggs are firm and cooked through. With large spoon loosen omelets and lift onto serving plate, keeping bacon in place to hold egg together.

Vegetable Omelet Torte

8 large eggs
6 tablespoons butter
1/3 cup green onion, chopped
1/3 cup zucchini, diced
1/2 cup mushrooms, sliced
1/4 cup cheddar cheese
4 cherry tomatoes, halved
4 tablespoons cream or milk

Sauté green onions in 1 tablespoon of butter; set aside. Do the same with each vegetable. Prepare one omelet, using eggs, milk, and 1 tablespoon of butter, and place on warm plate. (Do not fold). Top with sautéed onions. Make second omelet and place on top of onions. Top with zucchini. Repeat two more times, with final topping of grated cheese and tomatoes. Present torte whole, then slice to serve. Serves 4.

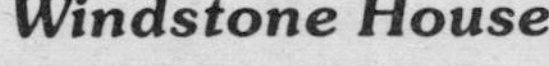

Windstone House

Barbara Kimes
539 Cleveland Road
Houston, MO 65483
(417) 967-2008

I especially enjoy serving omelets and this is a way to serve several people and yet have fresh omelet for everyone. You can use whatever fillings you prefer and as many layers as you like. Just allow two eggs per guest. If you are diet conscious you could use egg substitute.

Sara's Bed and Breakfast Inn

Donna and Tillman Arledge
941 Heights Boulevard
Houston, TX 77008
(713) 868-1130; (800) 593-1130;
FAX (713) 868-1160

This Queen Anne Victorian with its turret and widow's walk is located in Houston Heights, a neighborhood of historic homes, many of which are on the National Historic Register. Each bedroom is uniquely furnished, having either single, double, queen, or king beds. The Balcony Suite consists of two bedrooms, two baths, kitchen/ living area, and balcony. Breakfast is served in the beautiful garden room in the Inn. The sights and sounds of downtown Houston are five miles away.

Creamy Scrambled Eggs

8 eggs
1/4 cup of milk
1/4 teaspoon salt
dash of pepper
2 tablespoons of butter
1 - 3 ounce package of cream cheese
    with chives, cut into 1/2 inch cubes
chopped parsley, if desired

In a medium bowl, beat eggs, milk, salt and pepper until just combined. Melt butter in a large skillet over low heat. Pour in egg mixture. Cook over low heat. As eggs begin to set on bottom, gently lift cooked portion with spatula, letting uncooked portion flow to bottom of pan. Drop cream cheese cubes on top of eggs. Cook until eggs are no longer runny and cheese is melted. Sprinkle with chopped parsley, if desired. Makes 4 or 5 servings.

Cream cheese and chives add enjoyable flavor and color.

Special Scrambled Eggs

1 cup diced smoked turkey
1 cup sliced mushrooms
1/4 cup chopped green onion
12 eggs, well beaten
paprika
buttered bread crumbs with paprika

Spray six oven-proof au gratin dishes with cooking spray and set aside. Spray a large non-stick skillet with cooking spray and sauté green onions and mushrooms with smoked turkey until vegetables are tender. Add eggs and cook over moderate heat until eggs are soft set. Divide evenly into au gratin dishes. Top with Cheese Sauce and buttered crumbs. Cover and refrigerate overnight. In the morning, uncover and sprinkle with paprika. Bake at 350° for 20 minutes until bubbly and nicely browned.

Cheese Sauce

2 tablespoons butter
1/4 teaspoon salt
2 tablespoons flour
1 cup grated sharp cheddar cheese
dash each cayenne pepper and dry mustard
2 cups of scalded milk

Melt butter, add flour and seasonings and cook over moderate heat for a few minutes. Do not let brown. Add scalded milk, stirring constantly. Continue to heat and stir until smooth and thickened. Remove from heat, add cheese, and stir until cheese is melted.

The Yankee Tinker Bed and Breakfast

Jan and Ralph Wadleigh
5480 S.W. 183rd Avenue
Beaverton, OR 97007
(503) 649-0932 (voice and FAX);
(800) 846-5372

This dish is a favorite. It came from my Auntie Lee, a retired professor of nursing at Boston University. She used it frequently for entertaining at brunch since she could make it up the night before she wanted to serve it.

For the last eight years, guests here have had the opportunity to enjoy this special dish. I made minor modifications in the recipe that my aunt first gave to me. Substituting fresh mushrooms for canned and using smoked turkey instead of ham made this dish "ours."

By presenting this in individual au gratin dishes nestled between sprigs of fresh herbs each guest will have a piping hot but not dried out breakfast. We like to precede this with fresh squeezed orange juice and seasonal fruits or fruit soups served with our Gingered Yogurt Creme and garnished with herbs from our herb bed.

Hickory Bend Bed and Breakfast

Pat and Patty Peery
7541 Dupler Road, S.E.
Sugar Grove, OH 43155
(614) 746-8381

Nestled in the Hocking Hills of southeastern Ohio on ten wooded acres. "So peaceful, we got to go out to watch the car go *by on Sunday afternoon," says Pat. Guests come to the home for breakfast and conversation.*

"People write back to me for my scrambled egg recipe that is served with waffles, low-fat bacon, or sausage," says Patty, a spinner and a weaver. "Oh yes, waffles are served with maple syrup or strawberries/blueberries and low-fat topping."

Hickory Bend Scrambled Eggs

- 2 eggs per person
- 1/8 teaspoon, per egg, Molly McButter
- 1/8 teaspoon, per egg, Lawry's Seasoned Salt
- PAM or other low-fat cooking spray
- 1/4 teaspoon, per egg, chives

Break eggs in bowl, add Molly McButter and Lawry's seasoned salt and chives. Mix very well. Pour into hot (over medium heat) skillet sprayed with low-fat cooking oil. Stir continuously, pulling from the sides. Do not overcook! Serve hot from the skillet in warm awaiting bowl.

The Captain's Eggs

- 5 eggs
- 1/4 cup flour
- 1/2 teaspoon baking powder
- 3/4 cup cottage cheese
- 8 ounces Monterey Jack cheese, shredded
- 1/2 cup fresh mushrooms, sliced
- 1/2 cup broccoli florets, cut into small pieces (other seasonal vegetables can be substituted such as zucchini, or green or red peppers)

Preheat oven to 375°. Beat eggs with a wire whisk then add the flour and baking powder. Mix well. Stir in remaining ingredients and pour into an 8x8 inch baking dish that has been sprayed with a nonstick spray. Bake 25-30 minutes until set. Garnish with bacon or sausage links (cut in half). Serves 4-6.

This dish is great for breakfast right out of the oven, can be served for brunch as it keeps well on a warming tray and is perfect for a light supper. For supper I use a mix of red and green peppers and use shredded cheddar cheese in place of the Monterey Jack. Top with garden fresh tomatoes!

Captain Dibbell House

Ellis and Helen Adams
21 Commerce Street
Clinton, CT 06413
(860) 669-1646 (voice and FAX)

As more and more of our guests indicated they would like to splurge and have a full breakfast while enjoying a holiday, we started looking for recipes that would be different from the normal breakfast fare while keeping health and diet concerns in mind. This recipe is the result of the combination of several we tried. By using low-fat cheeses and vegetables we feel it offers an alternative to those who want to indulge but not feel guilty.

It has proven to be a favorite with our guests who frequently request the recipe. We like it, as it is easily prepared (vegetables can be cut up the night before), holds well on the warming tray on the sideboard and is versatile, so we can use the bounty from our garden in the summer.

North Coast Country Inn

Loren and Nancy Flanagan
34591 S. Highway 1
Gualala, CA 95445
(707) 884-4537; (800) 959-4537

Picturesque redwood buildings on a forested hillside overlooking the Pacific Ocean. The large guest rooms feature fireplaces, private baths, queen beds, decks, and mini-kitchens and are furnished with authentic antiques. There is a beautiful hilltop gazebo garden and romantic hot tub under the pines.

California Quiche

- 2 cans (7 ounces) whole green chilies, split
- 2 cups (8 ounces) shredded cheddar cheese
- 2 cups (8 ounces) shredded Monterey Jack cheese
- 3 large eggs
- 1 cup sour cream
- 1 tomato, medium, cored, and diced
- prepared salsa

Arrange half of the chilies, spread open, in a single layer on bottom of baking dish. Evenly sprinkle half of the cheddar and Jack cheeses over chilies. Lightly sprinkle with pepper. Repeat layers using remaining chilies and cheeses. In a bowl, beat together eggs and sour cream until blended. Pour evenly over chilies and cheese. Bake at 350° for about 30 minutes, until custard is set and jiggles only slightly in center, and edges are starting to brown. Cool 5 minutes before cutting.

Garnish with a band of the diced tomatoes across the top. Offer salsa in a side dish.

Country Quiche or "Garden Eggs"

dash Molly McButter
12 fresh eggs
1 small onion, diced
1 green or red bell pepper (optional)
6 scallions, snipped
1 carrot, shredded
1/2 cup chopped fresh spinach
6 slices whole wheat bread
1/2 cup sliced mushrooms
1 fresh tomato, diced (optional)
1/2 cup milk
1/2 teaspoon yellow-top Mrs. Dash
1/2 teaspoon garlic powder
Optional: diced ham, turkey or cheese

Save 2 slices bell pepper (flowers) plus "dot" of red tomato to decorate top.

Preheat oven to 350°. Scramble/whip eggs, milk, Molly McButter, Mrs. Dash, and garlic powder. Lightly oil 9x3 inch baking pan; line with bread. To egg mixture, add vegetables (and meat or cheese if desired). Pour over bread. Bake 1 hour. Garnish with bell pepper "flowers" before serving. Cut in squares. Serves 12.

May be baked in pie shells, whole or individual. Vegetables may be mixed in quantities and varieties to suit your taste and/or the season. May be served in a bowl after "scrambling" in a skillet (no baking) — called "Garden Eggs." Dress it up, make it elegant, or dress it down and make it homey!

The Northrop House Bed and Breakfast

Jean and Darrell Stewart with Gregory Northrup
358 East Main Street
Owatonna, MN 55060
(507) 451-4040; FAX (507) 451-2755

When our mother died in 1985 (and before we turned the old home place into a B&B) our longtime friend and neighbor asked if she could put her garden where Mom had hers. Our mother always gardened organically, composted long before it was popular, and the same is true of the neighbor.

We said, of course! . . . so "Granny's Garden" continues uninterrupted and we have the best garden *because all we have to do is pick it! The "Garden Eggs" are made with the organic produce from "Granny's Garden." Always a hit!*

Green Acres Farm Bed and Breakfast

Wayne and Yvonne Miller
1382 Pinkerton Road
Mount Joy, PA 17552
(717) 653-4028; FAX (717) 653-2840

Our 1830 farmhouse is furnished with antiques and offers a peaceful haven for your getaway. The rooster, chickens, Pigmy goats, lots of kittens, pony, and 1,000 hogs give a real farm atmosphere on this 160-acre grain farm. Children love the pony cart rides and the 8x 10-foot playhouse, and everyone enjoys the trampoline and swings. We offer tour information about the Amish Country and can arrange guests' dinner with an Amish family.

Green Acres Sunday Morning Quiche

6 cups cooked potatoes, grated
3 cups turkey, ham or other meat
3 cups medium cheddar cheese, grated
2 cups milk
6 eggs
1 cup Bisquick
1 small onion

Put grated potatoes in greased casserole dish. Add layer of meat, then top with cheese. For topping; put milk, Bisquick, onion, and eggs in blender and blend on medium for about 30 seconds. Pour over other ingredients and bake at 350° for 1 hour.

This is a good make-ahead dish — only put topping on just before you bake it. You can also use vegetables instead of meats, such as, pepper, celery, broccoli, mushroom, tomato, etc.

Nancy's Wonderful Quiche

1/4 cup melted butter
1 1/2 cups milk
1 teaspoon salt
dash pepper
3 eggs
1/2 cup Bisquick
1 cup shredded Swiss cheese
1/2 cup ham or bacon or asparagus or mushrooms

Mix first 5 ingredients together. Beat well, stir in Bisquick, pour into 9 inch pie dish (sprayed with PAM cooking spray). Add cheese and ham (bacon, asparagus, or mushrooms) on top of egg mixture. (Don't mix). Bake for 45 minutes at 350°.

White Lilac Inn

Mari Kennelly Slocum
444 Central Avenue
Spring Lake, NJ 07762
(908) 449-0211

Family tested, "Nancy's Wonderful Quiche" has been passed along to all the Slocums. Even real men like this one. Serve with fresh fruit, coffee or tea, orange juice, croissant, and jams. We like it and it's easy!

Harmony House Inn

Ed and Sooki Kirkpatrick
215 Pollock Street
New Bern, NC 28560
(919) 636-3810 (voice and FAX);
(800) 636-3113
Email: harmony@internet.net

Comfortable elegance in an unusually spacious Greek Revival inn built circa 1850 with final additions circa 1900. Guests enjoy a parlor, front porch with rocking chairs and swings, antiques and reproductions, plus a full breakfast in the dining room. Soft drinks and juice available throughout stay. All rooms have fully private, modern bathrooms. Located in the historic district near Tryon Palace, shops, and restaurants.

Apple, Bacon, and Cheese Quiche

fresh apples
2 cups grated cheddar cheese
1/2 pound bacon
1 1/2 cups Bisquick
1 1/2 cups milk
4 eggs

Preheat oven to 375°. Butter an 8x12 inch Pyrex baking dish. Peel and slice apples and layer them in the bottom of the dish in a single layer. Sprinkle grated cheese on top of the apples. Cook the bacon and break it into bite-sized pieces. Sprinkle bacon pieces on top of cheese. Beat four eggs. Add milk and beat to blend. Add Bisquick and beat into a batter. Batter should be fairly thin, but not watery. Add either more milk or Bisquick to adjust consistency. Pour batter over the apple, bacon and cheese. Bake for about 45 minutes, or until the top is browned. Serves 8.

Cameo Rose Quiche

1 - 9 inch frozen pie shell
6 eggs
1 cup Swiss cheese, shredded
1/2 cup nonfat sour cream
3/4 cup milk (2%)
2 tablespoons diced onion
6 strips lean bacon, cooked, fat cut off
1/3 cup fresh mushrooms
1/3 cup chopped fresh tomato
1/3 cup chopped fresh asparagus
1/2 teaspoon cach, salt and pepper
1 small clove of fresh garlic

Thaw pie crust while you sauté onion, mushrooms, garlic, asparagus, tomato, salt and pepper. Pour into crust and sprinkle with cheese and cooked bacon. Mix eggs, sour cream and milk well; pour into shell over cheese. Bake at 375° for 45-55 minutes or until puffed and golden brown. Remove and let stand 10 minutes before serving. Serves 8.

Cameo Rose Bed and Breakfast

Dawn and Gary Bahr
1090 Severson Road
Belleville, WI 53508
(608) 424-6340

I like to incorporate seasonal, fresh vegetables and fruits in my menus and this one is an especially nice treat in the spring when asparagus is fresh and tender. You can also do this without the meat for vegetarian guests or use sausage or ham for variety. I use a local baby Swiss cheese that has a very creamy, sweet taste adds to the ambiance of "America's Little Switzerland" in nearby New Glarus.

Country Rose Bed and Breakfast

Jack and Rose Lewis
5098 N. Mechanicsburg Road
Middleton, IN 47356
(317) 779-4501; (800) 395-6449

Our large home is a fully updated Victorian with lots of charm and original style. Located in the heart of Amish country, guests relax on the porch and watch buggies drive by or sit in the hot tub in our old-fashioned garden. In colder months, they may sit by the fireplace to chat or curl up with a good book. We offer evening refreshments and full breakfasts.

This quiche is very easy for innkeepers to make with little time. All our guests and family really enjoy it.

Easy Quiche

1 - 9 inch pie plate
3/4 cup chopped ham, sausage
1 cup grated cheese
4 eggs
1 cup milk
1/2 cup Bisquick
1/4 cup melted butter

Sprinkle cheese and meat on the bottom of pie plate. Mix remaining ingredients together and pour on top. Bake at 350° for 25-30 minutes. This recipe can be made with vegetables instead of meat (green pepper, mushroom, etc.)

Quick Quiche

Mix in blender:

3 eggs
1/2 cup Bisquick
1/2 cup melted margarine (optional)
1 1/2 cup milk
1/4 teaspoon salt
1/2 teaspoon lemon pepper

2 cups hash browns
cheddar or Monterey Jack cheese
optional: sausage, ham, bacon, vegetables
Parmesan cheese

Pour blended ingredients in round pan, or 9x13 inch stoneware baking dish coated with cooking spray oil. Cover bottom of dish with shredded hash browns. Layer with a generous portion of cheese. Can layer with meat or vegetables also. Push these ingredients under surface with the back of a spoon. Sprinkle with Parmesan cheese. Bake at 350° for 45 minutes. Let cool 10 minutes. Serves 6-8.

Park View Inn Bed and Breakfast

Gary and Jayne Hall
904-4th Avenue W, PO Box 567
Columbia Falls, MT 59912
(406) 892-7275 (voice and FAX)

A favorite dish at the Park View Inn consists of "Quick Quiche," freshly baked English muffin, toast with huckleberry jam, and a side dish of fresh fruit.

Top O' Triangle Mountain

Henry and Patricia Hansen
3442 Karger Terrace
Victoria, British Columbia
CANADA V9C 3K5
(604) 478-7853; FAX (604) 478-2245

This recipe was given to me by a guest from Ontario several years ago and is appreciated by my guests. I use salmon that we have caught and canned ourselves. Living on the west coast, where salmon is so readily available, gives this dish a special place on our menu.

Crustless Salmon Quiche

1 can salmon
1/2 cup flour
1/2 teaspoon salt
2 cups milk
1 1/2 cups grated cheddar cheese
1/4 cup green onion, chopped
6 eggs

Drain salmon, reserving liquid. Blend salmon liquid, flour, salt, eggs and milk until smooth. Pour into greased quiche pan. Sprinkle salmon, onion and cheese over egg mixture, pressing down lightly with a fork. Bake at 400° for about 35 minutes. Serves six. I serve this with English muffins or 12-grain toast.

Impossible All-In-One Quiche

1 1/2 cups milk
1/2 cup biscuit mix (Bisquick)
4 tablespoons butter or margarine
3 eggs
pinch of salt
1 cup grated cheddar cheese
optional: sprinkle of onion and parsley, bacon, sausage
optional: 1 cup any meat — ham, turkey, chicken — or 1 cup mushrooms

Heat oven to 350 degrees°. Mix well first 5 ingredients. Pour into a deep, lightly greased 9 inch pie pan. Add meat (optional) and poke into the batter. Sprinkle top with onions, mushrooms, cheese. Bake for 45 minutes or until golden brown. Let stand 10 minutes before cutting. Serves 6.

Lincoln Haus Inn Bed and Breakfast

Mary K. Zook
1687 Lincoln Highway, East
Lancaster, PA 17602
(717) 392-9421

Lincoln Haus Inn is the only inn in Lancaster County with a distinctive hip roof. It is furnished with antiques and rugs on gleaming, hardwood floors, and it has natural oak woodwork. I am a member of the Old Amish Church, serving family-style breakfast with a homey atmosphere.

Flowers & Thyme Bed and Breakfast

Don and Ruth Harnish
238 Strasburg Pike
Lancaster, PA 17602
(717) 393-1460

I love trying new and different recipes, noting on each the rating as to how we liked it. I was looking for a different type of quiche to serve and when I saw this it seemed to be one for me to try. My dad had been a big potato farmer and I still love potatoes served various ways. Using potatoes in this quiche cuts back on the fat from a regular crust, plus not as many eggs are required to fill up the pie. I've made adaptations though — usually I omit the meat because of guests' varied diet restrictions. I then serve the sausages separately. I also use the low-fat evaporated milk and it works quite well; 2% skim milk does not!

Meat-Potato Quiche

3 tablespoons vegetable oil
3 cups coarsely shredded raw potato
1 cup grated cheddar cheese
1 tablespoon dried onion flakes
1 cup evaporated milk
2 eggs
1/2 teaspoon salt
1/4 teaspoon pepper
1 tablespoon parsley flakes
optional ingredients: diced ham, chicken, or browned sausage can be added to cheese.

Preheat oven to 425°. In 9 inch pie pan, stir together vegetable oil, and raw potato. Press evenly into pie crust shape. Bake for 15 minutes until just beginning to brown. Remove from oven. Layer on cheese, and onion flakes. In a bowl, beat together milk, eggs, salt and pepper. Pour egg mixture onto other ingredients. Sprinkle with parsley flakes. Return to oven and bake about 30 minutes, until lightly browned. Allow to cool a couple of minutes before cutting. Serves 4-5.

I serve this quiche with meat on the side, usually sausage links along with asparagus tips or snow peas for color, and garnish with a strawberry sliced and flared. Bagels also go well with this dish.

Country Muffin Quiches (Crustless)

6 ounces cheddar cheese, grated
3 tablespoons flour
4 eggs, beaten
2/3 cup mayonnaise
1 package (10 ounces) frozen chopped spinach, thawed and drained
8 slices bacon, cooked and crumbled
4 ounce can chopped mushrooms, drained
1/2 teaspoon Greek all-purpose seasoning
dash fresh ground pepper
2 tablespoons chopped black olives (optional)

Toss cheese with flour. Add remaining ingredients; mix well. Grease muffin tins well. Fill with mixture. Bake at 350° for 20 minutes or until set. Makes about 8-10 average size muffins. You may want to substitute ham for the bacon, and onion for the mushrooms.

Country Victorian Bed and Breakfast

Diane Deardurff Weed
105 Tradd Street
Charleston, SC 29401-2422
(803) 577-0682

I like to serve these muffin quiches with a wedge of cantaloupe, slices of kiwi, large strawberries dipped in powdered sugar, and a sprinkle of fresh blueberries. Cornbread and chive muffins, juice, coffee, and tea complete this delightful breakfast which is served outdoors on the piazza in the morning, accompanied by the peaceful sounds of chirping birds and church chimes.

Historic Bennett House

Gail and Rich Obermeyer
825 Oak Street
Wisconsin Dells, WI 53965
(608) 254-2500

We named this recipe after pioneer photographer H.H. Bennett. His photographs adorn the walls of our 10 feet ceilings. His home was built in 1863, and Rich gives mini lectures on Mr. Bennett during the weekends. The Bennett Museum is one block from the home.

I serve this recipe in individual casseroles, with fresh fruit, specialty breads and homemade muffins.

Eggs Bennett

3 eggs
1 teaspoon water, added to beaten eggs
3 tablespoons real sour cream
1 slice honey ham
2 tablespoons medium cheddar cheese
salt and pepper to taste

Allow 3 eggs per person. Beat and scramble eggs. Spray PAM in ovenproof dish, add eggs. Spread on sour cream. Layer chopped honey ham over sour cream. Sprinkle grated cheese over ham. Bake in 350° oven about 10 minutes. Do not overbake.

Eggs Mey

4 ounces cream cheese
10 eggs, beaten
1 - 5 ounce can of evaporated milk
1 tablespoon chopped fresh dill
salt to taste (optional)
1/4 stick butter

Dice the cream cheese to 1/4 inch cubes. Combine with the remaining ingredients, except the butter, in mixing bowl. Melt butter in frying pan on medium heat. Add egg mixture. Fold mixture often in pan, until mixture is just set. Remove from heat and serve. Serves 5.

Captain Mey's Inn

George and Kathleen Blinn
202 Ocean Street
Cape May, NJ 08204
(609) 884-7793

This dish is named after Captain Cornelius Mey, the Dutch explorer, for whom Cape May is names. This dish can be served family-style in a casserole dish or individual portions. Looks nice with a sprinkle of finely chopped chives and fresh dill sprigs. Serve with hot croissants or bagels.

The Hostetler House Bed and Breakfast

Craig and Dea Hostetler
113 North Douglas Street
Glendive, MT 59330
(406) 365-4505; FAX (406) 365-8456

I serve these eggs with Brown 'n Serve sausages, fruit parfait, and sour cream muffins. I also serve fruit juice in iced wine goblets, tea, freshly ground coffee, or hot chocolate as desired. I use my grandma's china with matching placemats and cloth napkins. My husband and I often join our guests for coffee and try to make them feel as "at home" as possible.

Eggs Olympic

12 mushrooms, washed, sliced
2 tablespoons oleo
1 green onion, chopped
8 eggs
2 tablespoons water
1/2 cup tomato sauce
1 cup shredded cheddar cheese

Sauté mushrooms in 1/2 tablespoon oleo, set aside. Melt 1 1/2 tablespoons oleo in large pan. Add onion, sauté 30 seconds. Beat eggs with water, pour into frying pan, stirring continually. Just before eggs "set" divide into four oven-proof bowls. Top with mushrooms, tomato sauce, and cheese. Broil one minute until cheese melts and tomato sauce gets hot.

Mama Bear's Shirred (Baked) Eggs

1 tablespoon light cream (per individual baking dish)
1-2 eggs per serving
salt and pepper to taste
Swiss cheese, grated
paprika
butter

Heat oven to 350°. Butter individual shallow baking dishes. Pour 1 tablespoon light cream into each dish. Carefully break 1 or 2 eggs into each dish. Sprinkle with salt, pepper, paprika; dot with butter. Bake uncovered 12-15 minutes, or until desired doneness. Sprinkle 2 tablespoons grated Swiss cheese on each dish and bake 2 minutes longer.

Breitenbach Bed and Breakfast

Deanna Bear
307 Dover Road
Sugarcreek, OH 44681
(330) 343-3603; (800) THE-WINE (in Ohio); FAX (330) 343-8290

Located in the quaint Swiss village of Sugarcreek, we offer splendid accommodations in a comfortable, hospitable environment. Our new friends enjoy the cozy atmosphere and are served complimentary refreshments in the evening, and awaken to a full gourmet breakfast.

We always top these eggs with award-winning Swiss cheese from this unique area. With this we serve locally made German smoked sausage, homemade pastries and Apple Betty. We are committed to making your stay with us a cherished memory.

Custer Mansion Bed and Breakfast

Mill and Carole Seaman
35 Centennial Drive
Custer, SD 57730
(605) 673-3333

Guests to our B&B enjoy the nostalgia of an authentic 1891, Victorian Gothic home listed on National Register of Historic Places. Transoms, stained glass, and antiques feature Victorian elegance and country charm with western hospitality. Lovely, individually decorated rooms are named for songs. We serve an all-you-can-eat, delicious, home-cooked breakfast.

The recipe is one of our favorites. Best served hot — always with a muffin or coffee cake. A delicious hot dish. If vegetarian, just leave out the ham. Guests are always pleasantly surprised at how delicious it is.

Breakfast Soufflé

6 eggs
3 cups milk
1/2 teaspoon salt
1 cup shredded cheddar cheese
1/2 cup cooked, chopped ham
1/2 cup fresh, sliced mushrooms
1/4 cup onions, finely chopped
1/4 cup green pepper, finely chopped
6 slices white bread
butter

Line a 9x13 inch baking pan with 6 slices bread, buttered on both sides. Mix milk, eggs, salt. Beat well. Pour over bread slices and top with remaining ingredients. Cover with plastic wrap and set in refrigerator overnight. The next morning, bake at 300° for 1 hour. Serve hot. Serves 6-8.

Cheesie Breakfast Soufflé

- 9 eggs (or egg substitute), beaten or whisked
- 1 1/2 cups milk (whole, 1%, or 2%)
- 2-3 teaspoons sugar
- 1-1 1/2 teaspoons salt
- 12 ounces grated cheese (Monterey Jack or pregrated, 4-cheese Mexican combo)
- 4 1/2 ounce cream cheese, or 1/3 less fat, cubed or cut into small chunks.
- 12 ounces cottage cheese (lowfat or nonfat)

Mix above ingredients together, (may store this portion overnight in refrigerator).

- 1 1/2 teaspoons baking powder
- 3/4 cup flour (white or a blend with whole grain flour)
- 4 tablespoons butter, melted
- dash of dill, parsley, paprika (optional)

Mix baking powder and flour. With whisk, mix dry ingredients into wet mixture, lightly but thoroughly. Lastly, stir in butter and pour into lightly buttered or oiled 9x13 inch baking dish (oval or rectangular). Before placing in oven, sprinkle in diagonal lines: dried dill, parsley, and/or paprika in opposite diagonals to make lattice pattern. Pretty with green and red for Christmas breakfast or brunch. Bake at 325° for 40-50 minutes, or until lightly browned and knife come out clean when inserted in the center.

Goddard Mansion Bed and Breakfast

Debbie Albee
25 Hillstead Road
Claremont, NH 03743
(603) 543-0603; (800) 736-0603 (reservations); FAX (603) 543-0001

Circa 1905, this mansion with adjacent garden tea house is set amid acres of lawns and gardens with panoramic mountain views. This beautifully restored English manor style, 18-room mansion, with expansive porches, has 10 uniquely decorated guest rooms. The living room has fireplace and window seats for cuddling up with a good book and enjoying a vintage baby grand piano. A 1939 Wurlitzer jukebox lights up a corner of the walnut paneled dining room where a full, natural breakfast awaits guests each morning.

I serve my favorite soufflé garnished with fresh parsley and/or chives and with crusty bread or a fruity muffin.

Castle Garden Bed and Breakfast

Bruce and Kimmy Kloeckner
15 Shenandoah Street
St. Augustine, FL 32084
(904) 829-3839

Guests relax and enjoy the peace and quiet of "royal treatment" at our newly restored, 100-year-old castle of the Moorish Revival design. The only sound heard is the occasional roar of a cannon shot from the old fort 200 yards to the south or the creak of solid wood floors. Sleepers awaken to the aroma of freshly baked goodies as we prepare a full, mouth-watering, country breakfast just like "Mom used to make." We believe that every guest is a gift from God.

Castle Garden Soufflé

6 eggs
2 cups milk
6 slices white bread, crust removed, cubed
1 cup grated cheese
1 cup meat, bacon ham or sausage, fried and crumbled
may add broccoli or spinach

Beat eggs and milk together, and add cubed bread. Let soak overnight or longer. Next morning, pour into two loaf pans on top of half of the meat and cheese. Add rest of meat and cheese on top. Bake in a pan of water at 325° for 1 hour, or when a knife inserted in center comes out clean.

Artichoke Soufflé

6 tablespoons mild salsa
3 tablespoons grated Parmesan cheese
1 cup shredded sharp cheddar cheese
1 cup shredded Monterey Jack cheese
1 - 14 ounce can artichoke hearts, chopped
9 eggs
12 ounces cream cheese
vegetable or butter spray
optional: chopped tomatoes, parsley

Spray six 4-inch ramekins. Spread one tablespoon salsa in each ramekin cup. Distribute the chopped artichokes evenly over the salsa. Sprinkle 1/2 tablespoon of Parmesan cheese over artichokes. Sprinkle 1/6 of the sharp cheddar and 1/6 of the Monterey Jack cheeses over Parmesan cheese in each ramekin. Place the eggs in blender container and blend until smooth. Add the cream cheese to eggs and blend until smooth. Pour 1/6 of the egg mixture in each ramekin. Bake uncovered in 350° oven for 30-40 minutes.

Serve with dollop of salsa, 1 teaspoon of chopped tomatoes, and a piece of parsley on top. We usually serve this with hash brown potatoes, with a dollop of sour cream, topped with fresh chopped chives, and muffins. The colors on the plate are almost as wonderful as the breakfast. For people who don't like artichokes, this recipe works great if you substitute spinach and bacon (crisp and crumbled), or cooked sausage and onions, in place of the artichokes.

The Bed and Breakfast of Sumter

Suzanne and Jess Begley
6 Park Avenue
Sumter, SC 29150
(803) 773-2903; FAX (803) 775-6943

Charming, 1896 home facing a lush park in the historic district. Large front porch with swing and rocking chairs. Gracious guest rooms with antiques, fireplaces, and all private baths. Formal Victorian parlor and TV sitting area. FAX machine is also available. Gourmet breakfast includes fruit, entree, and home-baked breads.

Colonial Capital Bed and Breakfast

Barbara and Phil Craig
501 Richmond Road
Williamsburg, VA 23185
(757) 229-0233; (800) 776-0570;
FAX (757) 253-7667

Our Colonial Revival home in the architectural preservation District is only three blocks from the historic area. Guests enjoy our antiques, Oriental rugs, cozy canopied beds, and en suite baths. They indulge in a full, cooked breakfast before the days activities. Then relax afterwards on the porch, patio, or deck sharing tea and wine with friends, new and old.

Breakfast Soufflé for Hearty Appetites

- 12 slices coarse-grained white bread, crust removed
- 6 slices thin American cheese
- 6 slices thin Virginia ham
- 6 slices thin Swiss cheese
- 4 eggs, slightly beaten
- 1/2 teaspoon dry mustard
- 2 cups milk
- 1/3 cup butter or margarine, melted
- 2/3 cup corn flakes, crushed

Grease a 9x13x2 inch baking dish. Arrange 4 slices of bread at corners of dish and 4 half slices of bread in middle of dish. Top bread with American cheese, then ham, then Swiss, and cover with remaining bread, in the same arrangement as the bottom slices. Beat eggs and dry mustard, mixing well, and combine with milk. Pour over sandwiches. Cover and refrigerate overnight. Before baking, pour melted butter evenly over casserole, and sprinkle with corn flake crumbs. Bake in 350° oven for 55-60 minutes or until slightly brown and puffed. Cut into 4 servings, and serve at once. Present with garnish of melons and/or cluster of grapes. Makes 4 servings.

Fresh and Fast Frittata

4 eggs
1 green onion, chopped, place in small dish or teacup
1/4 bell pepper, chopped, place in small dish or teacup
1/4 tomato, chopped, place in small dish or teacup
3 mushrooms, sliced
4 drops Tabasco sauce
1 cup shredded cheddar cheese
salt and pepper to taste
3 tablespoons olive oil
1 tablespoon butter

Slice 3 mushrooms, sauté in 1 tablespoon of butter, drain. In a 4 cup measuring bowl, with pour spout, beat 4 eggs, add drops of Tabasco sauce. Turn burner on medium heat, place 3 tablespoons of olive oil in skillet with lid, and sauté the chopped green onions and the chopped bell pepper about 2 minutes, add the mushrooms and tomato, sauté about 1 more minute, pour in the egg mixture, toss on cheese, put on the lid and reduce heat to warm for 10 minutes (no peeking). When done, slice into four wedges and serve with fruit, muffins and fresh squeezed orange juice, for a golden "wakeup" breakfast.

Country Lane Bed and Breakfast

James and Ann Cornelius
Route 2 Box 94B
Royse City, TX 75189
(214) 636-2600; (800) 240-8757;
FAX (214) 635-2300

Just 28 miles east of Dallas, our country getaway has a private pond which is a favorite stopover of egrets and herons. Four guest rooms with private baths are themed to movie characters — Mae West, Roy Rogers, Natalie Wood, and Film Noir Mysteries. Hundreds of vintage and new movies are among the collectibles for guests' enjoyment.

1837
Bed and Breakfast

Sherri Weaver and Richard Dunn
126 Wentworth Street
Charleston, SC 29401
(803) 723-7166

Visitors to our 1837 B&B enjoy accommodations in a wealthy cotton planter's home and brick carriage house centrally located in Charleston's historic district. Featuring canopied, poster, and rice beds. Full, gourmet breakfast is served in the formal dining room and includes sausage pie, Eggs Benedict, ham omelets or frittata, and home-baked breads. The 1837 Tea Room serves afternoon tea to our guests and the public.

Ham Frittata

4 tablespoons margarine
1/2 cup onion, chopped
1/2 cup green pepper, chopped
4 ounces mushrooms
5 1/2 ounces ham, diced
10 ounces Monterey Jack cheese
12 ounces cheddar cheese
1 cup sour cream
20 eggs

Sauté first 4 ingredients. Whisk eggs and sour cream. Combine remaining frittata ingredients and pour into two 9 inch glass pie plates sprayed with PAM cooking spray. Bake at 325° for 50 minutes until pies are set in center, and blonde in color. Cool to room temperature and refrigerate.

Mornay Sauce

2 tablespoons margarine
6 tablespoons flour
1 chicken bouillon cube
1 1/2 cup milk
1 ounce Monterey Jack cheese
1 ounce Parmesan cheese

Dissolve bouillon cube in margarine in saucepan over medium heat. Slowly add flour (will thicken), add milk, blending until smooth. Add both cheeses and stir. Sauce should be thick. Cool and refrigerate.

Bread Crumbs

2 1/4 cup soft bread crumbs
1/4 cup Parmesan cheese
1/4 cup margarine, melted
2 tablespoons parsley, chopped

Put bread heels and slices along with parsley and Parmesan in food processor to make crumbs. Place in plastic container and add melted margarine. Toss lightly.

To serve: Microwave each pie on high for 1 minute. Spread Mornay Sauce over each pie and sprinkle with crumbs. Bake at 325° for 40-45 minutes. Crumbs should be brown. Slice and serve.

The William Catlin House

Robert and Josephine Martin
2304 E. Broad Street
Richmond, VA 23223
(804) 780-3746

Richmond's first and oldest bed and breakfast features antique, canopy poster beds and working fireplaces. Built in 1845, this richly appointed home is in the Church Hill historic district and was featured in Colonial Homes *and* Southern Living *magazines. Directly across from St. John's Church, where Patrick Henry gave his famous "Liberty or Death" speech. A delicious, full breakfast is served in the elegant dining room.*

Breakfast Frittata

3 medium potatoes
1/2 pound Italian sausage
6 large eggs
1/4 cup milk
2 tablespoons chopped, fresh parsley leaves
1/4 teaspoon salt
1/4 cup shredded mozzarella cheese

Peel, slice potatoes. Boil potatoes in 2 inches water until fork tender. Drain. Slice sausages into 1/2 inch pieces. In heavy 10 inch skillet, with oven-safe handle, sauté sausage until cooked. Drain fat. Add potatoes to sausage. In bowl beat eggs, milk, parsley, and salt. Pour egg mixture over potatoes and sausage. Cover. Cook over low heat 8 minutes or until center of frittata is set. Sprinkle with cheese. Broil until cheese is melted.

The Flip Side

French Toast, Pancakes, and Waffles

". . .For the Lord seeth not as man seeth; for man looketh on the outward appearance, but the Lord looketh on the heart."

1 Samuel 16:7

Back in Time

June and Ron Robinson
927 Cooper Avenue
Glenwood Springs, CO 81601
(970) 945-6183

This wonderful recipe is the favorite of our guests. Being located in the Rocky Mountains, a hearty breakfast is a must. It reminds us of Grandma's bread pudding. We call it the "Togtherness French Toast" as each person helps the other in serving from the serving dish. We always serve this to our "first timers" as it "hooks" the guests to return for more! Many requests for the recipe follow . . . another good reason as revenue goes to a charity in our area. We have adapted it for our health-minded friends. With serving granola, fruit and perhaps scones, this adds up to a bountiful breakfast.

This is truly a wonderful recipe and I am happy to share it with you.

Yummy French Toast

French bread cut in 2 inch slices
3 cups milk (I use 2% to reduce fat)
1 teaspoon vanilla
6 eggs (can use egg substitute)
1/2 teaspoon nutmeg
3/4 cup margarine
1 cup chopped pecan nuts
1 cup brown sugar
drizzle of dark corn syrup

Place the cut French bread in 8x13 inch pan sprayed with PAM cooking spray. Pour the next 4 ingredients that have been beaten together over the bread. Cover with plastic wrap and refrigerate overnight. In morning mix together topping of margarine, chopped pecan nuts, brown sugar and corn syrup. Turn over the drenched French bread so that the pieces are very moist on all sides. Place topping over bread. Bake at 350° for 40 minutes uncovered. Serve immediately. Serves 6-8. Can reduce amount by fourths and place in ramekins for servings for 1- 2.

Decadent French Toast

1/4 pound butter
1 cup brown sugar
2 tablespoons light corn syrup
1 loaf French or Italian bread
5 eggs
1 1/4 cups milk
1 teaspoon vanilla

In a saucepan, bring butter, corn syrup and brown sugar to a boil. Continue boiling for 1 minute, stirring constantly. Pour mixture into a 9x13 inch baking dish sprayed with PAM cooking spray. Cut bread into 1 inch slices and nestle into the syrup mixture. Combine eggs, milk, and vanilla in a blender and whip for 15 seconds. Pour over bread slices. Bake in a 350° oven for 30-35 minutes. Serves 6-8.

May be made the day before and refrigerated until ready for baking. Should be flipped upside-down prior to serving

The Victorian Lady Inn

Kate and Joe Bowski
421 Howard Street
San Antonio, TX 78212
(210) 224-2524; (800) 879-7116

Fabulous full breakfasts, served in the grand dining room amidst leaded glass windows and oak beamed ceilings, are a daily treat at The Victorian Inn. Decadent French Toast is a deliciously sweet blend of textures and tastes, sure to please any palette. Mornings will be savored while experiencing our casually elegant atmosphere and enjoying a variety of breakfast fare.

Singleton House Bed and Breakfast

Barbara Gavron
11 Singleton
Eureka Springs, AR 72632
(501) 253-9111; (800) 833-3394

Guests enjoy this dish on the balcony overlooking the fantasy wildflower garden below with its array of birds and butterflies, and lily filled goldfish pond. Music of birds in a meadow bring the local "chirpers" in to watch.

We serve Decadent French Toast with fresh watermelon, and Greek grapes on the side. Guest can choose butter, maple syrup, strawberry yogurt, fresh sliced strawberries, or bananas to top their toast. Whipped cream and sliced almonds are also an option.

Decadent French Toast

5 eggs
1/2 cup sugar
3 tablespoons cinnamon
1 quart milk
2-3 tablespoons almond extract
3 tablespoons vanilla
1/2 teaspoon nutmeg
2-3 slices, per person, French bread slices

Mix first 7 ingredients together, should be hot cocoa color. Dip bread, with tongs, into mixture. Cook with butter in iron skillet over medium heat until crisp.

Creamy French Toast

3 eggs
1 French loaf of bread
1/4 cup water
1/4 stick margarine
4 tablespoons peanut oil
2 1/1 ounce package walnut bits
8 ounces cream cheese, softened

Beat eggs with wire whisk. Add water and beat until well mixed. Slice French loaf into 1/4 inch slices. Spread cream cheese on one side of each slice. Sprinkle 1 1/2 teaspoon crushed walnuts on cheese side and place together like sandwiches. Dip in egg mixture until well coated. In iron skillet melt butter and oil; grill bread until golden brown. Serves 6-8.

Wilmar Manor Bed and Breakfast

Marise and Wilton Banks
303 West King Street
Shippensburg, PA 17257
(717) 532-3784

We offer guests accommodations in a beautiful Victorian mansion built in 1898. At Wilmar Manor we serve Creamy French Toast with warm maple syrup, accompanied with tea or coffee, fruit juice, and a serving of mixed fresh fruit. Guests enjoy the delicious breakfast in our formal Victorian dining room.

Alexander Bed and Breakfast Acres, Inc.

Jimmy and Pamela Alexander
Rt. 7, Box 788
Gainesville, TX 76240
(903) 564-7440; (800) 887-8794

Our charming, three-story Queen Anne home and guest cottage are nestled peacefully in the woods and meadows. The two-story cottage has three bedrooms and kitchen facilities. The main house features a wrap-around porch and offers five guest rooms.

We prepare a full breakfast for guests of the main house, and this recipe has been a real favorite with our guests.

Fluffy French Toast

1 cup flour
1 1/2 teaspoon baking powder
1 teaspoon salt
2 eggs
1 cup milk
10 - 1/2 slices bread

Combine fist 5 ingredients, mix well. Dip bread slices into batter and fry in 1/2 inch hot oil until lightly brown. Turn. Drain on paper towel before serving. Serves 5.

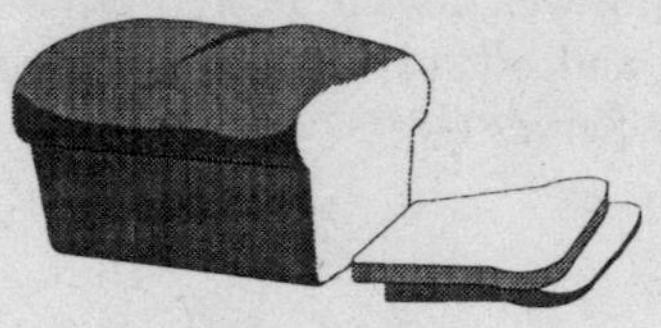

Crumb Topped Baked French Toast

2 eggs, well beaten
1/2 cup milk
dash salt
1-2 teaspoons vanilla
6 slices "Texas Toast," thick sliced bread
1 cup corn flake crumbs
1/4 cup melted butter (optional)

Whisk together eggs, milk, salt, and vanilla. Dip the bread slices into the egg mixture then coat bread slices both sides with corn flake crumbs; place on well greased cookie sheet. Drizzle bread with melted butter (optional). Bake in hot 450° oven for 10 minutes.

Piedmont House Bed and Breakfast

Sheri and Ron Morrill
165 Spring Street
Eureka Springs, AR 72632
(501) 253-9258; (800)253-9258

I came across this recipe nearly ten years ago when we first became B&B innkeepers. Our guests loved it so we still serve it when we have smaller groups. As you can double and triple the amount and serve up to ten or twelve people easily. We laughingly tell our guests we are seving them their cereal and toast today.

Serve with hot maple syrup, and any variety of jams taste great as a topping, especially strawberry.

The Doubleday Inn

Ruth Anne and Charles Wilcox
104 Doubleday Avenue
Gettysburg, PA 17325
(717) 334-9119

Situated directly on the Gettysburg battlefield, The Doubleday Inn is a fine country inn filled with comfortable antiques and Civil War accents. Enjoy the lovely grounds with splendid views overlooking Gettysburg and the National Military Park. The Inn has nine guest rooms. Guests enjoy a full country breakfast daily and can easily walk to many historic points. On selected evenings, licensed battlefield guides bring the battle alive.

Apple French Toast

1 large loaf Italian bread, sliced thickly
9 large eggs
1 cup sugar
3 1/2 cups milk
1 teaspoon vanilla
3 1/2 teaspoons cinnamon
1 teaspoon nutmeg
6-8 large Granny Smith apples
butter to dot on top

Spray an 11x15 glass dish with cooking spray. Place sliced bread together in bottom of dish, making sure they are arranged tightly together. In a bowl, whisk together sugar, milk, eggs and vanilla. Pour half of the egg mixture over bread. Peel, core and slice apples, then place on top of bread. Pour remaining egg mixture over apples. Dot with butter and refrigerate overnight. Bake 1 hour uncovered at 350°.

Apple-Cinnamon Baked French Toast

- 1 large loaf French bread
- 8 extra large eggs
- 3 1/2 cups milk
- 1 cup sugar
- 1 tablespoon vanilla
- 1 teaspoon nutmeg
- 6-8 MacIntosh or Cortland apples
- 1/8 stick butter

Slice bread into 1 1/2 inch slices. Spray 9x13 inch glass pan with nonstick spray. Place bread in glass dish, tightly. Beat together eggs, 1/2 cup sugar, milk and vanilla. Pour half mixture over bread. Peel, core, slice apples, and place on top of bread to cover. Pour remaining egg/milk mixture over apples. Mix remaining 1/2 cup sugar with cinnamon and nutmeg and sprinkle over top of apples. Dot with butter. Cover and refrigerate overnight. Next morning, preheat oven to 350°. Bake 1 hour. Remove and allow to rest 5-10 mintes before serving.

Serve with heated apple syrup and/or maple syrup. We serve with ham loaf patties and guests rave about the wonderful breakfast.

The Homeridge Bed and Breakfast

Sue and Howard Landon
1470 North State Street
Jerseyville, IL 62052
(618) 498-3442

One man said he would drive three hours for this breakfast any weekend.

We serve a full breakfast each morning to guests of our beautiful brick (1867) Italianate Victorian private home. We are located on eighteen acres in a comfortable country atmosphere. The historic estate features a tree-lined drive, pillared front porch, a large swimming pool, and much more.

Washington House Inn Bed and Breakfast

Mel and Nina Vogel
216 South George Street
Charles Town, WV 25414
(304) 725-7923; (800) 297-6957;
FAX (304) 728-5150
Email: mnvogel@intrepid.net
Web site: http://www.intrepid.net/wh/B&B

In charming Colonial Charles Town, nestled in the Blue Ridge Mountains where the Shenandoah and Potomac Rivers meet, the Washington House Inn is a wonderful example of late Victorian architecture. Built at the turn of the century, by descendants of President Washington's brothers, the Inn is graced with antique furnishings, carved oak mantles, seven fireplaces, and spacious guest rooms. Just 60 miles from Washington D.C.

Carmelized Apple French Toast

- 1 cup brown sugar
- 3 tablespoons light Karo syrup
- 6 tablespoons butter
- 3 Granny Smith apples, peeled, cored and sliced
- 18 slices day-old white bread
- 6 eggs
- 2 cups milk
- 1/2 teaspoon vanilla

Combine sugar, syrup and butter; boil in pan for 1 minute. Pour into greased 9x13 inch pan. Place sliced raw apples on top of caramel. Place bread three layers deep in pan. Mix eggs, milk and vanilla together; pour over bread. Refrigerate overnight. Bake at 325° for 45 minutes until brown and slightly puffy.

Washington House Inn

Blueberry Surprise Baked French Toast

8 thin slices or French or Italian bread
8 tablespoons cream cheese, softened
1 cup fresh or frozen "dry pack" blueberries
6 large eggs
1 1/2 cup milk
4 tablespoons blueberry syrup

Spray four individual casseroles with vegetable spray. Spread 4 slices of bread with cream cheese. Top with other 4 slices. Slice into 1 inch cubes and place in individual casseroles. Sprinkle on the blueberries. Mix eggs, milk and blueberry syrup. Pour over bread cubes and blueberries. Cover with foil (making sure foil doesn't touch bread) and refrigerate overnight. In the morning preheat oven to 350°. Place in oven and bake for 25-30 minutes. Remove foil and bake for an additional 15 minutes. Remove from oven and let cool 5 minutes. Drizzle with syrup. Serve with additional syrup for guests who like it sweeter. (This recipe stays hot for a long time and is great to serve on a winter morning.)

Colonial Gardens Bed and Breakfast

Scottie and Wilmot Phillips
1109 Jamestown Road
Williamsburg, VA 23185
(757) 220-8087; (800) 886-9715;
FAX (757) 253-1495

This recipe is always a hit with the guests and gets rave reviews. Although I change my menus seasonally, this is one recipe that does well all year long. I use fresh blueberries as long as they are available. Midwinter frozen "dry pack" blueberries may be used as well. The real secret in the flavor is the blueberry syrup. After testing many different brands of blueberry syrup I have settled on Maple Grove Farms of Vermont, Inc. It is very sweet and pure and the guests love it.

Hilltop Herb Farm at Chain-O-Lakes

Beverly Smith
One Victorian Place
Cleveland, TX 77327
(713) 592-5859; FAX (713) 592-6288

At Hilltop Herb Farm, the garden is where it all begins. Here you will learn the use of fine herbs in cooking, you can purchase seeds or cuttings for your own garden or just enjoy the nature trails.

Typically the "piece de resistance" on Saturday night is the "Traditional Dinner." This is a delicately prepared five-course meal complete with herb garden tour. If you are out for a weekend drive you might consider joining Beverly and her guests for a true "Country Inn" breakfast.

Hilltop Herb Farm is indeed an experience not to be forgotten.

Baked Blueberry-Stuffed French Toast

12 slices of homemade-type white bread
2 (8 ounce) packages cold cream cheese
1 cup blueberries, picked over and rinsed
12 large eggs
1/3 cup maple syrup
2 cups milk

Remove crusts from bread; cut into 1 inch cubes. Cut cream cheese into 1 inch cubes. Arrange half the bread cubes in a buttered 13x9 inch baking dish, scatter the cream cheese over the bread, and sprinkle the blueberries over cheese. Arrange remaining bread over blueberries. Whisk together the eggs, syrup, and milk; pour over bread and let chill, covered, overnight. Bake, covered with foil, in a preheated 350° oven for 30 minutes. Remove foil and bake for 30 minutes longer. Serve with blueberry sauce. Serves 6-8.

Blueberry Sauce

1 cup sugar
2 tablespoons cornstarch
1 cup water
1 cup blueberries
1 tablespoon unsalted butter

Combine sugar, cornstarch, and water in a saucepan. Cook over moderately high heat, stirring until mixture thickens. Stir in blueberries and simmer for 10 minutes, or until berries burst. Add unsalted butter and stir the sauce until butter is melted.

Blueberry and Cream Cheese Strata

- 1 - 16 ounce loaf sliced white bread, crusts removed
- 2 cups frozen or fresh blueberries (do not thaw)
- 1 - 3 ounce package cream cheese, cut into 1/4 inch cubes
- 4 eggs
- 2 cups milk
- 1/3 cup sugar
- 1 teaspoon vanila extract
- 1/4 teaspoon salt
- 1/4 teaspoon ground nutmeg

Butter an 8 inch square baking dish. Cut bread into 1/2 inch cubes (makes about 7 cups). Put half in baking dish. Top with half the blueberries, and all the cream cheese cubes. Top with remaining bread cubes, and blueberries. In a bowl beat eggs, milk, sugar, and flavorings. Beat well. Pour over bread mixture. Refrigerate covered 20 minutes, or overnight. Bake uncovered for 1 hour at 325°. Serves 8-10.

Blueberry Maple Syrup

- 2 cups blueberries
- 3/4 cup maple syrup
- 1 tablespoon cornstarch
- 2 tablespoons cold water

Mix blueberries and maple syrup. Mix cornstarch with cold water; add to syrup and cook until mixture boils. Simmer for one minute. Serve warm.

Eagleview Manor Bed and Breakfast

Bob and Pat Young
Box 3138, 178 Widder Street E.
St. Mary's, Ontario
CANADA N4X 1A8
(519) 284-1811

St. Mary's is a town time forgot." Our beautiful Victorian home overlooks a quaint, peaceful town. Minutes from London and Stratford. Sweeping staircase, stained-glass windows, Jacuzzi, quilts, antiques, fireplaces, in-ground pool, and four spacious guest rooms. Nanny's Tea Room available for afternoon or Victorian teas.

Maplewood Hotel

Catherine Simon and Jenna Schaeffer
428 Butler Street
Saugatuck, MI 49453
(616) 857-1771; (800) 650-9790, FAX (616) 857-1773

Unmistakeably Greek Revival in architectural design, the Maplewood Hotel includes a library, glass-enclosed porch, and a full-sized lap pool. We offer fifteen guests rooms, some with fireplaces and Jacuzzi tubs. Situated in downtown Saugatuck within walking distance to shops and restaurants. We serve a full gourmet breakfast that may include this favorite recipe.

Spiced French Toast
with Broiled Grapefruit

4 whole eggs
1 cup milk
1 teaspoon vanilla
1/2 teaspoon cinnamon
1/2 teaspoon nutmeg
1/2 teaspoon orange peel
1/2 teaspoon sugar
8 slices Brioche bread

Mix eggs, milk, vanilla, cinnamon, nutmeg, orange peel and sugar. Set aside. Slice bread into 1/2 inch thick slices and soak in egg mixture until just saturated. Brown in hot skillet filmed with canola oil.

Broiled Grapefruit

2 grapefruit
1/3 cup brown sugar

Cut grapefruit in half, section out into a flame-proof dish. Sprinkle brown sugar over fruit. Broil until bubbly, about 5 minutes. Serve Broiled Grapefruit on the side of French toast. Serves 4.

Oven-Baked Orange French Toast

1/4 cup butter or margarine
1/3 cup light brown sugar
1/4 teaspoon cinnamon
1 teaspoon grated orange rind
4 eggs, beaten
2/3 cups orange juice
8 slices French bread

In 9x13 inch pan melt the butter and sprinkle the mixture of brown sugar, cinnamon, and grated orange rind over the melted butter. Dip bread slices in the mixture of beaten eggs and orange juice. Place in pan and bake at 400° for about 20 minutes or until golden brown. Turn out of pan immediately.

Purviance House Bed and Breakfast

Robert and Jean Gernand
326 South Jefferson Street,
SR #5 and US #224
Huntington, IN 46750
(219) 356-4218

This is usually served with smoky links and fresh fruit. Although it makes its own syrup, extra syrup may be served as well. Our guests have really enjoyed this recipe — an architect from Chicago who didn't usually like French toast said it was so good it was worth the three-hour trip just to eat it! Another guest took one bite, got up and ran to the kitchen asking for the recipe! We once served this to 45 people at a prayer breakfast at our B&B!

Shady Lane Bed and Breakfast

Pat and Dennis Dougherty
PO Box 314, Allegheny Avenue
Eagles Mere, PA 17731
(800) 524-1248

This recipe stems from when I was a child and went to my nanny's house for the weekend. She would always make delicious French toast with some kind of fruit. This was a special breakfast! When Pat decided to go into the bed and breakfast business, I knew we would serve this special breakfast to our guests.

Peach or Apple French Toast

3 apples or peaches, peeled
1 cup brown sugar
1/2 cup butter or margarine
2 tablespoons water
5 eggs
1 1/2 cups milk
1 tablespoon vanilla
1 loaf of French bread (12-14 slices)
ground cinnamon

Slice apples or peaches and set aside. In a saucepan, heat butter and sugar over a mid-low heat until butter is melted, add water, and continue cooking until sauce becomes thick and foamy. Place in a 9x13 inch baking dish, cool 10 minutes. Place apple or peaches on top of cooled sauce and cover with slices of bread, placed closely together. Blend eggs, milk, and vanilla until well mixed. Pour over bread and sprinkle with cinnamon, cover dish with foil and refrigerate overnight. Place in 350° oven for 40 minutes loosely cover with foil the last 20 minutes. Serves 6-7.

Dust with powdered sugar and serve with warm maple syrup. Accompany the French toast with your favorite breakfast meat, fresh fruit and juice. This is fantastic for a very special breakfast or brunch. It is prepared the day before.

Pineapple Upside-Down French Toast

2 tablespoons butter or margarine, melted
1/4 cup brown sugar
1/2 cup crushed pineapple, drained
1 egg, beaten
1 1/2 cups milk
6 slices Texas toast
cinnamon

Pour melted butter into bottom of 9x13 inch pan. Sprinkle brown sugar and blend into butter. Layer pineapple onto mixture. Mix milk with beaten egg. Dip Texas toast into milk mixture but do not saturate. Lay toast on pineapple. Sprinkle top with cinnamon. Bake at 350° for 30 minutes or until golden brown. Sprinkle lightly with powdered sugar just before serving.

Mix equal portions of orange juice and cranberry together. Arrange a fruit platter with five or six slices of bananas and kiwi. Make strawberry fans by cutting four or five slits into a medium to large strawberry and fanning it out on the plate.

Terrace Hill Bed and Breakfast

Len, Cookie, Lenard, and Lynn Novak
922 River Road
Wisconsin Dells, WI 53965
(608)253-9363

When we first opened, some of our recipes required extensive prep time and baking time for best results — and prompt diners. We quickly realized our guests were on vacation and needed some flexibility. My son, Lenard, who enjoys puttering in the kitchen, set out to create some interesting breakfasts that would require less prep and baking time, and the Pineapple Upside-Down French Toast was one of the most popular creations. Our guest book comments support its popularity. If you like this recipe, get creative. Try it with whole berry cranberry sauce! That's another fantastic taste treat.

Serve with specialty coffee or tea, and homemade muffins or rolls, add soft music and candlelight and pamper yourself.

Captain's Quarters Inn

Bill and Phyllis Pepper
202 W. Queen Street
Edenton, NC 27932
(919) 482-8945; (800) 482-8945

We serve plenty of gourmet food to our guests, including welcome refreshments, continental breakfast, and a full three-course breakfast, as well as gourmet dinner on weekends. Our inn is a seventeen-room, circa 1907 home in the Edenton historic district with a 65-foot wraparound front porch (swings and rockers). Eight charming bedrooms with modern, private baths (seven queen beds, two twin beds).

Raspberry-Stuffed French Toast

1 - 10 ounce package unsweetened frozen raspberries (thaw, drain, saving juice)
2 - 8 ounce packages cream cheese, softened
1 tablespoon sugar
1 teaspoon ground allspice, or nutmeg
4 loaves day-old French bread, cut ends off
6 eggs
2 cups milk (could vary, depending on how dry bread is)
butter-flavored cooking oil

Mix together raspberries, cream cheese, sugar and spice. Cut bread lengthwise, part way through (as if making a hero sandwich.) Pull out a narrow trough (about 1/2 inch wide) of bread in center. Fill the trough with raspberry-cream cheese mixture and close the top over the bottom. Chill overnight or for several days. Can freeze for up to one month. Mix and beat together eggs and milk. Brush butter-flavored oil onto a 4-sided shallow cookie sheet. Cut stuffed French bread in 1 inch slices and dip into egg mixture. Bake in preheated 350° oven for 35 minutes, turning once after 20 minutes. Pour small amount of heated raspberry sauce over French toast. We serve with crisp bacon or light sausage. Serves 8-9 portions.

Raspberry Sauce

juice saved from 10 ounce package of frozen raspberries
1 1/2 cups sugar

Pour raspberry juice drained from frozen raspberries into saucepan. Add 1 1/2 cups sugar and heat slowly until melted. Boil for several minutes, until syrupy. Pour over French toast above.

You will probably have more raspberry sauce than you need for this recipe. Use part of extra for delicious salad dressing, by adding oil and vinegar.

Black Friar Inn

Perry and Sharon Risley, and Falke
10 Summer Street
Bar Harbor, ME 04609-4197
(207) 288-5091; FAX (207) 288-4197

This recipe I created from a melange of other stuffed French toasts, some were too sweet, and some not appropriate for New England. I wanted to use Maine ingredients as often as I could, so I sweetened with maple syrup and I use blueberries year-round (we can get flash frozen wild Main blueberries that work just fine for this recipe, when fresh ones aren't in season). The sourdough bread adds a tartness that offsets the maple syrup's sweetness well. We usually get requests for second helpings from this one, and it saves well throughout the entire breakfast serving. I have found that the bread is easier to cube if you freeze it partially.

Stuffed French Toast

6 slices sour dough bread, cut into 1/4 inch cubes
6 eggs
1/4 cup maple syrup
cinnamon and nutmeg to taste
4 ounce cream cheese, cubed
1 cup milk
blueberries/fruit as desired

Place 1/2 the bread cubes in a 8x8 inch lightly greased pan. Put cream cheese cubes on top, then fruit, and top with remaining bread cubes. Combine eggs, syrup, milk, cinnamon and nutmeg. Pour over bread. Cover with plastic wrap and refrigerate overnight. Heat oven to 350°. When ready to bake, remove plastic wrap and bake for 45 minutes, or until set.

Fruit Sauce

2 cups blueberries
1/2 cup orange juice
2 cups strawberries
2-3 tablespoons lemon juice
1/2 cup sugar

Combine berries, sugar, orange and lemon juices in saucepan over medium heat. Cook about 5 minutes. Puree in food processor or blender, return to saucepan, heat until warm.

Stuffed French Toast

8 ounces cream cheese, softened
2 tablespoons vanilla
2 tablespoons sugar
1/3 cup chopped nuts
1 loaf French bread
1/2 cup milk
1/2 teaspoon cinnamon
1/2 teaspoon nutmeg
6 eggs

Blend cream cheese, vanilla, sugar and nuts in a bowl. Slice bread into 1 inch thick slices, then slice a pocket in the center of each slice of bread. Spread about 1 tablespoon of this mixture in each pocket. In a bowl, beat eggs, milk, cinnamon and nutmeg. Dip each slice of bread into egg mixture. Let it soak a few minutes, then put on to a greased cookie sheet. Bake for 20 minutes at 375°. Serve with jam or syrup.

The Inn at Burg's Landing

Ken and Annie Burg
8808 Villa Beach Road
Anderson Island, WA 98303
(206) 884-9185

I serve this recipe along with an old-fashioned full breakfast consisting of juice, milk, coffee, meats, pastries or breads, and fresh fruit.

We serve Stuffed French Toast to our guest because this recipe brings to us memories of family times spent together. When we invite guests into our home we are inviting them to be a part of our family. Serving this meal for breakfast allows us to spend a relaxing morning savoring old memories and creating new ones with friends.

Friendship Manor Bed and Breakfast

Jack and Marylin Baker
349 South Main Street
Albion, NY 14411
(716) 589-7973

I serve this along with fresh pork sausage links heated with apple slices, sprinkled with lemon juice and brown sugar, and muffins and fresh fruit, for a lovely weekend brunch buffet style. It has always been a hit with my guests. The recipe has been requested numerous times and I am told it has become a tradition with my guests in their home at Christmastime.

Stuffed French Toast

1 - 1 pound loaf French bread
1 - 8 ounce package cream cheese
8 eggs
2 1/2 cups milk, light cream, or half and half
6 tablespoons butter or margarine
1/4 cup maple syrup

Cut bread into cubes. Grease a 13x9 inch pan. Place half of the bread cubes in pan. Top with cream cheese cubes and then with remaining bread. In blender mix eggs, milk, melted butter and maple syrup until well combined. Pour mixture over bread and cheese cubes. Using a spatula, slightly press layers down to moisten. Cover with plastic wrap and refrigerate for 2-24 hours. Remove wrap. Bake at 325° for 35-40 minutes. Serve with Apple Cider Syrup.

Apple Cider Syrup

1/2 cup sugar
4 teaspoons cornstarch
1/2 teaspoon ground cinnamon
1 cup apple juice, or cider
1 tablespoon lemon juice
2 tablespoons butter or margarine

In small pan, mix all ingredients, except butter. Cook until thickened and bubbly, then cook 2 minutes longer. Remove from heat and add butter. Stir until melted. Makes 1 1/3 cups.

Hillside Stuffed French Toast

1 loaf cinnamon raisin bread
1 tub pineapple cream cheese
1 cup eggnog

Make sandwiches with cinnamon raisin bread and pineapple cream cheese. Cut sandwiches diagonally in two. Dip in eggnog and fry in skillet using bacon drippings. Can be reheated in microwave. Freezes well.

Hillside Farm Bed and Breakfast

Gary and Deb Lintner
607 Eby Chiques Road
Mount Joy, PA 17552
(717) 653-6697; FAX (717) 653-5233 (call ahead)

In 1989 our B&B was asked to participate in a B&B Christmas tour. We choose to be the 8 Maids A-Milking (all 12 inns each chose which of the 12 days of Christmas they wanted to represent). Since everyone else was serving wassail or punch, we decided to go with the theme to serve eggnog. Not knowing how many people to anticipate, we got 20 gallons of eggnog. We had 18 gallons left over! After checking with the dairy and finding eggnog would freeze well, we decided it was the perfect dip for French toast. It works! We never have any leftovers.

The Royal Rose Inn Bed and Breakfast

Kenny and Cindy Vincent
41 Baltimore Avenue
Rehoboth Beach, DE 19971
(302) 226-2535

A charming and relaxing 1920s beach cottage, our bed and breakfast is tastefully furnished with antiques and a romantic rose theme. A scrumptious breakfast of homemade bread, muffins, egg dishes, and much more is served on a large screened-in porch. Air-conditioned bedrooms, guest refrigerator, and off-street parking are real pluses for guests. Centrally located one and one half blocks from the ocean and boardwalk.

Stuffed French Toast Strata
with Apple Cider Syrup

1 - 1 pound loaf unsliced French bread
1 - 8 ounce package cream cheese, cubed
8 eggs
2 1/2 cups milk, or half and half
6 tablespoons margarine, melted
1/4 cup maple syrup

Cut bread into cubes (12 cups). Place half of the bread cubes in a greased 13x9x2 inch baking dish. Top with the cream cheese cubes, then the remaining bread cubes. In a blender, mix the remaining ingredients well. Pour over bread and cheese cubes. Press down layers to moisten. Cover with plastic wrap and refrigerate 2-24 hours. Bake in a 325° oven for 35 to 40 minutes or until center is set. Serves 8-10.

Apple Cider Syrup

1/2 cup sugar
4 teaspoons cornstarch
1/2 teaspoon cinnamon
1 cup apple cider or apple juice
1 tablespoon lemon juice
2 tablespoons margarine

In a small saucepan stir together the sugar, cornstarch and cinnamon. Then stir in the apple cider and lemon juice. Cook and stir over medium heat until thick and bubbly. Cook and stir for 2 minutes more. Remove from heat and stir in the margarine. Makes 1 1/3 cups.

Stuffed French Toast
with Oven-Baked Eggs

1 - 1 1/2 to 2 pound loaf sourdough bread
3 ripe bananas, peeled
8 large eggs, beaten lightly
1/3 cup chopped walnuts
cinnamon
butter and oil
pure maple syrup, warmed
6 large eggs
3 scallions
3 teaspoons butter

Preheat oven to 350°. Cut six 1 1/2 inch thick pieces of bread on the diagonal. Make a slice 3/4 way through each piece to form a "pocket." Cut each banana in half, and cut each half into 3 long slices. Dip each slice of bread into the beaten egg, making sure to coat all 4 sides of each piece. Fill each "pocket" with bananas and place on a hot, oiled grill until browned (3-4 minutes each side). Place the slices on an ungreased cookie sheet.

Prepare Baked Eggs: Place 1/2 teaspoon butter in a small ramekin and top with a cracked egg. Sprinkle scallions over top and place in a pan. Surround the ramekins with 1/2 inch water. Bake eggs and toast in 350° oven for 15 minutes. Top toast with butter, and sprinkle of cinnamon, walnuts, and warmed NY state maple syrup. Yields 6 servings.

Giddings Garden Bed and Breakfast

Pat and Nancie Roberts
290 W. Seneca Turnpike
Syracuse, NY 13207
(800) 377-3452

Breakfast is served in the formal dining room during the cool months; and on summer days, guests can enjoy eating on the patio overlooking the gardens. Early risers can always enjoy a cup of rainforest coffee, herbal tea, or juice, as they stroll through the grounds. The following recipe is normally preceeded by peach yogurt topped with granola, served in champagne glasses. The stuffed toast is served with Oven-Baked Eggs and browned sausages, and breakfast is concluded by a cream filled chocolate cup topped with fresh berries.

The Inn at 410 Bed and Breakfast

Howard and Sally Krueger
410 North Leroux Street
Flagstaff, AZ 86001
(520) 774-0088; (800) 774-2008;
FAX (520) 774-6354

Carol Householder, previous owner of The Inn at 410, taught us how to make the elegant version of French toast. Guests rave every time we serve it. This is a very rich tasting French toast, so we serve one piece per person, especially if the French bread is a large loaf. However, a few hearty eaters may want a second piece.

Orange-Stuffed French Toast

1 - 16 inch long loaf French bread (about 1 pound), unsliced
orange marmalade
light cream cheese

Batter:
4 large eggs
1/2 cup skim milk
1 drop orange oil (or 1/2 teaspoon orange zest)
powdered sugar
orange slices, twisted for garnish

Preheat electric griddle to 350°. Slice French bread into 1 1/2 - 2 inch pieces. Using small knife, slit each top, going about 1/2 inch down to make a pocket in each slice. Fill each pocket with approximately 1 teaspoon cream cheese. Beat eggs, milk and orange oil or zest together. Dip each stuffed slice of French bread into the batter, then fry on heated, greased griddle until golden brown, turning once. Make sure it is on the griddle long enough to warm the marmalade and slightly melt the cream cheese. Place one piece on a plate. Sprinkle with powdered sugar and garnish with a twist of orange. Makes 12 servings.

Strawberry-Stuffed French Toast

2 large strawberries (fresh or frozen)
4 ounces cream cheese
1/2 cup powdered sugar

Put all three ingredients into a blender and mix on high until smooth.

2 large eggs
1 tablespoon milk
1/8 teaspoon ground cinnamon
1 teaspoon sugar
1/8 teaspoon vanilla
8 slices bread
oil

Beat eggs, milk, cinnamon, sugar, and vanilla with a whisk until well mixed. Spread all 8 slices of bread with the strawberry mixture. Put 2 slices of bread together sandwich style with the strawberry mixture in the middle. Dip each of the four sandwiches in the egg mixture. Pour oil on a hot griddle, 350°, and put the toast in the oil, cooking until golden brown, turning once. Serve either with maple syrup or fresh berries and whipped cream.

Sky-Vue Lodge

Glenn and Janice Jorgenson
22822 N. Highway 71
Winslow, AR 72959
(501) 634-2003; (800) 782-2003

A guest once told me, "If you're going to serve us eggs for breakfast, serve PLAIN eggs!" Plain good cooking is our specialty. We begin our breakfast with a first course of juice and fresh fruit in the summer, or piping hot cereal in the winter. This is followed by a hearty breakfast like fresh, homemade cinnamon rolls and scrambled eggs or fluffy buttermilk hotcakes and sausage. Sure, you may find something a little exotic like our Strawberry Stuffed French Toast, but we also serve thick slices of Texas Toast without the filling for those who like their food "just plain."

Bridgeford House

Denise and Michael McDonald
263 Spring Street
Eureka Springs, AR 72632
(501) 253-7853; FAX (501) 253-5497

Nestled in the heart of Eureka Springs' historic district, Bridgeford House is an 1884 Victorian delight. Outside are shady porches and beautiful gardens. A short walk to town on the trolley and horsedrawn carriage route. Each room or suite has private entrances and baths. Desserts in room as well as coffee. Large gourmet breakfasts served daily.

Fruit-Stuffed French Toast
with Strawberry Nut Sauce

12 slices raisin bread
3 eggs
1/4 cup milk
1 teaspoon vanilla
2 teaspoons sugar
6 teaspoons strawberry jam
6 ounces soft cream cheese

Spread cream cheese on six slices of raisin bread. Spread strawberry jam on six slices of raisin bread. Put bread slices together and set aside (cream cheese side to strawberry jam side.) Mix eggs, milk, vanilla and sugar. Dip sandwiches in egg mixture, then grill on both sides. Cut diagonally and spoon sauce over wedges before serving.

Strawberry Nut Sauce

1 cup strawberry jam
1/4 cup chopped walnuts
2 teaspoons lemon juice
2 teaspoons cornstarch
2/3 cups cold water

Mix cornstarch and water and wet aside. Heat jam to a boil and add water-cornstarch mixture. Stir constantly and bring to a boil, then simmer 3 minutes. Add lemon juice then chopped walnuts. Spoon approximately 1 tablespoon over 2 wedges of French toast. Serves 6.

Hidden Fruit French Toast

10 slices French bread, about 1/4 inch thick slices
3 eggs
1 tablespoon sugar
1/2 teaspoon cinnamon
1/8 teaspoon nutmeg
1 tablespoon baking powder
1 cup milk
1/2 cup flour
We offer these fruits: blueberry, strawberry, banana, banana nut, or chocolate chip, and Reese's Peanut Butter Chips.

Cut French bread and set aside to allow slices to dry a little. Using a wire whisk, whip eggs, sugar, cinnamon, nutmeg, baking powder and milk together. Add flour a little at a time, continue whipping batter as you do so. Dip a slice of bread quickly on both sides, allowing excess batter to drip off. Do not soak! Whip batter before dipping each slice. Place dipped bread into a medium hot skillet (I use an electric grill, set at 350°.) Add your choice of fruit generously over the top of each slice. Press fruit into bread with the back of a spoon. Cover fruit with about 1 teaspoon of batter. Turn slices when golden brown and cook fruit side until golden brown. Serve with a sprinkle of powdered sugar on top. Serves 5.

The Tuc' Me Inn Bed and Breakfast

Ernie, Terry, Tina and Foutz, and Idabel Evans
118 North Main St., PO Box 657
Wolfeboro, NH 03894
(603) 569-5702

We offer pancakes, waffles, and pockets with fruit inside them as one of our main course choices at breakfast. I felt there should be a way of baking the fruit inside the French toast. After I developed a batter thick enough to do so, our guests around the breakfast table started asking questions, such as "How does the fruit get inside the bread?" and "How early do you have to get up in order to bake the different kinds of fruit breads?"

Belle Aire Mansion Guest House

Jan and Lorraine Svec
11410 Route 20 West
Galena, IL 61036
(815) 777-0893

This is a delicious breakfast that my guests really enjoy. I serve it with a side of pork sausage and a piece of fresh melon and strawberries. Our guests love the fact that they can get a full breakfast, lovingly served, so different from their usual bowl of cereal, at home. It gives them a good start for a busy day visiting Galena.

Pecan Oven French Toast

1 (1 pound) loaf French bread
6 large eggs
1 1/2 cups half and half
1 1/2 cups milk
1 teaspoon vanilla
1 teaspoon cinnamon
1/8 teaspoon nutmeg

Topping:
1/2 cup butter, softened
1 cup light brown sugar, packed
2 tablespoons maple syrup
1 cup chopped pecans

Spray 9x13 inch baking dish with vegetable spray. Cut French bread into 1 inch slices. Layer bread into dish. Beat eggs, milk, half and half, vanilla, cinnamon and nutmeg well. Pour over bread and refrigerate, covered, overnight. Next morning prepare topping by mixing all ingredients well. Smooth topping over bread. Bake at 350°, uncovered, for 40 minutes. Remove from oven and let sit for 5 minutes before serving.

Honey-Glazed Pecan French Toast

1 loaf French bread (day old)
3 eggs
1 cup milk
1 1/2 teaspoon cinnamon
1 teaspoon vanilla
1 1/2 tablespoons honey

Topping:
2 tablespoons melted butter
1/2 cup light brown sugar
1/2 cup pecans, chopped
2 tablespoons honey

Grease two 9x13 inch glass pans. Slice French bread diagonally into 1 inch thick pieces. In a large bowl, whisk together the eggs, honey, and cinnamon. When thoroughly mixed, stir in the milk and vanilla. Dip the bread pieces in the mixture. Be sure to coat both sides. Arrange in greased pans, cover, and refrigerate overnight. In the morning remove from refrigerator, let stand 30 minutes before baking and uncover. Make topping: Drizzle butter over bread slices followed with a sprinkling of the brown sugar and pecan pieces. Top with a drizzling of honey. Bake for 20 minutes at 350°. Serve with warm maple syrup if desired. Smoked sausage is a great accompaniment.

The Kingsley House

Gary and Kari King
626 W. Main Street
Fennville, MI 49408
(616) 561-6425

Gary has always loved to cook and can remember helping his mother bake cookies when he wasn't even tall enough to see atop the kitchen counter.

Before we purchased the Kingsley House, we did a lot of experimentation with different recipes. We knew we wanted a French toast recipe so we tried many recipes from a variety of different cookbooks. We had French toast of a different variety everyday for 6 weeks! None of the recipes worked for us. Some were too sweet, others tasted good but looked awful, still others looked good and tasted awful. Finally Gary said he's have to come up with his own recipe that tasted and looked good! The result is Honey-Glazed Pecan French Toast.

Captain Nickerson Inn

Pat and Dave York
333 Main Street
S. Dennis, MA 02660
(508) 398-5966; (800) 282-1619

A special breakfast taste to bring back the memories of a special stay in a home that re-creates a simpler more elegant time gone by.

Hazelnut/ Amaretto French Toast

3 eggs well beaten
1/4 cup sugar
1 teaspoon vanilla extract
4-5 tablespoons Amaretto liqueur
3 heaping tablespoons Hazelnut Coffeemate
3/4 cup very hot water
1 cup milk

Beat eggs in bowl, add sugar and mix well. Add vanilla and Amaretto and mix well. Add Hazelnut Coffeemate to 3/4 cup hot water and blend until no lumps exist. Add to egg mixture slowly (so eggs don't cook) Add milk and blend well.

Serve cut in halves and sprinkle with confectioners' sugar.

Charleston House French Toast

1/4 cup melted butter
1 cup brown sugar
1 teaspoon cinnamon
5 eggs, beaten
1 1/2 cups skim evaporated milk (12 ounce can)
1 teaspoon vanilla
1/2 teaspoon salt
1 large loaf French bread cut into 1 inch slices

Pour melted butter on large jelly roll pan. Mix brown sugar and cinnamon together and evenly spread on top. Beat eggs, milk, vanilla and salt. Dip bread slices in liquid to coat each side. Place dipped bread on top of jelly roll pan, cover and refrigerate overnight, or 8 hours. Bake uncovered at 350° for 30 minutes. Invert and place on serving tray. Yield: 4-6 servings.

Charleston House Historic Inn

John and Helen Sullivan
918 College Avenue
Houghton, MI 49931
(906) 482-7790; (800) 482-7404;
FAX (906) 482-7068

Do not neglect to show hospitality to strangers, for by this some have entertained angels without knowing it." (Hebrews 13:2, NAS)

This wonderful easy French toast can be served without syrup as the brown sugar melts into the bread while baking. The Charleston House serves up breakfast buffet style to our guests, from 8:30 A.M. to 10:00 A.M. Our guests appreciate the flexible breakfast time and may choose from a variety of buffet offerings. We provide a hot entree that changes daily along with cereals, fresh fruits, juice and a homemade assorted bakery basket!

The Duck Pond Bed and Breakfast

Don and Toni Kohlstedt
6391 Morning Sun Road
Oxford, OH 45056
(513) 523-8914

Guests to our 1863 farmhouse agree that this is a favorite (made famous by repeat guests) among the breakfast recipes offered at our B&B. We serve the toast with coconut syrup and maple syrup.

Hawaiian French Toast

4 eggs
1/3 cup milk
2/3 cup orange juice
1/4 cup sugar
1/4 teaspoon nutmeg
1/2 teaspoon vanilla
8 - 1 inch slices Italian bread
1 stick butter
3 tablespoons ground Macadamia nuts

Whisk together first six ingredients. Place slices of bread in cake pan with tight fitting lid or cover with aluminum foil. Pour egg mixture over bread. Make sure each slice has been covered with egg mixture, turn slices over if necessary. Refrigerate overnight. Melt butter in jelly roll pan, place slices of bread in butter. Sprinkle with nuts. Bake 15-20 minutes.

Overnight French Toast

1/4 cup (1/2 stick) butter, room temperature
12 - 3/4 inch thick French bread slices
6 eggs
1 1/2 cups milk
1/4 cup sugar
1 teaspoon vanilla
1/2 teaspoon salt
powdered sugar
maple syrup

Spread butter over bottom of heavy, large baking pan with 1 inch high sides. Arrange bread slices in pan. Beat eggs, milk, sugar, syrup, vanilla, and salt to blend in large bowl. Pour mixture over bread. Turn bread slices to coat. Cover with plastic and refrigerate overnight. Next morning: preheat oven to 400°. Bake French bread 10 minutes. Turn bread over and continue baking until just golden brown, about 4 minutes longer. Transfer cooked toast to plates and sprinkle with powdered sugar. Serve immediately, passing maple syrup separately.

I use a glass Pyrex oblong baking dish, and let the dish get room temperature before baking.

Sugar Fork Bed and Breakfast

Mary and Sam Price
743 Garrett Road
Dandridge, TN 37725
(423) 397-7327; (800) 487-5634

Guests appreciate the tranquil setting of Sugar Fork, a short distance from the Great Smoky Mountains. Situated on Douglas Lake, the B&B has private access and floating dock. Enjoy warm-weather water sports and fishing year-round. Fireplace in common room, guest kitchenette, wraparound deck, swings, and park bench by the lake. A hearty breakfast is served family-style in the dining room or, weather permitting, on the deck.

Pheasant Field Bed and Breakfast

Denise (Dee) Fegan and Chuck DeMarco
150 Hickorytown Road
Carlisle, PA 17013
(717) 258-0717 (voice and FAX)
Email: pheasant@ pa.net

Our homey, old brick farm house welcomes guests to a quiet setting. This French toast smells so yummy while it's baking. The cinnamon aroma drifts up the stairs to become a wonderful wake-up call for our guests!

Overnight Baked French Toast

1 thin loaf of French or Italian bread
8 large eggs
3/4 teaspoon salt
3 cups milk
4 teaspoons sugar
1 tablespoon vanilla or almond extract
cinnamon
2 tablespoons butter, cut into small slices

Butter a 9x13 inch deep baking pan. Cut the bread into 1 inch thick slices and arrange in a single layer in the pan. In a large bowl, combine the eggs, salt, milk, sugar, and vanilla (or almond) extract, beating with an electric mixer. Pour the mixture over the bread. Sprinkle with cinnamon. Cover with foil and refrigerate overnight. Dot with butter and bake uncovered in a 350° oven for 45-50 minutes until the bread is lightly browned.

Serve with warm maple syrup or confectioners' sugar with fresh fruit.

Overnight Pecan French Toast

4 eggs
2/3 cup orange juice
1/3 cup milk
1/4 cup sugar
1/4 teaspoon ground nutmeg
1/2 teaspoon vanilla extract
1 - 8 ounce loaf Italian bread, cut into 1 inch slices
1/3 cup butter or margarine, melted
1/2 cup pecan pieces

With a wire whisk beat together eggs, orange juice, milk, sugar, nutmeg, and vanilla. Place the bread in a single layer in a casserole that just fits the slices. Pour the milk mixture over the bread. Cover and refrigerate overnight, turning once. Pour the melted butter on a jelly roll pan, spreading evenly. Arrange the soaked bread slices on the pan in a single layer. Sprinkle with the pecans. Bake at 400° until golden, 20-25 minutes. Serve with maple syrup and butter, if desired. Serves 4.

Indian Creek Bed and Breakfast

Shirley and Herman Hockstetler
20300 C.R. 18
Goshen, IN 46526
(219) 875-6606 or (219) 875-3968

Our newly built country Victorian home in the middle of Amish country is decorated with family antiques. Guests are invited to walk back to the woods or sit on the deck to watch for deer. They may also enjoy the great room, game room, and family room. Our full breakfast could include this easy favorite.

Scarlett's Country Inn

Scarlett Dwyer
3918 Silverado Trail
Calistoga, CA 94515
(707) 942-6669 (voice and FAX)

We serve this warm French toast on a platter sprinkled with powdered sugar. In addition we always serve a fresh fruit platter, fresh squeezed orange juice, and a choice of coffee, teas, or hot chocolate. Breakfasts are served on the deck by the pool, under the big apple tree in the summer, or in the main dining room in the winter. Our guests may always have this breakfast served in their rooms at whatever time they desire. Although the menu changes daily, this is the favorite of all.

Scarlett's Buttermilk French Toast

2 loaves fresh, sweet French bread
12 eggs
2 cups buttermilk
3 tablespoons vanilla
dash of salt, if desired
cinnamon
powdered sugar

Slice French bread into 18 pieces, each about 3/4 inch thick. Beat eggs, buttermilk and vanilla with a fork in a mixing bowl. Add salt, if desired. Grease hot griddle or frying pan with butter. Dip pieces of bread in mixture and place on griddle. Spoon more mixture on top of bread and sprinkle cinnamon on each piece. Pierce bread with a fork to help egg mixture saturate bread. Fry over medium high heat until brown on the bottom and turn over to brown the other side. Place immediately on plates or platter and sprinkle generously with powdered sugar. Garnish with strawberries. Serves 5-6 persons.

Carmelized French Toast

1 stick butter or margarine
1 cup brown sugar
1/4 cup pure maple syrup
16 slices bakery raisin bread or kuchen bread
4 ounces Neufchatel or cream cheese
6 large eggs
1 2/3 cups milk, skim is fine
1 teaspoon pure vanilla
cinnamon

In an 11x17 pan or dish, combine brown sugar, butter and maple syrup. Cook until dissolved and bubbly, approximately 5 minutes. Do not let butter burn. Meanwhile, spread 8 slices of bread with cheese and sprinkle with cinnamon. Place remaining 8 slices on top to make sandwiches, and cut sandwiches in half diagonally to fit the pan (do not overlap.) Blend eggs, milk, and vanilla; pour over sandwiches. Cover and let set for at least 40 minutes or overnight in refrigerator. Uncover and bake at 350° for 30-40 minutes. Flip bread over when removing from pan. If a crustier top is preferred, place back in oven for a few minutes longer. Top with a spoonful of yogurt or sour cream and sprinkle with fresh berries. Serves 8.

Victorian Rose Garden Bed and Breakfast

Don and Sherry Brewer
314 Washington Street
Algonquin, IL 60102
(847) 854-9667; (888) 854-9667;
FAX (847) 854-3236

Presentation of food is so important! It's fun to "decorate" the plate with a variety of colors and textures. First we serve a fresh fruit plate with a palette of colors — possibly cantaloupe, kiwi, strawberries, watermelon, bananas, and blueberries, or raspberries, topped with a sprig of mint. Next comes the main dish of Carmelized French Toast, with a clump of grapes and strips of bacon or sausages placed in fan shape. We always get raves from our guests!

The Gragg House

Judy and Robert Gragg
Kalmia Acres
210 Ridge Point Drive
Boone, NC 28607
(704) 264-7289; FAX (704) 265-0031

As a Christian who has always strived to keep the Ten Commandments, the one I have kept least well is "Thou shalt not covet." Coveting recipes is my downfall. My recipe for the French toast is a combination of recipes I have gathered. I liked the feature of baking the toast, rather than frying, from one recipe. From another, I like the cinnamon sprinkled on the baking sheet. From yet another recipe, I liked that the "toast" was actually large croissants. And then, the homemade cinnamon syrup was from another recipe source. Being a person who enjoys a creative approach in all that I do, I always enjoy the challenge of improving on others' ideas. So, that is what I have done with my collection of coveted recipes in coming up with my version of French toast. This breakfast is always overwhelmingly met with childlike enthusiasm . . . and a grown-up appetite.

Oven-Baked French Toast

and Cinnamon Syrup

3 eggs
1/2 cup orange juice
1/8 teaspoon salt
6 large croissants

Grease air-cushioned baking sheet with cooking spray then sprinkle cookie sheet very liberally with cinnamon. Combine beaten eggs, orange juice and salt. Split croissants and soak each piece in egg mixture. Drain and then put on cookie sheet. Bake at 325° for ten minutes. While baking cover with another cookie sheet to prevent overbrowning. Serve with your choice of syrups or with:

Cinnamon Syrup

1 cup granulated sugar
1/2 cup honey
1/4 cup water
1/2 teaspoon ground cinnamon
1/2 cup whipping cream, at room temp.

In a small saucepan, stir together sugar, honey, water and cinnamon. Stirring constantly, bring to a boil over moderate heat: boil for two minutes. Remove from heat, stir in cream and cool for at least 30 minutes. Syrup will thicken as it cools. Yield: 1 1/2 cups. Can be refrigerated for several months. Serve warm or at room temperature. I reheat mine in the microwave.

Oven-Baked French Toast

10 slices good French bread
6 large eggs
1 1/2 cup milk
1 1/2 half and half
1 teaspoon vanilla
1/8 teaspoon nutmeg
1/2 teaspoon cinnamon

Topping:
1/2 cup softened butter
1 cup packed brown sugar
2 tablespoon dark corn syrup (or maple syrup)
1 cup pecans, chopped

Butter 9 inch square baking dish. Fill with bread slices, mix eggs, milk, half and half, vanilla, nutmeg, and cinnamon. Pour over bread, cover and refrigerate overnight. In the morning, heat oven to 350°. Make topping: mix butter, brown sugar and syrup. Stir in pecans. Spread over bread. Bake until puffed and golden (about 50 minutes.) Serves 4 6.

States Inn

Garreth Jeffers
2039 West Valley Road
Friday Harbor, WA 98250
(360) 378-6240; FAX (360) 378-6241

The Oven-Baked French Toast recipe is a variation of a recipe used by a friend of mine at her Bed and Breakfast here on San Juan Island. After she passed away, I took over the running of her B&B for her estate. I always felt I was serving the French toast in her memory, and following in her footsteps.

Guests love the French toast, and I have given out many recipes, as I firmly believe in sharing.

Green Gables Bed and Breakfast

Bill and Marsha Wilkinson
504 Fancy Street
Covington, IN 47932
(317) 793-7164

The spicy aroma that permeates the house as this toast bakes literally draws guests to the dining room. This dish reminds guests of old-fashioned bread pudding and is a unique breakfast treat. Served with coffee or tea, fruit juice and a fresh fruit plate, and with homemade breads and cinnamon rolls, we promise that no guest will leave our table hungry.

Oven French Toast

1 load French bread, cut in 1 inch slices
2 cups milk
2 teaspoons vanilla
1/2 teaspoons cinnamon
8 eggs
2 cups half and half
1/2 teaspoon nutmeg
3/4 cup butter, softened
3 tablespoons corn syrup
1 1/3 cups brown sugar
1 cup pecans, chopped

Heavily butter 13x9x2 inch pan. Fill pan with bread slices. Blend eggs, milk, half and half, vanilla, nutmeg and cinnamon. Pour mixture over bread slices. Refrigerate covered overnight. Make topping by combining last four ingredients, set aside until ready to bake, then spread over toast. Bake at 350° for 50 minutes until puffed and golden brown. Serves 8-10.

Baked French Toast

1 egg
2 tablespoons salad oil
1/3 cup milk
pinch salt
1/2 teaspoon vanilla
4 slices bread

Orange Sauce

1 tablespoon cornstarch
1/2 cup sugar
pinch salt
1 cup orange juice
1/2 teaspoon nutmeg
1 tablespoon butter

Preheat oven to 450°. Combine all toast ingredients, except bread. Dip bread into mixture, coat well. Place on greased cookie sheet on top rack of oven. Turn and bake until brown. Make sauce: mix together cornstarch, sugar, and salt in saucepan. Stir in juice. Cook over medium heat until it boils. Stirring constantly.

The Shaw House

Mary and Joe Shaw
613 Cypress Court
Georgetown, SC 29440
(803) 546-9663

Everyone seems to enjoy this. I use a heart shaped-cutter on the bread and the hot orange syrup is poured out of an attractive container. Sausage and fresh fruit are very good with this. I usually serve a sprinkling of fresh herbs on top.

Asking God's blessings on food and conversation helps!

Scrubby Oaks Bed and Breakfast Inn

Mary Ann Craig
PO Box 1047
Durango, CO 81302
(90) 247-2176

Located on ten acres over looking the Animas River Valley, our sprawling ranch style inn has a quiet country feel with the convenience of being three miles from downtown Durango. Snacks are offered afternoons and a full country breakfast is served each morning. This recipe was a favorite with my six children when they were growning up, so now I serve it for my guests.

French Toast Strata

1 pound French bread, unsliced
8 ounces cream cheese, cubed
8 eggs
2 1/2 cups milk
6 tablespoons margarine, melted
1/4 cup maple syrup

Cut French bread into cubes (about 12 cups). Grease 3 quart rectangular baking dish. Place half bread cubes in dish. Top with cream cheese cubes and cover with remaining bread cubes. Combine eggs, milk, melted margarine, and maple syrup; beat together well. Pour egg mixture over bread and cheese cubes. Lightly press layers down to moisten, using a spatula. Cover with plastic wrap and refrigerate overnight. In morning, remove plastic wrap and bake, uncovered in a 325° oven for 35-40 minutes, or until slightly golden. Let stand 10 minutes before serving.

Serve in squares with bacon and sausage. I offer warm maple syrup and warm raspberry sauce as choices to pour over squares. Freezes well.

Buttermilk Pancakes

- 2/3 cup white flour
- 2/3 cup whole wheat flour
- 1 tablespoon baking powder
- 1/2 teaspoon soda
- 1/4 cup honey
- 2 cups buttermilk
- 2 eggs

Combine all the ingredients into a large bowl and mix for several minutes, until the mixture is smooth. Let it sit for about 30 minutes before putting onto the grill. Onto the grill add 1 tablespoon olive oil, to prevent sticking of the dough. Drop about 3 tablespoons of batter onto the hot surface. When bubbles appear on the surface, turn the pancake over to brown the other side. Serve immediately with pure maple syrup. Makes approximately 16 pancakes. These pancakes are very light and should be made small, otherwise they will fall apart.

The Victorian Veranda Bed and Breakfast

Nadine White
515 Cheyenne Avenue
Eaton, CO 80615
(970) 454-3890

We want to share with guests our beautiful two-story Queen Anne home with a wraparound porch. It also has a view of the Rocky Mountains which are 45 minutes away. Our guests enjoy the spacious and comfortable rooms, balcony, fireplaces, bicycles-built-for-two, baby grand, player piano, and one room that has a private whirlpool bath.

Sugar Fork Bed and Breakfast

Mary and Sam Price
743 Garrett Road
Dandridge, TN 37725
(423) 397-7327; (800) 487-5634

Guests appreciate the tranquil setting of Sugar Fork, a short distance from the Great Smoky Mountains. Situated on Douglas Lake, the B&B has private access and floating dock. Our guests enjoy warm-weather water sports and fishing year-round. Fireplace in common room, guest kitchenette, wrap-around deck, swings, and park bench by the lake. A hearty breakfast is served family-style in the dining room or, weather permitting, on the deck.

Apple Pancakes

2 1/4 cup self-rising flour
2 tablespoons sugar
1/2 teaspoon cinnamon
2 well-beaten egg yolks
2 cups milk
2 tablespoons margarine, melted
1 cup finely chopped apple
2 stiff beaten egg whites

Stir together flour, sugar, and cinnamon. Combine milk and egg yolks, then stir into flour mixture until just moistened. Add margarine and apples. Fold in whites. Let batter stand a few moments then bake on a lightly greased hot griddle using 1/3 cup batter. Serve with sauce.

Sauce:
2 tablespoons cornstarch
2 tablespoons brown sugar
dash salt
dash cloves
1 1/2 cups apple juice or cider
1/4 teaspoon cinnamon

Combine dry ingredients in saucepan. Gradually stir in juice or cider and cook until thickened and bubbly.

German Apple Pancake

Pancake:
- 3 large eggs
- 3/4 cup milk
- 3/4 cup flour
- 1/2 teaspoon salt

Filling:
- 1 pound tart apples
- 1/4 cup melted butter
- 1/4 cup sugar
- powdered cinnamon and nutmeg

Topping:
- 2 tablespoons melted butter
- powdered sugar

Preheat oven to 450°. Beat eggs, milk, flour, and salt, until smooth. In a heavy 12 inch skillet, melt 1 1/2 tablespoons butter; pour batter into skillet. Bake 15 minutes, lower temperature to 350°, bake 10 minutes more. Saute apples in 1/4 cup butter and 1/4 cup sugar, season to taste with cinnamon and nutmeg. Place pancake on serving dish, add apples to 1/2 of pancake; fold over. Top pancake with melted butter and powdered sugar. Serves 2-3.

The Apple Bin Inn Bed and Breakfast

Barry and Debbie Hershey
2835 Willow Street Pike
Willow Street, PA 17584
(717) 464-5881; (800) 338-4296;
FAX (717) 464-1818

What better way to enjoy the apples that surround you at The Apple Bin Inn than to eat them. We enjoy several small apple trees in our own back yard but can't keep up with the demand at the local orchard, just a few miles away.

This recipe came from a high school friend. While visiting her on vacation years ago, Mary prepared this dish as our evening meal. We really enjoyed it and of course it had to be included in our many morning meals.

Ann Starrett Mansion

Bob and Edel Sokol
744 Clay Street
Port Townsend, WA 98368
(360) 385-3205; (800) 321-0644;
FAX (360) 385-2976

Just as the Taj Mahal was built as a tribute to love, so was this mansion. The most photographed Victorian in the Northwest was awarded "The Great American Home Award" by the National Trust. A 60-foot octagonal tower with a free floating staircase leads to a celestial calendar and frescoed maidens dancing in the clouds depicting Ann. "The Crown Jewel of the Pacific Northwest." Step back in time to serenity and beauty.

German Pancakes with Apples

(Pfannkuchen)

German pancake recipes vary, but basically this is a large pancake puffed in a hot skillet in the oven. It is sometimes sprinkled with powdered sugar, topped with jam, fresh compote, or plum butter. It is delicious hot or can also be eaten cold.

3 eggs
3/4 cup all-purpose flour
1/2 teaspoon salt (optional)
1/8 teaspoon nutmeg (optional), may use zest of the lemon
1 cup milk
7 tablespoons butter
2 apples
2 tablespoons sugar
1 lemon sliced (optional)
1/2 cup powdered sugar

Preheat oven to 425°. Make a batter of the eggs, flour, salt, nutmeg, and milk. Whip them with a whisk or in a blender until smooth. Peel and core apples, thinly slice them and saute them in 4 tablespoons of butter. They should still be firm when you add them to the batter. Heat 3 tablespoons of butter in a large skillet. Don't burn it. Pour batter into the skillet and put skillet on the top rack of the oven. Bake until the edges are browned and crisp, about 20 minutes. Sprinkle with powdered sugar and decorate with slices of lemon. Serves 2-4.

German Apple Pancakes

3/4 cup all-purpose flour
3 tablespoons sugar
1/4 teaspoon salt
3 eggs
3/4 cup light cream
2 tablespoons melted butter
1 or 2 cooking apples
2 tablespoons brown sugar
1/2 teaspoon cinnamon
2 tablespoons melted butter

Heat ovenproof skillet, spray with PAM cooking spray. Combine sugar, salt, eggs, cream, and butter and mix well. Pour into hot skillet, and without removing skillet from heat, lay the apples (quartered and thinly sliced) over top, completely covering surface. Mix the brown sugar and cinnamon and sprinkle on top of apple slices. Drizzle 2 tablespoons melted butter over the brown sugar mixture. Bake at 400° until done (it puffs).

Bring the pancake to the table. It puffs up and looks wonderful. Let it cool a little, and cut into 4 to 6 wedges. Serve with bacon and maple syrup (it's just as good without the syrup).

Olde Stonehouse Bed and Breakfast Inn

Peggy Johnson
511 Main Street
Hardy, AR 72542
(501) 856-2983; (800) 514-2983;
FAX (501) 856-4036

Native stone house in historic district, one block from the Spring River, and Old Hardy Town's quaint antique and craft shops. Antiques, queen beds, private baths, central heat/air, ceiling fans, usual stone fireplace with "Arkansas Diamonds," player piano. Full breakfast served family style. Separate 1904 cottage with opulant Victorian-inspired suites.

Primrose Cottage

Inge Curtis
706 Richmond Road
Williamsburg, VA 23185
(804) 229-6421; (800) 522-1901;
FAX (804) 259-0717

Primrose Cottage is a nature-lover's delight. In the spring, the front walkway is lined with primroses. In cooler months, the front yard is abloom with banks of pansies. There are two bedrooms upstairs, each with a large, walk-in closet and private bathroom. Desks, chairs, and reading lamps add to the comfort of home. In the morning, the aroma of home cooking usually rouses even the sleepiest traveler.

Oven-Baked Apple Pancake

1/2 cup milk
1/2 cup all-purpose flour
1/2 teaspoon baking soda
3 eggs
1 teaspoon sugar
dash salt
3 tablespoons butter
1/4 cup sugar
1 teaspoon cinnamon
2 large apples, peeled, cored and sliced
1/3 cup golden raisins
1/3 cup chopped pecans
1/2 cup whipping cream

Mix milk, flour, baking soda, eggs, 1 teaspoon sugar, and salt together until smooth. Melt butter in 9 inch skillet with ovenproof handle. Saute apples lightly in butter, mix in 1/8 cup sugar and cup cinnamon mixture, raisins and pecans. Pour batter over apples. Bake in 400° oven for 10 minutes. Remove from oven, top with rest of sugar and cinnamon mixture and dot with butter. Return to oven for 15 minutes. Serve immediately topped with whipped cream. Serves 4.

Instead of apples, raisins and pecans, use 2 pears peeled, cored and sliced plus 1 cup of frozen or fresh cranberries and add 2 tablespoons of Grand Marnier before you finish sauteing.

Apple Puff Pancake

2 tablespoons butter
4 tablespoon sugar
3/4 teaspoon cinnamon
1 large apple, peeled, cored, and sliced
4 eggs
2/3 cup milk
1/3 cup flour

Melt butter in 9 or 10 inch microwave pie pan. Combine 3 tablespoons sugar and cinnamon and sprinkle over melted butter. Arrange apple slices over this mixture. Cook in microwave oven on high for 2 minutes. Cool slightly. Beat eggs, milk, flour, and remaining 1 tablespoon sugar, plus a dash of salt, until smooth. Pour over apple mixture and bake at 400° for 15-10 minutes until puffy and nicely browned. Serves 4.

Blue Spruce Inn

Pat and Tom O'Brien
2815 Main Street
Soquel, CA 95073
(408) 464-1137; (800) 559-1137;
FAX (408) 475-0608

Each time Laurie "inn sat" for us she would leave the menus she had prepared for breakfast and I kept seeing this "Apple Puff Pancake" on her list. Finally I asked her about this recipe and she shared it with me. I use it often and it is always well received. In her other life, Laurie is an outstanding seventh-grade language arts teacher. She makes me proud to have shared her profession. "Thanks, Laurie, for your dedication and devotion to those wonderful children who are richer for having been in your class."

The Graham Bed and Breakfast Inn

Roger and Carol Redenbaugh
150 Canyon Circle Drive
Sedona, AZ 86351
(520) 284-1425; (800) 228-1425;
FAX (520) 284-0767

The Graham Inn is an impressive contemporary Southwest inn with huge windows allowing great views of Sedona's red rock formations. Each guest room has a private bath, balcony, and TV/VCR and some rooms have a Jacuzzi and fireplace. All rooms have many individual features which make each unique and delightful. Pool and spa invite guests outdoors.

Red Rock Puffed Apple Pancakes

6 large Granny Smith apples, peeled and cored
1/2 cup butter, plus 3 tablespoons, butter
3 tablespoons cinnamon
1/2 cup sugar
1 1/2 cups flour
1 1/2 cups milk
9 eggs

Saute apples in 1/2 cup butter until tender. Mix cinnamon and sugar and pour 3/4 mixture onto apples, stir. Mix flour, milk, and eggs with mixer until smooth. Place sauteed apples in ovenproof 9x11 inch pan. Pour egg mixture over top. Bake at 400° for 15 minutes. Pull from the oven, dot with 3 tablespoons butter and sprinkle remaining sugar/cinnamon mixture over the top. Return to the oven for about 10 minutes longer, until puffed. Serve immediately with your favorite syrup. Serves 8-10.

Banana-Poppyseed Pancakes

3 cups whole wheat flour
2 teaspoons baking powder
2 teaspoons baking soda
1 teaspoon salt
1/2 cup brown sugar
1/2 teaspoon nutmeg
4 eggs
2 cups milk
1 teaspoon vanilla
2 bananas
1/4 cup poppyseeds

Combine the dry ingredients, except for poppyseeds, and bananas (even the night before to save time.) Quarter the bananas lengthwise and then chop into pieces, add these and poppyseeds to dry ingredients. In blender, mix wet ingredients. Fold wet ingredients into dry ingredients to form batter. Note: batter consistancy will vary, wetter will spread more on griddle and thicker will stay more compact. Fry about 3 tablespoons of batter on a nonstick electric griddle, turning once.

Golden Dreams Bed and Breakfast

Ann Spence
6412 Easy Street
Whistler, British Columbia
CANADA V0N 1B6
(604) 932-2667; (800) 668-7055;
FAX (604) 932-7055
Email: golden@whistler.net

These hearty pancakes have been served to our skiers since we opened in 1987. I recently added in the poppyseeds for a new twist, and they are a great hit!

Be creative on the size and the extras that you have on hand (chocolate chips, toasted almonds, coconut, sunflower seeds, raisins, etc.) Serve sprinkled with powdered sugar and a generous slathering of flavored yogurt! Garnish with fresh of frozen strawberries and top with toasted almonds. Enjoy!

Inn at Blush Hill

Pamela Gosselin
RR#1, Box 1266
Waterbury, VT 05676
(802) 244-7529; (800)736-7522;
FAX (802) 244-7314
Email: innatbh@aol.com

This recipe was the Blue Ribbon Breakfast Winner from the American Bed and Breakfast Association's Recipe Contest. It is published in the Innkeeper's Finest Breakfast *by Jessica Bennett, which is a collection of the Blue Ribbon Breakfast Recipes from innkeepers around the country. We hope you will enjoy preparing it for your special breakfast, just as much as our guests enjoy it here at the inn!*

Our inn is located "back to back" to Ben & Jerry's ice cream factory, Vermont's top tourist attraction.

Four-Berry Pancakes

1 1/2 cups flour
2 tablespoons sugar
1 teaspoon salt
1 teaspoon baking powder
3 tablespoons oil
2 whole eggs
1/2 cup plain yogurt
3/4 cup milk
3 cups fresh berries in any combination desired (blueberries, raspberries, strawberries, blackberries)

Mix all the dry ingredients in a bowl. In a separate bowl, mix the wet ingredients, except for fruit. Combine wet and dry ingredients to make the pancake batter. Reserve 2 cups of the berries and add the remaining 1 cup to the batter. Mix gently, being careful not to break up the fruit. Pour 1/4 cup batter per pancake onto a hot, oiled griddle. Turn the pancakes when the edges are dry and bubbles appear. Arrange 3 pancakes on a plate, for each person. Top with a scoop of Ben & Jerry's Vanilla Ice Cream, 1/2 cup of reserved berries, and warmed Vermont maple syrup. Add a sprig of fresh mint to garnish. Recipe may be doubled.

People-Pleasin' Peach Puff Pancake
with Cherry-Almond Sauce

6 eggs
1 1/2 cups milk
1 cup all-purpose flour (not self-rising)
4 tablespoons sugar
1 teaspoon vanilla
1/2 teaspoon salt
1 teaspoon cinnamon
2/3 stick butter or margarine
12 canned peach halves (approx.) sliced thin

Preheat oven to 425°. Slice butter into baking dish, add peach slices and place in oven until butter is melted and bubbly. Meanwhile, mix eggs, milk, flour, sugar, vanilla, salt, and cinnamon until blended. Pour batter over peaches. Sprinkle with brown sugar. Bake approximately 25 minutes until brown and puffy. Serve immediately with Cherry Almond Sauce on top.

Cherry-Almond Sauce

1 can cherry pie filling
1/2 stick butter or margarine
1/3 cup brown sugar
1/4 cup light corn syrup
1/2 teaspoon almond extract

Cook all ingredients, except almond extract, in saucepan until blended and bubbly. Remove from heat, add almond extract. Mix well and pour over Peach Puff Pancake. (Optional: garnish with slivered almonds.)

Hilton's Bluff Bed and Breakfast Inn

Jack and Norma Hilton
2654 Valley Heights Drive
Pigeon Forge, TN 37863
(423) 428-9765

Tastefully decorated in a romantic mingling of the old and new, our inn boasts truly elegant country living. Private balconies, covered decks with rockers and checkerboard tables. Den with mountain-stone fireplace; game room/conference room. We prepare a full southern gourmet breakfast each morning.

Berry Hill Gardens Bed and Breakfast

Jean Fowler and Cecilio Rios
RD1, Box 128, Ward-Loomis Rd.
Bainbridge, NY 13733
(607) 967-8745 (voice and FAX);
(800) 497-8745

Our restored 1820s farm house on a hilltop is surrounded by extensive herb and perennial gardens and 180 acres where guests are welcomed to hike, swim, birdwatch, skate, cross-country ski, or sit on the wraparound porch and watch nature parade. Our rooms are furnished with comfortable antiques.

We serve a full breakfast to our B&B guests. These pancakes are very light and a hit with everyone.

Yogurt-Orange Pancakes

1 tablespoon grated orange rind
2 teaspoons sugar
1/3 cup orange juice
3/4 cup plain yogurt
1 large egg
2 tablespoons unsalted butter, melted and cooled
1 cup all-purpose flour
1 teaspoon baking soda
1/2 teaspoon baking powder
1/4 teaspoon salt

Combine the orange rind, orange juice, yogurt, egg, sugar, and melted butter. Beat until well combined. In another bowl, sift together flour, baking soda, baking powder, and salt. Add to yogurt mixture, and stir until well combined. Batter will be thick.

Topping: Slice a cup of fresh strawberries or peaches and combine with 2 teaspons of sugar. Let stand 30 minutes.

Heat heavy griddle over moderately high heat and brush it with melted unsalted butter. Spoon batter onto the griddle and spread to form 3 inch round pancakes. Cook for 1-2 minutes, until tops are bubbly. Turn the pancakes and cook for 1 minute longer, or until golden brown. Transfer to platter, brush with melted unsalted butter, cover and keep warm in oven (200°).

Arrange pancakes in clusters on the platter, garnish each with a dollop of yogurt and top with the fruit. Sprinkle the fruit with orange zest. Serves 4.

Corn Pancakes

1 cup cornmeal
1/2 cup flour
1/4 cup sugar
1 teaspoon salt
4 teaspoons baking powder
1 egg
1 1/2 cups milk
1/4 cup soft shortening

Mix flour, sugar, salt, baking powder, and cornmeal. Add egg, milk, and shortening. Spoon batter onto a hot, greased griddle and cook until bubbles appear, then flip. Serves 4.

Ponda-Rowland Bed and Breakfast Inn

Jeanette and Cliff Rowland
RR 1, Box 349
Dallas, PA 18612-9604
(717) 639-3245; (800) 854-3286;
FAX (717) 639-5531

We are a farm. Pancakes are expected! Children (and parents) love the "free hand" animal shapes that cakes can be served in. They compliment the animals they can visit and add to their learning process (children and adults)!

Carriage Corner Bed and Breakfast

Mr. and Mrs. Gordon Shuit
3705 E. Newport Rd., PO Box 371
Intercourse, PA 17534-0371
(717) 768-3059

Our Saturday favorite actually came to us by way of one of our regulars, Irene Dietlin from New England. One of the sheer delights of an innkeeper is a familiar voice on the other end of the phone asking if there's room in the inn for a particular period. With Irene, and some others, a call results in a caravan of women, each interested in quilting, Pennsylvannia Dutch foods, and the beauty of this tranquil village. Irene and other returnees have often established connections with Amish women and their families, whom they've come to love, so that such a visit means renewed "fellowship" (the Old English meaning of the word Intercourse*). Whether that fellowship and communication occurs around oatmeal pancakes at breakfast, or out in the Amish-Mennonite community, it makes a venture to Lancaster County all the richer for those who visit the area.*

Oatmeal Pancakes

Dry ingredients:
- 4 cups rolled oats
- 1 cup flour
- 1/4 cup sugar
- 2 teaspoons baking powder
- 2 teaspoons baking soda
- pinch salt

Wet ingredients:
- 4 cups (1 quart) buttermilk
- 4 eggs
- 1/2 cup melted butter
- 2 teaspoons vanilla

Combine all dry ingredients in a large bowl. Combine wet ingredients in a bowl. Add liquid all at once to dry ingredients. Stir with fork to blend (do not overbeat). Let stand 45 minutes. Batter will thicken. If too thick, add a little more milk. Cook on hot griddle. Serves 8-12.

We often serve our pancakes with a peach ginger sauce. Grated, fresh ginger is cooked in butter for several minutes, sliced peaches added. After testing I sometimes thicken with cornstarch, add a touch of Vermont maple syrup. The pancakes are accompanied with fresh made sausage links from a farm across from us.

Raised Pecan Flapjacks

1 package dry yeast
1/4 cup warm water
1 egg
1 cup milk
2 cups Bisquick
1/2 cup pecan pieces

Dissolve yeast in warm water, add egg, milk, and Bisquick. Beat with mixer until smooth; cover, let stand at room temperature for 1 hour, or refrigerate overnight. Just before baking, stir in pecans. Bake on hot griddle. Serve with hot maple syrup. Serves 2.

The Redbud Inn

John and Donna Morris
815 N. Locust Street
Denton, TX 76201
(817) 565-6414; (888) 565-6414;
FAX (817) 565-6515

The Redbud Inn has grown into a B&B cluster group which includes The Magnolia Inn and Ginseppe's Italian Restaurant. All are side by side. We have two large, luxury suites which include dinner on the balcony from Ginseppe's. We recently added a hot tub. Inn available for weddings and family reunions.

Mountain Home Bed and Breakfast

PO Box 234
10 Courtland Boulevard
Mountain Home, NC 28758
(704) 697-9090; (800) 397-0066

We serve our Ginger Pancakes with strips of thick sliced bacon, a scoop of soft butter and flavored margarine on top, and a small container of syrup on the side of each plate. Pancakes can be made a little ahead and put in oven between sheets of paper towels to keep warm. Plates put in oven on warm keep pancakes hot up to the end of breakfast — but warn guests the plates are hot! These smell great cooking.

Ginger Pancakes
with Maple-Pecan Sauce

3 1/3 cups all-purpose flour
2 1/4 teaspoons baking powder
2 1/4 teaspoons baking soda
3/4 teaspoon salt
1 1/2 teaspoon cinnamon
3/4 teaspoon ground cloves
1 1/4 teaspoons ground ginger
1 cup water
1 1/4 cups buttermilk
2 eggs, lightly beaten
1/4 cup plus 2 tablespoons butter, melted
1/3 cup brown sugar, packed

Maple-Pecan Sauce

2 cups maple syrup
1/2 cup honey
3/4 cup chopped pecans
1/2 teaspoon cinnamon

Sauce: mix ingredients in medium saucepan. Heat until boiling. Keep warm over low heat.

Pancakes: mix first seven ingredients well in large bowl. Combine eggs, water, buttermilk, butter, and brown sugar. Add to dry ingredients. Mix well. For each pancake, pour about 1/3 cup on greased (with butter) griddle. Cook until done. Serve with Maple-Pecan Sauce. Batter keeps in refrigerator 3-4 days if covered.

Pumpkin Pancakes

2 cups flour
2 tablespoons brown sugar
1 tablespoon baking powder
1 teaspoon salt
1 teaspoon ground cinnamon
1/4 teaspoon nutmeg
1/4 teaspoon ground ginger
1 1/2 cup milk
1/2 cup cooked pumpkin
1 large egg
2 tablespoons vegetable oil

In large bowl, combine dry ingredients. In small bowl, combine milk, pumpkin, egg and oil. Stir liquid mixture into flour mixture, until dry ingredients are moistened. Batter will be thick. For each pancake, pour 1/4 cup batter onto hot griddle; using a spatula, spread the batter into a 4 inch circle before mixture sets. Cook until surface appears dry. Turn; cook another two to three minutes.

Breezy Acres Farm Bed and Breakfast

Joyce and David Barber
R.D. #1, Box 191
Hobart, NY 13788
(607) 538-9338

Breezy Acres is a crop farm in addition to being a bed and breakfast. Two of the products we make are maple syrup and pumpkins. In the spring, guests may watch while sugar is being evaporated to make syrup; come back in the fall to pick out their own pumpkin, and can enjoy pumpkin pancakes with our delicious maple syrup, year-round! The fields of pumpkins are a glorious sight when combined with the colors of the leaves in the fall.

Pinehurst Inn Bed and Breakfast

Roger and Phyllis Ingold
50 Northeast Drive
Hershey, PA 17033
(717) 533-3603; (800) 743-9140;
FAX (717) 534-2639

I serve these with pure maple and tiny sausage. Because I get so many requests for the recipe, I made (hastily one morning) papers to hand out. I use 2 cups of pancake mix that you add water to rather than Bisquick mix, oil, eggs, and evaporated milk. It's quicker and just as good.

Good-Morning Pumpkin Pancakes

2 cups biscuit mix
2 tablespoons pack light brown sugar
2 teaspoons ground cinnamon
1 1/2 cups (12 ounce can) undiluted Carnation Evaporated Milk
1 teaspoon ground allspice
1/2 cup Libby's Solid Pack Pumpkin
2 tablespoons vegetable oil
2 eggs
1 teaspoon vanilla extract

In large mixer bowl, combine biscuit mix, sugar, cinnamon, and allspice. Add evaporated milk, pumpkin, oil, eggs, and vanilla; beat until smooth. Pour 1/4 to 1/2 cup batter (depending on size of pancake desired) onto heated and lightly greased griddle. Cook until top surface is bubbly and edges are dry. Turn, cook until golden. Keep pancakes warm. Serve with syrup or honey. Makes about 16 pancakes.

Pumpkin Pancakes
with Apple Cider Syrup

1 1/2 cups flour
1 teaspoon baking powder
1 1/2 teaspoon pumpkin pie spice
1/4 teaspoon baking soda
1/4 teaspoon salt
1 egg
1/4 cup canned pumpkin
1 1/2 cups milk
3 tablespoons cooking oil

In medium bowl stir together first 5 ingredients. In another bowl beat the next 4. Add flour mixture to the milk mixture and stir just until blended, but still lumpy. Pour about 1/4 cup of batter for each pancake onto a hot griddle or heavy skillet. Cook over medium heat until browned on both sides. Makes about 10 pancakes.

Apple Cider Syrup

1/2 cup sugar
1 cup apple cider or apple juice
1/2 teaspoon cinnamon
2 tablespoons butter or margarine
4 teaspoons cornstarch
1 tablespoon lemon juice

In a small saucepan stir together the sugar, cornstarch, and cinnamon. Then stir in the apple cider and lemon juice. Cook and stir the mixture over medium heat until mixture is thickened and bubbly. Then cook and stir for 2 minutes more. Remove saucepan from heat and stir in the butter or margarine until melted. Makes 1 1/3 cups.

The Dickey House Bed and Breakfast

William and Dorothy Buesgen
331 S. Clay Street
Marshfield, MO 65706
(417) 468-3000

The stately, three-story antebellum mansion situated on one acre of parklike grounds, is one of Missouri's finest bed and breakfast inns. Four antique-filled guest rooms with private baths, plus two spectacular suites with luxuriously appointed decor, double Jacuzzi, fireplace, and cable TV. The Inn and dining room are enhanced by a display of fine American and European art and antiques. A gourmet breakfast is served in true Victorian style, amid fine china, silver, and crystal.

Gone With the Wind Bed and Breakfast Inn

Linda and Robert Lewis
453 West Lake Road, Rt. 54A
Branchport, NY 14418
(607) 868-4603

The serving of these pancakes starts in the fall and continues throughout the wintertime (by popular request). I don't know if Aunt Pitty Pat ever made pancakes, but on a fall day on Aunt Pitty Pat's porch, these pumpkin pancakes are quite a tongue twister.

Aunt Pitty Pat's Pancake

(Pumpkin)

Mix in blender:

- 1 cup milk
- 1 tablespoon olive oil
- 1 large brown egg

Add:

- 1 tablespoon brown sugar
- 1/2 teaspoon cinnamon
- 1/8 teaspoon ginger
- 1/8 teaspoon nutmeg
- 1/4 cup pumpkin (cooked and pureed) or canned
- 1/2 teaspoon vanilla

Add above mixture to:

- 1 cup pancake mix (Aunt Jemima original)

Stir with whisk until well blended; and grill, using canola oil. Yield: 12 cakes.

Serve with sauted pecan-apple rings or pure New York State maple syrup. Definitely a new taste!

Whole Grain Pancakes

- 1/2 cup uncooked oatmeal
- 1/2 cup cornmeal
- 1/4 cup wheat bran
- 1 cup Bisquick
- 1 egg
- 2/3 cup milk
- 1 cup boiling water

Put oats, cornmeal, and wheat bran in medium bowl. Pour boiling water over and stir. Mixture should be thin. Add more water if necessary. Cover bowl and let stand for 15 minutes. Mix in egg and milk, using whisk. Add Bisquick and stir. If too thin, add more Bisquick. If too thick, add more milk. Fry on hot griddle which has been sprayed with cooking spray. Serves four. May add chopped apples, blueberries, or other fruit if desired.

We serve this with pure maple syrup, made at a local farm. We tell our guests these are "good for you" pancakes, because of all the fiber and low fat content.

The Inn at Ludington

Diane Shields and David Nemitz
701 E. Ludington Avenue
Ludington, MI 49431
(616) 845-7055; (800) 845-9170

Here at the Inn, I try to serve an abundant and varied menu each morning, and have developed several different kins of pancakes. Most of them are quite rich, and with the addition of butter and real, locally made maple syrup, while delicious, are not exactly "health food." Whole Grain Pancakes are a way to indulge in pancakes, while still feeling virtuous, because of the high fiber content. This is Diane's original recipe!

Our buffet breakfast is meant to please hearty eaters, picky eaters, and those with special dietary needs. Anyone who requests a special dish in advance, such as vegetarian or nondairy, will be accommodated. I try to incorporate these dishes into the regular menu, so everyone can try them.

I believe that the second "B" in bed and breakfast is every bit as important as the first "B."

Deacon Timothy Pratt Bed and Breakfast

Shelly Nobile
325 Main Street
Old Saybrook, CT 06425
(860) 395-1229

I serve these heart-shaped pancakes on guests' special occasions, such as birthdays (with a candle), anniversaries, weddings, or for couples on a romantic get-away. These are healthy, light and fluffy, low cholesterol but very tasty pancakes! Breakfast is served on fine china, crystal and silver. Fresh flowers and breakfast by candlelight adds to the mood and ambiance.

"Heart" Healthy Pancakes

1 1/2 cups flour
1/3 cup sugar
2 teaspoons baking powder
1/8 teaspoon salt
1 1/2 cups milk, skim
2 tablespoons corn oil
2 egg whites

Combine dry ingredients in large bowl. Add milk and corn oil, mix until just moistened. Beat egg whites in small bowl until stiff peaks form. Fold into batter. Place greased Teflon heart shaped molds on lightly greased griddle (medium high temperature.) Pour batter into molds. When bubbles begin to form, remove mold and flip pancakes. When done, trim pancakes with knife, if necessary, for perfect shapes. Serve with strawberry garnishes and warm maple syrup.

German Pancakes

6 large eggs
1 cup all-purpose flour
1 cup milk
1/4 cup melted butter
1 teaspoon salt
1/2 cup powdered sugar
6 lemon wedges

Beat eggs in mixer on high for 5 minutes. Alternately add the flour and milk. Add the salt, and melted butter. Continue to mix the ingredients for another minute or two. Spray 6 baking dishes with nonstick cooking spray. Ladle 4 ounces of batter into each baking dish. Bake in a 425° oven for 10-15 minutes, until brown. Sprinkle with powdered sugar.

Mansion on Main

Lee and Inez Hayden
802 Main Street
Texarkana, TX 75501
(903) 792-1835

This dish is conveniently served from the oven to the table. It is delicately delicious and makes a great presentation. When the pancakes are removed from the oven, sprinkle with powdered sugar and a squeeze of lemon juice. Serve with an all-fruit syrup style topping.

These pancakes receive rave reviews from our guests at "The Mansion." Team them with parfaits made from berries and yogurt.

Hexagon House

Ron and Lois Duncan Hart
419 Cincinnati Avenue
Lebanon, OH 45036-2123
(513) 932-9655

Built in the mid 1850s, Hexagon House is located 30 miles north of Cincinnati; easy to reach from interstates and convenient to local attractions. The house is listed on the National Register of Historic Places due to its unique six-sided exterior and its interesting interior floor plan. Rooms are spacious, comfortable, and tastefully decorated. The objective of the full-time hostess is to provide each guest with a pleasantly memorable experience.

German Pancake Puff

1 large, or 2 small apples, peeled, sliced thinly
3/4 cup flour
3 eggs
3/4 cup buttermilk
cinnamon sugar
1/4 teaspoon nutmeg
1/4 cup butter
powdered sugar

Mix apple slices with cinnamon sugar. Set aside. Mix flour, eggs, buttermilk and nutmeg together, leaving batter slightly lumpy. Melt butter in 9 inch pie plate; pour batter on top of it. Arrange apple slices on top of batter. Bake at 425° for 20 minutes, or until golden brown and puffy. Optional: sift powdered sugar on top, serve with extra cinnamon sugar or maple syrup. Variation: substitute canned or fresh peach slices for the apple.

Swedish Pancakes
with Huckleberry Sauce

Pancake:
- 2 eggs, beaten
- 1 cup milk
- 1 cup flour
- 1 teaspoon sugar
- 1/4 teaspoon salt
- 1/3 cup butter

Combine eggs, milk, flour, sugar and salt; beat until smooth. Add melted butter to batter. Use 1/4 cup batter on hot grill for each pancake. Flip and roll up pancake, serve with sauce and whipped cream. Makes 8 pancakes.

Huckleberry Sauce

- 1/2 cup sugar
- 1 1/2 tablespoon cornstarch
- 2 cups huckleberries
- 1/3 cup water
- 2 tablespoons lemon juice

Combine sugar and cornstarch in pan; stir in berries. Add water and lemon juice. Stir while cooking until thickened.

To serve, sprinkle whipped cream with dash of nutmeg or mace; add a fresh pansy or sprig of peppermint herb on the plate. Add a ham slice and fruit cup to this menu.

Paradise Gateway Bed and Breakfast and Log Guest Cabin

Pete and Carol Reed
PO Box 84
Emigrant, MT 59027
(406) 333-4063

We offer quiet, charming, comfortable guest rooms in the shadow of the majestic Rocky Mountains. Also a modern two-bedroom log cabin with 25 acres of Yellowstone River frontage, decorated in country charm and extremely private. As day breaks, guests enjoy a country, gourmet breakfast by the banks of the Yellowstone River, a noted blue ribbon trout stream. A "cowboy treat tray" is served in the afternoon. We are near the only entrance open to Yellow-stone year-round.

The Manor House Bed and Breakfast

Rick and Liz Latshaw
57 Maine Avenue
West Yarmouth, MA 02673
(508) 771-3433
(800) 9-MANOR-9

This is an easy breakfast recipe that looks great when it is served and is healthy too! I usually use strawberries, peaches, and blueberries as toppings but you can be creative, as just about any type of fruit will work. Sometimes I even put out a little homemade whipped cream with extra cinnamon added — guests love this!

Cinnamon Swedish Pancakes

- 1/4 cup butter
- 6 eggs
- 1 cup milk
- 1 cup all-purpose flour
- 1 teaspoon cinnamon
- 1/8 teaspoon salt

Preheat oven to 400°. Melt butter in a 9x13 inch baking pan until bubbly, but not brown. Mix the remaining ingredients together and pour into the pan. Bake for 20 minutes or until puffed up and brown on edges. Cut up into squares and serve with assorted fresh fruit and homemade whipped cream. Enjoy!

Puffed Oven-Baked Pancakes

2 tablespoons unsalted butter
1 egg
1/4 cup low-fat milk
1/4 cup all-purpose flour
1/4 teaspoon almond extract
1/2 teaspoon grated lemon peel

Preheat oven to 475° (Yes, 475°!) Place butter in a 6 inch cast iron pan and heat in oven until butter is melted. Beat egg in blender, or with whisk, until light yellow. Gradually add milk, then flour, beat until smooth. Stir in extract and lemon peel. Pour into the hot pan of butter and return to oven. Cook until puffed and golden, about 12 minutes. Remove from oven (it will "fall"), and fill with fresh fruit. Sprinkle with powdered sugar and serve at once. Top with your choice of fresh sliced fruit, warmed pie filling, and/or toasted almonds.

Addie's Attic Bed and Breakfast

Fred and Marilyn Huhn
117 S. Jackson Street
Houston, MN 55943
(507) 896-3010

Beautiful turn-of-the century home, circa 1903; cozy front parlor with curved glass window. Games, TV, and player piano available. Guest rooms decorated and furnished with "attic finds." Hearty, country breakfast served in dining room. Guests "Ooh, and aaah!" when I serve this dish! I serve it with ham.

The Ice Palace Inn

Giles and Kami Kolakowski
813 Spruce Street
Leadville, CO 80461
(719) 486-8272

This breakfast is not only elegant, but it is also healthy and hearty. After a warm full breakfast, our guests are ready for either taking in the sights or enjoying the beautiful Rocky Mountains.

Palace Puff Pancake

3 egg
3/4 cup flour
3/4 cups milk
1/2 teaspoon salt
3 tablespoons butter
2 tablespoons sugar
1/4 teaspoon cinnamon
1 apple, cored, and thinly sliced

Preheat oven to 400°. Place a 12 inch skillet in oven. Beat eggs, then add flour, milk, and salt; mix until smooth. Remove skillet from oven. Put butter in skillet and coat all sides. In a small bowl, mix sugar and cinnamon. Toss with apple slices then arrange slices in skillet. Pour batter over apples. Bake uncovered for 25 minutes, or until pancake is puffy and golden brown. Makes one large pancake, which serves four.

Best if served hot out of the oven, sprinkled with powdered sugar, and hot maple syrup.

Lavendar Hill Puffed Pancake

Pancake:
- 3 eggs
- 1/2 cup milk
- 1/2 cup flour
- 1/4 cup sugar
- 2 tablespoons oil
- dash salt (optional)
- 1/2 cube (4 tablespoons) butter
- sprinkle powder sugar

Blend first six ingredients in food processor or blender. Meanwhile, melt butter in 9 inch round or fluted dish in oven at 425°. When butter begins to sizzle, but not brown, pour blended ingredients into center of dish and bake 20 minutes.

Lavendar Hill Special Sauce

- 3 tablespoons red raspberry preserves
- 1 tablespoon Karo syrup
- 1 cup red raspberries, fresh or frozen
- 1 cup chopped black mission figs
- 1 tablespoon Amaretto

Mix raspberry preserves, Karo syrup, and Amaretto and put in microwave 45 seconds, making a raspberry framboise. Add raspberries and figs and microwave an additional 1-1 1/2 minutes, depending upon if frozen.

Lavendar Hill Bed and Breakfast Inn

Jean and Charlie Marinelli
683 S. Barretta
Sonora, CA 95370
(209) 532-9024
(800) 446-1333, ext. 290

Lavendar Hill Puff Pancake makes a wonderful presentation. First, out of the oven, sprinkled with powdered sugar it is shown to guests who are impressed to see the puffed pancake rising 2-3 inches above dish. Second, after topping with special sauce, it is as eye appealing as delicious. Most guests have not experienced this dish in any restaurant! While the special sauce was invented by Charlie, this dish is very versatile for you can make your own topping, of peaches, strawberries, etc. Each new fruit seems to taste better than the last!

Sand Dollar Bed and Breakfast

Bob and Nita Hempfling
606 N. Holladay Drive
Seaside, OR 97138
(503) 738-3491; (800) 738-3491

Our historic Craftsman bungalow includes two upstairs bedrooms with private baths and comfy beds, or some guests may prefer our cottage with its spectacular view and full kitchen. Only a short walk to the beach, shops, or restaurants. We are a retired minister and wife.

Since sand dollars are found on our beach and we give them to guests as souvenirs, these dollar-sized cakes are a very popular part of our breakfasts.

Sand Dollar Brancakes

2 cups 100% bran cereal
2 cups hot water
1/2 cup flour
1/3 cup sugar
1 1/2 teaspoons baking powder
1 teaspoon ground cinnamon
1/4 teaspoon ground allspice
2 large eggs
1 1/2 tablespoons salad oil
1 teaspoon vanilla
1/2 cup chopped walnuts

Add water to bran; let stand until absorbed and cool. Add eggs, oil and vanilla to bran. In another bowl mix flour, sugar, baking powder, cinnamon, allspice, and nuts. Add these dry ingredients to bran and egg mixture and stir until smooth. Heat griddle to 375° and rub lightly with oil. Use 1 heaping tablespoon butter for dollar-size cakes. Cook until browned on both sides, about 2 minutes per side. Serves 6. Makes 36 pancakes.

Serve with sliced strawberries, in season, or warm maple syrup. I also serve a fruit salad and sausage links.

McElhinney House Pancake

1/2 cup flour
1/2 cup milk
2 eggs
4 tablespoons butter
2 tablespoons confectioners' sugar
pinch nutmeg
juice of 1/2 lemon
jam

Preheat oven to 425°. Combine flour, milk, eggs, and nutmeg. Beat lightly. Leave batter lumpy. Melt butter in 12 inch skillet with heat proof handle. When very hot, pour in batter. Bake in oven 15-20 minutes until golden brown. Sprinkle with confectioners' sugar. Return briefly to oven. Sprinkle with lemon juice. Serve with jam. Serves 2.

This pancake looks beautiful when served on a tray with fresh raspberries, strawberries, kiwi or fruit in season. This is a McElhinney House specialty.

McElhinney House

Mary and Jim McElhinney
10533 Fairway Ridge Road
Charlotte, NC 28277
(704) 846-0783 (voice and FAX)

The McElhinney House Pancake has been tested and refined several times. Its lightness pleases our weight conscious guests. I serve it with fresh raspberries, kiwi, strawberries and melon or other fruit in season, and sometimes with freshly grown herbs. It is also delicious with homemade jam and a dash of fresh lemon juice. One of our guests commented that the pancake was "filled with homemade flavor."

The Wooden Duck

Bob and Barbara Hadden
140 Goodale Road
Newton, NJ 07860
(201) 300-0395; FAX (201) 300-0141

When The Wooden Duck Bed and Breakfast opened Feather Pancakes were one of the three standard breakfast offerings. The recipe was acquired from Barbara's brother Jack, who experimented and changed the ingredient proportions many times. In trying to get the pancakes even lighter, Jack kept adding more baking powder until your mouth "tingled" when you ate them — too much baking powder!

The joke at The Wooden Duck when guests compliment the Feather Pancakes is Bob's reply, "Barbara doesn't let me make the pancakes, mine are so light that I can't keep them on the griddle!"

These pancakes are served with maple syrup, homemade jams, and fresh peach or strawberry sauce. It is important to make the batter ahead of time, it needs to "rest" for about ten minutes before cooking.

Feather Pancakes

3/4 cups flour
1/3 teaspoon salt
1 tablespoon baking powder
1 1/3 tablespoons sugar
1 egg, beaten
3/4 cup milk
1 1/3 tablespoons salad oil

Mix flour, salt, baking powder, and sugar together. Blend together in blender or food processor egg, milk, and salad oil; add to flour mixture and beat until smooth. Allow batter to sit for ten minutes. Cook on griddle. Serves 4.

Colonial Jonnycakes

(from a circa 1750 recipe)

1 cup dark rum
1 cup whole milk (or half and half)
1 tablespoon dark molasses
1 tablespoon sugar
1 teaspoon salt
1 1/2 cups Jonnycake meal (this is rare white flint corn found only in parts of Rhode Island and Connecticut; one source is Carpenter's Grist Mill, Inc. 35 Narragansett Avenue, Wakefield, RI 02879. Note: this meal must be kept in the freezer, otherwise it will quickly spoil.)

Mix all ingredients. Cover and let stand overnight. In morning, stir up well. The batter needs to be about the consistency of runny mashed potatoes, so you may need to add a little more milk. Drop about a tablespoon of the batter at a time onto a greased griddle heated to 375°-400°. Cook a few minutes on each side until the cakes have reached a medium tan. Serve with butter and molasses on top. Serves 4-6 people.

Newport House Bed and Breakfast

Cathy Millar and John Fitzhugh Millar
710 South Henry Street
Williamsburg, VA 23185-4113
(757) 229-1775; FAX (757) 229-6408

Newport House was built to museum standards in 1988 from a 1756 design. The house is furnished totally in the period with English and American antiques and reproductions, most of which are available for sale (to guests only) upon request.

A full breakfast in the morning usually includes an interesting historical lecture by your host. Visitors to Colonial Williamsburg, by staying at Newport House, can thus immerse themselves in the colonial period more completely than anywhere else without sacrificing comfort.

The word Jonnycake (note no h in it) is short for Journey cake, as some people used to carry them in their pockets for a snack on the road, but we don't recommend that.

The "B and J" Bed and Breakfast

William and Jeananne Wintz
HCR52, Box 101-B
Hot Springs, SD 57747
(605) 745-4243

Nestled in the Southern Black Hills, this charming 1880 log cabin, decorated in antiques, provides guests with a unique pioneer setting. Guests enjoy the peaceful mountain scenery while listening to the Fall River that never freezes. Early mornings, deer and wild turkey may be seen. True western hospitality and a good home-cooked breakfast are always available in Jeananne's kitchen. Beautiful and delicious, this recipe is a treat to eat by our bubbling Fall River.

Mr. Morning's Famous Pancakes and Waffles

6 eggs, separated
1 quart buttermilk
1/3 cup liquid shortening or oil
1 teaspoon vanilla
3 cups flour, white or whole wheat
3 tablespoon sugar
1 teaspoon salt
2 teaspoons baking powder
2 teaspoons baking soda

Mix: egg yolks, buttermilk, oil, and vanilla. Set aside. Sift together: 3 cups flour, sugar, salt, baking powder, and baking soda. Mix into first mixture. Beat egg whites until stiff. Carefully fold into above batter. Batter makes excellent light waffles or pancakes. You may add blueberries, blackberries, or nuts.

Serve with real butter, and real maple syrup. Mound up whipped cream, with a cherry on top, with 2 fresh mint leaves on each side.

Gingerbread Waffles

1 cup flour
1 1/2 teaspoon baking powder
1 teaspoon pumpkin pie spice
3/4 teaspoon cinnamon
1/2 teaspoon baking soda
pinch salt
1/3 cup brown sugar, packed
1 egg, separated
3/4 cup buttermilk
1/4 cup molasses
3 tablespoons margarine, melted
milk

Combine flour and spices. In separate bowl, combine brown sugar, egg yolk, molasses, margarine, buttermilk, and enough milk for right consistency. Beat egg white in small bowl for one minute. Stir gently into batter. Bake in preheated waffle iron until golden and done. Set on rack in warm oven for crispier waffles. Top with Cool Whip before serving with syrup. Makes 2 large waffles.

Victoria Rose Bed and Breakfast

Linda and Foy Shahan
415 E. Cleveland
Guthrie, OK 73044
(405) 282-3928

Our breakfast is our signature. We serve a three-course Victorian decorated breakfast. These waffles receive great reviews! They are light, and mild flavored. These would be a second course. I usually serve a fruit cup, waffles, and then an egg and meat dish.

Lafayette House Bed and Breakfast

Bill Daffield, Nancy Buhr, Anna Millet, Cameron Samm
2156 Lafayette Avenue
St. Louis, MO 63104
(314) 772-4429; (800) 641-8965;
FAX (314) 664-2156

These waffles are great served with a warm fruit compote and whipped honey butter. We also like to serve a warm cinnamon vanilla syrup that the guests really love.

Our guests look forward to breakfast and never leave hungry which is great fuel for a day of sightseeing.

Malted Belgian Waffle

2 cups sifted flour
2 tablespoons sugar
1 1/2 tablespoons baking powder
1 teaspoon salt
2-3 tablespoons malt
2 eggs, separated
1 3/4 cup milk
6 tablespoons melted butter

Preheat waffle iron. Sift flour, sugar, baking powder, salt, and malt into bowl. Combine egg yolks, milk, and butter; mix until smooth. Add to dry ingredients; mix until smooth. Beat egg whites until soft peaks form and fold into batter. Pour into iron and bake until steaming stops and waffle is golden brown. Serves 8.

Not by Bread Alone

Yeast Breads
Sweet Breads
Muffins
Biscuits and Scones
Other Breads

"He maketh peace in thy borders, and filleth thee with the finest of the wheat."

Psalm 147:14

Norwood Bed and Breakfast

Roland and Pat Jensen
201 Norwood Court
Wetaskiwinn, Alberta
CANADA T9A 3P2
voice and FAX (403) 352-8850; (888) 352-7880

Country charm and old-fashioned hospitality are combined in Norwood Bed and Breakfast, a modern home decorated with antiques and memorabilia. Guests will enjoy extra special amenities that include Jacuzzi on outside deck and a baby grand piano, library, and CD system in the sitting room. A full breakfast is served in the formal dining room or on a sunny patio and includes homemade breads and jams.

Two-Hour Bread or Buns

Add altogether:

- 3 cups hot tap water
- 1/2 cup sugar
- 6 tablespoons light olive oil
- 1 teaspoon salt
- 2 eggs or 100 ml Egg Beaters
- 2 tablespoons Fast Rising Instant Fermipan yeast
- 2 cups whole wheat flour

Mix all of the above with a wooden spoon in a large mixing bowl. Add 7-8 cups of white flour to get it past the sticky stage. After you get past the stirring stage with the spoon, just use your hands and knead it.

Cover the lightly oiled bowl with a tea towel and let rise for 15 minutes. Punch down and do this same step two more times.

Divide the risen dough into four equal parts and make into loaves and place in lightly oiled loaf pans. Let rise until doubled (about 30 minutes). Bake at 350° for approximately 25 minutes.

This can also be made into buns or cinnamon buns. You can use only white flour (makes a lightweight bread or buns). This is a single recipe which makes four loaves or four dozen buns. I have doubled this recipe and also tripled it, which then makes 12 loaves. The produce freezes well and you can pop a loaf in the microwave for about 1 1/2 minutes for the fresh out of the freezer loaf. Tastes like it just came out of the oven.

Grandma's Homemade Bread

2 tablespoons dry yeast
1/2 cup + 1 tablespoon white sugar
5 cups water
4 tablespoons Crisco shortening
10 cups bread flour
1 teaspoon salt
1/2 cup butter (melted)

Dissolve yeast plus 1 tablespoon sugar in 1 cup warm water. Cover and set aside. In large saucepan melt Crisco, 1/2 cup sugar, and salt in 2 cups *hot* water. Add 2 cups cold water and 5 cups flour. Mix together. Add dissolved yeast mixture to warm dough and knead. Knead for twenty minutes, adding remaining five cups of flour gradually. Let rise in covered pan 1 1/2 hours; punch down and divide into bread pans. Let rise 2 hours in cold oven; bake at 325° for 30 minutes. Brush with melted butter and remove from pans to rack.

Texas Star Bed and Breakfast

David and Marie Stoltzfus
Mail: Route 1, Box 187-1
Edgewood, TX 75117
Physical: County Road VZ3103
Canton, TX
(903) 896-4277

This recipe has come down through the Stoltzfus family for generations and remains a favorite of our guests. We leave a complimentary small loaf in each room on arrival to reflect our country ranch setting and German background. Sliced thicker, this bread makes delicious French toast for breakfast as well. Excellent compliment for our homemade jams. Best served warm from microwave.

Olde English Tudor Inn B&B

Larry and Kathy Schuh
135 West Holly Ridge Road
Gatlinburg, TN 37738
(423) 436-7760; (800) 541-3798;
FAX (423) 430-7308

The Olde English Tudor Inn Bed and Breakfast is set on a hillside overlooking the beautiful mountain resort of Gatlinburg. It is ideally located within a few minutes walk to downtown and a few minutes drive to the Great Smoky Mountain National Park. The Inn has seven spacious guest rooms with their own modern bath and cable TV (HBO). Each guest is made to feel at home.

Grandma's White Bread

1 package active dry yeast
2 cups milk, scalded
2 teaspoons salt
6 1/4 to 6 1/2 cups sifted all-purpose flour
1/4 cup warm water
2 tablespoons sugar
1 tablespoon shortening

Preheat oven to 350°. Soften yeast in warm water. Combine hot milk, sugar, salt, and shortening. Cool to lukewarm. Stir in 2 cups flour, beat well. Add yeast and mix. Add enough flour to make a moderately stiff dough. Knead on a lightly floured surface until smooth, about 8 minutes. Shape in a ball and place in a bowl that has been rubbed with margarine, turn over to "grease" entire surface. Cover with towel and let rise until double in size, about one hour. Punch down.

Cut dough in half. Shape in two smooth balls, cover and let rest 10 minutes. Shape in loaves. You may freeze in an airtight bag until ready for use. If frozen, place in greased (margarine) loaf pan and cover. Let rise overnight. If not frozen, place dough in greased loaf pan and cover. Let rise until doubled in size, about 1 hour. Bake in 350° oven about 20 minutes or until done.

Focaccia

2 cups lukewarm water
1 tablespoon sugar
1 tablespoon dry yeast
1 1/2 tablespoons olive oil
1 tablespoon salt
4 cups flour, or more if needed

Topping:
1 tablespoon dried basil
1 tablespoon oregano
4 cloves garlic, minced
2 cans chopped tomatoes, well drained
1/2 cup Parmesan cheese

Mix water, sugar and yeast. Set aside for five minutes. Add oil, salt and flour. Knead on lightly floured surface until soft and silky, adding more flour, if needed. Place in greased mixing bowl and let stand in warm place until doubled in bulk (about 2 hours). Mix topping ingredients. After dough has risen, roll out into two equal-sized rounds about 1/2 inch thick. Place them on oiled baking sheet. Spread topping over the rounds, pressing lightly into dough. Let rise for about 20 minutes. Bake at 450° until bread is nicely browned (20-30 minutes). Serve hot. Yield: 8 servings.

Wuanita Hot Springs Ranch

The Pringle Family
8007 County Road 887
Gunnison, CO 81230
(970) 641-1266

I can't say that there's much unusual about this recipe, except that we enjoy serving it at our guest ranch on "Spaghetti and Shrimp w/Alfredo Sauce" Day.

Bay View Farm

Helen Sawyer
337 Main Highway
Route 132, Box 21
New Carlisle West, Quebec
CANADA G0C 1Z0
(418) 752-2725; (418) 752-6718

On the coastline of Quebec's picturesque Gaspe Peninsula, guests are welcomed into our comfortable home. Our country breakfast is complete with fresh farm, garden, and orchard produce.

Bay View Pretzels

1 tablespoon yeast
1 1/4 cup warm water
3 3/4 cups flour (no salt)
egg white
coarse salt
oil

Dissolve yeast in warm water. Let stand ten minutes. Mix in 3 3/4 cups flour. Knead 7-8 minutes, adding flour to make a smooth stiff dough. Place in oiled bowl. Cover with damp towel and let rise until doubled. Divide into 12 equal parts. Roll each part into a long, thin rope. Form into a pretzel. Place on oiled cookie sheet. Brush with egg white and sprinkle lightly with coarse salt. Let rise, covered, about 20 minutes, then bake 10-12 minutes at 475°. Cool on racks.

We make these rather thick so they turn out rather like rolls. Great at breakfast served with yogurt, cottage cheese, or fruit cup.

Stollen

- 1 cup (2 quarters) softened butter
- 1 cup sugar
- 4 eggs
- 1 teaspoon salt
- 8 cups flour
- 2 cakes yeast
- 1 pint lukewarm milk
- 1/2 lemon, grated
- 1/2 cup currants or raisins (washed or soaked)

Crumble yeast in a bowl which has been warmed; add lukewarm milk and 1 cup flour; let rise. Cream butter and add sugar and eggs one at a time, stirring well after each addition. Then add salt, lemon, and the remainder of the flour and the yeast mixture alternately. Fold in currants.

Mix well, adding only enough flour to knead, and knead until elastic. Set aside in warm place until double in bulk. Place on lightly floured board; knead and shape into loaves; place in pans and let rise until double in bulk. Bake 1 hour in 350° oven. Chopped pecans may be placed in the bottom of the pan before the dough is put in. The nuts add a special taste to the Stollen.

St. James Inn

Ann and J. R. Covert
723 St. James
Gonzales, TX 78629
(210) 672-7066

A former cattle baron's mansion, the Inn is a welcome respite from the busy life. Furnished with antiques, colorful collections, and warm hospitality. The rural area offers hiking, biking, antiquing, and roaming. Enjoy cold lemonade on the front porch or spiced tea in front of a fire.

Vintage Country Vacations

Doug and Donna Bernard
Box 537
Norquay, Saskatchewan
CANADA S0A 2V0
(306) 594-2629; FAX (306) 594-2629

This recipe has special significance because the four generations of family history we feature at Vintage Country Vacations are of Swedish ancestry. I love this recipe because it is so convenient to prepare the night before. My guests love the fresh aroma as it bakes in the morning and they also look beautiful. I usually serve them with fresh orange juice and a fresh fruit salad for a light, elegant, and delicious breakfast.

Swedish Cream Dough

(for coffee breads and miscellaneous buns and pastries)

This terrific refrigerator dough is the basis for a variety of sweet rolls, cakes, and danish pastries. You can make it up to four days in advance. It handles best when thoroughly chilled.

- 1 envelope of active, dry yeast
- 1/4 cup warm (115° F) water
- 1 cup heavy cream*
- 1/4 cup evaporated milk
- 3 egg yolks, slightly beaten
- 3 1/3 cups flour
- 1/4 cup sugar
- 1 teaspoon salt
- 1/2 cup butter or margarine at room temperature

* Instead of cream and milk 1 1/4 cups of evaporated milk can be used

Stir yeast into warm water to dissolve. In small bowl, mix well the dissolved yeast, cream, milk, and egg yolks then set aside. In a large bowl, stir flour, sugar, and salt. Cut in 1/2 cup butter with pastry blender or two knives until mixture resembles coarse crumbs. Stir yeast mixture into flour mixture just to moisten. Spread dough with light film of butter to prevent drying. Cover bowl with plastic and refrigerate overnight or up to four days. Dough needs just a few minutes kneading on lightly floured surface before shaping and baking.

Cinnamon Orange Twists

Roll dough into rectangle 24x 6 inches. Spread with soft butter. In small bowl stir together brown sugar and cinnamon and sprinkle over bottom of long half of dough. Fold top half and cut 24 vertical strips (1 inch wide). Pinch ends of each strip to seal twist in opposite directions. Place on greased baking sheet. Let rise one hour or until almost doubled. Bake twists in 375° oven for 12-15 minutes or until brown. Spread with glaze while still warm.

Glaze:

- 1/2 cup icing sugar
- 2 tablespoons + 1 teaspoon of orange rind
- 1 tablespoon orange juice

In a small bowl, cream together sugar and orange rind. Gradually beat in orange juice until smooth.

Licking Riverside Historic Bed and Breakfast

Lynda L. Freeman
516 Garrard Street
Covington, KY 41011
(606) 291-0191 call first; (800) 483-7822; FAX (606) 291-0939

We use this recipe to make numerous items. Especially good are the Cinnamon Buns. Guests love them! They are delicious with or without icing. Serve warm to melt their hearts and stomachs.

Basic Foundation Dough

2 cakes compressed yeast
1 tablespoon sugar
1 cup warm (not hot) water
flour
1 cup milk, scalded
3/4 cup shortening
1/2 cup sugar
1 teaspoon salt
7 cups sifted all-purpose flour
3 eggs beaten

Dissolve yeast and one tablespoon sugar in lukewarm water. Add shortening, sugar and salt to scalded milk and cool to lukewarm. Add 3 cups flour to make a batter, and beat with wooden spoon. Add the yeast mixture and beaten eggs; beat well. Add enough of the remaining flour to make a soft dough, turn out on a floured surface and knead lightly. Place in greased bowl, turn so that all sides are greased and rise until doubled in bulk, about 2 hours. When light, punch dough down and shape as desired for Coffee Cake, Swedish Tea Ring, or Cinnamon Buns. When ready to bake, bake in preheated 425° oven for 12-25 minutes depending on size.

Fruit Bread

Combine the following:

- 5 cups flour
- 3/4 teaspoon baking powder
- 2 1/4 teaspoon salt
- 3 teaspoon cinnamon
- 4 1/2 cups sugar
- 3 teaspoons baking soda
- 3 teaspoons cloves
- 1 1/2 teaspoon nutmeg

Stir in:

- 1 1/2 cups vegetable oil
- 6 eggs
- 1 1/2 cups water

Add:

- 3 cups canned pumpkin or applesauce or mashed bananas
- 1 1/2 cups chopped nuts

Stir until well blended. Bake at 325° about one hour or until done. Makes five loaves.

Vanilla Pancake Sauce

- 1 cup sugar
- 1/2 teaspoon cinnamon
- 2 tablespoons butter
- 3 tablespoons flour
- 2 cups water
- 1 teaspoon vanilla

In a saucepan combine sugar, flour, and cinnamon. Whisk in water, and bring mixture to a boil until sugar is dissolved. Let mixture simmer for two minutes. Remove pan from heat, whisk in vanilla and butter until butter is melted. Serve immediately over pancakes or store in a tightly closed jar for up to a month.

Genesee Country Inn

Glenda Barcklow
948 George Street, Box 340
Mumford, NY 14511-0340
(716) 538-2500; (800) 697-8297;
FAX (716) 538-4565

Our classic, but cozy inn is a historic stone mill. Nine-room B&B inn with all private baths, some fireplaces, canopy beds, A/C, and TV. Serenity and privacy just one mile from Genesee Country Village Museum and 30 minutes from downtown. Woods, waterfalls, and trout fishing on the property. Gourmet breakfasts.

The Oak and Apple Bed and Breakfast

Jana Brown
208 N. Second Street
Oakland, MD 21550
(301) 334-9265

This is an old family recipe that my guests love!

Circa 1915, our restored Colonial Revival sits on a beautiful large lawn with mature trees and includes a large, columned front porch, enclosed sunporch, parlor with fireplace, and cozy gathering room with television. Awaken to fresh continental breakfast served fireside in the dining room or on the sunporch. The quaint town of Oakland offers a wonderful small-town atmosphere.

Banana Bread

1/2 cup shortening
1 cup sugar
2 eggs
1 cup mashed bananas
1 teaspoon lemon juice
1 teaspoon vanilla
2 cups flour
3 teaspoons baking powder
1/2 teaspoon salt
3/4 cup walnuts

Cream shortening and sugar. Mix eggs, bananas, lemon juice, and vanilla and add to creamed mixture. Mix dry ingredients and add to mixture. Fold in nuts. Bake in greased loaf pan at 375° for about 1 hour. Cool in pan for 10 minutes then transfer to rack.

Banana Butterscotch Bread

1/2 cup butter
3/4 cup sugar
1 egg, large
3 bananas, ripe
2 cups flour
1 teaspoon baking powder
1/2 teaspoon baking soda
1/2 teaspoon salt
3/4 teaspoon cinnamon
1/8 teaspoon nutmeg
1/2 to 3/4 cup butterscotch morsels
1/2 cup chopped walnuts (optional)

Grease or spray two loaf pans. Cream butter, egg, and sugar. Add mashed ripe bananas. Sift flour, baking powder, baking soda, salt, cinnamon and nutmeg. Add to creamed mixture, blend. Add butterscotch morsels and nuts by folding in gently. Pour into pans, bake at 350° for 25-28 minutes.

National Pike Inn

Tom and Terry Rimel
9W Main Street
PO Box 299
New Market, MD 21774
(301) 865-5055

This is a wonderful bread for breakfast, luncheon, or teas. You can even serve it as a dessert. I have given this recipe out to hundreds of people over the years. Everyone loves it. I found a version of this recipe years ago in a magazine and I changed it to my tastes. It is easy to make and keeps beautifully. You will enjoy this special banana bread.

Sanctuary Ministries

Emil and Barbara Schoch
20277 Schick Road
Defiance, OH 43512
(419) 658-2069

I serve this with a breakfast of eggs, juices, coffee or tea and spreads, such as margarine, jams, apple butter or cream cheese. I also include toast and/or bagels for variety of tastes. This is not only delicious, it is nutritious and filling. Is adds to the down home style of our table.

Banana-Zucchini Bread

3 large bananas (mashed)
3/4 cup white sugar
1 cup shredded zucchini (drained)
1 egg, (beaten lightly)
2 cups all-purpose flour
1 teaspoon baking powder
1 teaspoon baking soda
1/2 teaspoon salt
1 teaspoon cinnamon
1/2 cup raisins
1/2 cup chopped nuts
2 tablespoons melted margarine

Mix together first four ingredients. In another bowl mix together next five ingredients and combine with banana mixture. Mix thoroughly. Add margarine. Mix in. Add raisins and nuts. Put into greased loaf pan. Bake at 350° for 1 hour. Test with toothpick for doneness inside.

Zucchini Quick Bread

- 3 eggs
- 1 cup honey
- 1 cup brown sugar
- 3 teaspoons vanilla
- 1 cup Wesson oil
- 2 cups shredded zucchini
- 2 1/2 cups flour
- 1 teaspoon cinnamon
- 1/4 teaspoon baking powder
- 1 teaspoon salt
- 1 cup chopped nuts

Preheat oven to 350°. Beat eggs until light and fluffy. Add honey, brown sugar, vanilla, oil and blend well. Stir in squash. Add flour, baking powder, salt, soda and cinnamon to above mixture. Fold in nuts. Pour in greased loaf pans. Bake for 45 minutes to 1 hour until done. Makes 2 large loaves or 5 small loaves.

Jeanette's Bed and Breakfast

Jeanette and Ray West
3380 E. Lockett Road
Flagstaff, AZ 86004-4043
(520)527-1912; (800) 752-1912

I have served this bread to friends and family for over 20 years. When I opened my bed and breakfast in the spring of 1996, the Zucchini Quick Bread became an instant hit. It is yummy and nutritious at the same time. Serve it for breakfast, lunch, dinner, desert time or for a snack. Enjoy!

Annabelle Bed and Breakfast

George and Carolyn Mayer
501 Speed Street
Vicksburg, MS 39180
(601) 638-2000; (800) 791-2000

When baking Cranberry-Orange Bread, the wonderful aroma wafts through the house, usually around check-in time. While enjoying our home baked cookies and special teas in the parlor upon arrival, the guests anticipate the complete southern breakfast of the next morning, served in our formal dining room.

This sweet bread is a delightful accompaniment to our daily changing breakfasts which may include Eggs Benedict, Garlic Cheese Grits, French toast or a variety of omelettes.

Cranberry-Orange Bread

1 3/4 cups all-purpose flour
3/4 cup sugar
1 teaspoon baking soda
1/3 teaspoon baking powder
1 teaspoon salt
1 teaspoon grated orange rind
1 egg
2/3 cup orange juice
3 teaspoons butter, melted
1 cup cranberries
1/3 cup water

Preheat oven to 325°. Grease loaf pan and dust with flour. In large bowl, sift together flour, sugar, baking soda, baking powder, salt, and orange rind. In separate bowl combine eggs, orange juice, cranberries, melted butter and water. In center of dry mixture, stir in wet ingredients until combined. Fold in cranberries. Pour mixture into loaf pan and bake for 1 hour or until test shows done.

Orange-Cranberry Tea Bread

- 2 cups all-purpose flour
- 2 teaspoons baking powder
- 1/4 teaspoon salt
- 4 tablespoons cold unsalted butter, cut into small pieces
- 3/4 cup + 2 tablespoons sugar
- 4 ounces chopped walnuts
- 1 tablespoon grated orange zest
- 1 egg
- 2/3 cup orange juice (preferably fresh)
- 2 cups fresh cranberries
- 1 tablespoon milk

Preheat oven to 350°. Butter 9x5 inch loaf pan and line bottom with waxed paper. Combine flour, baking powder, and salt. Cut in butter to resemble cornmeal. Add 3/4 cup of sugar, walnuts and orange zest. In small bowl, beat egg until frothy, beat in orange juice. Pour liquid over dry ingredients, mix until dough masses together. Add cranberries and combine. Pour batter into prepared pan. Brush with milk and sprinkle with remaining sugar. Bake for 1 hour or until firm and golden brown. Transfer to cooling rack.

The Cranberry Inn at Chatham

Ray and Brenda Raffurty
359 Main Street
Chatham (Cape Cod), MA 02633
(508) 945-9232; (800) 332-4667;
FAX (508) 945-3769

At the Cranberry Inn we like to use native "Cape Cod" cranberries in special recipes such as this. This bread is extremely moist and is best served cold. I am asked for the recipe so often that I finally typed it on our computer and printed copies to hand out! One guest told me she thought her grandmother had the best recipe for cranberry bread, but this one will replace it!

Homestead Lodging

Robert and Lori Kepiro
184 East Brook Road (Rt. 896)
Smoketown, PA 17576
(717) 393-6927; FAX (717) 393-6927

This Pecan Orange Bread is delicious served warm from the oven. The bread creates a tantalizing aroma in your bed and breakfast. It simply melts in your mouth as you discover the hidden cream cheese in each bite!

Pecan-Orange Bread

3/4 cup sugar
1/2 cup chopped pecans
1 tablespoon grated orange rind
2 11 ounce cans refrigerated buttermilk biscuits
1 3 ounce cream cheese, cut in 20 squares
1/2 cup butter, melted
1 cup confectioners' sugar
2 tablespoons orange juice

Combine sugar, pecans, and orange rind in a small bowl; set aside. Separate each biscuit and place a cream cheese square into half of the biscuit and pinch sides together. Dip in butter and dredge in sugar mixture. Stand on edge in greased bundt pan; space evenly. Drizzle remaining butter and sprinkle with sugar mixture. Bake at 350° for 35-45 minutes. Invert on serving plate. Combine confectioners' sugar and orange juice and drizzle over bread.

Lemony Yogurt Bread

1 cup vegetable shortening
2 cups sugar
4 eggs, well beaten
3 cups flour
1/2 teaspoon salt
2 teaspoons baking powder
1 8 ounce lemon yogurt
1 lemon, juice and rind (I use 2 teaspoons "grated, dried lemon peel" + 1 tablespoon juice)

Topping:
Lemon juice (about 1 tablespoon)
1/3 cup sugar

Preheat oven to 350°. Grease two 8 inch loaf pans. Cream shortening and sugar and add beaten eggs and mix well. Sift flour, salt, and baking powder and add to egg mixture alternating with yogurt. Grate rind of lemon and add to mixture with 1/2 the juice from the lemon. Pour mixture into greased loaf pans and bake 45 minutes. As soon as loaves are baked, drizzle top with lemon-sugar mixture. Cool in pan.

The Boulevard Bed and Breakfast

Judy and Charles Powell
1909 Baynard Boulevard
Wilmington, DE 19802
(302) 656-9700; FAX (302) 656-9701

We serve this sweet bread with juice and a dish of fruit while we are cooking guest's order for main course at breakfast. The bread is very good in the summer or spring served with strawberries or any other berry or the melon group such as cantelope (because it is not overwhelming as far as flavor).

White Pillars Bed and Breakfast

John and Donna Clark
395 Old State Road
PO Box 185
Canton, NY 13617
(315) 386-233; (800) 261-6292;
FAX (315) 386-2353

Our guests tell us it is hard to get out of bed in the morning because of the delightful comfort of extra-thick mattresses, down comforters, and luxurious pillows. But the aroma of these freshly baked cinnamon rolls lures them down to the kitchen where they gather around the warm AGA stove and watch their made-to-order omelets be prepared.

Refrigerator-Rise Cinnamon Rolls

2 tablespoons active dry yeast
2 cups warm water
1/2 cup sugar
1/2 cup canola oil
1/3 cup powdered milk
1 egg, beaten
1 1/2 teaspoons salt
6 cups white flour, approximately

Filling:
2 teaspoons cinnamon
1 cup sugar
6 tablespoons softened butter or margarine

Dissolve yeast in water. Add remaining dough ingredients, forming a soft dough. Knead. Roll out to a large rectangle and spread with filling ingredients which have been mixed together. Roll up long side, then slice into 24 pieces. Place on greased cookie sheet. Let rise overnight in refrigerator. Next morning, remove from refrigerator, set at room temperature for 15 minutes, then bake at 350° for about 30 minutes. Frost with confectioners' sugar and water if desired.

Shamrock Cinnamon Rolls

1 tablespoon butter, softened
1/2 cup marmalade
2 tablespoons chopped nuts
1 cup packed brown sugar
1/2 teaspoon cinnamon
2 10 ounce refrigerated buttermilk flaky biscuits
1/2 cup melted butter

Preheat oven to 350°. Grease 12 cup or 6 cup Bundt pan with tablespoon butter. Place teaspoonfuls of marmalade in pan. Sprinkle with nuts. In small bowl mix well sugar and cinnamon. Separate biscuits an dip in melted butter and then into brown sugar mixture. Stand biscuits on edge in pan and space evenly. Sprinkle with remaining sugar mixture and drizzle remaining butter. Bake near center of rack for 30-40 minutes or until golden brown. Cool upright for five minutes and invert onto serving plate. Yield: 6-8 servings

Shamrock Bed and Breakfast

Tom McLaughlin
5657 Sunbury Road
Columbus, OH 43230-1147
(614) 337-9849

Our bed and breakfast is one half mile from I-270, close to the airport, and 15 minutes from downtown. The B&B is handicapped accessible and it is all on one floor. There are one and one fourth acres of landscaped gardens, trees, patio, and arbor for enjoyment. For entertainment guests can choose from the large library of books, videos, and CDs or just relax in front of the fireplace. There is easy access to downtown activities like Polaris Amphitheater, shopping, parks, gardens, galleries, and country.

Lithia Springs Lodge Bed and Breakfast

Paul and Reita Johnson
Route 1 Box 77A
Gassville, AR 72635
(501) 435-6100

We have a lovingly restored, early Ozark health lodge, six miles southwest of Mountain Home in north central Arkansas. Fishing, boating, and canoeing in famous lakes and rivers. Scenic hills, valleys, and caverns. Silver Dollar City, Branson, and Eureka Springs are within driving distance. Enjoy walking in the meadow and woods and browse through the adjoining Country Treasures Gift Shop.

Almost Goof-Proof Caramel Rolls

9 frozen dinner rolls

Mix and set aside:
1/2 cup chopped pecans or walnuts
1 3 ounce box butterscotch pudding (not instant)
cinnamon

Melt 1/4 cup butter. Set aside.

In a 9 x 9 pan, place frozen dinner rolls 1/2 inch apart. Sprinkle dry ingredients over top and drizzle butter over top. Night before, put in oven on lower rack. In the morning, turn on oven to 350°. Do not open the oven door. Bake 25 minutes or 5-10 minutes more. Take out of oven, let set a few minutes. Turn upside down on plate.

Plantation Quickie Sticky Buns

- 1 8 ounce tube refrigerated cresent roll dough
- 1 tablespoon margarine, softened
- 1 tablespoon granulated sugar
- 1/2 teaspoon cinnamon
- 1/4 cup margarine
- 1/2 cup brown sugar
- 1/4 cup water
- 1/2 broken pecans or walnuts, if desired

Unroll the dough, leaving it in two rectangles, pushing triangles together if necessary. Spread with the softened margarine and sprinkle with the granulated sugar and cinnamon. Re-roll dough.

Melt 1/4 cup margarine and mix in water and brown sugar. Divide evenly in 10 regular size greased muffin cups. Cut the dough into 10 equal slices and place in muffin cups. Bake in preheated 350° oven for 12-15 minutes. Remove from oven, quickly run a knife around each bun and immediately invert on to a cookie sheet or waxed paper.

Plantation House

Merland and Barbara Clark
RR 2 Box 17
Elgin, NE 68636-9301
(402) 843-2287

Breakfast is served family style in our formal dining room. Coffee is available early and our guests often take a cup to the backyard gazebo to enjoy the fresh country air. Merland does the meats and toast and I do the egg dishes and the baking. These mouth-watering rolls are an adaptation from a recipe found in a magazine and are so easy. Our guests seem to love them and never guess that they are made from a commercially prepared dough.

A Laber of Love

Lori Laber
11030 County Road 10
Middlebury, IN 46540
(219) 825-7877

These rolls are best when served warm out of the oven. The aromas of fresh rolls baking and coffee brewing greet my bed and breakfast guests as they come down to breakfast.

My Cape Cod home is located in northern Indiana Amish farm country on three acres, two of which are wooded. Screened-in gazebo in woods is ideal for quiet time or just relaxing.

Sticky Pecan Rolls

6 tablespoons margarine or butter
1 cup evaporated milk
1 cup water
2 packages yeast
2 teaspoons salt
1/2 cup sugar
2 eggs
6 1/2 to 7 cups flour

Topping (per 9 inch pan):
2 tablespoons margarine or butter
1/4 cup packed brown sugar
1 tablespoon white corn syrup
1/2 cup pecan halves or broken pieces

Heat milk and water to lukewarm. Add yeast and dissolve before adding salt, sugar, and melted margarine. Stir in two cups of flour; add eggs and mix well. Add the remaining flour to make a soft dough. No need to knead. The dough may either be refrigerated overnight to rise or left out to rise until double in size.

Topping: For each pan, melt two tablespoons of margarine right in the pan over low heat. Add brown sugar, and the corn syrup. Stir as mixture heats. Leave on stove just until mixture begins to bubble. Remove from heat before adding the pecans.

Prepare rolls and place on top of topping mixture. Allow to raise before baking. Bake at 350° for 15-20 minutes or until golden brown. When baked, place a large dinner plate on top of rolls and turn rolls out onto plate. Yields about 30 rolls or three 9-inch pans.

Sticky Buns

- 1 package Betty Crocker golden pound cake mix
- 3 cups all purpose flour
- 2 packages regular yeast
- 1 1/2 cups very warm water (105°-115°)
- 1/2 cup butter
- 3/4 cup brown sugar (light gives better appearance)
- 1/2 cup light corn syrup
- 3/4 cup chopped pecans

Mix cake mix (dry), flour, yeast in large bowl. Stir in water, dough may seem dry. Cover and let rise 30 minutes (dough will not double in size).

Melt butter in a 13 x 9 glass pan. Stir in brown sugar and corn syrup. Sprinkle pecans over mixture. Stir down dough. Turn onto lightly floured surface. Divide into 15 or more equal pieces; shape each piece into a ball. Dip pieces in a mixture of 1/2 cup brown sugar, 2 tablespoons cinnamon and 1/4 cup sugar. Arrange pieces on bottom of pan. (You can cut down on these ingredients if you want to.)

Bake 35-40 minutes at 350°. This can be refrigerated overnight and baked in the morning.

Bailey House

Jenny Bishop
28 South 7th Street
Amelia Island, Fernandina Beach, FL 32034
(904) 261-5390; (800)251-5390;
FAX (904) 321-0103

Our elegant Queen Anne home is furnished in Victorian period decor. The beautiful home, with magnificent stained-glass windows, turrets, and a wraparound porch, was built in 1895 and is on the National Register of Historic Places. The location in Fernandina's historic district is within walking distance of excellent restaurants, antique shopping, and many historic churches.

Queen Anne Inn

Robert and Pauline Medhurst
420 West Washington
South Bend, IN 46601
(219) 234-5959; (800) 582-2379

These sticky buns are our Sunday morning tradition at the Queen. This easy recipe adds 15 minutes more to sleep in.

Our 1893 Victorian house features antiques, original Frank Loyd Wright bookcases, silk cloth wall covering, and a beautiful tiger oak staircase. An abundant breakfast, afternoon tea, and snacks are provided. Near downtown, Notre Dame, local attractions, and good restaurants. Our guests relax and relive earlier days.

Easy Sticky Buns

3/4 cup whipping cream (unwhipped)
3/4 cup brown sugar (packed)
2-3 teaspoons cinnamon
11 frozen small yeast roll dough (Roundy's or Rhoades for example)
1/4 cup nuts (sliced almonds, pecans or walnuts)

Combine whipping cream, brown sugar and cinnamon. Pour into ungreased 9 inch round cake pan. Put 7 round frozen dough balls around edge of pan and 4 frozen dough balls in middle. Let rise in kitchen overnight.

Bake at 350° for 15-20 minutes or until golden brown. Turn out onto serving plate. Top with nuts. You may select whichever kind you like.

Then you just sit back and wait for the raving comments.

Apple Bread

1/2 cup oil
1 cup applesauce
3 cups flour
2 cups sugar
3 eggs
1 cup apple pie filling
1 teaspoon salt
1 teaspoon cinnamon
1 teaspoon baking soda
1 teaspoon vanilla

Mix ingredients together. Pour into two greased and floured loaf pans and bake at 350° for 1 hour. Makes two loaves.

The Columbian, A Bed and Breakfast Inn

Chris and Becky Will
360 Chestnut Street
Columbia, PA 17512
(717) 684-5869; (800) 422-5869

The part of running a bed and breakfast that I find the most enjoyable is finding new recipes and trying them out. I'm always on the lookout for new and unusual breakfast recipes and this is one I found that has become a guest favorite. I serve it as part of a very full breakfast to our guests. When I first started making this recipe, it called for a lot more oil which made it very greasy and heavy, so as I do with many recipes that are just not quite what I want, I experimented. I found that by adding applesauce in place of oil it was much lighter and more cakelike.

Old Thyme Inn

George and Marcia Dempsey
779 Main Street
Half Moon Bay, CA 94019
(415) 726-1616; FAX (415) 712-0805

Our inn is a restored 1889 Queen Anne Victorian, located on historic Main Street in the downtown area. Some rooms have fireplaces and double-size whirlpool tubs. The theme is our English-style herb garden; all rooms are named after herbs. Atmosphere is friendly and informal. We serve beverages in the evening and a hearty breakfast each morning.

Glazed Apple Bread

1/2 cup canola oil
1 cup sugar
1 teaspoon vanilla
1 large egg
2 cups sifted unbleached flour
1/2 teaspoon cinnamon
1/2 teaspoon salt
2 teaspoons baking powder
2 tablespoons milk
1/2 cup raisins
2 large apples finely chopped (use good baking apples)
1/2 cup walnuts, chopped

Glaze:
1/2 cup powdered sugar, sifted
1 tablespoon water
2 tablespoons melted butter

Combine oil, sugar, and vanilla. Cream until light and fluffy. Add eggs and beat well. Sift together flour, cinnamon, salt and baking powder. Add milk, raisins, apples, nuts and dry ingredients to mixture and stir only until flour is well dampened. Bake in well-greased 9x5x4 inch loaf pan at 350° for 50-60 minutes. Cool; remove from pan. Combine glaze ingredients; mix well and pour over loaf. Let glaze set before wrapping loaf tightly. Best if made day prior to serving.

Apple-Cheese-Nut Bread

1/4 pound butter, room temperture
1/4 cup brown sugar
3/4 cup white sugar
1/4 teaspoon nutmeg
2 cups sifted flour
1 teaspoon baking powder
1/2 teaspoon baking soda
1 teaspoon salt
2 eggs
1 1/2 cups apples; unpeeled, chopped
3/4 cup sharp Cheddar, grated
1/2 cup walnuts or pecans, chopped

Preheat oven to 350°. Grease and flour a 3x5 loaf pan. Cream butter, sugars, and nutmeg until smooth. Sift flour with baking powder, soda, and salt and set aside. Add eggs to butter-sugar mixture and beat with mixer until smooth and light. Add apples, cheese, and nuts. Combine. Add dry ingredients and mix until just combined. Pour into prepared pan (batter will be thick). Bake 1 hour or until tester comes out clean.

Five Gables Inn

Mike and De Kennedy
PO Box 335
East Boothbay, ME 04544
(270) 633-4551; (800) 451-5048

This recipe has been in my family so long I don't know who created it. It's great served warm with butter at breakfast or at tea time. And it can be frozen.

Ridgeland

Carl and Michele Nicholson
6875 126th Avenue
Fennville, MI 49408
(616) 857-1633

Our bed and breakfast is located in the fruit belt along Lake Michigan. One of the major crops is blueberries; they were even raised on our land near the turn of the century as Ridgeland was a working fruit farm and resort. The guesta in the 1890s to approximately 1920 were served dishes that included fruit raised on the farm. Ridgeland is no longer a fruit farm but our blueberries are locally grown.

Blueberry Bread

1 1/2 cup brown sugar
2/3 cup vegetable oil or applesauce
1 egg
1 cup sour milk
1 teaspoon vanilla
2 1/2 cups flour
1 teaspoon salt
1 teaspoon baking powder
1 1/2 cup fresh or frozen blueberries
1/2 cup chopped nuts

Topping:
1 tablespoon margarine, melted
1 tablespoon cinnamon
1/2 cup sugar

Mix ingredients in order given. Pour into two well-greased bread pans and set aside. Mix topping and sprinkle over top of loaves. Bake at 350° for 40 minutes, reduce heat to 250° for 10 minutes. Let cool before removing from bread pans.

Muffin Coffee Cake Caps

1/4 cup butter
1 cup sugar
1 egg, well beaten
1 1/2 cups all purpose flour
2 teaspoons baking powder
1/4 teaspoon salt
1/2 cup milk

Topping:
1/2 cup brown sugar
2 tablespoons flour
2 teaspoons cinnamon
1/2 cup melted butter
1/2 cup chopped nuts

Cream butter. Beat in sugar and egg. Sift flour, baking powder, and salt. Add sifted flour mixture alternately with milk, beat until smooth. Prepare topping, mixing all ingredients well. Prepare six cup muffin cap baking tray. Place 3/4 cup batter in each cup. Place about 2 tablespons of topping on each cap. Bake at 375° for about 15-18 minutes or until done.

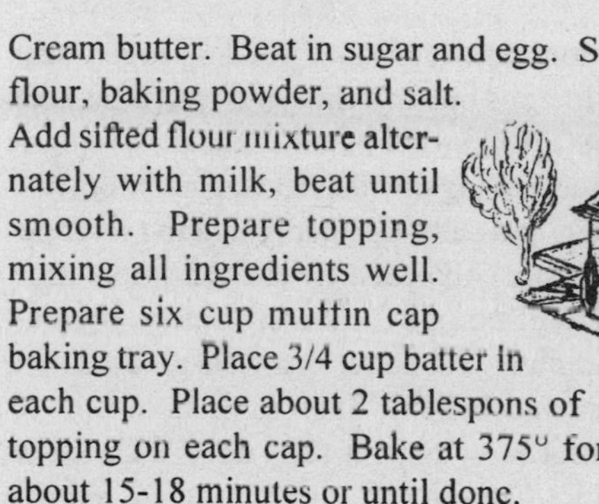

Holly Hedge House

Lynn and Marian Thrasher
908 Grant Avenue South
Renton, WA 98055
(206) 226-2555; FAX (206) 226-2555

Muffin Coffee Caps are the ideal size to enjoy with your first cup of coffee of the day.

Maplewood Inn

Cindy and Doug Baird
Route 22A South
Fair Haven, VT 05743
(802) 265-8039; (800) 253-7729;
FAX (802) 265-8210

Guests rave about this wonderful tea bread. It looks and tastes fantastic. Spread with cream cheese and it's a winning combination.

Our guests rediscover romance in this exquisite, Historic Register Greek Revival. Elegant rooms and suites boast antiques, fireplaces, A/C, color cable TVs, radios, optional phone, and turn-down service. Keeping foom with fireplace, gathering foom with library, parlor with games and complimentary cordials. Hot beverages and snacks anytime.

Sweet Potato Bread

1 cup butter or margarine, softened
2 cups sugar
4 eggs
2 1/2 cups cooked, mashed sweet potatoes
3 cups flour
2 teaspoons baking powder
1 teaspoon baking soda
1 teaspoon cinnamon
1/2 teaspoon nutmeg
1/4 teaspoon salt
1 teaspoon vanilla
1/2 cup flaked coconut
1/2 cup walnuts or pecans, chopped

Cream butter, gradually adding sugar, beat. Add eggs one at a time and beat after each one. Add sweet potatoes, beat. Combine flour, baking powder, soda, cinnamon, nutmeg, and salt. Gradually add to sweet potato mix and beat after each addition. Batter will be stiff. Stir in vanilla, coconut and nuts. Put batter in a well-greased tube pan and bake at 350° for 1 hour and 15 minutes, or until it tests done with toothpick. Cool in pan for 15 minutes, remove from pan and let cool completely. Can also be baked in two standard loaf pans. Check after 50 minutes and cook until it tests done.

Tea Bread for All Seasons

8 cups flour
2 tablespoons baking soda
2 tablespoons baking powder
1 tablespoon salt
3 tablespoons cinnamon or nutmeg
6 cups sugar
3 cups oil
6 eggs
6 cups fruit
2 cups water or milk (according to fruit used)
6 tablespoons grated orange rind

Fruit may be zucchini, carrots, bananas, pumpkin, prunes, peaches, apples, etc. You can also add raisins if you desire.

Mix all dry ingredients together. Mix oil, eggs, and fruit together, then blend all ingredients with the water or milk. Mix well. Makes about seven loaves of bread. You can also use this recipe to make muffins. Bake bread at 350° for about 45 minutes. Use greased loaf pans or aluminum foil pushed in place. You can wrap well and freeze up to two months. I make several different kinds so guests that stay several nights have a variety.

The Pickford House Bed and Breakfast

Anna Larsen
2555 MacLeod Way
Cambria, CA 93428
(805) 927-8619

I serve this bread with wine at our 1860 bar and all enjoy it. You could add icing if you want it a little fancy. For banana bread, I leave out the spice. This is a great way to use up over-ripe bananas. Just freeze until you get enough for six cups.

Serendipity Inn

Terry and Sheila Johnson
407-71st Avenue North
Myrtle Beach, SC 29572
(803) 449-5268; (800) 762-3229

The Serendipity Inn serves its full complimentary breakfast buffet style in our Garden Room. Everything we serve is homemade and baked just before our guests arrive at 8:00 A.M. Judging by the comments, the way to someone's heart is still through his or her stomach!

The carrot loaf recipe is just one of the many baked goods we prepare at the Serendipity. It is moist and delicious, freezes well and is a big hit with our guests. The Serendipity also offers fresh baked bread, fresh fruit, juice, coffee, cereal, bagels, and boiled eggs.

Carrot Loaf

3 cups all-purpose flour
2 teaspoons baking soda
2 teaspoons baking powder
1/2 teaspoon salt
1 teaspoon cinnamon
4 eggs
2 cups sugar
1 1/2 cups corn oil
1 teaspoon vanilla
2 cups grated raw carrots
1 cup chopped walnuts
1 can crushed pineapple

Preheat oven to 350°. In large bowl, sift together flour, baking soda, baking powder, salt, and cinnamon. In separate bowl, beat together eggs and sugar until pale yellow; beat in oil and vanilla. Stir in sifted ingredients. Fold in carrots, walnuts and pineapple. Butter and lightly flour a 10 inch bundt pan or two loaf pans. Pour batter into prepared pan. Bake 1 hour and 10 minutes or until cake tester comes out dry.

Morning Glory Muffins

1 1/4 cup sugar
2 1/4 cup flour
1 tablespoon cinnamon
2 teaspoons baking powder
1/2 teaspoon salt
1/2 cup shredded coconut
1/2 cup raisins
1 apple shredded
8 ounces crushed pineapple drained
2 cups grated carrots
1/2 cup pecans or walnuts
3 eggs
1 cup vegetable oil
1 teaspoon vanilla

Sift together sugar, flour, cinnamon, baking powder and salt in large bowl. Add coconut, fruits, carrots and nuts. In separate bowl, whisk eggs with oil and vanilla. Pour this mixture into bowl of dry ingredients. Blend well. Fill muffin tins 3/4 full. Bake in 350° oven for 35 minutes. Test with toothpicks. Cool in pan 10 minutes. Turn out onto rack. Best if allowed to ripen 24 hours. Freezes well.

Joy's Morning Glory Bed and Breakfast

Merle and Joy Petersen
4308 Main Street
Elk Horn, IA 51531
(712) 764-5631

I read LaVyrle Spencer's book Morning Glory *during the time we were restoring our 1912 home for a bed and breakfast. I liked the book so much that I decided to name our new business "Joy's Morning Glory Bed and Breakfast." The guest room that faces the morning sun is also named Morning Glory. Shortly after I chose the name, my mother found the Morning Glory recipe for me. I have served Morning Glory Muffins ever since and have received many compliments.*

Ridgetop Bed and Breakfast

Bill and Kay Jones
PO Box 193
Hampshire, TN 38461
(615) 285-2777; (800) 377-2770

We grow our very own blueberries; and guests may pick some to nibble on or take home with them. This dish capitalizes on the blueberries, but guests will also find them in their fruit cup, in waffles, and atop the individual baked French toast we serve.

Ridgetop Oatmeal Blueberry Muffins

1 egg
1/4 cup oil
1/4 cup brown sugar
1 cup buttermilk
1 cup oatmeal (not instant)
1/2 cup whole wheat flour
1/2 cup all-purpose flour
1 teaspoon baking powder
1/2 teaspoon baking soda
1/2 teaspoon salt (optional)
1 cup blueberries (fresh or frozen)

Mix first four ingredients. Add oatmeal. Stir baking powder, soda, and salt into flours and stir into other ingredients. Add blueberries. Spoon into greased muffin tins. Bake in 400° oven for 20-25 minutes. Let cool in pan a minute or two before attempting to remove. Makes 1 dozen.

Blueberry Muffin Cakes

Cream:
- 1/2 cup softened Imperial Margarine
- 3/4 cup granulated sugar

Add:
- 2 eggs, beat well

Mix together:
- 2 1/3 cups flour
- 2 1/2 teaspoons baking powder
- 1/2 teaspoon salt
- 1/2 teaspoon ground nutmeg

And add, alternating with:
- 3/4 cup milk

Fold in:
- 1 1/2 cups blueberries

Divide batter evenly into 18 greased muffin tins. Bake at 350° for 20-25 minutes. Cool slightly after removing from muffin tins. Dip top in melted butter. Dip into cinnamon-sugar mixture (3/4 cup sugar, 1/4 teaspoon cinnamon).

Katy's Inn

Bruce and Kathie Hubbard
503 South Third
PO Box 869
La Conner, WA 98257
(360) 466-3366; (800) 914-7767

Charming 1876 Victorian two blocks up hill from quaint LaConner that has 100 unique shops, galleries, and antique stores. Four lovely guest rooms upstairs (two with private bath) with access to wraparound porch through French doors. Romantic suite with private bath, located by gardens and pond, has a private entrance. Warm hospitality, full breakfast, and hot tub. Great for small retreats (18 max.), weddings, and/or receptions.

Shearer Hill Farm Bed and Breakfast

Bill and Patti Pesey
PO Box 1453
Wilmington, VT 05363
(802) 464-3253; (800) 437-3104

I have a large raspberry patch. I pick, crush, and freeze berries in ice cube trays. Pop out when frozen. Store in freezer bags to use all winter. Guests love fresh raspberry muffins in January.

Patti's Vermont Blueberry Muffins

1 cup butter
2 cups sugar
4 eggs
1 cup milk
4 cups flour
1/4 teaspoon salt
2 teaspoons baking powder
1 teaspoon vanilla extract
1 1/2 cups blueberries

Beat butter until smooth. Cream with sugar until well blended. Add eggs, one at a time. Beat well. Add flour alternately with milk. Beat well. Add salt, baking powder, vanilla, and mix well. Blend in blueberries. Bake in muffin pans at 350° for 30-40 minutes, until light golden. Makes 24 muffins. Bon appétit.

Two-Berry Muffins

1/2 cup milk
1/4 cup vegetable oil
1 egg
1 cup flour
1/2 cup sugar
1/2 cup oat bran
2 teaspoons baking powder
1/4 teaspoon salt
1/2 cup blueberries (fresh or frozen)
1/2 cup red raspberries (fresh or frozen)
1/2 cup pecans, chopped (optional)

In small bowl, combine milk, oil and egg. Set aside. In large bowl, stir together flour, sugar, oat bran, baking powder and salt. Add liquid ingredients. Stir until just moistened. Gently fold in fruits and nuts. Spray muffin tins with no-stick spray. Fill until 2/3 full. Bake at 400° for 18 minutes. Let sit for 2-3 minutes before removing from pan. Makes 12.

The Parsons House Bed and Breakfast

Al and Carol Keyes
211 Lee Street
PO Box 38
Defiance, MO 63341
(314) 798-2222; FAX (314) 798-2220

These muffins are tender and tasty as well as colorful with their red and blue berries. Best of all, when guests request a low-fat menu, these muffins easily comply by simply using skim milk, egg substitute and applesauce (for the oil).

Linden Manor Bed and Breakfast

Linda and Gregg Molloy
267 Charlotte Street West
Saint John, New Brunswick
CANADA E2M 1Y2
(506) 674-2754

Our Seasonal Fruit Muffins are a real hit with our guests. Guests enjoy coming downstairs in the morning to the smell of fresh muffins, hot out of the oven, with coffee or tea and a plate of fresh fruit. While our guests linger over their muffins, we prepare their choice of eggs any style, French toast, or cereal.

Seasonal Fruit Muffins

2 cups white flour
1 tablespoon baking powder
1/2 teaspoon salt
1/2 cup white sugar
1 teaspoon cinnamon
1/2 teaspoon nutmeg
1 egg
1 cup milk
1/3 cup melted butter
1-1 1/2 cups fruit, peaches, blueberries, or raspberries

Preheat oven to 400°. Combine first 5 ingredients (Note: for peaches replace cinnamon and nutmeg with 1/4 teaspoon mace.) Beat egg lightly, add milk and melted butter. Make a well in dry ingredients and pour in liquid mixture. Stir just enough to combine. Sprinkle with Topping. Bake 15-20 minutes.

Topping

Mix together:
2 tablespoons brown sugar
1/2 teaspoon cinnamon
1/4 teaspoon nutmeg

Sugarless Fruit Muffins

- 2 cups unbleached flour (or 1 1/2 cups white and 1/2 cup whole wheat)
- 1/2 teaspoon baking soda
- 2 teaspoons baking powder
- 1/2 cup nuts
- 1/2 teaspoon nutmeg
- 1/2 teaspoon cinnamon
- 1/2 cup chopped golden raisins
- 2 tablespoons grated orange or lemon zest
- 2 tablespoons frozen apple or orange juice concentrate
- 1/4 cup canola or olive oil
- 2 egg whites or 1 egg
- 1 1/4 cups pureed fruit (bananas, apples, berries, pumpkin, etc.)

In food processor bowl combine dry ingredients, raisins and orange or lemon zest. Process until raisins and zest are chopped. Set aside. In food processor, puree fruit (if using berries, use directly from freezer), add rest of liquid ingredients, blend. Add dry ingredients and nuts. Use on/off to blend or blend by hand as for any muffins. Preheat oven to 400°. Spray 12 cup muffin pan with nonstick coating. Fill cups evenly and bake 17-18 minutes. Remove from pan and serve warm or cool and freeze. Recipe freezes well. May be doubled. If frozen, remove from freezer 3 to 4 hours before serving or night before. To heat, place on cookie sheet, and heat in 300° oven 10-15 minutes. Makes 12 muffins.

Maggie's Bed and Breakfast

Maggie Leyda
2102 N. Keebler
Collinsville, IL 62234
(618) 344-8283

Owner Maggie Leyda seasons with herbs, never fries, and offers a primarily vegetarian, organic menu. Among its highlights are fresh strawberries and raspberries, as well as salt- and cholesterol-free muffins and crepes. Guests can soak in Maggie's hot tub and stroll the inn's two acres (including a fishpond).

Twin Oaks Bed and Breakfast

Norman and Sarah Glick
73 South Dryhouse Road
Belleville, PA 17004
(717) 935-2026

Most of my guests enjoy hot homemade muffins or breakfast breads and rolls. I find this muffin recipe easy and delicious.

We are located in the heart of the Kishacoquillas Valley only 30 minutes from Penn State. Norman and I welcome our guests to a new facility with clean, spacious rooms. In a quiet country setting with a panoramic view of Stone and Jacks mountains.

Streusel-Topped Banana Muffins

1/4 cup packed brown sugar
1/4 cup chopped nuts
1 teaspoon ground cinnamon
1 cup mashed ripe bananas (2-3 medium)
1/2 cup vegetable oil
1/3 cup milk
1 teaspoon vanilla
1 egg
2 cups all purpose flour
3 teaspoons baking powder
1 teaspoon salt
1/3 cup chopped nuts if desired

Heat oven to 400°. Grease bottoms only of 12 muffin cups or use paper liners. Mix brown sugar, 1/4 cup nuts and cinnamon. Reserve. Beat bananas, oil, milk, vanilla, and egg. Stir in remaining ingredients (except reserved mixture) all at once, just until flour is moistened. Batter will be lumpy. Divide batter evenly among muffin cups. Sprinkle with reserved mixture. Bake 15-20 minutes or until golden brown. Remove from cups.

BJ's Banana-Nut Muffins

1/4 cup melted butter
1 cup sugar
1 egg
3 bananas (mashed)
1 1/2 cups flour sifted
1 teaspoon soda
3/4 cup chopped pecans
1 teaspoon salt (optional)

Beat egg and add to melted butter and sugar. Mix well. Add mashed bananas. Sift together flour, soda, and salt. Mix together with egg mixture and add nuts. Pour into muffin tins sprayed with PAM. Bake at 350° for 20-25 minutes or 375° for 45 minutes for Banana Bread. Cool and "sprinkle with powdered sugar."

Gazebo Country Inn

Don and Bonnie Johannnsen
507 East Third
Salida, CO 81201
(719) 539-7806

These muffins are the Gazebo Country Inn's most requested and were created by my mother, Georgia Alice Bernback. (Use for banana bread or muffins.)

Our restored Victorian home (1901) is located in the heart of the Rockies and boasts magnificent views. We are committed to guests' comfort and relaxation.

Mountain View Inn

Fred and Susan Spencer
RD #1 Box 69
Waitsfield, VT 05673
(802) 496-2426

The Mountain View Inn is an old farmhouse, circa 1826, that was made into a lodge in 1948 to accommodate skiers at nearby Mad River Glen. Today it is a country inn with seven rooms. Meals are served family style around the antique harvest table where good fellowship prevails. Sip mulled cider around a crackling fire in our living room when the weather turns chilly.

Bran Banana Muffins

2 cups unbleached white flour
1 teaspoon baking powder
1/2 teaspoon baking soda
3 ripe mashed bananas
1 1/2 cup All Bran Cereal
1/2 cup cooking oil
3/4 cup sugar
2 eggs
1 cup nuts (add after previous ingredients are well mixed)

Combine all ingredients in bowl of electric mixer and beat for two minutes. Spoon into paper lined muffin cups. I find an ice cream scoop works well as one scoop just fills a muffin cup. Bake in preheated 375° oven 20-25 minutes or until well browned. Yield 18 muffins.

These are great with scrambled eggs and bacon or as an accompaniment to hot cereal on a cold blustery morning before heading out to ski. They also pack well for a mid-morning snack on the ski trails.

Banana-Chocolate Chip Muffins

2 cups flour
1/3 cup sugar
1 1/2 teaspoons baking powder
1 1/2 teaspoons baking soda
1/4 teaspoon salt
1/2 cup chopped walnuts or pecans
1/2 cup chocolate chips
2 large (or 3 small) bananas
2 eggs
1/4 cup oil
1/3 cup milk

Preheat oven to 375°. In a large bowl, mix together flour, sugar, baking powder, baking soda, and salt. Stir in the nuts and chocolate chips. In a separate bowl, mash the bananas and add the eggs, oil and milk. Whisk together then add all at one time to dry ingredients. Stir only until dry ingredients are moistened. Fill 12 greased muffin cups. Bake for 15-18 minutes.

Beaver Lake Bed and Breakfast

David and Elain Reppel
Route 2, Box 318
Eureka Springs, AR 72632
(501) 253-9210

For many people, chocolate denotes a special occasion and chocolate for breakfast is just plain neat! This recipe was developed to delight our chocolate loving guests on their birthdays and anniversaries. A Banana Chocolate Chip Muffin is a treat that does not compromise nutrition. Enjoy!

Bluff Point Bed and Breakfast

Walter and Edna Parfitt
26 Fort Hill Road
Groton, CT 06340
(860) 445-1314

A restored Colonial bed and breakfast (circa 1850) located on U.S. Route #1 and adjacent to Bluff Point State Park Coastal Preserve. Conveniently located four miles from Mystic Seaport Museum. Large common area with shared TV is available for our guests. We give warm and friendly service.

Zucchini Muffins

3 eggs
1 cup corn oil
1 teaspoon vanilla
2 cups unpeeled grated zucchini
1 1/2 cups sugar
2 cups flour
1 tablespoon cinnamon
1 1/2 teaspoons baking soda
1/4 teaspoon baking powder
1 cup nuts (optional)

Mix all ingredients in order. Beat well. Grease well and flour pans, including around the top of muffin pan. Fill muffin tins 3/4 full. Bake at 400° for 20 minutes. Sprinkle with confectioners' sugar. This makes 1 dozen plus 9 muffins. NOTE: Be sure to bake correct amount of time. They are very moist and delicious.

Carrot and Raisin Muffins

- 1 1/4 cups sugar
- 2 1/4 cups flour
- 1 tablespoon cinnamon
- 2 teaspoons baking soda
- 1/2 teaspoon salt
- 1/2 cup shredded coconut
- 1/2 cup raisins
- 1 apple, shredded
- 8 ounces crushed pineapple, drained
- 2 cups carrots, grated
- 1/2 cup pecans or walnuts. chopped
- 3 eggs
- 1 cup vegetable oil
- 1 teaspoon vanilla

Sift together sugar, flour, cinnamon, baking soda, and salt in large bowl. Add coconut, fruits, carrots and nuts. In separate bowl, whisk eggs with oil and vanilla. Pour mixture into bowl of dry ingredients. Blend well. Fill greased muffin tins 3/4 full. Bake at 350° for 35 minutes. Cool in pan for 10 minutes, turn out onto rack. Best if allowed to ripen for 24 hours. Freezes well.

Ship's Knees Inn

Jean and Ken Pitchford
186 Beach Road
PO Box 756
East Orleans, MA 02643
(508) 255-1312; FAX (508) 240-1351

Our 170-year-old restored sea captain's home is a three minute walk to beautiful sand-duned Nauset Beach. Inside the warm, lantern-lit doorways are 19 rooms individually appointed with special Colonial color schemes and authentic antiques. Some rooms feature authentic ship's knees, hand painted trunks, old clipper ship models, braided rugs, and four-poster beds. Tennis and swimming are available on the premises. Three miles away overlooking Orleans Cove, the Cove House property offers three rooms, a one-bedroom efficiency apartment, and two cottages.

Victorian Treasure Bed and Breakfast Inn

Todd and Kimberly Seidl
115 Prairie Street
Lodi, WI 53555
(608) 592-5199; (800) 859-5199;
FAX (608) 592-7147

Fall brings the scent of fallen leaves, pumpkin patches, and laden apple trees to the Wisconsin River Valley. Autumn is a special time in the rolling hills of Lodi, located between Madison and Baraboo/Devil's Lake — where scenic vistas, quiet waterways, and wooded hikes await you. It is also a time when the harvest is celebrated at the breakfast table of Victorian Treasure. This is a favorite apple recipe, with wonderful textures and flavors provided by crunchy walnuts and soft, sweet golden raisins.

Apple-Nut Muffins

3/4 cup vegetable oil
1 cup sugar
2 eggs
1 teaspoon vanilla
2 cups all-purpose flour
3/4 teaspoon baking soda
3/4 teaspoon ground cinnamon
dash mace
1/2 teaspoon salt
1 1/2 cups diced apples, preferably MacIntosh
1/2 cup golden raisins (can use regular, but these are nicer)
1/2 cup chopped walnuts

In large bowl, beat oil and sugar with electric mixer until smooth (2 minutes). Add eggs and vanilla, beat one minute. In a second bowl, mix remaining dry ingredients, then add to oil mixture. Stir just to combine. Stir in apples, raisins, and nuts. Spoon into muffin cups, bake at 400° for 20-25 minutes. Yields 12 muffins. These muffins look nice if topped with either dry oatmeal or a sugar streusel — equal parts of flour and sugar, cut in butter until crumbly.

Oatmeal Applesauce Muffins

1/2 cup butter/margarine
3/4 cup brown sugar
1 egg
1 cup flour
1/2 teaspoon cinnamon
1/4 teaspoon cloves
1/4 teaspoon nutmeg
1 teaspoon baking powder
1/4 teaspoon soda
1/4 teaspoon salt
1 cup applesauce
1 cup oatmeal, quick or regular
1/2 cup nuts
1/2 cup raisins

Cream butter and brown sugar, add egg. Mix together dry ingredients. Add alternately with applesauce. Add oatmeal, nuts and raisins. Bake at 350° for 25 minutes. Makes 1 dozen

Lamb's Inn Bed and Breakfast

Dick and Donna Messerschmidt
Route 2, Box 144
Richland Center, WI 53581
(608) 696-4301

This recipe was given to me by a high school friend for my bed and breakfast breakfasts. It is one of my favorites to serve because it is not a sweet muffin. Also it uses ingredients I always have on hand and is a smaller recipe. Our guests love them.

Nauset House Inn

Al and Diane Johnson, John and Cindy Vessellt
143 Beach Road
PO Box 774
East Orleans, MA 02643
(508) 255-2195

Nauset House Inn serves a full and a continental breakfast everyday. We love variety and different foods to make breakfast special. Our Oatmeal Butterscotch Muffins added a new twist. Lots of guests can't figure out what is in there, and always ask for the recipe. We hope you will enjoy surprising your family and guests with our muffins.

Nauset House Oatmeal Butterscotch Muffins

1 18 ounce box regular rolled oats
1 quart buttermilk
1 pound brown sugar
3 sticks margarine (melted and cooled)
6 eggs, slightly beaten
3 cups flour
4 teaspoons baking powder
1 teaspoon salt
1 1/2 teaspoons baking soda
1 package butterscotch chips

In a large bowl, combine oats, buttermilk and brown sugar. Set aside and let stand for 1 hour. Combine, margarine and eggs. Set aside. Sift flour, baking powder, salt, baking soda. Add margarine and eggs to oats. Mix together well, then mix in flour mixture. Add 1-2 cups butterscotch chips. Bake at 400° for 15-20 minutes. Makes 3 dozen. Raisins may be substituted for chips.

Pear-fection Muffins

1 cup oat bran
1 cup skim milk
2 egg whites
1/2 cup brown sugar
3 tablespoons oil
1 large ripe pear
1 cup flour
1 teaspoon baking powder
1 teaspoon cinnamon
1/2 teaspoon nutmeg (optional)
1/2 cup nuts (optional)

Soak oat bran in milk for one hour. Mix dry ingredients. Mix all others in a blender at low speed, including pear. Add to dry ingredients. Bake at 400° for 30 minutes.

This is good with other fruit that gets a little too ripe. Makes 1 dozen.

Cloverhill Bed and Breakfast, Inc.

Carolyn Young
401 North Clay Street
Green Springs, OH 44836
(419) 639-3515

There are always fresh muffins at the breakfast table, with fresh fruit, cereal and juice.

Cloverhill sits on a hill overlooking the community of Green Springs located in northern Ohio between Fremont and Tiffin on State Route 19—an area rich with history. Nice quiet stay in a small village. It's 15 minutes from Tiffin University and Seneca Caverns; 30 minutes from Lake Erie and Cedar Point.

The Country Club Inn

Barbara Ann and Norman Oliver
5170 Lewiston Road
Lewiston, NY 14092
(716) 285-4869; FAX (716) 285-4869

At the Country Club Inn, breakfast is served at our guests' convenience. As you awaken to your new surroundings, the smell of fresh brewed coffee will greet you. Juice and fruit begin your full breakfast in the elegant semi-circular dining room, overlooking one of several bird feeders on the property. Before leaving for sightseeing or shopping, you may enjoy your extra cup of coffee on the patio overlooking the golf course.

Date and Nut Muffins

1 1/2 cups flour
1 cup wheat bran
1/2 cup brown sugar
1 tablespoon baking powder
1/2 teaspoon salt
1/4 teaspoon cinnamon
1 cup pitted dates, chopped
1/2 cup walnuts or pecans, chopped
1 egg
1 1/2 cups milk
1/3 cup butter, melted
3 tablespoon molasses or honey
12 walnut or pecan halves (optional)

Combine flour with bran, sugar, baking powder, salt and cinnamon. Stir in dates and nuts. In another bowl whisk egg with milk, melted butter and molasses. Stir milk mixture into flour mixture just until combined. Spoon batter into 12 greased or paper lined muffin cups. Place a nut on each muffin if desired. Bake in preheated 400° oven for 20-25 minutes.

Salt can be omitted for low sodium diets, also egg substitute can be used, along with skim milk for a low-fat diet. Individually wrapped these muffins freeze well up to 1 month.

Mandarin Muffins

1 - 11 ounce can Mandarin orange segments
1 tablespoon orange extract
2 cups all-purpose flour
2 teaspoons baking powder
1/2 teaspoon baking soda
1/2 teaspoon salt
1/2 cup brown sugar, packed
1/4 cup sugar
1 egg, well-beaten
18 ounce carton sour cream
1/3 cup shortening, melted

Drain orange segments, reserving liquid. Cut the segments into halves and place in a measuring cup, add orange extract and reserved liquid to make 8 ounces. Set aside.

Combine flour, baking powder, soda, salt and sugars in a large bowl. In a separate bowl, combine egg, sour cream, orange mixture and melted shortening. Make a well in the center of dry ingredients. Add orange mixture and pecans. Stir just until moistened. Spoon into greased or lined muffin pans, filling 2/3 full. Bake in a 400° oven for 20-25 minutes. Makes 1 to 1 1/2 dozen muffins.

Hacienda Vargas Bed and Breakfast Inn

Paul and Julie DeVargas
PO Box 307
1431 El Camino Real
Algodone/Santa Fe, NM 87001
(505) 867-9115; (800) 261-0006;
FAX (505) 687-1902

Our chef is my sister-in-law, Frances Vargas. One day she did not have her regular muffin ingredients and decided to use whatever she had on hand. She found a can of mandarin oranges and the rest is history. For five years our guests have asked over and over for this muffin recipe. Now we are famous for it. We had a guest from Austria that told all her friends and now we have a good percentage of our business from Europe

Oakwood House Bed and Breakfast

Robert and Judy Hotcakiss
951 Edgewood Avenue NE
Atlanta, GA 30307
(404) 521-9320; FAX (404) 688-6034

We generally serve muffins in a basket wrapped in fresh linens. If serving these, be sure you don't use perfect linens (oil and chocolate can ruin them). For ones with powdered sugar, a simple silver tray looks elegant. We believe in offering the best home style hospitality. These muffins are straight forward and great—like us.

Judy's Double Chocolate Muffins

1 1/2 cups all purpose flour
1/4 teaspoon salt
3 teaspoons baking powder
3/4 cup milk
1/2 cup mini or semisweet chocolate chips
powdered sugar, optional
1/2 cup powdered cocoa
1/3 cup + 2 tablespoons sugar
2 eggs
1 teaspoon vanilla
1 teaspoon almond extract
4 tablespoons margarine or butter

Melt butter with sugar in bowl to cream together (use microwave). Sift together flour, cocoa, salt and baking powder. Put eggs in with sugar/butter and mix well. Add extracts, sift in dry ingredients then fold in milk. Stir until well-mixed. Stir in chips.

Grease muffin pans with spray product. Bake at 425° about 15-20 minutes, or until a toothpick comes out clean. Serve with sifted powdered sugar on top or pats of butter on the side.

Pecan Mini Muffins

1 cup light brown sugar
1/3 cup all purpose flour
1 pinch of salt
1 cup chopped pecans
2 eggs
1/2 teaspoon vanilla

Mix by hand just until moist. Oil or spray muffin pans generously. Bake at 350° for 20 minutes. Remove from pans immediately. Makes 24 mini muffins.

Miss Betty's Bed and Breakfast Inn

Betty and Fred Spitz
600 West Nash Street
Wilson, NC 27893-3045
(919) 243-4447; (800) 258-2058

Once known as the "City of Trees" with its giant evergreens towering over Nash Street, the main street in town, Wilson, North Carolina, also includes in its repertoire of trees numerous pecan trees, particularly the large Stewart variety. These plentiful hometown pecans serve as the basis of the locally derived "Pecan Mini Muffins," a favorite at "Miss Betty's."

Arbor Rose Bed and Breakfast

Christina Alsop
8 Yale Hill Road
Stockbridge, MA 01262
(413) 298-4744

We had some return guests checking in and all in the same breath requesting our corn muffins for breakfast the next day. It wasn't until the next morning that I realized we were out of the frozen corn I usually ground up in the meat grinder to make them so nice and moist. It was mid August and our organic garden had been pumping out produce at a pace we could hardly consume, so among the other odd fruits and vegetables bursting the seams of the ice box were some mighty fine looking specimens of summer squash. They were yellow, after all. So I added a handsome amount of squash to the muffin batter and those corn muffins came out better than ever.

Summer Corn Muffins

Combine (#1):

- 1 cup unbleached flour
- 1 cup whole wheat flour
- 2 cups corn flour
- 1 teaspoon baking powder
- 1 1/2 teaspoons baking soda
- shake salt
- 2/3 cups sugar

Combine (#2):

- 2 eggs
- 2/3 cup vegetable oil
- 2/3 cup yogurt
- 2/3 cup buttermilk
- 2 cups grated summer squash

Combine #1 and #2 and bake in 325° oven in greased tins until just firm on top. Rest five minutes before popping from tins. Serve with butter and raspberry jam.

Raspberry Corn Muffins

1 cup yellow cornmeal
1 cup all-purpose flour
1/2 cup sugar
1 teaspoon baking powder
1 teaspoon baking soda
1/4 teaspoon salt
2 large eggs
1 1/4 cups plain yogurt
1/2 stick (1/4 cup) unsalted butter, melted and cooled
1 cup fresh raspberries

Preheat oven to 375°. Butter 12 muffin cups. In a bowl, whisk together the cornmeal, flour, sugar, baking powder, baking soda and salt. In another bowl whisk together the eggs, yogurt, and butter; add to flour mixture and stir the batter until it is just combined. Fold in the raspberries gently, divide the batter among the muffin cups and bake in the middle of the oven for 20 minutes or until a tester comes out clean. Let the muffins cool in the cups on a rack for three minutes. Turn out on a rack and serve.

Bayview Hotel A Country Inn

Gwen Burkard
8041 Soquel Drive
Old Aptos Station, CA 95003
(408) 688-8654
(800) 4-BAYVIEW
FAX (408) 688-5128
Internet: http://BlueSpruce.com.

The Bayview Hotel is proud to be the oldest operating inn on the Monterey Bay. This elegant Victorian-Italianate structure was built in 1878 by Joseph Arano who imported fine furniture for his "grand hotel." All rooms have private baths, some have fireplaces and extra-large soaking tubs. Some of the original furniture is still at the Inn. One of the Bayview's contemporary amenities is the Bayview Grill and Bar which serves breakfast to inn guests as well as lunch and dinner.

Bee Hive Bed and Breakfast

Herb and Treva Swarm
Box 1191
Middlebury, IN 46540
(219) 825-5023; FAX (219) 825-5023

Enjoy a family setting in the country. Treva has decorated the Bee Hive with interesting collectibles and primitives including original paintings by Miss Emma Schrock. Herb collects antique farm machinery. Ask to see his "Old Baker" tractor. After the farm chores are done, Herb may be coaxed to play his diatonic accordion for a sing-a-long.

We serve these muffins every morning. Our guests enjoy the hearty country breakfast. Many of our guests return for the breakfast.

Refrigerator Bran Muffins

Combine in a large bowl:

- 1 - 10 ounce package raisin bran cereal
- 5 cups flour
- 5 teaspoons soda
- 2 teaspoons salt
- 3 cups sugar

Add:

- 1 quart buttermilk
- 1 cup vegetable oil
- 4 eggs, beaten

Mix until all ingredients are moistened. Fill muffin tins 3/4 full and bake at 350° for 15-20 minutes. Store in covered container in refrigerator.

Bran Muffins

Mix together:

1 cup sour cream or yogurt
1 cup (scant) maple syrup
2 eggs

Mix together and add to above:

1 3/4 cup flour
2 teaspoons baking powder
1 cup bran
1/8 teaspoon salt

Stir in 1/3 cup raisins and/or 1/3 cup nuts gently. Bake in greased muffin tins at 400° for 20 minutes.

Ski Inn

Mrs. Larry Heyer
Route 108
Stowe, VT 05672
(802) 253-4050

The story behind the muffin recipe is the story of satisfied customers. Many of our guests bought and enjoyed these muffins at our local health food store "Food for Thought." They persuaded me to ask the owner, Suzanne Smith, for the recipe so I could serve the muffins here for breakfast or dinner.

El Presidio Bed and Breakfast Inn

Patti Toci
297 North Main Avenue
Tucson, AZ 85701
(520) 623-6151; (800) 349-6151

During the house and garden restoration of the 1980s, I planted a lemon tree in the courtyard. It has become large and productive and I have designed many recipes using my fresh lemons. I often send guests home with bags of lemons which is a first for them to pick themselves.

Lemon Muffins

Mix in a large bowl:

- 1 3/4 cups flour
- 1 cup chopped walnuts
- 1/3 cup sugar
- 2 teaspoons baking powder
- 2 teaspoons grated lemon rind

Mix in small bowl:

- 1/2 teaspoon salt
- 1 egg
- 1/2 cup milk
- 1/3 cup melted butter
- 1/4 cup yogurt

Add to dry mixture. Stir just to blend.

Fill 12 muffin tins; sprinkle with streusel. Bake at 375° for 20 minutes. Drizzle with syrup while still warm.

Streusel Topping

Mix until crumbly:

- 3 tablespoons each flour, sugar, and wheat germ
- 2 tablespoons soft butter
- 2 teaspoons grated lemon rind

Lemon Syrup

Boil together:

- 1/3 cup sugar
- 1/3 cup lemon juice

Six-Week Muffins

15 ounces bran cereal with raisins
3 cups sugar
5 cups flour
5 teaspoons baking soda
2 teaspoons salt
4 eggs, or Egg Beaters
1 quart buttermilk
1 cup oil
1 large orange, rind grated to use juice

Combine cereal, sugar, and flour, sifted with soda and salt in a large bowl. Add mixture of eggs, buttermilk, oil, orange juice, orange rind and juice. Mix well. Fill muffin tins 2/3 full or use paper lined muffin/cupcake holders. Store in refrigerator and take out only what you need each morning, baking just the right amount for the guests present. Bake 15 minutes at 400°. Makes about 6 dozen.

This is a low-fat, moist muffin. You may add nuts, fresh chopped apple or any other fruit on hand to vary the flavor.

Doll House Inn and Historical Bed and Breakfast

Barbara and Joe Gerovac
709 E. Ludington Avenue
Ludington, MI 49431
(616) 843-2286; (800) 275-4616

Our Six-Week Muffin recipe came to us through a family friend who knew we were very interested in eating healthy. Our inn serves a full, healthy and tasteful breakfast which we emphasize is good for your heart and body. When the quiet season is upon us, we can always serve the fresh muffins for two or four guests and it's prepared on hand to pop in the oven freshly baked in the morning. Or it's very handy to serve guests with tea in the afternoon as well. We prepare special needs diets for our guests as they request. Breakfast with us is an event, not just an afterthought!

King George IV Inn and Guests

Debbie, Mike, and BJ
32 George Street
Charleston, SC 29401
(803) 723-9339

Step into the past and feel the history of Charleston around you. The King George Inn is a 200-year-old (circa 1790s) "Charleston Historic House" located in the heart of the historic district.

Jelly "Donut" Muffins

2 tablespoons shortening
1/2 cup sugar
1 egg
2 cups flour
3 teaspoons baking powder
1/2 teaspoon salt
1/2 teaspoon cinnamon
1/2 cup milk
1/4 cup jelly
1 cup chopped nuts or pecans
melted butter

Cream shortening and sugar. Add egg and beat. Add remaining dry ingredients alternately with milk. Spray muffin pans, fill 1/2 full. Place a spoon of jelly on each, then top with more batter. Brush with butter, then sprinkle nuts and more cinnamon on top. Bake at 400° for 20-25 minutes or so.

Little Cheese Hots

- 1/2 cup water
- 1/4 cup butter
- 1/16 teaspoon cayenne
- 1/2 teaspoon vegetable seasoning salt
- 1 tablespoon dried parsley
- 1/2 cup flour
- 2 large eggs
- 12 pieces sharp cheddar cheese (1/4x 1/2 inch)

Boil water and butter until butter melts. Add flour all at once. Beat with a spoon until mixture leaves the sides of the pan. Remove from heat. Beat in eggs, one at a time. Beat in cayenne, vegetable seasoning salt, parsley. Spoon dough onto a greased 12x15 inches baking sheet, making 12 mounds. Place a piece of cheese inside each mound being sure to cover the cheese completely. Bake at 425° for 12 minutes. Reduce heat to 375° for another 12 minutes, or until golden brown. Serve warm. Yields 12 cheese puffs.

These cheese puffs are fun to eat and attractive to serve. Placed on a salad plate next to the salad, eyes light up. At breakfast time, these puffs go nicely with fresh or cooked fruit or with sausage and eggs.

Hannah Marie Country Inn

Mary Nichols
4070 Highway 71
Spencer, Iowa 51301
(712) 262-1286; (800) 972-1286;
FAX (712) 262-3294

Through the years of innkeeping we have seen the enjoyment of couples having a truly good time together. Many couples tell us of their whirlwind days and how good it is to be refreshed in a rural setting.

To add more choice as to when and where our guests eat their evening refreshment, we've created a snacking plate. This replaces our all-sit-down, and eat-together dessert. As delicious as those evening desserts were, the snacking plate is far more popular.

This plate usually includes fruits dipped in chocolate, crackers and cheese. Our Little Cheese Hots are a unique way to add cheese to any snacking plate. Larger Little Cheese Hots appear with our salads at our small bistro. Everyone loves them.

Lone Cone Elk Ranch Bed and Breakfast

Bob and Sharon Hardman
PO Box 220
Norwood, CO 81423
(970) 327-4300

The year-round Elk Ranch is located in the small agricultural town of Norwood where cattle ranches and farms dot the landscape. The complete downstairs of the two-story home is yours during your stay. It includes two bedrooms, a bathroom with a shower, a spacious living area with a fireplace a private entrance, and a TV in the common area. Our ranch is less that one hour from Telluride Colorado Ski Village.

We serve a country breakfast including sausage and eggs and the following biscuits, which all fit in beautifully with our charming country decor.

Biscuits

2 cups unbleached flour
1/2 teaspoon soda
1 1/2 teaspoons garlic salt
1 1/2 cup grated sharp cheddar cheese
1 1/4 cup buttermilk
1/2 cup butter
3 teaspoons baking powder
1/4 teaspoon cream of tartar

Mix and combine dry ingredients. Cut in butter, add grated cheese. Stir in milk. Dough can be rolled in 1/4 cup flour and cut in rounds or spooned onto greased baking pan. Bake at 400° for 15 minutes or until golden brown.

Pat's Baking Powder Biscuits

Stir together with fork until mixed well:

2 1/2 cups flour
4 teaspoons baking powder
1/2 teaspoon salt

Cut in with pastry blender until mixture resembles cornmeal: 2/3 cup plus 1 tablespoon yellow Crisco. (You cannot overdo this part. Be sure all flour is mixed in with shortening.)

Add 1 cup milk and stir with fork until mixture follows fork around bowl. Do not work dough any more than absolutely necessary at this point or biscuits may be tough. Roll or pat out on pastry cloth to 3/4 inch thick. If you pat instead of roll, use the side of a glass to smooth the tops, then use the same glass to cut out the biscuits. DO NOT OVERWORK BISCUIT DOUGH. Bake on ungreased baking sheet 12-15 minutes at 475° or until lightly browned.

Note: Buttermilk biscuits may be made by adding 1/4 teaspoon soda to dry ingredients and using sour or buttermilk. If you do not have sour milk on hand, add a teaspoon or so of vinegar to regular milk.

Grandpa's Farm Bed and Breakfast

Keith and Pat Lamb
Box 476, HCR1
Lampe, MO 65681
(417) 779-5106; (800) 280-5106

This recipe is adapted from the old flour-sack biscuit recipe common in the Ozarks in the old days. When biscuits were to be made, usually every morning for breakfast and perhaps another meal or two during the day, a well was made in the middle of the flour right in the sack and the biscuits were mixed by hand there. This saved dishwashing but necessitated careful sifting of the flour before making a cake or something else as hard bits of biscuit dough were often left in the flour sack! Rather than have to worry about the hard dough tags, I experimented and came up with the following.

Grandpa tells our guests to get their forks ready to stab these biscuits to hold them on their plates or they're liable to fly right off since they're so light and fluffy.

Harborlight Guest House Bed and Breakfast

Bobby and Anita Gill
332 Live Oak Drive
Cape Carteret, NC 28584
(800) 624-VIEW; FAX and voice
(919) 393-6868

I serve the tea biscuits on a clear 6 inch dessert plate with an orange slice, which has a cherry centered on it. This is my morning sunshine and tea biscuits!

Cinnamon Tea Biscuits

1 - 8 ounce can crescent rolls
2 tablespoons butter, melted
1/3 cup sugar
1/2 teaspoon ground cinnamon

Orange Glaze

1/3 cup powdered sugar
1 tablespoon frozen orange juice concentrate, thawed
1 teaspoon water

Unroll dough on floured wax paper. Press perforations to seal (each square will include 2 crescent rolls). Brush with melted butter. Combine sugar and cinnamon; sprinkle over dough. Roll up dough and cut each roll into 4 biscuits. Place in greased muffin cups. Bake at 375° for 8-10 minutes. Remove from pan. Drizzle with orange glaze. Makes 16 tea biscuits.

Cedar House English Scones

1 cup self-rising flour
1/8 teaspoon salt
1 tablespoon margarine
2 tablespoons sugar
1 tablespoon raisins
1 egg
1/4 cup milk

Mix flour and salt, cut in margarine. Stir in sugar and raisins. Mix egg and milk together, reserve a little to brush over tops of scones, add rest to above dry ingredients and blend but do not overmix. Fill 6 cup muffin tin with mixture and brush on reserved egg/milk mixture. Bake at 425° for approximately 10 minutes.

The Cedar House Inn

Russ and Nina Thomas
79 Cedar Street
St. Augustine, FL 32084
(904) 829-0079; (800) 233-2746;
FAX (904) 825-0916
Email: russ@aug.com

The Cedar House English Scones are a key element in our "St. Augustine Heritage Breakfast" which consists of fresh citrus fruit salad, Spanish egg ensemble, sliced tomatoes and southern fried sweet potatoes. This breakfast suggests the rich cultural diversity of St. Augustine. We converted the original recipe given to us by English friends, from English weights to American measurements and methods. One English travel writer who was a guest at the inn declared that the Cedar House English Scones were better than any he'd ever had in England!

Captain Dexter House of Edgartown

Carl and Denise
35 Pease's Point Way
PO Box 2798
Edgartown, MA 02539
(508) 627-7289; FAX (508) 627-3328

These scones are best served warm, fresh out of the oven. Scones are a welcome change from the homemade muffins and breads served most mornings. A wonderful aroma wafts up the stairs, to gently awaken guests. Scones are traditionally English and very reminiscent of a by-gone era.

Scones

2 cups all-purpose flour
2 tablespoons sugar
1/2 teaspoon salt
1/4 teaspoon baking soda
1 teaspoon baking powder
6 tablespoons butter or margarine
1/2 cup "filler" of dried currents or raisins or cranberries or chocolate chips
1/2 cup buttermilk
2 eggs

Preheat oven to 425°. In a large bowl, combine flour, sugar, baking powder, salt, and baking soda. Using a pastry blender, or two knives scissor fashion, cut in the butter until the mixture resembles coarse crumbs.

Stir in your choice of "filler" until well mixed. In a small bowl, combine the buttermilk and eggs. Add this to the dry ingredients and stir to form a soft dough. With floured hands, knead gently and briefly to combine. Divide dough in half.

On an ungreased cookie sheet, pat each piece of dough into a 6 inch round. Cut each round into 6 pieces. DO NOT separate. Bake until golden brown, about 12-15 minutes. Separate wedges and serve warm. Yields 12 scones.

The Campbell House Scones

- 3 cups all-purpose flour
- 1/3 cup sugar
- 2 1/2 teaspoons baking powder
- 1/2 teaspoon baking soda
- 3/4 teaspoon salt
- 3/4 cup firm butter (1 1/2 sticks) cut into small pieces
- 3/4 cup chopped dried fruit or nuts
- 1 teaspoon grated orange peel (optional)
- 1 cup milk

Mix first five ingredients. Cut in butter. Stir in fruit, nuts, and/or orange peel. Make a well in center of mixture; add milk all at once. With fork, stir until dough pulls away from the bowl. Gather dough into ball; turn onto a lightly floured board. Divide dough into four parts and pat each part into a circle. Cut each circle into four parts and place on a greased cookie sheet. Sprinkle with cinnamon-sugar (optional). Bake at 400° for 12 minutes. Makes 16 scones. Serve warm. Enjoy!

The Campbell House, A City Inn

Myra Plant
252 Pearl Street
Eugene, OR 97401
(541) 343-1119; (800) 264-2519;
FAX (541) 343-2258

Splendor and romance in the tradition of a fine European hotel. Each of the elegant rooms feature private bath, TV/VCR, telephone, and robes. Selected rooms feature a four-poster bed, fireplace, and jetted or clawfoot tub. Take pleasure from the Old World ambiance of the parlor and library with a fine selection of books and videos to choose from. Walking distance to restaurants, theaters, museums, and shops. Two blocks from nine miles of riverside bike paths and jogging trails.

Fairhaven Inn

Susie and Dave Reed
RR 2, Box 85, North Bath Road
Bath, ME 04530
(207) 443-4391

This recipe came from Roland Messiner, the White House Pastry Chef. At our pastry shop, Sweet Surrender, we refined it and the Washington Post *declared them "the best in Washington" in 1993.*

Scones

2 cups all-purpose flour
1/4 cup powdered sugar
1 1/2 tablespoons baking powder
1/4 teaspoons salt
1/4 pound cold unsalted butter
1 cup heaviest whipping cream you can find
1/2 cup currants

Preheat oven to 375°. Combine flour, sugar, baking powder, and salt. Cut in the butter until the pieces are no larger than the tip of your little finger. Add the currants. Add the cream and mix until blended. Knead gently on a well floured surface. Roll to about 3/8" and cut out with a glass or biscuit cutter. You can mix this all by hand or with a heavy-duty mixer like a Kitchen Aide, but it doesn't work well in the Cuisinart. Bake for 10 minutes, turn and finish for 5-8 minutes until nicely browned. If you find that the scones are not rising properly, check your oven temperature. Too hot is better than too cool.

I sometimes use diced dried apricots and a little nutmeg. The scones tend to flatten out but they taste great. Any dried fruit will work. Fresh apple is good too. Sprinkle a little cinnamon sugar on top before cooking.

If you want to try savory, cut the sugar back a little. Fresh rosemary is out of this world. Sun-dried tomatoes with fresh basil is good too.

Tea Scones

- 2 cups flour
- 2 tablespoons sugar
- 3 teaspoons baking powder
- 1/2 teaspoon salt
- 1/3 cup butter
- 1 egg beaten
- 3/4 cup milk

Sift dry ingredients. Cut in butter until size of coarse cornmeal. Add egg and about 3/4 of the milk. Stir quickly until no flour shows. Add more milk if necessary. Knead gently about 15 times on floured surface. Shape into 2 balls. Press each ball into a round about 1/2 inch thick. Cut each round into 8 pie-shaped pieces. Bake on cookie sheet lined with parchment. Bake at 425° for about 12 minutes.

This basic scone adapts well to adding currants or any other dried fruit. One tasty variation is to press a pineapple chunk and a mandarin orange segment into the top of each scone before baking. These taste great with a spread of equal parts cream cheese and whipped cream or whipped topping. A compliment to any meal or tea.

Thorn's Cottage Bed and Breakfast

Larry and Beth Thorn
RD #1, Box 254 Seaton Road
Stahlstown, PA 15687
(412) 593-6429

A short drive through Rolling Rock Farms and the town of Ligonier is very much like rural England on Ireland. What would breakfast be in this setting without scones? A family favorite for over 20 years, Tea Scones compliment any meal, require no special ingredients and adapt well to additions of fruit or flavorings.

Greenville Inn

Elfi, Michael and Susie Schnetzer
PO Box 1194 Norris Street
Greenville, ME 04441
(888) 695-6000; FAX and voice
(207) 695-2206

Our scones are excellent served with tea and accompanied by strawberry jam and whipped cream. The flaky inside is enhanced by the crispy outside and the delicate aroma of orange-scented scones wafts throughout the inn.

Scones

1 3/4 cup all-purpose flour
2 teaspoons baking powder
1/2 teaspoon salt
1 tablespoon sugar
2 teaspoons grated orange zest
8 tablespoons cold unsalted butter
3/4 cup buttermilk
2 tablespoons sugar

Preheat oven to 400°. Combine the flour, baking powder, salt, sugar and orange zest. Cut butter into flour mixture with pastry knife or fingers. Butter chunks should remain about 1/4 inch in size. Stir in 2/3 cup buttermilk until just absorbed. Shape dough into a ball and pat into a 7 inch diameter disk. Cut disk into eighths and place on a baking sheet lined with parchment paper. Brush tops with remaining buttermilk and sprinkle with sugar. Bake for 15-20 minutes.

English Breakfast Scones

1 1/2 cups all-purpose flour
1/2 cup currants or raisins
1 teaspoon baking powder
1/2 teaspoon salt
1/2 teaspoon baking soda
1 cup cheddar cheese, grated
3/4 cup buttermilk or sour milk
2 tablespoons olive oil (or any kind)
1 egg

Heat oven to 375°. Spray round pan (9 inch diameter) with nonstick cooking spray. Mix flour, raisins, baking powder, salt and baking soda in large bowl. Stir in remaining ingredients. Spread in pan. Bake 30 minutes or until golden brown. Cool 10 minutes before cutting. Drizzle confectioners' sugar and milk glaze over top after cooled. Serve warm. 12 wedges.

The Country Victorian Bed and Breakfast

Mark and Becky Potterbaum
435 South Main Street
Middlebury, IN 46540
(219) 825-2568

The basis for this recipe was discovered in one of my "health-conscious" cookbooks. It was called Cheese Currant Wedges or something unimaginative like that. I made up a batch (substituting, changing and experimenting — as usual before even trying it the real *way first . . .). They were wonderfully flaky and tender and so easy and quick that I thought they'd work out great as a new breakfast item. I served them several times and upon being asked for the recipe I, of course, had to come up with an elegant and fitting name . . . .*

Breakfast is always served on my grandmother's china in the dining room. Our guests have a wonderful view of our quaint little town in the middle of Indiana's Amish Country.

1909 Heritage House at Berwyn

Meriam and Dale Thomas
PO Box 196, 101 Curran
Berwyn, NE 68819
(308) 935-1136

A warm welcome awaits guests to our lovely three-story Victorian/Country home with air-conditioned rooms. Heritage House is located in Central Nebraska, on Highway 2, which is one of the most scenic highways in America. A country breakfast is served in an elegant dining room, country kitchen, sunroom, or Garden Room. Guests relax in a therapy spa and visit the country chapel and gift shop in Heritage House Park.

Almond Toast

2 tablespoons unsalted butter (for pans)
6 large eggs
1 cup sugar
1/2 cup vegetable oil
1/2 teaspoon vanilla extract
1 lemon, juice and rind
3 cups all-purpose flour
3 teaspoons baking powder
3/4 cups almonds, shelled
pinch of salt
cinnamon to taste

Preheat oven to 350°. With the butter, grease two 8x4 inch loaf pans. In a large mixing bowl, beat eggs lightly. Fold in the sugar, oil, and vanilla. Add lemon juice and grate the rind into mixture. Add flour, baking powder, almonds, and salt, stirring well. Pour mixture into pans and bake 45 minutes. Remove from oven. When cool, slice the loaves and sprinkle the slices with cinnamon. Makes 10-12 servings.

House in the Woods Anise Toast

2 eggs
2/3 cup sugar
1 cup flour
2 teaspoons anise seed
butter or margarine

Beat eggs and sugar together until lemon yellow. Add flour and anise seed. Bake 20 minutes at 375° or until toothpick tester is clean. Slice in 1/2 inch slices. Spread lightly with softened margarine or butter. Bake at 350° for five minutes. Turn over and bake five minutes longer.

Kjaer's House in the Woods

George and Eunice Kjaer
814 Lorane Highway
Eugene, OR 97405
(541) 343-3234

This recipe has been a hit both for breakfast with our fruit course and also with tea, hot or iced when guests check in during the afternoon. It can be doubled and freezes nicely. It's a versatile recipe and has "saved" me several times when drop-in guests have appeared.

Berrywick II

Helen and Jack Weber
RD 2 Box 486
Cooperstown, NY 13326
(607) 547-2052

After winning a cruise to Bermuda on a St. Patrick's Day Church raffle, this Irish Soda Bread became my personal thanks to the Irish. Everyone has always enjoyed it. I originally received the recipe from a Polish girl and I am of German descent. It's a small wonderful world — thank God and thank the Irish!!

Irish Soda Bread

3 cups all-purpose flour
1/2 cup sugar
2 teaspoons caraway seeds
1 teaspoon baking powder
1/2 teaspoon baking soda
2 eggs
1/2 sugar
1/2 pint sour cream
1/2 cup milk
1/2 cup raisins

Stir dry ingredients in large bowl. Beat eggs well in mixer. Add and beat in sugar. Add sour cream, milk; blend well. Add raisins and stir to moisten. Mix wet ingredients into dry ingredients. Mix to blend well with spoon. Put in baking bowls. Complete recipe fits in one 8 inch pie plate which bakes for 1 hour. I usually make 3-4 loaves using 1 to 1 1/2 quart bowls lightly greased. Bakes at 350° for 45-60 minutes depending on bowl size. Test for doneness with toothpick. Serve warm with butter.

Irish Bread

- 4 cups flour
- 4 teaspoons baking powder
- 1 cup sugar
- 1/2 teaspoon salt
- 2 eggs
- 1/2 cup butter
- 1 cup milk
- 1 cup raisins

Preheat oven to 350°. Sift the flour, baking powder, sugar, and salt together. Cut in butter with a pastry cutter, then add eggs slightly beaten and the milk. Place mixture into a greased loaf pan. Bake for one hour. Remove bread and let cool for one hour. Yields approximately 10 slices.

The Inn at Crystal Lake

Richard and Janice Octeau
Route 153, PO Box 12
Eaton Center, NH 03832
(603) 447-2120; (800) 343-7336;
FAX (603) 447-3599

Most people have fond memories of Mother cooking that special something in her kitchen; something that nobody else could do quite like Mom. It was her secret recipe and it was made with love. Such is the case with this recipe. As a little girl of Irish descent, I remember Momma making her Irish Bread. The aroma of the bread baking permeated the house as I waited with anticipation for it to come out of the oven. I learned that the Irish Bread recipe had been handed down for many, many generations. Momma has long been gone but her recipe and memories of her live on. I wonder what she would say if she knew I was giving her recipe away. I now have my daughter making it and the Irish Bread is served to guests at our inn as they wait for their breakfast to be prepared.

Hibernia Bed and Breakfast

Mrs. Aideen Lydon
747 Helvetia Cr.
Victoria, British Columbia
CANADA V8Y IMI
(604) 658-5519; FAX (604) 658-0588

We ate this bread everyday growing up in Ireland. It still takes pride of place on the breakfast table. The smell of Irish bread is one of nostalgia. I couldn't live without it! I have given this recipe to people from around the world!

Aideen's Irish Soda Bread

4 cups white flour
1 cup wheat germ
2 teaspoons salt
3 teaspoons sugar
2 1/2 cups flour with wheat bran
3 teaspoons baking soda
4 cups buttermilk, approximately

Mix dry ingredients in bowl. Add buttermilk GRADUALLY stirring as you go. Dough should not be too wet but rather like biscuit dough. Bake in two loaf pans at 350° for 10 minutes, then 300° for 15-20 minutes. Bread is done when brown. Do not overcook. Spread a little butter on the hot bread to make a glaze or wrap in clean tea cloth and let cool. It is also delicious served warm from the oven although it dissappears quickly! It also freezes well.

Irish Soda Bread (Farls)

1 1/2 cups flour
1 teaspoon baking soda
1/2 teaspoon salt
1 cup buttermilk

Heat electric griddle to 375°. Mix dry ingredients in medium bowl. Add buttermilk all at once. Stir together with a knife until mixture clings together. Turn out onto floured surface and roll in flour. Pat into 10 inch circle. Cut into four pie shaped wedges. Transfer to hot griddle. Bake until brown and crusty, flip onto other side and bake again until crusty. Serve warm with butter and homemade jam.

Carriage House Bed and Breakfast

Ray and Dorothy Spriggs
1133 Broad Street
Grinnell, IA 50112
(515) 236-7520

These farls make a wonderful breakfast bread. Cut each pie-shaped wedge in half and then slice each piece horizontally in half. Spread butter and jam on the cut surface. This is an authentic Irish bread made in the north of Ireland. It differs from many soda bread recipes which are baked in the oven. Originally this would have been baked on a griddle on a crock over an open peat fire.

Harborside House

Susan Livingston
23 Gregory Street
Marblehead, MA 01945
(617) 631-1032

Guests often ask for the recipe for this delicious and unusual breakfast bread. It is easy to make and freezes well. The almond flavor is enticing when the loaf is warmed before serving. For the most healthful version, skim milk and egg substitute may be used.

Morning Muesli Bread

1 cup sugar
3/4 cup milk
1/3 cup safflower oil
2 large eggs
1/2 teaspoon almond extract
2 cups Ralston Muesli cereal, crushed
2 teaspoons baking powder
1/2 teaspoon salt
1 1/2 cups flour

Preheat oven to 350°. Grease 9x5x3 inch pan (or two small). Crush cereal in blender or Cuisinart to equal 1 1/3 cups. Reserve 1/3 cup. Combine sugar, milk, eggs, oil, and almond extract in small bowl. Combine flour, cereal, baking powder and salt in large bowl. Add sugar mixture to flour mixture. Pour into pan and press reserved cereal on top. Bake 50-60 minutes. Cool 10 minutes and turn out on wire rack. Serves six.

Blessed Beginnings

Appetizers

". . . Every man should eat and drink, and enjoy the good of all his labour, it is the gift of God."

Ecclesiastes 3:13

Thomas Mott Homestead Bed and Breakfast

Patrick J. Schallert, Sr.
Route 2, Box 149-B
(Blue Rock Road on Lake Champlain)
Alburg, VT 05440-9620
(802) 796-3736 (voice and FAX);
(800) 348-0843

In the large cities celery root can be found in selective produce departments. In highly rural areas it must be sought. (The root will keep three to four weeks in the refrigerator.) But if you find it and serve it at your small inn, guests, in turn, will seek you out.

Celery Root

Quarter, trim, and peel one celery root. Boil in salted water almost to cover until fork tender — watch carefully! Cook and dice while warm (save cooking water).

Sauce:

- 1/3 cup mayonnaise
- dash of sugar
- dash of pepper
- 1 diced green onion
- 1/2 teaspoon green bell pepper, finely chopped
- 3 tablespoon red wine vinegar

Mix mayonnaise with sugar and pepper. Add onion, green pepper, and vinegar and stir until creamy. Combine sauce with celery root using the cooking water to thin if necessary.

Cool overnight or longer in the refrigerator. Serve using toothpicks.

Olive Cream Cheese Spread

8 ounces Philadelphia cream cheese
1 onion, grated
3/4 cup olives, sliced
1 tablespoons Durkees Dressing
1 tablespoons mayonnaise

Cream the cheese. Add sliced olives, dressing, mayonnaise, onion, and the juice from the grated onion. Stir all together. Chill.

Spread on crackers or bread cubes. Makes a great in-between-meals snack, and guests love it.

1857's Bed and Breakfast

Deborah Bohnert
127 Market House Square
Mail: PO Box 7771
Paducah, KY 42002-7771
(502) 444-3960; (800) 264-5607;
FAX (502) 444-3960

My grandmother Camilla is always there for me and stays at the bed and breakfast when I have to be out of town. She makes the guests' muffins and dips. She is also acts as tour guide for our guests. The following is Grandmother Camilla's recipe.

The Captain Lord Mansion

Bev Davis/Rick Litchfield
PO Box 800
Kennebunkport, ME 04046
(207) 967-3141; FAX (207) 967-3172

Christians, as well as gracious hosts and innkeepers, Bev Davis, husband Rick Litchfield, and their friendly, helpful staff are eager to make your visit enjoyable. The Captain Lord Mansion is an intimate and stylish inn situated at the head of a large village green, overlooking the Kennebunk River. Built during the War of 1812 as an elegant, private residence, it is now listed on the National Historic Register. Family-style breakfasts are served in an atmospheric, country kitchen.

Bacon-Wrapped Water Chestnuts

2 cans whole water chestnuts
1 pound trimmed bacon
1/2 cup soy sauce
3 tablespoons brown sugar, packed
toothpicks

Cut bacon long enough to just go around chestnuts and fasten with toothpick. Place in a container to accommodate the number you are making. Mix sugar and soy sauce until sugar is dissolved. Pour over chestnuts. With baster, drench each chestnut with the sauce. Place in refrigerator for 6-24 hours, basting periodically. Just prior to serving, place on broiler pan and broil 10 minutes or until bacon is crisp. Make sure toothpicks are not too close to heat. Serve immediately.

Brie en Croute

6 inch wheel of Brie
1 sheet of Pepperidge Farm puff pastry
1 egg

Preheat oven to 400°

Remove one sheet of puff pastry from freezer. Save second sheet for other use. Thaw at room temperature for 20 to 30 minutes. Unfold pastry on lightly floured surface. Roll in approximately 12x12 square and place on baking sheet. Place Brie in center of pastry. Bring corners of pastry together over Brie and twist slightly to seal. Be sure Brie is totally sealed in pastry. Brush pastry with egg wash and bake at 400 for 25 to 30 minutes, until pastry is golden. Remove from oven and let cool for 15 minutes before serving.

Serve with crusts of French bread and a glass of your favorite Chardonnay or other preferred wine. Grapes and other fresh fruits go well with this.

We would often have this in my home in Belgium, especially for special parties or holidays.

"An Elegant Victorian Mansion" B&B Experience

Doug and Lily Vieyra
1406 'C' Street
Eureka, CA 95501
(707) 444-3144; FAX (707) 442-5594

To complete the magic of your stay, a delicious full multi-course French-gourmet breakfast awaits you each morning. The inn's innkeeper/chef, Lily, is a native of Belgium, where she trained under family friend and 4-Star Chef, Jacques Debecker in his renowned restaurant, St. Nicolas, which produced the finest French cuisine in the Flanders region. Here, as there, Lily uses only the finest and freshest of ingredients, most of which come from the Inn's own organic gardens and orchard.

"Nothing more illustrates this culinary reinforcement of Belgium culture than does our Brie en Croute. In addition to occasionally serving it at breakfast, we more often serve it during our Victorian "High Tea" afternoon "Check-in" period. And now, we wish to share it with you . . . BON APPETIT!"

Strater Hotel

Roderick E. Barker
699 Main Avenue
Durango, CO 81301
(970) 247-4431; (800) 227-4431;
FAX (970) 259-2208

Strater Hotel has been around since 1887. Authentic Victorian walnut antiques and architecture. Romance and charm. Cable TV, telephones, private baths, jacuzzi, restaurant, and Old West saloon. Located in the heart of the historic downtown shopping and entertainment district. Two blocks from D&SNG RR depot. Free parking. Near historic sites and outdoor activities. Melodrama on site.

Baked Brie en Croute

1 kilo French Brie
1 cup raspberry preserves
1 ounce bleu cheese crumbles
1 ounce toasted pine nuts
1 12 ounce sheet "Pennant" puff pastry (10x 15 inch)
1 large egg
1/2 cup all purpose flour

Mix whole egg with 1/2 cup of water (mix thoroughly). Place Brie on table, spread raspberry over top evenly, sprinkle on bleu cheese crumbles and then toasted pine nuts. Set aside.

Spread flour out on table, place pastry on floured table and roll out (approximately 3 inches larger than Brie). Place Brie in center of pastry, raspberry side down. Cut corners to round off, approximately 2 inches. Egg wash pastry and fold over Brie, overlapping as you wrap. Turn pastry-wrapped Brie over and place on parchment-covered sheet pan and finish egg washing.

Poke 10-12 holes in top of pastry. Refrigerate 2 hours. Preheat oven (convection oven) to 350°. Bake 12-15 minutes or until golden brown. Serve.

Golden Delight Appetizer for Breakfast

12 tablespoons Almond Delight cereal
1/4 banana, cubed
20 golden raisins
12 tablespoons Dannon vanilla yogurt
4 tablespoons honey

Use 4 sherbet glasses to serve in. Put Almond Delight Cereal in bottom of sherbet glasses (3 tablespoons). Put 4 to 5 golden raisins on top of cereal. Put several several pieces of diced banana in each serving glass. Then put three tablespoons of Dannon yogurt on top of banana. Drizzle honey over the yogurt. Serve as an appetizer for breakfast. It is yummy and healthy.

Sugar River Inn Bed and Breakfast

Jack and Ruth Lindberg
304 So. Mill Street
Albany, WI 53502
(608) 862-1248

Our turn-of-the century inn, with many original features, has the charm of yesteryear and Christian fellowship. We are located in a quiet village in southern Wisconsin along the Sugar River. We have spacious lawn, canoeing, and fishing in the backyard. We are minutes away from the bike trail. Comfortable, light, airy rooms await you with queen-size beds, fine linens, afternoon refreshments, and wake up coffee. We are near New Glarus, House on the Rock, Little Norway, and the state capital in Madison. Only two hours from Chicago.

Treasures of Eden

Salads and Vegetables

"And he shall be like a tree planted by the rivers of water, that bringeth forth his fruit in his season; his leaf also shall not wither; and whatsoever he doeth shall prosper."

Psalm 1:3

Laurel Hill Plantation

Jackie and Lee Morrison
PO Box 190, 8913 N. NWC 17
McClellanville, SC 29458
(803) 887-3708

You are cordially invited to indulge in a full country breakfast served in the dining room or perhaps on the porch, to enjoy afternoon refreshments, to crab from the dock, to fish in the fresh water pond, to prop up your feet, to simply soak in the serenity afforded by spectacular scenery and a leisurely lifestyle.

The following is a great salad when fresh fruits are hard to find. It looks beautiful served in a glass compote or bowl. I serve this with a grits casserole, lemonade, breads, and jams.

Fruit Salad

1 - 20 ounce can pineapple tidbits, drained. Can use chunks but cut them in half.
1 - 11 ounce can mandarin oranges, drained
1 - 8 ounce jar maraschino cherries, drained and cut in half
1 small can coconut or 1 cup of packaged variety
1/4 cup chopped pecans
1/4 cup seedless raisins
1 pint sour cream
2 tablespoons granulated sugar (sometimes I use brown sugar for a different flavor)

Mix sour cream and sugar until well-blended. Add fruits and mix well. Chill. Serves 8.

Dabney House Chicken Salad

4 chicken breasts, boiled, deboned and cooled (2 cups meat)
1/2 cup chopped celery
1/2 cup chopped green onions
1 cup seedless red grapes
2 cups uncooked corkscrew pasta
1/2 cup chopped walnuts (optional)

Dressing:
1/3 cup mayonnaise
2 teaspoons lemon juice
1 1/2 cups lemon yogurt

Cook pasta according to package directions (be sure not to overcook!). Chill in cold water. Drain. In a small bowl, mix dressing ingredients thoroughly — set aside. Toss together chicken, celery, onions, grapes, pasta and nuts. Pour dressing over chicken mixture and mix. Chill. Serve on a bed of decorative lettuce. Serves 4.

Dabney House Bed and Breakfast

John and Gwen Hurley
106 South Jones
Granbury, TX 76048
(817) 579-1260; (800) 566-1260

Our Craftsman-style one-story home was built in 1907 by a local banker and is furnished with antiques, hardwood floors, and original woodwork. We prepare a romance dinner (by reservation only). We also offer custom, special occasion baskets in room upon guests' arrival, by advance order only.

I serve this to ladies bridge groups for a light lunch with assorted crackers. It is easy and quick to make! I do not recommend making the night before. This salad is at its best when served fresh!

Sharon's Lakehouse Bed and Breakfast

Sharon and Vince DiMaria
4862 Lakeshore Road
Hamburg, NY 14075
(716) 627-7561

We love sharing our home with guests. Built on the shore of Lake Erie, both guest rooms and sitting room offer a magnificent view of Buffalo city skyline and the Canadian border only fifteen minutes west of the city. Rooms are new and beautifully decorated with waterfront view. All prepared food is gourmet quality style. Many of our guests have enjoyed this salad as a quick lunch or a little snack at different times.

Fresh Ziti Pasta Salad

3 large ripe tomatoes, chopped
4 large cloves of garlic, chopped
1 small sweet onion, finely chopped
20 fresh basil leaves, cut into strips
1/2 cup extra virgin olive oil
1/4 teaspoon of each: anise seed, fennel seed, oregano, fresh grown black pepper.
1 pound pasta or small shells or Ziti pasta

Cook pasta, drain and cool. Just before cooling pour three tablespoons olive oil over pasta and mix. This will keep the pasta from sticking together. Put balance of oil in a bowl. Mix all ingredients into olive oil. When pasta is cool, pour oil mix over it and mix well. Serve. If desired, sprinkle Italian cheese over prepared pasta.

Spring Festival Salad

1 1/2 cups mixed seasonal greens (romaine, endive, arugula, radicchio)
2 tablespoons dried cranberries
2 tablespoons raisins
2 tablespoon toasted sliced almonds
2 tablespoons Gorgonzola cheese, crumbled
3 large grapefruit sections

Fluff mixed greens on salad plate. Sprinkle next four ingredients on top of the greens. Arrange grapefruit sections in a spiral on top of greens. A fanned strawberry can also be added to the center of the grapefruit wedges for extra pizazz. Serve with salad dressing of your choice. Here at the Inn, we always use a honey-walnut-raspberry vinaigrette, yet more fat-free or low-cal alternatives could be enjoyed. Serves 1 generously.

The Inn at Olde New Berlin

John and Nancy Showers
321 Market Street
New Berlin, PA 17855-0390
(717) 966-0321; FAX (717) 966-9557

Actually, we began in the winter months here by calling this our "Winter Festival Salad." It was so popular we merely changed the name in the spring to make it more seasonal. Guess what — it's summer and you can predict what just might happen!

Little Britain Manor

Fred and Evelyn Crider
20 Brown Road
(Village of Little Britain)
Nottingham, PA 19362
(717) 529-2862

We are a farm B&B surrounded by Amish and Mennonite farms in beautiful southern Lancaster County. Guests relax in our quiet, restful, country home away from noise, busy crowds, and city traffic. They gather in the large farm kitchen to enjoy a full country breakfast and experience the warmth of heartfelt hospitality.

Oven Roasted Vegetables

10 small new potatoes, quartered
1 small chopped onion
1 cup baby carrots

Combine:
1/4 cup oil
1 tablespoon oregano
3 tablespoons lemon juice
3 minced garlic cloves
1 teaspoon pepper
1 teaspoon salt

Combine oil and other listed ingredients. Drizzle over potatoes, onions, and carrots. Bake 20 minutes at 350°. Optional: Add one medium red pepper cut in strips. Bake 10 minutes more (30 minutes total). Wonderful with beef, chicken, or fish entrees.

Marinated Carrots

2-3 pounds carrots
1 medium green pepper (sliced thin)
1 medium onion (sliced thin)
3/4 cup vinegar
1 can tomato soup
1 tablespoon Worcestershire sauce
2/3 cup sugar
1/2 cup oil
1 tablespoon Dijon mustard
1/2 teaspoon salt

Peel carrots and slice on diagonal. Cook for ten minutes or until partially soft. Drain. Add sliced green pepper and onion to hot carrots. Mix together the rest of the ingredients and blend well. Pour over carrots making sure they are covered with sauce. Put in airtight container and put in refrigerator. Will keep up to four weeks in refrigerator. Best if kept in refrigerator for 1-2 days before serving.

Inn St. Gemme Beauvais

Janet Joggerst
78 North Main Street
Sainte Genevieve, MO 63670
(573) 883-5744; (800) 818-5744;
FAX (573) 883-3899

Jacuzzis, hors d'oeuvres, and private suites filled with antiques only begin the pampering stay in Missouri's oldest, continually operating bed and breakfast. The romantic dining room, complete with working fireplace, is the perfect setting for an intimate breakfast.

This dish makes a beautiful luncheon plate. The color is outstanding. Serving them chilled is amazing and guests are very surprised.

Silver Wood Bed and Breakfast

Larry and Bess Oliver
463 County Road 512
Divide, CO 80814
(719) 687-6784; (800) 753-5592
Email: silver1007@aol.com

Breakfast is served at 8:30 to our guests and is a leisurely, social occasion with a hearty entree, fresh seasonal fruit and an abundance of homemade muffins or sweet breads. Our guests are then ready for a day of hiking our trails or visiting the many attractions of the Pikes Peak/Colorado Springs area.

Creamy Asparagus Casserole

8 eggs
3/4 cup milk or cream
1/2 cup chopped onion
3/4 cup ham cubes (optional)
8 ounce cream cheese, cubed
8 mushrooms
12 asparagus spears (canned works best)
Mrs. Dash

Spray four individual casseroles with PAM. Layer three asparagus spears, two sliced mushrooms, chopped onion, cream cheese cubes, and ham. Sprinkle with Mrs. Dash. Beat eggs, add milk. Pour over vegetables in casseroles to almost cover. Bake at 350° for 10 minutes. Stir edges into center. Bake 20-25 minutes more until golden and puffy. Serve at once on warm plates.

I use oblong Corning Ware casserole dishes so that the whole asparagus spears fit well. This casserole is very good without the ham for vegetarian guests.

Yellow Squash Casserole

3 pounds fresh or frozen yellow squash, sliced
1 large onion, sliced
2 cups water
1/2 cup butter
15 soda crackers, crushed
1 pound Velveeta, cut into small pieces
1/8 cup sugar
1/2 teaspoon salt
1 teaspoon black pepper

Put squash, onion, and water in pot and cook until tender. Remove from heat; drain well. Add remaining ingredients. Mix well. Pour into greased baking dish. Bake at 325° until lightly golden. Makes 10-12 servings.

Namaste Acres Barn Bed and Breakfast

Bill, Lisa, and Lindsay Winters
5436 Leipers Creek Road
Franklin, TN 37064
(615) 791-0333; FAX (615) 591-0665

Quiet valley setting. Poolside deck and hot tub, hiking, horseback trails. Our country inn offers four theme suites, including the Loft, Bunkhouse, Cabin, and Franklin. In-room coffee, phone, and refrigerator, TV/VCR (movies). Private entrance and bath. Featured in Southern Living, Horse Illustrated, *and* Western Horseman.

I usually serve this casserole with supper or take it as a dish for a potluck. The recipe is from a local restaurant in Historic Franklin.

Vintage Comfort Bed and Breakfast

Helen R. Bartlett
303 Quapaw
Hot Springs, AR 71901
(501) 623-3256; (800) 608-4682

Guests enjoy our comfortably restored Queen Anne house built in 1907. Four spacious rooms are available upstairs, each with private bath, ceiling fan, and period furnishings. We serve a delicious full breakfast each morning in the inn's dining room. Vintage Comfort B&B is known for its comfort and gracious southern hospitality.

Baked Mushroom Delight

1/2 pound fresh mushrooms, sliced
2 tablespoons butter
8 strips bacon, fried crisp, drained and crumbled
1/4 teaspoon thyme
3 cups (12 ounce) shredded Monterey Jack cheese
8 eggs, beaten
1/4 teaspoon rosemary
pepper to taste

Preheat oven to 275°. Sauté mushrooms in butter; place on bottom of a well-greased 8 inch square baking dish. Top with bacon and then the cheese. Combine eggs, pepper, thyme and rosemary, pour over layered ingredients. Bake 45 minutes to 1 hour or until center is set and top is golden. Serves 4-6.

To prepare in advance: Assemble up to the point of pouring the egg mixture over the layered ingredients.

Mushroom Business

(Compliments of Carolyn Williams, Valley Forge Mt. B&B.)

1 pound coarsely sliced mushrooms
2 tablespoons butter
6 slices white bread, buttered
1/2 cup each — chopped green pepper, celery, and onion, sautéed
1/2 cup mayonnaise
3/4 teaspoon salt
1/4 teaspoon pepper
2 eggs
1/2 cup milk
1 can mushroom soup
optional: grated cheese

Sauté mushrooms in butter only until they start to smell. Cut bread into 1 inch squares and put into deep 2 1/2 quart casserole. Combine mushrooms with the chopped vegetables. Stir in mayonnaise, salt and pepper. Put Mushroom Business on bread cubes in casserole. Top with 3 more cubed slices white bread. Beat eggs with milk, pour over casserole; refrigerate overnight. Before baking, pour one undiluted can mushroom soup over casserole. Bake at 325° for 1 hour. Optional: sprinkle with grated cheese before serving if desired.

Association of B&B's in Philadelphia, Valley Forge, and Brandywine

Carolyn Williams, coordinator
Box 562
Valley Forge, PA 19481
(610) 783-7838; (800) 344-0123;
FAX (610) 783-7783

There is a B&B for you! — whether business, vacation, getaways, or relocating. Also serving Bucks and Lancaster Counties. Over 500 rooms available in historic city/country inn, town houses, unhosted estate cottages, and suites. Request a free brochure or descriptive directory ($3).

This recipe is like a strata; it is prepared and refrigerated the day before it is baked. The Brandywine Valley is the mushroom capital of the country. Excellent served with poultry in lieu of stuffing a hen or turkey; as a breakfast side dish with ham or pork sausage.

Hearthside Bed and Breakfast

Don and Lu Klussendorf
2136 Tanbe Road
Sturgeon Bay, WI 54235
(414) 746-2136

Our 1800s farmhouse has a blend of contemporary and antique furnishings. The old barn still stands nearby. Within easy driving distance are fantastic state parks, beaches for swimming in summer, or areas for skiing in the winter. Lighthouses, U.S. Coast Guard Station, lake cruises, airport, ship building, and weekend festivals. The rooms are charming; three with queen beds. Our family room has twin beds with an adjoining room that has a double bed. Guests may use TVs, VCRs, living room, and sun room.

Potato Pancakes

3 1/2 tablespoons flour
2 pounds potatoes
3/4 grated onion
1 egg beaten
3/4 teaspoon salt
pepper

Measure flour in bowl. Over flour, grate potatoes with fine grater. Add rest of ingredients. Mix, fry in 1 cup oil. Serve with applesauce, butter, ham, fish, or bacon.

Raised Potato Pancakes

2 packages yeast, dry
1/4 cup luke warm water
2 eggs, beaten
2 cups warm milk
3 tablespoons instant potato flakes
2 1/2 cups sifted flour
1 tablespoon sugar
1 teaspoon salt
2 tablespoons wheat germ or bran
1/4 cup salad oil

Dissolve yeast completely in warm water and set aside. Beat eggs and warm milk together. Then mix with yeast. Add instant potatoes, flour, sugar, salt, and wheat germ or bran. Mix until smooth. Stir in salad oil. Let stand for 1/2 hour or until double in bulk. Fry in greased skillet, serve as for first recipe.

Sumptuous Selections

Soups and Main Dishes

"When thou hast eaten and art full, then thou shalt bless the Lord thy God for the good land which he hath given thee."

Deuteronomy 8:10

The Manor at Taylor's Store B&B Country Inn

Lee and Mary Lynn Tucker
Rt 1 Box 533
Smith Mountain Lake, VA 24184
(540) 721-3951; (800) 722-9984;
FAX (540) 721-5243

When Lee and I first started the bed and breakfast, there were no restaurants in the Smith Mountain Lake area. So, rather than send our guests all the way into Roanoke for dinner, we decided to offer dinner meals as well as breakfast. Our original idea was just to have a simple "hearty soup and crusty bread" waiting for them on arrival, but our adventurous nature quickly led us into offering a full six-course gourmet dinner. However, as our business grew . . . and the lake area grew with new restaurants . . . we decided to concentrate on the bed and breakfast rather than developing a full scale restaurant.

This Virginia Peanut Soup was the traditional second course of our six-course meal. We adapted the recipe from the old Virginia recipe to make it more heart healthy.

Heart Healthy Virginia Peanut Soup

2 ribs of celery, chopped
1 medium onion, chopped
2 tablespoons safflower margarine
2 tablespoons flour
2 cups chicken broth
2 cups skim milk
1 cup peanut butter (natural, freshly ground, without added oil, sugar, salt, or additives) either crunchy or smooth
salt, pepper, paprika

Brown celery and onions in margarine. Add flour and chicken broth and bring to a boil. Add milk and combine well, reduce heat to medium low. Add peanut butter (whisking helps it combine better) and simmer for five minutes.

Ladle the soup into a blender in small batches and blenderize until smooth. Return it to the pan, reheat and season with salt and pepper to taste. Serve sprinkled with paprika. Yields 8 cups or 6-8 servings.

Tomato Soup
with Cognac and Orange

3 tablespoons butter
1 large onion, chopped
1 clove minced garlic
1 1/2 teaspoons dried basil
2 tablespoons honey
1 large can marinara sauce
3 tablespoons cognac
grated zest and juice of 1 orange
1/2 cup heavy whipping cream
1/2 cup sour cream

Melt butter, saute onions and garlic about three minutes. Turn down heat, add basil and honey. Stir. Cook about two minutes, add marinara, cognac, and orange zest and juice. Season to taste. Simmer about twenty minutes. Just before serving, add cream and sour cream. DO NOT BOIL. Can be garnished with toasted seasoned bread crumbs!

Historic Nickerson Inn

Gretchen and Harry Shiparski
262 Lowell, PO Box 986
Pentwater, MI 49449
(616) 869-6731; FAX (616) 869-6151

The Historic Nickerson Inn has been serving guests with "special hospitality" since 1914. Our inn was totally renovated in 1991. All our rooms have private baths and air-conditioning. We have two Jacuzzi suites with fireplaces and balconies overlooking Lake Michigan. Two short blocks to Lake Michigan beach, and three blocks to shopping district. Casual, fine dining in our 80-seat restaurant.

Brass Lantern Inn

Andy Aldrich
717 Maple Street
Stowe, VT 05672
(802) 253-2229; (800) 729-2980;
FAX (802) 253-7425
Email: brasslantern@aol.com

The Inn carries the traditional Vermont bed and breakfast theme throughout — from its decor of period antiques, handmade quilts, and locally crafted amenities to the food and beverages reflecting local and Vermont state products. In addition, guests are treated to a unique ambiance and casual, attentive service. The Inn's setting provides panoramic views of Mt. Mansfield and its valley from nearly every room.

Butternut Squash Soup

2 pounds butternut squash, trimmed, seeded, and cleaned
4 cups water
1 tablespoon salt
1/2 cup diced celery
1/2 cup diced onions
1/2 cup diced green bell peppers
1/4 cup melted butter
1/4 cup white wine
1 teaspoon tarragon leaves
1/2 teaspoon ground cinnamon
1/2 teaspoon ground nutmeg
1/4 teaspoon ground cloves
4 cups chicken stock
1/4 cup all-purpose flour
1/4 cup melted butter
1/2 cup Vermont maple syrup
1/4 cup dry sherry

Add squash to a large pot with salted water, and cook until soft (approximately 40 minutes). Strain out the squash, reserving 2 cups of liquid and discarding the rest. In the large pot, saute the diced vegetables in 1/4 cup butter and wine for 5 minutes. Add the herbs and spices. Add the chicken stock and 1 cup of reserved liquid. Bring to a boil, then thicken with a roux made by mixing the flour with 1/4 cup melted butter. Puree the cooked squash in a blender or food processor with the remaining 1 cup of reserved liquid. Add to the pot and cook on low heat for 5 minutes, stirring often. Add the syrup and sherry. Mix well and serve. Serves 12-16.

Pumpkin Bisque

1 tablespoon butter
1 large onion, diced
3 cups pumpkin puree
6 cups chicken stock
3 tablespoons flour
1/2 teaspoon salt
1/4 cup chopped, fresh parsley
croutons

In a large saucepan, melt butter and saute onion for 4-6 minutes or until golden. Mix pumpkin and chicken stock into saucepan and cook on medium heat for ten minutes. Remove 1 cup liquid and whisk in flour. Return mixture to soup and cook stirring occasionally for 5 minutes. Stir in salt and parsley. Serve immediately with croutons as garnish.

Castle Marne — A Luxury Urban Inn

The Peiker Family
1572 Race Street
Denver, CO 80206
(303) 331-0621; (800) 92-MARNE; FAX (303) 331-0623

A bisque is usually quite rich with cream. This is delicious with not nearly as many calories. It can be served year-round but is especially nice served in the late fall. We always have it on the menu for our Candlelight Dinners around Halloween and Thanksgiving.

Applebrook Bed and Breakfast

Sandra Conley and Martin Kelly
Route 115A
Jefferson, NH 03583-0178
(603) 586-7713; (800) 545-6504

This is one of our most requested soup recipes. We served it to a group of Appalachian Mountain Club bicyclists who visit us often. Now they request it every time they visit our casual bed and breakfast in a large Victorian farmhouse.

Applebrook's Aztec Corn Soup

3 can kernel corn (do not drain) OR for a creamier soup use 4 pound frozen kernel corn
6 cans chicken or vegetable stock
2-3 large tomatoes
1 cup onions, chopped
3 cloves garlic, chopped
1 tablespoon dried oregano
1 can Mexican stewed tomatoes
vegetable cooking spray
1 - 7 ounce can green chilies, chopped
1/2 cup salsa, mild or hot depending on your preference
1 tablespoon cumin powder
1/2 bunch fresh marjoram, chopped, (or 2 tablespoons dried marjoram)

Puree all but one cup of the corn. In large pot combine corn and stock. Bring to a boil. Reduce heat. Simmer covered for 20 minutes. Cut tomatoes in 1/2 inch slices. Place on cookie sheet. Broil until partially blackened. Chop into chunks. Puree onion, garlic, oregano, and stewed tomatoes. Spray pan with PAM, add pureed onion mix, and slowly cook for 20-30 minutes. Add onion mixture, chilies and salsa to corn. Bring to boil. Reduce heat. Simmer 20 minutes. Remove from heat. Add cumin and marjoram. Serve.

Onset Bay Quahog Chowder

Zachariah Eddy House

51 South Main Street
Middleboro, MA 02346
(508) 946-0016

This recipe is the specialty of the house at the Zachariah Eddy House Bed and Breakfast. We usually use the freshest of clams from Onset Bay. The flavor of chowder made with fresh quahogs cannot be duplicated with canned ingredients or bottled broth!

Directions for seafarers:

Take I495 South to Exit #1 and follow signs to Onset Beach! Wait for low tide and then get ready to dig. A good catch should take no more than an hour.

Directions for landlubbers:

At your local fish market or supermarket, buy about two dozen large fresh quahogs (hard-shelled clams) and shuck. Be sure to save all liquid for this is the key to the flavor. The faint of heart can substitute fresh chopped clams in their own juice. You need at least one full quart and even as much as two. The more clams and natural juices, the more flavor.

In large skillet, melt one stick of butter. Add two chopped onions and saute until cooked but not browned. Meanwhile, cut 6-8 potatoes into bite-size pieces for chowder. Cook for 10 minutes in boiling water. Do not overcook or they will fall apart in chowder. Drain immediately and set aside. When onion is cooked, add 1/2 cup of flour and blend in well with wire whisk. Continue cooking for two to three minutes longer. Cut clam meat into small pieces. Strain clam liquid with fine strainer to be sure there are no shells, and pour gradually into butter and flour mixture, stirring constantly. Add the clam pieces and continue to cook over low heat for about 10 more minutes, long enough to cook the clams.

Gradually add one quart of light cream to roux (butter and flour mixture), stirring constantly. Heat through over low heat, being careful not to boil. Add salt, pepper, and parsley to taste, then add the potatoes and serve. Chowder will be thick. If a thinner consistency is desired, add more cream or milk. Although milk will thin more easily than cream, it will curdle if chowder should get by you and come to a boil.

Butcher House in the Mountains

Hugh and Gloria Butcher
1520 Garrett Lane
Gatlinburg, TN 37738
(423) 436-9457

Nestled 2,800 feet above the main entrance to the Smokies, Butcher House in the Mountains offers mountain seclusion as well as convenience. The Swiss-like cedar and stone chalet enjoys one of the most beautiful views in the state. Antiques are tastefully placed throughout the house and a guest kitchen is available for coffee and lavish dessert. European gourmet brunch served.

Chicken Glorious

2 large onions sautéed
12 ounce package fresh mushrooms
1 whole frying chicken, skinned and cut in pieces
1 1/2 cups low-fat mozzarella cheese
Italian seasoning
granulated garlic

Place skinned chicken in a baking dish, add 1/3 cup water. Sprinkle chicken with Italian seasoning and granulated garlic. Bake at 325° for 25 minutes. Turn chicken and repeat process. Sauté onions until soft and transparent. Add washed and sliced mushrooms. Remove chicken from oven, spoon mushroom mixture over it evenly. Sprinkle with 1 1/2 cups of low-fat mozzarella cheese. Return to oven just until cheese is melted. Enjoy! This is a wonderful dish to take to church as a dish to pass. You'll have rave reviews.

The Williamsburg Sampler Ranch Chicken

1 dozen corn tortillas
1 large onion
1 large bell pepper
1/2 pound grated cheese
1 can cream of mushroom soup
1 teaspoon chili powder
1 chicken, boiled and boned
chicken broth
1 can chopped tomatoes
1/2 teaspoon garlic salt

Boil and bone chicken into bite-size pieces. Reserve broth for 10 minutes. Line 13x9 inch pan with softened tortillas. Layer onion, bell pepper, cheese, and soup over tortillas. Sprinkle with chili powder, garlic salt, and tomatoes. Bake at 350° for 30 minutes. Serves 8-10 persons.

Williamsburg Sampler Bed and Breakfast

Helen and Ike Sisane
922 Jamestown Road
Williamsburg, VA 23185
(804) 253-0398; (800) 722-1169

In 1988, while working for the Department of Defense, I was assigned to a position in Worms, Germany. While there I traveled throughout Europe and indulged in eating the local foods. After a year, I just wanted some good old home cooking. One of my German staff overheard me relating this to another member in my office. This wonderful lady gathered with her friends to come up with a meal that would have many of the ingredients I like.

I was invited to her home for dinner thinking that it would be the traditional native meal. To my surprise, all of my staff and their family members were there. At the table they served this wonderful meal that I can taste today. The recipe I have provided you is from memory and tastes close enough to the real thing.

Adams Edgeworth Inn

Wendy and David Adams
Monteagle Assembly
Monteagle, TN 37356
(615) 924-4000; FAX (615) 924-3236

Circa 1896, Adams Edgeworth Inn celebrates 100 years of fine lodging and still is the region's leader in elegance and quality. Recently refurbished in English Manor decor, the Inn is a showcase for fine antiques, important original paintings and sculptures, and a prize-winning rose garden. Five-course, fine dining by candlelight every night. "One of the best inns I've ever visited anywhere . . ." (Sara Pitzer, recommended by "Country Inns" in Country Inns Magazine).

While we are lucky to have fresh, wild mountain blackberries in abundance during the summer, others may have to settle for the frozen or cultivated berries. Either way, the dark purple glaze on these game hens is striking for a family picnic or a formal evening dinner. However, more impressive than its color, is the tart, but savory taste of the meat of these tender birds.

Mountain Blackberry Cornish Game Hens

4 - 18 ounce Cornish Game Hens
1 1/2 cups olive oil
1 cup apple cider vinegar
1/2 cup balsamic vinegar
3 tablespoons fresh or dried thyme
2 tablespoons honey
2 teaspoons salt seasoning
1 1/2 pints fresh or frozen blackberries
string

Preheat oven to 350°. Puree 1 pint of the blackberries in a food processor to a chunky texture. Add 1/2 cup of the olive oil and pulse until slightly emulsified, 1-2 minutes. Pour blackberry puree into a large bowl. Add the hens and remaining ingredients to the bowl. Saving a handful of blackberries for garnishing. Marinate the birds for at least 3 hours, stirring and rearranging occasionally. Truss the hens with baking string. Place birds and half of the marinade in a shallow roasting pan. Place in oven and cook birds for 45 minutes or until the juices run clear, remembering to baste every 10-15 minutes. Serve with garnish with remaining blackberries. Serves 8 lunch portions, or 4 dinner portions.

Buffalo Burgundy

2 1/2 pounds buffalo stew meat
1 can mushroom soup
1 cup burgundy
1 package onion soup mix

Put in covered casserole and bake 3 hours at 300°. Serve over rice. Beef may be substituted if buffalo is unavailable.

Spahn's Bighorn Mountain Bed and Breakfast

Ron and Bobbie Spahn
PO Box 579
Big Horn, WY 82833
(307) 674-8150

Towering log home and secluded guest cabins on the mountainside in Whispering Pines. Adjacent to a million acres of forestland which is home to deer, moose, and eagles. Gracious mountain breakfast served on the deck with binoculars to enjoy the 100 mile view. Owner was a Yellowstone Ranger. Ten minutes from I-90 near Sheridan. Evening cookout and wildlife safari available.

Blue Belle Inn Bed and Breakfast

Sherrie C. Hansen
513 W. 4th Street, PO Box 205
St. Ansgar, IA 50472
(515) 736-2225

We serve Rahm Schnitzel with Heaven and Earth Soup (apples and onions in a light broth spiked with apple brandy), German Potato Salad, homemade spaeztle noodles, red cabbage, and Black Forest Cheesecake. Candlelit, lace-covered tables, heirloom china and festive foodstuffs featuring German, English, French, Italian, Scandinavian, and American theme cuisines provide an unforgettable dining experience for the Blue Belle Inn's overnight guests and local patrons alike.

Rahm Schnitzel

8 pork or veal cutlets (thin sliced or tenderized cuts)
1/4 cup butter
salt and pepper to taste

Gravy:
2 cups beef broth
1 cup sour cream
4 teaspoons beef bouillon granules
1 cup milk or half and half
2 heaping tablespoons cornstarch

Sauté cutlets in butter over medium heat until meat is done and lightly browned on both sides. Sprinkle with salt and pepper.

Whisk gravy ingredients together. Pour into hot frying pan with meat drippings. Whisk until smooth thick and bubbly. Place meat in lightly sprayed roasting pan. Pour gravy over meat, add sautéed mushrooms if desired. Cover and bake at 350° for 1½ hours. Serve over favorite pasta or homemade spaeztle noodles.

Pygmalion Party Plum Meatballs

1 pound ground pork sausage
1 pound ground beef
2 eggs
1/2 cup chopped shallots
2 tablespoons chopped parsley
2 teaspoons salt
2 cups Italian flavored bread crumbs
2 tablespoon margarine

Mix first 7 ingredients; make into meatballs 1 inch in diameter. Brown in margarine.

Sauce:
1 cup Pygmalion House Plum Jam
1/2 cup barbecue sauce

Mix sauce and pour over meatballs. Bake for 30 minutes in 350° oven. (Freezes well.)

Pygmalion House Inn Bed and Breakfast

Caroline
331 Orange Street
Santa Rosa, CA 95401
(707) 526-3407 (voice and FAX)

Our own plum jam is made from our own trees surrounding the house. The trees are nearly as old as the house, about a hundred years old. We can see the plums maturing out of our second floor windows. And this is a tall Victorian! Our jam is on sale here.

Virginia Rose Bed and Breakfast

Jackie and Virginia Buck
317 East Glenwood
Springfield, MO 65804
(417) 883-0693; (800) 345-1412

This two-story farmhouse, built in 1906, offers country hospitality right in town. Situated in a tree-covered acre, our home is furnished with early-twentieth-century antiques, quilts on queen-sized beds, and rockers on the porch.

We use this recipe when we have brunches or lunches. It is something a little different and goes with many food items.

Mexican Lasagna

1 can cream of chicken soup
1 pint sour cream
6 ounce can diced chilies
1 pound grated cheddar cheese
1 package small flour tortillas

Mix first 3 ingredients. Assemble a layers, starting with tortillas on the bottom of a greased 9x13 inch pan and adding soup mixture topped with cheese. Repeat 2 more layers. Bake at 350° for 30 minutes. Cool for 5 minutes. Cut in bite-size pieces for an appetizer or large squares for a main course dish. Serves 8-10. Good hot or cold. May be made ahead of time and refrigerated, then bake as instructed.

Beth's Black Beans and Pita

8 ounces black beans, dried
1 red pepper
1 medium onion
1 teaspoon minced garlic
1/4 teaspoon oregano
3 tablespoons olive oil
1/4 cup red cooking wine
4 cups shredded romaine lettuce
1/4 cup sour cream
1/2 cup salsa
4 pita breads
1 cup mozzarella cheese

Cook black beans according to package directions. Sauté pepper, onion, and garlic in olive oil. Add sautéed vegetables, oregano, and wine to beans. Place beans in four shallow bowls, top with shredded lettuce, salsa, and sour cream. Top pita with mozzarella cheese; melt in oven and cut in four pieces. Arrange around beans. Serve at room temperature.

Womble Inn

Steve and Beth Womble
301 W. Main
Brevard, NC 28712
(704) 884-4770

The Womble Inn invites guests to relax in a welcoming, comfortable atmosphere. Each of our six guest rooms is especially furnished in antiques and decorated to make each guest feel cared for.

We serve breakfast on a silver tray or, if guests prefer, they may be seated in the dining room.

My lunch customers really like this dish. I also use the black beans on a salad of mixed greens with chicken and make it a Mexican salad.

Grafton Inn

Liz and Rudy Cvitan
261 Grand Avenue South
Falmouth Heights (Cape Cod), MA 02540
(508) 540-8688; (800) 642-4069; FAX (508) 540-1861

We serve our Clam Fritters with lobster Newburgh sauce on a bed of Boston lettuce. Fresh fruit compote makes a nice accompaniment. Garnish with a nasturtium flower. Hollandaise sauce may also be used.

Oceanfront, the Grafton Inn faces Nantucket Sound. Cape Cod and clams are synonymous. You can walk 30 steps from our front door and rake your own clams at low tide.

Clam Fritters

8 large shucked clams
1/4 cup clam liquor
1 egg, slightly beaten
3 tablespoons melted butter
3 tablespoons milk
1 cup sifted flour
4 teaspoons baking powder
1/2 teaspoon salt
1/8 teaspoon pepper

Put clams through food processor; add clam liquor, egg, butter, and milk. Mix and sift dry ingredients and add to clam mixture, stirring until smooth. Drop by spoonfuls into hot fat (375°), and cook 2-3 minutes or until golden brown. Drain on unglazed paper. Serves 6.

Haddock De Journée

2 pounds haddock, filet
4 ounces shrimp, chopped fine
4 ounces scallops, chopped fine
2 ounces lobster, chopped fine
pinch of salt and pepper
1/2 ounce (1 tablespoon) lemon juice
1 ounce (2 tablespoons) white wine
1 tablespoon Worcestershire sauce
pinch of thyme
1/2 cup heavy cream

Hollandaise Sauce

1/2 cup melted, warm butter
1 1/2 tablespoons lemon juice or tarragon vinegar
3 egg yolks
4 tablespoons boiling water
1/4 teaspoon salt
pinch of cayenne

Colonial House Inn

Malcolm Perna, Tony Malcolm
277 Main Street, Route 6A
Yarmouth Port, MA 02675
(508) 362-4348; (800) 999-3416;
FAX (508) 362-8034

The Colonial House Inn features traditional New England cuisine with a continental flair. It also features gracious hospitality and old world charm. This registered historical landmark has antique appointed guest rooms, private baths, and air-conditioning.

Combine all ingredients except haddock and heavy cream in a stainless steel mixing bowl. Place bowl over ice. Add cream slowly whipping constantly with wire whisk until mixture is well blended. Butter an ovenproof baking dish. Slit haddock to make a pocket, and stuff with mixture. Place in dish and bake at 350° for 20 minutes or until fish flakes when tested. Before serving top with Hollandaise Sauce. Serves 4.

Sauce: Place egg yolks in double boiler (cook over hot water — NOT boiling water), stirring constantly with wire whisk until they begin to thicken. Add 1 tablespoon boiling water. Repeat until all 4 tablespoons of water have been added. Beat in warm lemon juice. Remove from heat. Add warm melted butter very slowly, beating constantly with wire whisk. Add salt and cayenne. Serve at once. Hint: Can be stored in large-mouth Thermos jar until serving time. Makes 1 cup.

Adams Hilborne

Wendy and David Adams
801 Vine Street
Chattanooga, TN 37403
(423) 265-5000; FAX (423) 265-5555

We offer Old World charm and hospitality in a tree-shaded setting rich with Civil War history and turn-of-the-century architecture. The inn has a rarely seen Victorian Romanesque design with original coffered ceilings, hand-carved oak stairway, beveled glass windows, and ceramic tile embellishments.

This is a favorite dish at brunch at the Repertoire Restaurant and also at dinner at the Cafe Alfresco—light, delicious, and unusual. Hilborne's Lobster Cakes are one of our most popular signature dishes.

Hilborne's Lobster Cakes

with Mustard Sauce

1/2 pound cooked lobster, chopped
3 carrots, chopped
1 large onion, chopped
1/2 cup mayonnaise
1/4 cup honey
1/4 cup Dijon mustard
salt to taste
garlic powder to taste
3-6 cups bread crumbs

Combine all ingredients, adding bread crumbs as needed to bind. Form into little cakes, fry in sauté pan with oil halfway up lobster cake. Test fry one cake first and adjust consistency of cake as needed to hold firm in oil. Serve with mustard sauce.

Mustard Sauce

1 cup favorite mustard
1/2 cup mayonnaise
1/2 cup sour cream
garlic powder to taste
Tabasco to taste

Combine all ingredients. Refrigerate 1-2 hours before serving.

Salmon Stroganoff

4 tablespoons butter
2 tablespoons vegetable oil
1/2 pound fresh mushrooms
salt and white pepper
1/2 cup white wine
1 teaspoon curry powder
2 cups cream
1 pound salmon, boned and skinned
1/4 cup chopped parsley
1 cup thinly sliced onion

Fettuccini with Dill Butter:
4 tablespoons butter
1 tablespoon chopped fresh dill, or 1 teaspoon dried dill
1 pound egg fettuccini

Yukon Don's Bed and Breakfast Inn

Yukon Don and Kristan Tanner
1830 E. Parks Hwy., Suite 386
Wasilla, AK 99654
(907) 376-7472; (800) 478-7472;
FAX (907) 376-6515

We are proud to own "Alaska's most acclaimed B&B inn." Each spacious, comfortable guest room is decorated with authentic Alaskana.

This recipe is one of my favorites from Kristan's collection.

Melt butter with oil in 12 inch skillet or sauté pan. Slice and sauté mushrooms in butter and oil over medium heat about 5 minutes, stirring. Season to taste with salt and pepper. With slotted spoon remove mushrooms to a small bowl. Deglaze pan with white wine and boil rapidly, about 1 minute. Add remaining butter and sliced onion. Cook over medium heat until soft, about 5 minutes, stirring. Remove onions from pan and set aside on small plate. Add curry powder and cook over low heat about 30 seconds. Pour in cream and bring to gentle boil. Reduce volume by half; this will take about 20 minutes. Slice salmon into 1/2" strips and set aside. When cream is reduced, add salmon strips and poach until tender, about 5 minutes. Add mushrooms, onions, parsley and serve immediately over fettuccini.

Fettuccini: In large kettle, bring 4 quarts of water to a boil. In large saucepan, melt butter over low heat. Add dill. Lightly salt water, and cook noodles. Drain noodles in colander and toss in warm dill butter. Turn onto serving platter and top with Salmon Stroganoff.

Carter House Victorians

Mark and Christi Carter
301 L Street
Eureka, CA 95501
(707) 444-8062; (800) 404-1390;
FAX (707) 444-8067

Carter Victorians encompasses three lovely Victorians: the Carter House Inn, an exact replica of a circa 1884 San Francisco house that was destroyed in the 1906 earthquake; the classic 25-room Hotel Carter, and the newest addition, the three-room, single-level Bell Cottage. Each offers a distinctly clean and artful blend of classic Victorian architecture with stylish, contemporary interior settings, all in a warm, hospitable environment. A great variety of luxurious rooms, each appointed with original local art, fine antiques, and generous amenities such as fireplaces, whirlpools, bay views, skylights, double-head showers, soaking tubs with marina views, king-size beds, telephones, VCRs and a video tape library, honor bars, and minifridges. "The best of the best," according to California Living Magazine.

Fresh Salmon Cakes
with Spicy Lemon/Mustard Sauce

1/2 red bell pepper, finely chopped
1/2 green bell pepper, finely chopped
2 garlic cloves, chopped
1 tablespoon olive oil
2 tablespoons white wine, or water
1 pound fresh salmon meat
1/2 cup fresh fine white bread crumbs
3 scallions, thinly sliced
3-4 tablespoons heavy cream
salt and pepper, to taste
dash of Tabasco sauce
1-2 dashes Worcestershire sauce
olive oil, for frying

Sauté peppers and garlic in olive oil. Add white wine and cook until liquid evaporates. Remove from heat. Break up salmon meat, but do not chop. Mix salmon with bread crumbs. Mix in sautéed peppers, garlic, and raw scallions. Add cream until mixture binds, but is not mushy. Season to taste with salt, pepper, Tabasco, and Worcestershire. Cover and refrigerate for at least 1 hour. Fifteen minutes before you are ready to cook salmon, make sauce.

Spicy Lemon/Mustard Sauce

4 garlic cloves, finely chopped
juice of 1 lemon
2 tablespoons white wine, or water
1 cup heavy cream
1 tablespoon Dijon mustard
salt and pepper, to taste
Tabasco sauce, to taste
Worcestershire sauce, to taste

Cook garlic, lemon juice and wine over medium heat until very little liquid is left in the saucepan. Add cream and bring to a boil. Reduce heat and simmer about 10 minutes until sauce is thickened. Stir in mustard, salt, pepper, a dash of Tabasco, and a dash of Worcestershire sauce. Set aside in a warm place.

Shape salmon mixture into 3 ounce patties and fry in olive oil until golden brown. Drain on paper towels. Serve cakes with sauce while still warm. Makes 8 cakes, serves 4.

Carter Hotel

Grandma's House Bed and Breakfast

Charlie and Hilda Hickman
734 Pollard Road, PO Box 445
Kodak, TN 37764
(423) 933-3512; (800) 676-3512;
FAX (423) 933-0748

This is a favorite at Grandma's House as a part of our farm-style, "loosen your belt" breakfast. I am asked for this recipe almost every time I serve it. As you know, we like grits in the South and this goes really well with grits and home-made buttermilk biscuits.

Impossible Ham 'n Swiss Pie

(the pie that does the impossible by making its own crust)

2 cups cooked smoked ham, cut-up fully
1 cup shredded natural Swiss cheese (4 ounce)
1/2 cup chopped green onions or chopped onion
4 eggs
2 cups milk
1 cup Bisquick baking mix
1/4 teaspoon salt
1/8 teaspoon pepper

Heat oven to 400°. Grease pie plate, 10x1 1/2 inches. Sprinkle ham, cheese, and onions in plate. Beat remaining ingredients until smooth (15 seconds in blender on high or 1 minutes with hand mixer). Pour into plate. Bake until golden brown and knife inserted in center comes out clean, 35-40 minutes. Cool 5 minutes. Makes 6 servings. High altitude: bake about 45 minutes.

Quiche

1 tablespoon butter
1/2 cup bacon
1 unbaked pie shell
4 eggs
2 cup whipping cream
3/4 teaspoon salt
1/8 teaspoon ground nutmeg
1 cup Swiss cheese
1/2 cup mushrooms
1 small can of mild Hatch Brand Chilies
2 tablespoon parsley

Cook bacon and crumble in bottom of uncooked pie shell. Beat eggs, cream, parsley, salt, and nutmeg with wire beater. Add cheese, mushrooms, and a small can of mild Hatch Brand Chilies into pie crust. Mushrooms and chilies may be omitted. Bake 15 minutes at 425°, then lower temperature to 325° for 35 minutes.

Monjeau Shadows

Billie and Gilbert Reidland
HC 67, Box 87
Nogal, NM 88341
(505) 336-4191

Our guests enjoy the year-round comfort of Monjeau Shadows, a four-level Victorian farmhouse located on ten acres of beautiful, landscaped grounds. When I have guests who stay two or three nights, this dish is a welcome change. I serve it with a fruit plate containing three or four different fruits.

Victorian Harvest Inn

Linda and Robert Dahlberg
Locust Lane, PO Box 2763
North Conway, NH 03860
(603) 358-3548; (800) 642-0749;
FAX (603) 356-8430

This can be served as breakfast, but does very well on a brunch table, with home fries or fried potatoes and fresh raisin/cinnamon toast. "Real men" may not eat quiche, but there are many exceptions. I don't remember ever having a slice turned down.

Crustless Quiche with Crab and Onion

3 large eggs
1 1/2 cups half and half
1/4 cup melted butter
dash pepper
dash salt
1 small can crab meat
1/2 cup Bisquick
1/4 cup chopped onion
1 cup Monterey Jack cheese, shredded

Preheat oven to 350°. Spray a 9 inch quiche dish or pie plate with oil and set aside.

In a medium bowl, combine the eggs, half and half, then whisk in the salt, pepper, butter and Bisquick. Pour mixture into quiche dish, add crab, onion, then cheese. Push into liquid with fork to cover. Place in 350° oven for 30 minutes. Check with knife inserted one inch from edge. Knife should come out clean. Let sit 10-15 minutes to set up cheese.

Quiche Lorraine

10 inch pie shell
1/2 pound bacon
1 1/2 cup grated Swiss cheese
4 eggs, beaten
1 cup whipping cream
1 cup half and half
1 tablespoon all-purpose flour
3/4 teaspoon salt
dash black pepper
dash ground nutmeg

Bake pie shell at 400° for three minutes. Remove from oven and prick gently with a fork. Bake five more minutes. Remove. Cool on rack. Cut bacon into small pieces, fry until crisp. Drain. Place bacon in pie shell evenly. Cover with the Swiss cheese. Combine remaining ingredients, stirring well. Pour over cheese in pastry shell. Sprinkle lightly with additional nutmeg. Bake at 375° for about 45 minutes, until set in center. Test by inserting knife. Nothing should stick on knife if done.

Benson Bed and Breakfast

Stan and Norma Anderson
402 North Oakland Avenue
Oakland, NE 68045
(402) 685-6051

This quiche is a real favorite at Benson Bed and Breakfast. We serve it beautifully by cutting 3 orange slices, laying two slices side by side, then cutting one slice from center outward and twisting it across other two slices. Add a fresh strawberry and a slice of kiwi, perfectly placed along with a sprig of fresh parsley. Place two cooked sausage patties and a fresh made muffin or biscuit. It is served immediately to our wonderful bed and breakfast guests.

Pleasant Valley Bed and Breakfast

Tim and Peg Lowman
7343 Pleasant Valley Road
Camden, OH 45311
(513) 787-3800

The first time I made this recipe was for our family Christmas. It was the first time we had all been together in twenty years. There were twenty-six of us. Now that we have this big place, we all get together every other Christmas.

I serve this with sausage links and fresh fruit. Every time I serve this to our guests, I get the warm good feeling I get with my family.

Christmas Quiche

1/4 cup margarine
18 eggs
1 cup sour cream
1 cup milk
2 teaspoons salt
1/4 teaspoon dried basil leaves
2 cups shredded cheddar or American cheese
1 - 4 ounce can mushrooms drained
4 green onions with tops, thinly sliced about 1/4 cup
1 - 2 ounce jar diced pimento, drained

Heat margarine in a 13x9x2 inch baking dish in a 325° oven until melted, coat dish. Beat eggs, sour cream, milk, salt, basil, in large bowl until blended. Stir in cheese, mushrooms, green onions and pimento. Pour into baking dish. Bake uncovered until omelet is set but still moist; 40-45 minutes. Cut into 18 three inch squares.

Ham-Asparagus Quiche

2 packages (10 ounces each) frozen asparagus
1 pound fully cooked ham
2 cups shredded Swiss cheese
1/2 cup chopped onion
6 eggs
2 cups milk
1 1/2 cups Bisquick
2 tablespoons dried vegetable flakes
1/4 teaspoon pepper

In two greased 9 inch pie plates, layer the ham, asparagus, cheese, and onion. Add remaining ingredients and mix well. Divide in half and pour over asparagus mixture in each pie plate. Bake at 375° for 45 minutes. Yield: 12 servings. You can easily substitute the ham and asparagus for spinach, mushroom, sausage, bacon, etc. I make this up the previous evening and bake it in the morning.

Union Hill Inn Bed and Breakfast

Tom and Mary Kay Moular
306 Union Street
Ionia, MI 48846
(616) 527-0955

I serve this quiche with fresh-baked muffins, and fresh fruit. My guests love it! I give the recipe to them. They are anxious to make it because they do not have to make a crust — it's self-rising and easily interchangeable.

Antique City Inn Bed and Breakfast

Sylvia Reddie
400 Antique City Drive
PO Box 584
Walnut, IA 51577
(712) 784-3722

I serve my Ham and Cheese Strata with sticky buns and fried potatoes, and a few slices of orange on plate.

I cook the things I like, and this is a very popular recipe. I have used it for about thirty years. I love it because it can be made the night before.

Ham and Cheese Strata

6 eggs
2 cups milk
1 teaspoon dry mustard
1 teaspoon Worcestershire sauce
10 slices bread (white)
2 cups grated cheddar cheese
1 pound ham slices

Grease 9x13 inch casserole dish, layer 1/2 bread, ham, cheese and bread. Beat eggs, add milk, mustard, Worcestershire sauce, mix and pour on top of bread-ham mixture. Refrigerate 4 hours or overnight. Bring to room temperature. Bake 45-60 minutes at 350°. Let stand 15 minutes. Makes 8 servings.

You can substitute one cup of cream of celery soup for one cup of milk.

Ham and Swiss Phyllo

with 1-2-4 Sauce

1/8 cup butter
1/8 cup flour
1 cup whole milk
3 cups Swiss cheese
2 tablespoons chives
1 tablespoon Dijon mustard
4 cups cured ham
16 sheets phyllo pastry (makes 8 individual servings)
melted butter

Filling: Melt butter, add flour and make roux. Add milk to roux and let thicken, then add cheese, chives and mustard; stir and let thicken. Add ham and stir.

Phyllo: Use two sheets per serving. Butter first sheet, lay second sheet on top and butter. Put 1 tablespoon (approximately) of filling at one end of sheets, in center, then fold sheets in thirds and roll. Baste with butter and bake on greased pan at 350 ° for 10 minutes in convection oven. Can be cooked in conventional oven, but it will not brown as well.

1-2-4 Sauce

1/8 cup honey
1/4 cup Dijon mustard
1/2 cup sour cream

Mix together and pour 1 teaspoon across the top of cooked phyllo.

The Stovall House Country Inn and Restaurant

Hamilton (Ham) Schwartz
1526 Highway 255 N.
Sautee, GA 30571
(706) 878-3355

This Greek pastry, phyllo, is a signature item for our restaurant. We use it for luncheon groups, wedding receptions, and cocktail parties, in addition to its being a regular menu appetizer and entree. We have over a dozen of our own filling recipes including vegetarian, chicken, beef, seafood, and dessert. The 1-2-4 sauce served with the ham and Swiss phyllo can also be used as a basting sauce for grilling chicken or as a dipping sauce for ham sandwiches.

10th Avenue Inn Bed and Breakfast

Francie and Vern Starkey
125-10th Avenue
Seaside, OR 97138
(503) 738-0643 (voice and FAX);
(800) 569-1114

Our 1908 ocean view home is just steps from the beach and a short walk on the promenade to restaurants and shopping. Light, airy guest rooms are decorated in soft colors and sprinkled with antiques.

We serve this sandwich when asparagus appears in early spring to have a change from the egg dishes served in winter.

To add even more color to the plate, we serve two or three large slices of tomato alongside.

Baked Asparagus-Cheese Sandwich

- 6 (3/4 inch thick) slices firm-textured bread, trim crust
- 6 (3 1/2 square) slices process Swiss cheese
- 4 eggs
- 2 cups milk
- 1 teaspoon salt
- 1/8 teaspoon pepper
- 1/4 teaspoon nutmeg
- 1 tablespoon chopped onion
- 18 cooked asparagus spears
- 1/2 cup shredded cheddar cheese

Arrange bread in 9x13 inch pan. Top each slice with cheese slice. Beat eggs slightly; add milk, seasonings, and onion. Pour over sandwiches and bake in slow oven 325° for 25 minutes. Remove from oven. Top each slice with 3 asparagus spears. Sprinkle with cheddar cheese. Return to oven and bake 10-15 minutes, until custard is set and top is golden. Let stand 5 minutes before serving. Serves 6.

’Tis So Sweet

Desserts

“How sweet are thy words unto my taste! yea, sweeter than honey to my mouth!”

Psalm 119:103

The Gables Inn

Mike and Judy Ogne
4257 Petaluma Hill Road
Santa Rosa, CA 95404
(707) 585-7777; (800) GABLES;
FAX (707) 584-5634

We make two to three pans of these every few days, and our guests just love them. I think part of their appeal is their size. We've tried making smaller ones, but they just don't have that "showstopper" look. When Mike carries in the silver baskets just overflowing with these huge, golden brown popovers, I can hear the oohs and aahs all the way back to the kitchen!

The Gables Inn's Famous Popovers

2 cups whole milk
4 extra large eggs
1/2 tablespoon sugar
1/2 teaspoon salt
2 cups flour

In blender container, whirl eggs and milk together. Add remaining ingredients and blend just until flour is incorporated. Pour into muffin cups which have been well greased with a vegetable cooking spray. (At the Gables, we use this recipe to fill six "Texas" size muffin cups.) Place pan in cold oven and turn oven to 425°. Bake 20 minutes, then turn oven down to 375° and bake approximately 35-40 minutes more until popovers are standing about two to three inches over tops of pan and are golden brown. Serve immediately with fresh butter and homemade jams.

Apple Popover

Popover:

1/2 cup all-purpose flour
1/2 cup milk
1 tablespoon butter
1/8 teaspoon salt
4 egg whites

Topping:

1 1/2 cups of any fresh fruit
1/2 cup jelly (pick a jelly that will mix with fruit flavor)
1/8 teaspoon cinnamon

Heat oven to 400°. Spray 8 inch square baking dish with nonstick cooking spray. In medium bowl, beat flour and milk with wire whisk until blended. Add butter, salt, and egg whites; beat well. Pour into spray coated dish. Bake at 400° for 25-30 minutes or until puffed and golden brown.

Meanwhile in small saucepan combine all topping ingredients: heat over low heat until jelly is melted and mixture is hot. Stir while heating. Immediately after popover is out of oven cut into fours and serve with hot topping.

Bielenda's Mars Avenue Guesthome

Joanne and Michael Bielenda
515 Mars Avenue
Galena, IL 61036
(815) 777-2808; FAX (815) 777-1157

Our full breakfast includes two juices, three breads, a fruit dish and Apple Popover, served on a romantic candlelight table with china, crystal, and flowers. Our guests enjoy our breakfast because they never go away hungry, and also because of the various table settings which fit the season at the time of their visit.

The Red House

John and Dorothy Towns
PO Box 164
Cranberry Isles, ME 04625
(207) 244-5297

Enjoy the breathtaking beauty of Maine, while experiencing the relaxing, quiet atmosphere of The Red House on Great Cranberry Island. Situated on a large saltwater inlet, guests need only look outside for beautiful scenery and extraordinary ocean views. At The Red House there are six guest rooms and each is distinctively decorated in traditional style; some with shared baths and some private with baths. Come and share your hosts' island home and experience the tranquil peace of God's creation.

Popovers

3 eggs
1 1/4 cups milk
1 1/4 cups flour
1/2 teaspoon salt
1 tablespoon melted butter

Have ingredients at room temperature. Whisk eggs, milk and add flour, salt, and melted butter. Whisk again (small lumps are OK). Pour into large muffin pans. Bake at 400° about 40 minutes. Serve hot from oven. Makes 6.

Popovers are impressive served with homemade orange marmalade and strawberry jam.

Almond Pastry

Crust:
1 cup all-purpose flour
1/2 cup butter or margarine
2 tablespoons water

Puff pastry layer:
1/2 cup butter or margarine
1 cup flour
3 large eggs
1 teaspoon almond extract
1 cup water

Frosting:
1 cup confectioner's sugar
1/2 teaspoon almond extract
1-2 tablespoons half and half

Crust: Cut 1/2 cup butter into 1 cup flour until crumbly. Sprinkle water over mixture and blend until a ball forms. Divide in half and form 2 rectangles on 12x3 inch ungreased cookie sheet; set aside.

Puff pastry layer: Boil butter and water in saucepan. Remove from heat and add 1 cup flour all at once, stirring until mixture leaves sides of pan. Add eggs one at a time blending well after each. Blend in almond extract, then spread on crusts. Bake 60 minutes until golden and puffy.

Frosting: Mix all frosting ingredients. Frost pastry when cool. Top may be sprinkled with chopped walnuts or chopped maraschino cherries before glaze hardens.

The Cameo Manor North

Greg and Carolyn Fisher
3881 Lower River Road
Niagara Falls (Youngstown), NY 14174
(716) 745-3034

Our guests simply devour these! This is a pastry that my grandmother made at Christmas time when we were young. I think of her everytime I make them. I honor her memory and her love of baking by including this treat in my repertoire of Cameo Confections!

Kaltenbach's Bed and Breakfast

Lee Kaltenbach
RD6, Box 106A Stony Fork Road, Kelsey Street
Wellsboro, PA 16901
(717) 724-4954; (800) 722-4954

This sprawling, country home with room for 32 guests offers visitors comfortable lodging, home-style breakfasts, and warm hospitality. Set on a 72-acre farm, Kaltenbach's provides ample opportunity for walks through meadows, pastures, and forests; picnicking; and watching the sheep, pigs, rabbits, and wildlife. All-you-can-eat country breakfasts are served. Honeymoon suites have tub or Jacuzzi for two. Hunting and golf packages are available. Near Pennsylvania's Grand Canyon. Kaltenbach's was awarded a three-Crown rating from the American Bed and Breakfast Association for its accommodations and hospitality.

Pumpkin Roll

3 eggs
1 cup sugar
2/3 cup pumpkin
1 teaspoon baking soda
1 teaspoon cinnamon
3/4 cup flour

Filling:
8 ounces cream cheese
4 tablespoons butter
1 cup powdered sugar
1 teaspoon vanilla

Mix eggs and sugar together. Add remaining ingredients. Bake on a greased cookie sheet (grease pan and put waxed paper on top, then grease and flour waxed paper). Bake at 350° for 15 minutes. This bakes very quickly, so keep an eye on it.

Remove warm cake from pan onto a dish towel covered with powdered sugar. Wrap up and let cool. Mix filling ingredients. Unwrap and spread with filling. Roll up like jelly roll and wrap in aluminum foil and keep refrigerated. Slice and serve.

Quick Cobbler

- 1/2 cup butter
- 1 cup sugar
- 1 cup self-rising flour
- 1 cup buttermilk (or substitute 1 teaspoon vinegar into a glass, add milk to make 1 cup; set for 5 minutes)
- 1 teaspoon vanilla
- dash of cinnamon
- 2-4 cups fresh fruit (sweetened slightly if necessary)

Melt butter in 10 inch pie dish or 8x10 glass pan. Mix sugar, flour, buttermilk, and vanilla in a bowl, pour into center of melted butter. Add fruit to center. Carefully spread fruit to sides of batter. Dash cinnamon sugar over fruit. Bake at 350° for 35-45 minutes. Crust will be light brown and fruit will bubble. Serves 4-6. Great side dish for eggs, or makes a great dessert!

Garratt Mansion

Royce and Betty Gladden
900 Union
Alameda, CA 94501
(510) 521-4779; FAX (510) 521-6796

We use the fresh fruit of the season, apples in fall and winter, berries in July, strawberries and peaches in June, nectarines and blueberries in August. We have a buffet breakfast at least once a week with cobbler as the feature in addition to rolls, cereals, yogurts, and fruit and fresh squeezed orange juice.

Buck Bay Farm

Rick and Janet Bronkey
Star Route Box 45
Olga, WA 98279
(360) 376-2908

Wild blackberries are abundant in the Northwest so guests from other parts of the country are fascinated to be able to pick them along the roads and hiking paths. They love a dish of fresh berries with breakfast or served warm in a recipe like this.

Wild Blackberry Cobbler

4-6 cups blackberries (or apple slices)
2 1/3 cup sugar
2-3 teaspoons cinnamon
2 cups Bisquick
2 eggs, lightly beaten

Spread fruit in rectangular baking dish. Cover with 1 cup sugar. Sprinkle with cinnamon if desired (with apples add 1/4-1/2 cup water). Prepare topping by combining Bisquick with 1 1/3 cup sugar, stir in eggs to make crumbly topping. Spread topping over fruit. Bake at 400° until well browned.

Apple Cobbler

Sky Chalet Mountain Lodge

Ken and Mona Seay
PO Box 300, Route 263
280 Sky Chalet Lane
Basye, VA 22810
(540) 856-2147; FAX (540) 856-2436

Homemade cobblers have been a tradition at Sky Chalet Mountain Ledge, a mountain top inn, since 1937. This recipe has been revised some through the years, and we found this recipe combination is delectable. Our guests love to have some of the "Sky Chalet Cobbler" served with ice cream while dining by the warm fireplace, or taking their dessert on the verandah (with rocking chairs) overlooking the unchallenged, breathtaking, panoramic views of the mountains and valleys.

Filling:
- 2 teaspoons cinnamon
- 1 teaspoon nutmeg
- 4 cups light brown sugar
- 1 1/3 tablespoons lemon juice
- 5 tablespoon cornstarch
- 1 gallon fresh sliced apple, or canned sliced apples, drained

Crust:
- 2 1/4 cups flour
- 1 teaspoon salt
- 2 tablespoons sugar
- 3/4 cup shortening, room temperature
- ice water

Topping:
- 1 cup flour
- 1 cup sugar
- 1 teaspoon baking powder
- 1/2 teaspoon salt
- 1 egg, beaten
- 2 tablespoons butter, room temperature

Filling: Mix all ingredients for filling together, and place in large pan (approx. 18x10 inch rectangle, 2 1/2 inches deep).

Crust: Sift flour, sugar, and salt together. Cut in shortening until size of peas. Sprinkle ice water into mixture, 1 tablespoon at a time, and work mixture until it sticks together when pressed with a fork. Chill dough in the refrigerator for at least 15 minutes. Roll out on lightly floured board; place over filling; using a fork, poke holes in crust (this allows steam to escape), and bake in 350° oven for 20 minutes or until brown.

Topping: Sift flour, sugar, baking powder and salt together in a bowl and mix until thoroughly combined. Add egg, working into mixture with fork or pastry blender. Cut butter into mixture until it reaches a pebbly consistency. Add topping on crust after cobbler and crust have baked until brown. Continue baking until topping is brown.

The Alexander House

Ruth Ray and Woody Dinstel
210 Green Street., PO Box 187
West, MS 39192
(601) 967-2266; (800) 350-8034

Fried pies are an old-fashioned Mississippi treat. They may be served at breakfast, tea, or supper. Just what one might imagine a bed and breakfast in Mississippi might serve-along with tea cakes, hot biscuits and ham and eggs!

Mississippi Fried Pies

2 cups all-purpose flour
1 teaspoon salt
1/2 cup milk
1/2 cup vegetable oil
1 can Lucky Leaf apple, or peach, or cherry pie filling

Combine flour and salt, combine milk and oil. Pour milk mixture into flour mixture. Stir until blended: make ball. Divide ball in half, then fourths, then eighths; make eight 5 inch circles. Fill each pie with 2 1/2 tablespoons of fruit mixture. Moisten circle edges with milk and seal with fork. To fry, use 1 inch of oil in skillet heated to 375°. Turn once. Drain on paper towels. Don't skimp on towels. Sprinkle with sugar if desired.

Our Family Tart

Combine:
1 1/4 cup flour
1/4 cup sugar
1/4 pound butter

Add:
1 egg yolk
1 teaspoon vanilla

Apricot Glaze

1 cup dried apricot, cut up
1/2 cup sugar
1/2 cup water
1 teaspoon lemon juice

Press dough into tart pan. Decoratively place fruit such as fresh apple, blueberries, peaches, cherries, on top. Bake at 350° for 30 minutes.

Glaze: Bring to a boil and boil until syrupy. Glaze cooled tart and serve.

I garnish the tart with kiwi, grapes, or whatever fruit is in season.

The Edge of Thyme, A Bed and Breakfast Inn

Eva Mae and Frank Musgrave
6 Main Street
Candor, NY 13743
(607) 659-5155; (800) 722-7365

We serve this as a signature dish at the end of breakfast or at high tea in late afternoon. Sometimes I spread lemon curd on the top of the base before adding the fruit. It is a versatile and attractive dish enjoyed by many and often requested by returning guests. Serves 8-12.

Pleasant Lake Bed and Breakfast

Richard and Charlene Baerg
2238 60th Avenue
Osceola, WI 54020-4509
(715) 294-2545; (800) 294-2545

When we started in the bed and breakfast business six years ago, we were looking for different and unique recipes. We came across this one in a brunch cookbook. It's so nice to be able to use fresh fruit, and the berry combination with the bananas and whipped topping is very colorful and makes the table look pretty.

Fresh Fruit Tarts

15 ounce package Pillsbury All Ready Pie Crusts, or use your own crust
1 teaspoon flour

Filling:
5 cups assorted fresh fruit (blueberries, strawberries, bananas)
16 ounce jar strawberry glaze
1/2 cup frozen whipped topping, thawed

Allow both crust pouches to stand at room temperature 15-20 minutes. Heat oven to 450°. Remove crusts from pouches; unfold and remove plastic sheets. Sprinkle flour over crusts. Using fluted round cookie cutter, cut five 4 inch circles from each crust. Fit circles, floured side down, over backs of ungreased muffin cups. Pinch 5 equally spaced pleats around sides of each cup. Prick each crust generously with fork. Bake at 450° for 9-13 minutes or until light golden brown. Cool completely; remove from muffin cups.

In large bowl, combine fruit and strawberry glaze. Refrigerate until thoroughly chilled. Before serving, spoon 1/2 cup fruit mixture into each cooled crust; top with whipped topping. Serves 10.

Peach or Pear Tart

1 1/4 cup unbleached flour
1/2 teaspoon salt
1/2 cup butter
2 tablespoons sour cream
3 fresh pears or peaches
3 egg yolks, or 1 whole egg + 1 yolk for less cholesterol
1 cup sugar
2 tablespoons flour
1/3 cup sour cream

Place first 4 ingredients in Cuisinart and process until it forms a ball. Pat into a buttered 9 inch tart or pie plate and bake 10 minutes at 425°. Put eggs, sugar, flour and sour cream in Cuisinart and blend until smooth. Remove tart from oven and reduce temperature to 350°. Pour egg/sugar mixture over sliced fresh peaches or pears (about 3). Cover with foil and bake about 10 minutes more or until set.

The Gallery Bed and Breakfast at Little Cape Horn

Carolyn and Eric Feasey
4 Little Cape Horn
Cathlamet, WA 98612-9544
(360) 425-7395; FAX (360) 426-1351

I put this in fancy dessert saucers topped with a bit of sour cream lightly sweetened with brown sugar and topped with a crystallized violet and fresh mint leaf.

Dutch Treat Bed and Breakfast

Ria and Peter Stroosma
1777 W. Big Lake Boulevard
Mt. Vernon, WA 98273
(360) 422-5466

We serve an expanded continental breakfast of 5-6 different varieties of breads. Cheese, cold cuts, eggs and the traditional sweet sprinkles and jam are always on a Dutch breakfast table. There is always homemade granola and fresh fruit.

In summer, breakfast is served out on the deck overlooking the lake. Some of our guests have enjoyed this hearty breakfast after having cast their lines from the dock or rowboat into the lake, that in the early morning hours is only shared with other creatures, human and winged, that are hunting for the fish.

For those who plan to spend a day on or by the water, a picnic lunch can be provided.

Appeltaart

5 cubes of margarine
700 grams (5 to 5 1/2 cups) of flour
325 grams (1 1/3 to 1 1/2 cups) of sugar
pinch of salt
firm, tart apples
raisins
cinnamon

Mix margarine, flour, sugar, and salt into a stiff dough and line a large roasting pan with it. Save some of the dough. Peel, core, and slice as many apples as needed to fill the dough lining. Mix apples, raisins and cinnamon (sprinkle a few drops of lemon juice on the apples to keep them from turning brown) and fill the pan. Crumble the remaining dough over the top of apple mixture. Bake at 350° for 30-40 minutes, or until lightly browned.

This is the Dutch variant of apple pie and just as popular. I only get a baking urge once in a while, so I like to make large batches. I wrap several squares into small packages and freeze them. That way there are always homemade treats on hand.

Tart Cherry Crepes

1 cup all-purpose flour
1 tablespoon sugar
4 eggs
1 1/2 cup milk
2 tablespoons oil

Put all ingredients in a blender and blend until smooth. Lightly oil an 8 inch frying pan over medium high heat, pour about 2 tablespoon of batter in pan and swirl to coat bottom of the pan. When the top of the crepe is dry, flip and cook for 45 seconds. Crepes should be very thin. Keep warm in oven, cover with another plate.

Tart Cherry Sauce

2 cups frozen or fresh tart cherries
1/2 cup sugar
1 tablespoon cornstarch

Combine ingredients and heat over medium high heat stirring until sugar melts and sauce thickens. Fold crepes in half and in half again to form triangles. Place 2 on a plate and ladle sauce in the center. Dust with confectioners' sugar around the edges and serve. Makes enough to serve 6 people.

Blueberries or raspberries may be substituted for the cherries. For a gourmet touch, add 2 tablespoons of cherry liquor to the sauce before serving.

In the summer, I serve them with our local blueberries, strawberries, and tart cherries. In the winter, a warm apple cinnamon sauce is perfect with crepes , or I stuff them with cheese and sausage and top with a sour cream sauce.

Pentwater "Victorian" Inn

Quintus and Donna Renshaw
180 E. Lowell, PO Box 98
Pentwater, MI 46449
(616) 869-5909; FAX (616) 869-7002

The inspiration for Tart Cherry Crepes comes from our local cherry orchards and the crepes are a specialty of the Pentwater Inn. My husband and I lived in England for six years and often traveled to France for holidays where we enjoyed French crepes. They are usually served in France as a dessert or enjoyed as a snack in the same way we enjoy an ice cream cone. They can be purchased from local shops, where they are cooked while you wait, and then filled with a multitude of sauces of fruits or chocolate. They are rolled into a cone shape and wrapped in paper to be eaten on the go.

The Pentwater Inn, with it's lovely Victorian warmth, compliments the international antiques that fill the rooms. We call it a "Victorian Inn with a touch of Europe." Specialties like Tart Cherry Crepes, and Scottish Scones are asked for when guests return.

Maggie's Bed and Breakfast

Maggie Leyda
2102 N. Keebler
Collinsville, IL 62234
(618) 344-8283

Maggie Leyda has adjusted many of her favorite recipes to reduce the fat and calorie content — something she did several years ago when her health began to fail. She has adjusted to life with very little salt in her diet, and she said the food tastes better now than it ever did because of her creative use of herbs and spices. The end result was that Maggie, who is over the age of 60, is in better health now than at any period in her life.

Maggie's Strawberry Crepes

Batter:
- 1 cup cold water
- 1 cup cold skim milk
- 4 eggs or 6 egg whites
- 1/2 teaspoon or less salt
- 2 cups stone ground unbleached flour
- 4 tablespoons canola oil

Filling:
- 2 - 8 ounce packages light cream cheese
- 1 pint light sour cream
- 1/2 cup powdered sugar

Sauce:
- 2 cups fresh crushed strawberries
- 1/3-1/2 cup sugar

Topping:
- 3-4 cups lightly sweetened whole strawberries
- Dollops of filling or sour cream
- Mint sprig for garnish

Put water, skim milk, eggs salt, flour, and oil in blender and mix until smooth. Refrigerate at least two hours or overnight. When ready to cook, heat six-inch nonstick skillet or crepe pan that has been sprayed with PAM. Pour crepe batter into skillet, lifting and tilting just until bottom of pan is coated with batter.

When edge starts to curl and crepe looks dry, turn and cook other side lightly. Gently lift out crepe and rest on waxed paper. Continue cooking crepes, stacking each one between waxed paper until done.

Combine the filling ingredients of cream cheese, sour cream and sugar. Beat until smooth; set aside. Crush strawberries and mix with sugar; set aside.

Preheat oven to 325°. To assemble crepe, place two to three tablespoon of filling on one side of crepe and gently roll up. Place seam side down in baking dish. Bake for 5-7 minutes. Remove from oven and top with sauce, sweetened whole berries, a generous dollop of filling or sour cream, and a sprig of mint. Leyda usually places three filled crepes on a serving plate for each person. The end result is almost too pretty to eat, but too tempting not to devour the whole thing.

Mowreys' Welcome Home Bed and Breakfast

Paul and Lola Mowrey
4489 Dover-Zoar Road, NE
Dover, OH 44622
(330) 343-4690

This apple crisp is frequently on the breakfast menu at Mowreys', complemented by hot sweet rolls, fresh fruit, and real, down home atmosphere. "As American as apple pie," it smells of grandma's house, recalling memories of a gentler time.

Served meals in the large dining room beside a bay window, our guests enjoy the lovely view, inside and out, warmed by good food and friendly company.

Apple Crisp

4 cups apples, sliced
1 teaspoon cinnamon
1 teaspoon salt
1/4 cup water
1 tablespoon lemon juice
3/4 cup all-purpose flour
1/2 cup granulated sugar
1/2 cup brown sugar
1/3 cup oleo

Place apples in buttered 10x6x2 inch baking dish. Sprinkle with cinnamon, salt, water, and lemon juice. Rub together flour, sugars, and oleo until well mixed. Place mixture evenly over apples.

Bake at 350° for 40 minutes. May be served warm with milk, if desired, or as dessert with vanilla ice cream.

Apple au Gratin

2 pounds apples, peeled and sliced
1/2 cup raisins
1/2 teaspoon cinnamon
1/4 cup lemon juice
3/4 cup brown sugar, packed
1/2 cup flour
1/2 teaspoon salt
1/4 cup butter softened
1 cup sharp cheddar cheese, grated

Arrange apples in a well-buttered 1-quart casserole dish. Sprinkle with raisins, cinnamon and lemon juice. Stir together with a fork the brown sugar, flour, salt, butter, and cheese. Sprinkle over the apples. Bake at 350° for 30 minutes or until apples are tender. Yields 6 servings.

Donna's Bed and Breakfast Cottages

Johannes and Donna Marie Schlabach
PO Box 307, East Street
Berlin, OH 44610
(330) 893-3068; (800) 320-3338

We have beautifully appointed country decor rooms, log cabin, honeymoon/anniversary cottages, elegant and luxurious chalets. Most accommodations have heart-shaped waterfall Jacuzzi, fireplace, cathedral wood ceiling with skylights, deck, kitchenette, cable TV, VCR, stereo — all rooms have private bath and air.

Line Limousin Farmhouse Bed and Breakfast

Bob and Joan Line
2070 Ritner Highway
Carlisle, PA 17013
(717) 243-1281

Over the years we have had great guests. One was a lady from Virginia who also had a bed and breakfast and shared her recipe for Monkey Bread which was three times all the ingredients. I cut the recipe into a third the size calling it "Petite" (our cattle are from Limoges, France, so I like to stick to as many French things as I can).

The 15 minutes bake time is perfect for preparing just before serving breakfast and serving hot from the oven for this dessert. We had one guest and his wife return, telling me he came back just for Line Limousin Petite Monkey Bread.

Petite Monkey Bread

1 - 10 ounce can buttermilk biscuits
3/4 cup sugar
1 teaspoon cinnamon
raisins
chopped nuts
1 cup brown sugar, firmly packed
1/2 cup (1 stick) butter or margarine

Cut each biscuit into fourths. Put the sugar and cinnamon into a plastic bag: shake well. Shake the biscuit pieces a few at time in mixture and place in a well-greased 8 inch round cake pan. Sprinkle raisins and nuts over the biscuits. Melt the brown sugar and butter; boil for 1 minutes, no longer. Pour over the biscuits, nuts and raisins. Bake in a 350° oven for 15 minutes or until done. Turn out on plate. Do not cut this creation. Just pull the biscuits apart with a fork and enjoy!

Frozen Strawberry Dessert

3 cups graham cracker crumbs
1 stick oleo, melted
1/2 cup brown sugar
3 egg whites
1 1/2 cup sugar
1 1/2 package frozen strawberries or 1 pints of your fresh strawberries
3 tablespoons lemon juice
1 1/2 cup whipping cream, whipped

Stir graham cracker crumbs, melted oleo, and brown sugar together and pat into a 10x13 inch baking dish. Beat 3 egg whites, gradually adding sugar until egg whites are stiff. Fold strawberries and lemon juice and whipped cream together and pour over crumb crust. Freeze 1 night. Serve with a spoonful of whipped cream and a strawberry on top of each piece.

Strawberry Lace Inn

Jack and Elsie Ballinger
603 North Water Street
Sparta, WI 54656
(608) 269-7878

This recipe has been in our family for years and since our bed and breakfast is called the Strawberry Lace Inn , this recipe fits our menu nicely. All of our menus have strawberries included somehow. The home at 603 North Water Street is an excellent example of an Italianate Victorian residence. The home was built in the 1870s for Major James Davidson, a Civil War veteran who helped organize the Fifth New York Cavalry and became a prominent figure in the Wisconsin lumbering and merchandising business. Let Jack and Elsie Ballinger take you back in more detail of why this is one of Wisconsin's most historic homes. Partake of their crystal and linen presentation of a four-course breakfast.

The 1890 Queen Anne Bed and Breakfast

714 Wayne Street
Sandusky, OH 44870
(419) 626-0391

Since we've converted our home of 34 years into a bed and breakfast, our six grown children have shown a real interest in our operations. Two have voiced an interest in continuing it when we desire to completely retire.

It's not unusual for them to send us recipes they believe will add to our breakfasts. This "escalloped pineapple" came from daughter-in-law Dana. We find it delicious with ham or as a side dish. It could also be used as a dessert with some ice cream.

Escalloped Pineapple

1 cup sugar
1/2 cup margarine or butter, melted
1 - 5 1/2 ounce can evaporated milk
3 eggs, beaten
4 cups bread, cubed
1 - 20 ounce can chunk pineapple, drained

Combine sugar, margarine, milk, and eggs. Toss with bread and pineapple. Place in a buttered 8x12 inch pan. Bake at 350° for 45 minutes. Serves 6-8. This is good hot for breakfast. Delicious with ham. Great for dessert with whipped cream or ice cream.

Escalloped Pineapple

3 eggs
1 stick butter
1 1/3 cup sugar
6 slices bread, cubed
1 - 15 1/2 ounce can pineapple, crushed

Heat oven to 350°. Beat eggs, cut butter into small pieces. Mix all ingredients together and place in a 2 quart casserole dish. Bake 45-45 minutes.

Skoglund Farm

Alden and Delores Skoglund
Rt. 1, Box 45
Canova, SD 57321
(605) 247-3445

Skoglund Farm brings back memories of Grandpa and Grandma's home. It is furnished with antiques and collectibles. A full, home-cooked evening meal and breakfast are served. Guests can sightsee in the surrounding area, visit Little House on the Prairie Village, hike, or just relax. Several country churches are located nearby.

Since we serve a evening meal, this is a side dish that everyone likes.

Simpson House Inn

Dixie Adair Budke
121 East Arrellaga Street
Santa Barbara, CA 93101
(805) 963-7067; (800) 676-1280;
FAX (805) 564-4811

Our Victorian estate is considered one to the most distinguished homes of its era in southern California. It features the elegant 1874 home, restored 1878 barn, and three garden cottages. The Inn is elegantly appointed with antiques, English lace, Oriental rugs, and fine art.

This is an Davies family recipe. It comes from southeast London where Glyn was born and his family still loves.

Lemon Curd

6 ounces sugar
4 egg yolks
1 egg white
2 ounces butter
grated rind and juice of 1 large lemon

Whip yolks and white well. Melt butter, sugar, lemon juice and rind in saucepan (double boiler). Add eggs, mix well. Cool slowly — stirring constantly until thick (about 15 minutes). Refrigerate in air tight jar. Will store 2 weeks if kept refrigerated.

Nectarine-Blueberry Crisp

1 pound blueberries
3/4 pound nectarines, sliced
6 tablespoons sugar
2 1/2 tablespoons cornstarch
1/2 teaspoon lemon zest
1 1/2 teaspoon lemon juice
3 tablespoons dark brown sugar
3 tablespoons white sugar
3/4 teaspoons cinnamon
1/4 teaspoon nutmeg
1/8 teaspoon cardamon
1/2 cup rolled oats
1 cup flour
1/2 cup butter, softened

Heat oven to 375°. Mix fruit, sugar, and starch, zest and juice. Pour in greased 8x8 inch baking dish, set aside. Mix sugar, cinnamon, nutmeg, cardamon, and stir in. Add oats, flour and butter; mix until crumbly. Cover fruit with mix. Bake 30 minutes. Serve with whipped cream.

Summit Place Bed and Breakfast

Marlene and Douglas Laing
1682 W. Kimmel Road
Jackson, MI 49201
(517) 787-0468

Guests enjoy warmth and elegance at Summit Place, where the past blends with the present in a beautiful, quiet countryside. We specialize in service, comfort, and a full breakfast, served in our formal dining room and prepared the old-fashioned way — from scratch. Bedrooms are lovely and comfortable with reading chairs, desk, color cable TV, extra quilts, and phones. Tea with treats served in afternoons and wake-up coffee and muffins are delivered to guests' doors.

Wood Haven Manor Bed and Breakfast

Jolene and Bobby Wood
809 Spruce Road
Leadville, CO 80461
(719) 486-0109; (800) 748-2570;
FAX (719) 486-0210

I serve this in the winter in place of a fruit or with a garnish of fruit. Many of my guests send me recipes to try and this was one of them. It's a wonderful change of pace.

Bread Pudding

4 eggs
1 cup sugar
4 cups milk
2 teaspoons vanilla
1 1/2 loaves bread, cubed
3 ounces raisins
1/2 cup brown sugar

Butter Sauce

3/4 cup sugar
3 beaten egg yolks
3 tablespoons butter
2 tablespoons cornstarch dissolved in 1/4 cup water
1/2 cup boiling water
2 teaspoons vanilla
1/8 teaspoon salt

Beat eggs and sugar. Add vanilla and milk and beat. Add bread and raisins. Mix well. Put in two 9x9x2 inch loaf pans. Sprinkle each loaf with 1/4 cups brown sugar. Bake at 350° for 30 minutes or until pudding has risen to top of pan. Serve warm, topped with butter sauce.

Butter Sauce: In double boiler, cream sugar, eggs, and butter. Add cornstarch mixture. then add boiling water slowly. Cook until thickened stirring constantly. Add vanilla and salt.

Country Bread Pudding

8 cups cubed bread

Beat slightly together:
- 8 eggs
- 2 teaspoons cinnamon
- 1 teaspoon nutmeg
- 1 teaspoon salt

Mix:
- 6 cups milk, scalded
- 1 1/3 cups sugar
- 3 teaspoons vanilla

Arrange bread cubes in a 9x13 inch pan. Sprinkle with raisins. Combine egg and milk mixtures. Pour over bread. Bake in 350° oven for 55-60 minutes. Serve warm with whipped cream or vanilla sauce.

Happy Lonesome Log Cabins

Christian and Carolyn Eck
HC 61 Box 72
Calico Rock, AR 72519
(501) 297-8764

A favorite in Calico Country Tearoom Bake Shop — Calico Rock, AR. It is served there with vanilla sauce, a white sauce with sugar and vanilla added to make a sweet sauce. Sprinkled with nutmeg.

Apple Country Bed and Breakfast

Mark and Shirley Robert
4564 Old Naches Highway
Naches, WA 98937
(509) 965-0344; FAX (509) 965-1591

Our bed and breakfast sits in a beautiful setting of apple orchards in the heart of Washington State. I try to use all the apple recipes I can. My husband bakes the bread. Homemade bread really adds to the flavor of this recipe. We serve this with 3-4 kinds of fruit and juice and rhubarb muffins, a full hearty breakfast. We can make this ahead and serve warm or cold. It is excellent. I hope all of you will try this!

Bread Pudding with "Apple" Sauce

2 cups homemade bread crumbs, toasted
4 cups milk, scalded
2 eggs
1/2 cup or less sugar
1/4 teaspoon nutmeg
1/4 teaspoon salt
1 teaspoon vanilla
1/2 cup dried cranberries, nuts, and raisins

Soak bread in milk. Beat eggs until light; add sugar, salt, nutmeg, vanilla, raisins, or cranberries, and nuts. Mix thoroughly with bread mixture. Pour into greased baking dish and set in pan of hot water. Bake at 350° for 1 hour or until knife inserted in center comes out clean. Serve warm or cold with sauce.

Apple Sauce

1 cup peeled and chopped apples, Golden Delicious or Granny Smith
1/2 cup sugar
1/4 teaspoon cinnamon
1 teaspoon grated lemon rind

Combine apples and sugar. Cook until tender. Add water if needed. Add next two ingredients. Spoon over bread pudding warm or cold. Also excellent with raspberry sauce.

Butterscotch Bread Pudding

1 tablespoon margarine or butter
1/2 cup brown sugar, light
3-4 slices of bread, buttered
2 cups milk
3 eggs, beaten
pinch of salt
1 teaspoon vanilla

In top of double boiler, put margarine. Add brown sugar. Do not stir! Add bread, buttered, and broken up. Mix milk, eggs, salt and vanilla together and pour over bread (DO NOT STIR AT ANY TIME.) Cook over hot water at least 1 3/4 hours. Run a knife around the edge of pan to loosen. Place pan or bowl on top of double boiler and turn upside down. Sauce will drizzle over pudding.

The Moorings Lodge

Ernie and Shirley Benard
207 Grand Avenue South
Falmouth Heights, MA 02540
(508) 540-2370

This recipe has been in my family for at least 50 years. Tips: A hearty bread, like homemade, is best. This is no problem at our place because we make our own. Keep your serving bowl close to the size of your double boiler — it holds the pudding together and makes a better presentation. This is a recipe that our return guests always ask for. Enjoy!

Anderson Creek Inn

Rod and Nancy Graham
12050 Anderson Valley Way
PO Box 217
Boonville, CA 95415
(707) 895-3091; (800) 552-6202;
FAX (707) 895-2546

A variety of nut breads has often been a part of our hearty breakfast, but I've always been disturbed by wasting the "heels." This recipe was born as a result of my reluctance to throw away the unsightly or day-old breads that would otherwise still be good. It has now become one of our most popular dishes and goes quite nicely with our Lamb Sage Sausage and plenty of fresh fruit. This recipe can be adapted to use with almost any kind of leftover nut bread, and lend itself quite well to experimentation. It's fun and easy!

Banana-Nut Bread Pudding

with Rich Cream

1/2 loaf or more day-old banana bread
6-8 eggs
1 1/2 cup whole milk
1/2 cup chopped walnuts
3 tablespoons sugar
1 teaspoon cinnamon

Break banana bread into small pieces and place in an 8x8 or 9x9 inch baking dish which has been lightly sprayed with a non-stick spray. Beat eggs and milk together and pour over bread cubes. Mix nuts, sugar, and cinnamon together and sprinkle over top. Can be refrigerated overnight. Bake at 350° for 45 minutes or until toothpick comes out clean. Let sit for 5-10 minutes before cutting into squares. Serve with cream drizzled over top.

Rich Cream Sauce

1 cup heavy cream
1/4 cup sugar
4 tablespoon butter

Place ingredients in heavy saucepan. Allow to boil up, stirring constantly. When mixture begins to boil down, remove from heat and allow to cool.

Orange Bread Pudding
with Warm Maple Sauce

3 eggs
2 egg whites
1 3/4 cups milk
1/3 cups orange marmalade
1/4 cup sugar
1/2 teaspoon vanilla
4 slices dry bread, cut into small pieces
1/3 cup raisins
1/2 cup coconut
1/2 teaspoon cinnamon

Whisk together the eggs, egg whites, milk, orange marmalade, sugar, cinnamon and vanilla. Place bread in ungreased 8 1/2 inch round baking dish. Sprinkle raisins and coconut over bread. Pour egg mixture over all. Bake at 325° for 40 minutes or until knife comes out clean.

Maple Sauce

1/3 cup maple syrup
1 tablespoon cornstarch
1/4 teaspoon shredded orange peel
3/4 cup orange juice

Cook and stir the maple sauce ingredients until thick and bubbly. Remove from heat, stir in 2 tablespoons butter, serve warm.

This dish can be prepared the night before. Store in refrigerator and bake before breakfast.

Historic Charleston Bed and Breakfast

Bob and Jean Lambert
114 Elizabeth St.
Charleston, WV 25311
(304) 345-8156; (800) CALL WVA; FAX (304) 342-1572

This is a wonderful side dish for breakfast! Day old cinnamon rolls can be used in place of bread. Guests request this bread pudding on return visits. Serve it warm in individual dishes — with a spoonful of whipped topping.

Swans Court Bed and Breakfast

Monty Dixon
421 Court Street
Belleville, IL 62220
(618) 233-0779

This recipe came to the Dixon family from the boarding school my aunt Jewel attended in Ewing, Illinois about 1920. It has become part of the family dinners at Thanksgiving and Christmas and now is enjoyed as a late dessert at Swans Court Bed and Breakfast.

Date Pudding

2 egg yolks
1 cup sugar
1 cup pecans, chopped
1 cup dates, chopped
2 tablespoons flour, heaping
1 teaspoon baking powder
2 egg whites, stiffly beaten

Mix the first six ingredients together well. This mixture will be stiff. Fold in the stiffly beaten egg whites. Bake in a greased 8x8 inch pan at 275° for 30 minutes. This will fall as it cools. Do not overbake or it will be too hard. Serve with whipped cream.

McLeran House Peach Custard

2 cups sliced frozen peaches, thawed and drained
1 tablespoon lemon juice
1 tablespoon powdered sugar
1/4 cup margarine, softened
1 cup skim milk
3 egg whites (or 1/2 cup cholesterol-free egg product)
3/4 cup granulated sugar
1 cup Bisquick Reduced Fat baking mix
1 tablespoon vanilla
1 tablespoon almond extract

Heat oven to 350°-375°. Grease 8x8x2 inch square pan. Place peaches in pan. Sprinkle with lemon juice and powdered sugar. Set aside. Mix remaining ingredients in separate bowl until well blended. Pour mixture over peaches. Bake 40-45 minutes or until edges are light brown and toothpick inserted in center comes out clean. Custard will not look smooth.

Serve warm, sprinkled with powdered sugar. 6-8 servings.

1909 McLeran House Bed and Breakfast & Collectibles Shoppe

Robert and Mary Ryals
12408 County Road 137
Wellborn, FL 32094
(904) 963-4603

This recipe is the result of a diligent search for healthful recipes which are also delicious. Prior to retirement, Mary and I were employed for many years in the public school system in south Florida. The stress, plus the sedentary aspect of our jobs, led to weight problems for both of us and heart disease for me. To combat both problems, we radically altered our eating habits and Mary made a concerted effort to prepare tasty, healthful meals. When we opened our bed and breakfast, we determined to provide our guests with such dishes. Peaches being a traditional favorite in the south, it seemed appropriate to include them. The custard is not overly sweet and is healthful and nutritious as well as delicious. We feel a responsibility to provide our guests with food that will contribute to their well-being.

Emerald Isle Inn Bed and Breakfast

Marilyn and Ak Detwiller
502 Ocean Drive
Emerald Isle, NC 28594
(919) 354-3222 (voice or FAX)

Located at the ocean, this jewel of a Crystal Coast inn is truly a treasure to be discovered. A peaceful haven to all who seek a quiet, restful, and sun-filled getaway. Each stay includes a full gourmet breakfast with freshly ground coffee and other tempting samplings. Swings and porches with ocean and sound views add to your enjoyment. With direct beach access,guests are only steps away from discovering the gentle shoreline treasures. "Come to your home away from home for a visit you'll always remember!"

Bananas Detwiller

3 bananas
6 tablespoons heavy cream
3 tablespoon light brown sugar
1 tablespoon favorite liqueur
1 tablespoon sweet butter

Melt butter in Teflon frying pan. Add brown sugar, heavy cream, and liqueur. Cook over medium heat until sauce starts to bubble. Cut bananas in half lengthwise. Cut in half again crosswise. Place in saucepan and cook for about 3-4 minutes, depending on the ripeness of your bananas. Serve as a side dish to your entree. Will serve 6 people.

Variations on this dish can be made with peaches. You can also substitute different liqueurs for a unique flavor each time.

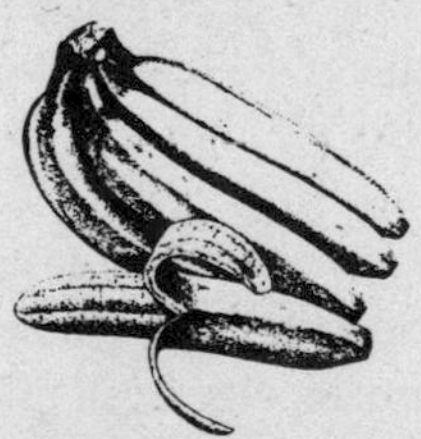

Chocolate Strawberry Shortcake

(featured in Bon Appetit*)*

The 1785 Inn

Becky and Charlie Mallar
PO Box 1785
North Conway, NH 03860-1785
(603) 356-9025; (800) 421-1785;
FAX (603) 356-6081

The Inn's famous scene of Mt. Washington is virtually unchanged from when the Inn was built over 200 years ago. The Inn's homey atmosphere makes guests feel right at home, and the food and service makes them eagerly await their return.

2 cups flour
2 teaspoons baking powder
4 tablespoons unsweetened cocoa
1/3 cup sugar
1/2 teaspoon baking soda
1/2 teaspoon salt
5 tablespoons cold unsalted butter, cut into 5 portions
4 ounces chocolate chips
3/4 cup milk

Combine flour, baking powder, cocoa, sugar, baking soda, and salt in a food processor. Add butter and chocolate chips and process until crumbly. Begin processing and add milk until mixture is crumbly but will hold together when pinched with fingers. Turn moistened dough out onto counter, form into a ball, and flatten into a circle approximately one inch thick.

Using a 2 inch round cutter, make 12-15 shortcakes. Place on cookie sheet lines with parchment paper Bake in a 450° oven for 13 minutes. When slightly cooled, place on plate and cover with plastic wrap to keep them moist.

Strawberry Sauce: Puree 2 quarts strawberries in a food processor. Remove from processor, pour into bowl, and add 2 cups sugar, and 1/2 cup orange juice. Add 2 quarts sliced berries to the pureed mixture.

Whipped Cream: Whip 2 cups heavy cream in bowl of electric mixer on high speed. When the mixture begins to thicken, add 1/2 cup confectioners' sugar and 2 teaspoons vanilla extract.

Assembly of Individual Shortcakes: Place a tablespoon of sauce in the bottom of a dish. Place the bottom half of the shortcake on the sauce. Continue on with 2 tablespoons sauce, 1 tablespoon whipped cream, the top of the shortcake, 2 more tablespoons sauce, and top with 1 tablespoon whipped cream. Garnish with fresh mint leaves.

Lindgren's Bed and Breakfast on Lake Superior

Shirley Lindgren
County Road 35, PO Box 56
Lutsen, MN 55612-0056
(218) 663-7450

Shirley and husband Bob bought this log home on Lake Superior's North Shore in 1967. But when they sold their Twin Cities' nursery businesses in 1987, they had major restoration done on the home and moved north for good. Bob bought a boat and Shirley headed for the trout streams. The bed and breakfast allows them to share their home and landscaped grounds with people and their policy is, "When you are away from home, our home is your home."

Lindgren's Caramel Torte

6 egg yolks
1 1/2 cups sugar
1 teaspoon baking powder
2 teaspoons vanilla
6 egg whites, beaten stiff
2 cups graham crackers, finely crushed
1 1/4 cups chopped nuts, we use pecans
1 pint heavy cream, whipped

Beat egg yolks well, adding sugar, baking powder and vanilla. Fold beaten egg whites into egg yolk mixture. Fold in graham cracker crumbs and nuts. Blend. Line two 9 inch round cake pans with waxed paper. Pour in batter. Bake at 325° for 35 minutes. Cool on wire racks. Cut each layer in half to make four layers. Stack each layer with whipped cream and spread to with whipped cream. Drizzle entire cake with caramel sauce. Serves 10 persons.

Lindgren's Caramel Sauce

1 1/4 cups lightly packed brown sugar
1 tablespoon flour
1/4 cup butter
1/4 cup orange juice
1/4 cup water
1 beaten egg
1 teaspoon vanilla

Combine sugar, flour, orange juice, butter, water, and egg in top of double boiler. Cook uncovered over low heat, stirring until boiling and thickened. Add vanilla. Cool and drizzle over entire cake.

Bella Rose Mansion's Crepes

- 1/2 cup all-purpose flour
- 2 eggs
- 1 tablespoon granulated sugar
- 1/2 cup milk
- 1/2 cup water

To make the crepes, combine all ingredients in a blender and blend until well-mixed. Heat a 6-inch non-stick fry pan. Ladle a small amount of batter over the bottom of the pan, tilting the pan to evenly coat it with the batter. Place pan over the heat and cook until batter appears dry, about 15 seconds. Invert the pan to remove the crepe. Place the cooked crepe on a plate between layers of paper towels and repeat until batter has been used. Yields 10-12 .

Cream cheese filling:

- 2 - 8 ounce packages cream cheese, fat-free or regular, softened
- 2/3 cup sugar
- 4 egg yolks
- 2 teaspoons vanilla extract
- fresh strawberries or other fruit, sliced
- fresh fennel (optional)

To make the filling, place first 4 ingredients in large bowl and beat, using an electric mixer, until smooth. Refrigerate.

To assemble, place crepe on work surface. Spoon about two tablespoons of filling onto center of crepe and roll. Decorate filled crepes with sliced strawberries or your favorite fresh fruit. Garnish with fresh fennel. Serves 8-10.

Bella Rose Mansion

Rose James/Michael Ray Britton
255 North 8th Street
Ponchatoula, LA 70454
(504) 386-3857
Internet: http://cimarron.net/vsa/la.bella.html

Rose James, proprietor of Ponchatoula's Bella Rose Mansion, says the key is having everything fresh — fresh flowers on the table and fresh herbs on the plate. James also is conscious of her guests' eating habits. Even though they are on vacation, they often are watching their weight.

Rose James serves these crepes in her glass-walled, plant filled veranda overlooking the swimming pool. A few sliced strawberries and a sprig of fresh fennel on the plate makes the dish as appealing as the surroundings.

Rosedale Bed and Breakfast

Katie and Jim Haag
1917 Cypress Street
Paris, KY 40361
(606) 987-1845

This torte can be partially prepared in advance. The crust can be made and pressed into the pie pan. The cream cheese filling can also be mixed together as long as an egg substitute is used. It is an easy, yet elegant, recipe to prepare that is always a favorite of our guests. Apples can also be used.

Bavarian Pear Torte

1/2 cup margarine
1/3 cup sugar
1/4 teaspoon vanilla
1 cup flour
8 ounce cream cheese
1 egg
1/4 cup sugar
1/2 teaspoon vanilla
4 cups peeled pears, sliced thin
1/3 cup sugar
1/2 teaspoon cinnamon
1/4 cup sliced almonds

Mix margarine, sugar, vanilla, and flour, and press into bottom of a 10 inch deep-dish pie pan. Mix cream cheese, egg, sugar, and vanilla. Pour into pastry-lined pan. Toss together pears, sugar, and cinnamon. Arrange over cream cheese mixture as desired. Sprinkle almonds on top.

Bake at 400° for 10 minutes and 350° for 25 more minutes. Allow to cool before removing from pan. This is good served as a dessert or at breakfast/brunch.

Pear Clafouti

3 cups sliced firm but ripe pears, can use peaches, cherries, blackberries, and so on.
1 1/4 cup milk
1/3 cup white sugar
3 large eggs
2 teaspoons vanilla
1/2 teaspoon grated lemon rind
2/3 cup all-purpose flour

Place all ingredients except pears in blender. Blend for one minute at full speed, or beat with a mixer until smooth.

Butter a glass or pottery pie dish. Spread fruit into the dish and pour the batter on top of the fruit. Bake in a preheated oven at 350° for about 40 minutes, or until the clafouti has puffed, browned, and the custard has set. Lovely served hot or warm and even cold!

Spring House

1264 Muddy Creek Forks Road
Airville, PA 17302
(717) 927-6906

Pear Clafouti makes a French country dessert that is a lovely second course to a leisurely breakfast on the porch of Spring House, where guests savor both the food and the view of the Muddy Creek Valley.

Olde World Bed and Breakfast

Jonna Sigrist
2982 State Route 516 NW
Dover, OH 44622
(330) 343-1333; (800) 447-1273

To serve individual pieces, put each piece on plate and drizzle chocolate and caramel over, letting topping fall on the plate. Sprinkle with pecans. To achieve an even thin drizzle, place toppings in plastic bag and snip a corner to use like a pastry bag. This is the best way to individualize each piece for those who don't want a specific topping. For the best flavor, serve with cheesecake cold and topping warm. Enjoy!

Turtle Cheesecake

2 cups crushed chocolate cookies
1/4 cup butter, melted
2 1/2 8 ounce packages cream cheese
1 cup sugar
1 1/2 tablespoons flour
1/4 teaspoon salt
1 teaspoon vanilla
3 eggs
2 tablespoons whipping cream
1 cup pecans

Caramel Topping:
7 ounces caramels
1/3 cup whipping cream

Chocolate Topping:
4 ounces German Sweet chocolate
2 tablespoons whipping cream

Combine cookie crumbs and 1/4 cup butter and press into 9 inch springform pan. Beat cream cheese. Add sugar, flour, salt and vanilla; mix well. Add eggs one at a time. Stir in cream. Pour over crust. Bake for 10 minutes at 450°, then reduce heat to 200°. Continue baking 35-40 minutes. Let cool in pan. Refrigerate. For caramel topping, melt caramels and cream over medium heat. For chocolate topping, mix chocolate and cream over medium heat. Top it all with pecans.

Heavenly Delights

Cakes and Pies

"And thou shalt rejoice in every good thing which the Lord thy God hath given unto thee, and unto thine house. . . ."

Deuteronomy 26:11

The Rose Garden Bed and Breakfast

Dawn Mann
195 South Academy
New Braunfels, TX 78130
(210) 629-3296; (800) 569-3296

Our half-century old home is only one block from downtown. We offer two designer guest rooms. The Royal Rose Room has a four poster rice, queen bed with a crystal chandelier and country French decor. The Country Rose Room has a Victorian-style, iron-and-brass queen bed with pine walls also done in country French. A full gourmet breakfast is served in the formal dining room.

Oatmeal Cake

1 1/2 cup oatmeal
2 cups water
1 1/2 sticks butter
1 1/2 cups sugar
2 cups flour
1 1/2 teaspoons soda
1 1/2 cups brown sugar
3/4 teaspoon salt
3/4 teaspoon cinnamon
3 eggs

Boil the water, stir in oatmeal and let stand 20 minutes. Mix together sugar, flour, soda, brown sugar, salt and cinnamon. Mix eggs and butter into oatmeal. Then mix with dry ingredients. Mix, DO NOT BEAT! Bake 35 minutes at 350° until cake tests done. Dust with powdered sugar. Also makes wonderful muffins.

Buttermilk Cake

- 2 cups sugar
- 3 cups flour
- 1 cup buttermilk
- 2 sticks butter
- 1 teaspoon vanilla (Imitation vanilla and butternut flavoring are excellent.)
- 1/2 teaspoon baking soda
- 1/2 teaspoon baking powder
- dash of salt
- 1 tablespoon lemon juice (optional)
- 2 eggs
- 2 egg whites

Cream butter well. Add sugar gradually. Add buttermilk. Then add flour gradually. In last cup of flour sift all dry ingredients. Add eggs and whites, one at a time. Beat well. Then add lemon juice if desired. For added flavor, I add some grated orange rind and some chopped walnuts. Bake in a tube pan for the first half hour at 325°. The second half hour at 350°. These temperatures are based on gas ovens. If using electric oven, please adjust baking time for 15 minutes extra.

Glaze: Pour approximately 1/2 cup of orange juice (fresh squeezed is best) into pot and put in about 1/2 cup sugar. Let come to a full boil and then simmer for 10 minutes. Let cool a bit and pour over cooled cake.

Gaithersburg Hospitality Bed and Breakfast

Suzanne and Joe Danilowicz
18908 Chimney Place
Gaithersburg, MD 20879
(301) 977-7377

This luxury host home just off I-270 with all amenities, including private parking, is located in the beautifully planned community of Montgomery Village, near churches, restaurants, and shops, and is 10 minutes from D.C. Metro. This spacious bed and breakfast has two rooms with private baths. Also offered are a large, sunny third room with twin beds, and a fourth room with a single bed. Hosts delight in serving full, home cooked breakfasts with guests' pleasure and comfort in mind.

Logwood Bed and Breakfast

Debby and Greg Verheyden
3506 US Highway 550
Durango, CO 81301
(970) 259-4396; (800) 369-4082

This cake was called our "contagious" cake here at Logwood. Once you had a piece, you would come back time and again for more. Guests are welcome into the kitchen in the afternoon and evenings after dinner in town to sample all the tasty and tantalizing treats the Verheydens make for just their sweet taste buds. They are also welcome to take their dessert choices into the living room or out on the 700 square foot deck to view the Animas Valley by day and bright stars at night.

Logwood Pineapple Cake

2 cups flour
2 cups sugar
1 teaspoon baking soda
1 teaspoon salt
2 eggs
1 large can crushed pineapple with juice
3/4 cup Wesson oil

Sift dry ingredients together. Add oil, pineapple, and eggs. Mix by hand. Pour batter into a greased and floured 9x13 inch pan. Bake at 350° for 30-40 minutes or until toothpick comes out clean.

Cream Cheese Icing

1 small cream cheese
1/2 stick butter
2 cups powdered sugar

Mix ingredients with a mixer in a large bowl. For consistency, you may need to add a small amount of milk. Spread icing on cake while warm — not hot.

Rhubarb Cake

1 1/2 cup packed brown sugar
2/3 cup liquid shortening
1 egg
1 cup sour milk (1 cup milk and 1 tablespoon lemon juice or vinegar)
1 teaspoon baking soda
1 teaspoon salt
1 teaspoon vanilla
2 1/2 cups flour
1 1/2 cups diced, fresh rhubarb
1/2 cup finely chopped walnuts

Mix ingredients in order given. Pour into a well-greased and floured 9x13 inch pan. Top with small squares of butter, evenly spaced, and sprinkle with sugar. Bake in 325° oven for 40 minutes (don't overbake). Freezes well.

Linden Tree Inn

Jon and Dawn Cunningham
26 King Street
Rockport, MA 01966
(508) 546-2494; (800) 865-2122

Our inn is located on one of Rockport's many picturesque streets and offers a haven for a restful and relaxing vacation. Inside our Victorian-style home guests find 14 individually decorated guest rooms, all with private baths. Guests enjoy the Inn's formal living room, sun porch, the bay and pond views from the cupola, the spacious yard, and Dawn's "made from scratch" continental breakfast served buffet-style in the dining room. This recipe is made with fresh rhubarb from our garden.

New Life Homestead Bed and Breakfast

Carol and Bill Giersch
1400 East King Street
Lancaster, PA 17602-3240
(717) 396-8928

This apple cake is cut into squares about 2 1/2x2 1/2 inches. Grandma always had a plate full on the table at every holiday. It was the kind of cake you could pick up with your hands and run off with. My grandmother was from the Ukraine and a wonderful cook. She taught me to use only the best *for our family dinners and that's what I use for my bed and breakfast friends now. I miss her very much!*

Grandma Katie's Apple Cake

- 4 cups flour
- 4 teaspoons baking powder
- 1 teaspoon salt
- 1 cup lard or 1/2 cup oil with 1/2 cup milk
- 2 eggs
- 3/4 cup sugar
- 3/4 cup milk if using lard
- 10-12 apples, sliced and peeled
- 1-2 teaspoons apple pie spice
- 1 teaspoon salt
- 4 tablespoons butter

Cream lard (or oil) with sugar, and eggs. Add milk, flour, baking powder, and salt. Add more flour if needed to hold dough together. Chill. Roll out chilled dough 1/2 at a time. Place in greased cookie sheet with sides. Fill with apples mixed with spices and salt. Dot butter over top, as making a pie. Roll rest of dough into a rectangular shape, place over apples, cut air slits in top. Bake at 350° for 45 minutes to 1 hour until apples are tender. Cool and slice into squares.

Northwest Apple Cake

2 cups all-purpose flour
1 1/4 cups sugar
1 tablespoon baking powder
1 1/4 teaspoons ground cinnamon
1 teaspoon salt
1/2 teaspoon baking soda
1/2 teaspoon ground allspice
1/4 teaspoon ground cloves
1/2 cup butter, melted and cooled
1 cup sour cream
2 large eggs
1 cup finely diced apple

Crumb topping:
1/4 cup sugar
3 tablespoons all-purpose flour
1/4 teaspoon ground cinnamon
2 tablespoons butter

Heat oven to 350°. Butter 9 inch tube or bundt pan. Prepare Crumb topping: In a small bowl, combine the sugar, flour and cinnamon. Cut in butter until mixture resembles coarse crumbs. Set aside.

In a large bowl, combine the flour, sugar, baking powder, cinnamon, salt, baking soda, allspice, and cloves. In a small bowl, stir the butter, sour cream, and eggs until they are well combined. Stir the butter mixture into the flour mixture just until the batter is smooth and satiny. Stir in the apples. Spread the batter into the prepared pan. Sprinkle with the crumb topping. Bake the cake 1 hour, or until the crumbs are lightly browned and a cake tester comes out clean. Cool the cake in the pan for 20 minutes. Invert onto a work surface and remove the pan. Turn it over onto a serving plate.

North Island Bed and Breakfast

Jim and Maryvern Loomis
1589 North West Beach Road
Oak Harbor, WA 98277
(360) 675-7080

Begin the day with a walk or jog on the beach, then join us in the dining room between 8:30 and 9:30 A.M. for a hearty breakfast buffet. We are pleased to serve fresh fruit in season, juice, homemade breads and muffins, cereals, and freshly ground coffee or tea. Many of the fruits are grown here on the island, including the apples for our Northwest Apple Cake.

Thorpe House Country Inn

Mike and Jean Owens
PO Box 36
19049 Clayborne Street
Metamora, IN 47030
(317) 647-5425

A dear friend, whose last name is Apple, shared this scrumptious recipe with us. It's very popular during autumn when apples are plentiful in our beautiful Whitewater River Valley. It can be enjoyed warm on crisp evenings, but it is also a welcome addition to our breakfast buffet.

Fresh Apple Cake

2 cups peeled, chopped apples
1 cup sugar
1 egg
1 cup flour
1 teaspoon cinnamon
1 teaspoon soda
1/2 teaspoon salt
1/2 cup brown sugar
2 tablespoons cornstarch
1/2 cup sugar
1 cup water
2 tablespoons vanilla
2 tablespoons butter

Mix apples and sugar; let stand 1 hour until syrup forms. Mix first 7 ingredients. Pour into prepared 8 inch pan. Bake 35 minutes at 375°. Mix brown sugar, cornstarch, 1/2 cup sugar, and water in saucepan. Boil until clear, then add vanilla and butter. Cover cake with sauce while it's still hot.

Peach Dessert Cake

1 cup sifted cake flour
1 teaspoon baking powder
1/4 teaspoon salt
1/2 cup shortening
1/2 cup granulated sugar
1 teaspoon grated lemon rind
2 eggs, unbeaten
4 fresh peaches
1/3 cup granulated sugar
1/2 teaspoon cinnamon
1/4 cup chopped walnuts

Heat oven to 350°. Sift together first three ingredients. Work shortening with spoon until creamy. Slowly add 1/2 cup sugar, working until light and creamy. Add lemon rind, the eggs, one at a time, beating well. Add flour in fourths, beating after each addition. Spread 1/2 batter in greased 8x8x2 inch pan. Peel, pit and slice peaches. Arrange on batter. Spread rest of batter on top. Combine 1/3 cup sugar, cinnamon, and walnuts; sprinkle over all. Bake in moderate oven for 50 minutes. Cut into 9 squares. Serve warm with cream or ice cream.

Port City Victorian Inn

Barbara and Fred Schossau
1259 Lakeshore Drive
Muskegon, MI 49441
(616) 759-0205; (800) 274-3574;
FAX (616) 759-0205

I serve this as a coffee cake for breakfast and guests rave about how delicious it is! The recipe is about as old as the bed and breakfast — 120 years, and is also an elegant dessert served warm with ice cream. We serve breakfast in our formal dining room, or on our enclosed sun porch between 8:30 and 10 A.M. with coffee and tea always available for evening or early risers.

Evergreen The Bell-Capozzi House

Rocco and Barbara Bell-Capozzi
201 East Main Street
Christiansburg, VA 24073
(540) 382-7372; (800) 905-7372;
FAX (540) 382-4376

Our guests are always pleasantly surprised when I serve this cake for breakfast. Many of our guests are parents of nearby Virginia Tech students who join us for breakfast from time to time. They love the "Killer Cake" and usually take extra pieces back to the dorms. This is the moistest chocolate cake I have ever baked.

Chocolate Cherry Cake

1 box fudge cake mix
2 eggs, beaten
1 teaspoon almond extract
1 teaspoon vanilla
21 ounce can cherry pie filling

Mix by hand until well blended. Spray vegetable spray and flour a bundt pan. Bake at 350° for 25-30 minutes.

Frosting:
1 cup sugar
5 tablespoons butter
1 tablespoon cocoa
1/3 cup milk
1/2 cup pecan pieces

Frosting: Mix sugar, butter, cocoa, and milk. Cook 5 minutes to boiling, stirring constantly. Remove from heat and add pecans. Stir for desired consistency. Drizzle over cake.

Couscous Cake
with Strawberry Sauce

2 cups couscous
pinch salt
6-8 tablespoons AgarAgar flakes
(High protein tasteless seaweed that gels like Arrowroot. Get from health food store.)
toasted slivered almonds
5 cups apple juice
1 lemon, grated, rind and juice
1 pint strawberries

Bring apple juice and salt to boil in saucepan. Add lemon rind and juice, then AgarAgar and cook until flakes dissolve. Add couscous, lower flame, stir until semi-thick. Remove from heat and stir in sliced strawberries (save some for sauce). Oil a mold and pour in mixture. Cool and unmold.

Strawberry Sauce

1 cup apple juice
5 tablespoons AgarAgar
strawberries
slivered almonds

Heat apple juice to boil. Add AgarAgar, Stir and add chopped strawberries. Remove from heat when mixture thickens. Spoon glaze over cake top with slivered almonds.

Gardeners Cottage

Barbara Gavron
11 Singleton
Eureka Springs, AR 72632
(501) 253-9111; (800) 833-3394

Tucked away in a private, wooded, historic district location, this delightful cottage is decorated in charming country decor with romantic touches, cathedral ceilings, skylight, full kitchen, and a Jacuzzi for two. The spacious porch with its swing and hammock is for leisurely lounging. Great for honeymooners or a long peaceful stay.

Tweedy House Bed and Breakfast

Ed and Kathy Greiner
16 Washington Street
Eureka Springs, AR 72632
(501) 253-5435; (800) 346-1735

Built in 1883, Tweedy House is an elegant Victorian home located on the Historic Loop. Inside Tweedy House guests find three stories of antiques, family heirlooms, and quality furnishings.

This is our most requested dessert recipe! It is easy to make and tastes like you spent hours in the kitchen.

Rave Review Coconut Cake

1 package yellow cake mix
1 1/3 cup water
1/4 cup oil
1 small package vanilla instant pudding
4 eggs
1 cup flake coconut
1 cup pecans, chopped

Mix cake mix, pudding, water, eggs, and oil. Beat at medium speed for four minutes. Stir in coconut and nuts. Pour into greased/floured 9x13 inch pan. Bake at 350° for 35-40 minutes. Cool and frost.

Coconut Cream Cheese Frosting

3 tablespoons softened margarine
2 teaspoons milk
1 teaspoon vanilla
1 - 8 ounce package cream cheese
3 1/2 cups confectioners' sugar
1 cup flake coconut

Cream margarine and cream cheese. Cream cheese must be soft. Add milk, beat sugar in gradually. Blend in vanilla and coconut.

Poppy Seed Cake

- 1 yellow cake mix
- 1 box instant lemon pudding
- 1/4 cup poppy seeds
- 3/4 cup oil
- 1 cup water
- 4 eggs

Mix all ingredients together for three minutes. Bake at 350° in a bundt pan for 40 minutes. Let cake cool in pan for 10 minutes or more before removing from pan.

Lantana Guest House

Cynthia A. Sewell
22 Broadway
Rockport, MA 01966
(508) 546-3535; (800) 291-3535

This recipe was given to me about twelve years ago by a guest and her clergyman husband. The recipe came from their church recipe book. I have served this cake to my guests for breakfast and used it also for dessert at my church. I always have a request for the recipe. This is a very light cake and not too sweet.

Riverwalk Inn

Johnny Halpenny and Tammy Hill
329 Old Guilbeau
San Antonio, TX 78204
(210) 212-8300; (800) 254-4440;
FAX (210) 229-9422

The Riverwalk Inn is comprised of five two-story homes, circa 1840, which have been restored on the downtown San Antonio Riverwalk. Decorated in period antiques which create an ambience of "country elegance." Rock on our 80-foot porch lined with rocking chairs. Enjoy Aunt Martha's evening desserts and local storytellers that join us for our expanded continental breakfast. A Texas tradition with a Tennessee flavor awaits guests.

Ooey Gooey Cake

Step 1:
- 2 eggs
- 1 box yellow or chocolate cake mix
- 1 stick or butter

Step 2:
- 2 eggs
- 1 package cream cheese (8 ounces)
- 1 box powdered sugar

Step 1: Mix 2 eggs, cake mix, and slowly add melted butter. Spread in bottom of a well-greased springform pan.

Step 2: Mix cream cheese, eggs, and slowly add the box of powdered sugar. Mix until creamy, pour on top of first layer of mixture, covering first mixture completely. Bake at 350° for approximately 40-45 minutes.

Frozen Chocolate Mousse Cake

9 eggs, separated
1 cup sugar
zest of 1/2 orange
12 ounces sweet cooking chocolate
3/4 cup butter
1 tablespoon + 1 teaspoon Cointreau
    or other orange flavored liqueur
pinch of salt
1 cup whipping cream

Melt butter and chocolate, separately. In large mixer bowl, beat egg yolks and sugar until thick and lemon colored. Add melted chocolate, orange zest, melted butter and 1 tablespoon orange liqueur. Beat well. In another bowl, beat the egg whites and salt until stiff but not dry. Spoon 1/4 of the whites into the chocolate mixture, fold in well, add the remaining egg whites and fold in gently but thoroughly. Spread half the mixture in sprayed or greased 10 inch springform pan. Bake for 30 minutes. Cool.

While cake is baking, refrigerate the remaining chocolate mixture. Beat 1 cup whipping cream in bowl until slightly thickened, add 1 teaspoon orange liqueur, beat until thick. Fold gently but thoroughly into remaining chocolate mixture. Spread over the baked cooled shell. Freeze. Allow to thaw in refrigerator for 2 hours before cutting. Serves 10-12.

Silas Griffith Inn

Paul and Lois Dansereau
RR1 Box 66F
Danby, VT 05739
(802) 293-5567; (800) 545-1509

Our frozen Chocolate Mousse cake is a wonderful dessert, I love it. And best of all it can be made ahead, in fact, several can be kept in the freezer for those busy times. A friend gave me the recipe many years ago. It has become a staple recipe here at the Inn. This dessert gets rave reviews. I serve it with a fresh strawberry and a little whipped cream for garnish.

Adams Hilborne

Wendy and David Adams
801 Vine Street
Chattanooga, TN 37403
(423) 265-5000

Old World charm and hospitality in a tree-shaded setting rich with Civil War history and turn-of-the-century architecture. Rare Victorian Romanesque design with original coffered ceilings, hand-carved oak stairway, beveled glass windows, and ceramic tile embellishments. Small European-style hotel accommodation in 15 tastefully restored, exquisitely decorated guest rooms. Private baths, fireplaces, and complimentary breakfast for guests. Fine dining nightly at the Repertoire Restarant and casual dining at Café Alfresco.

Chocolate Mousse Cake

Cake:

1 cup all-purpose flour
1 teaspoon baking powder
1/2 teaspoon salt
1 cup butter, softened
1 cup sugar
2 eggs
1 tablespoon Amaretto
1/2 cup sour cream

Sift together flour, baking powder, salt and set aside. Whip eggs and sugar together until they are light and fluffy. Beat in the eggs, butter, and Amaretto. Alternately add in the dry ingredients and sour cream, beginning and ending with the flour. Pour into a buttered and floured 9 inch cake pan and bake at 350° for 45 minutes or until a cake tester comes out dry. Allow it to cool for 15 minutes before removing to a cake rack to cool for at least 1 hour.

Mousse:

1 pound chocolate morsels
3 egg yolks, slightly beaten
1/4 cup butter, melted
1 pint heavy cream
1 tablespoon brandy
1/4 sugar

In a double boiler over low heat, melt the chocolate. Whisk in the butter and then

the cream, sugar, and brandy together until stiff. Fold in the chocolate.

Cut the cake in half, horizontally, and place half in a nine inch springform pan. Pour the mousse over the cake. Top it with the other half of cake, or use it to make a second Chocolate Mousse Cake. Place it in the refrigerator to set for at least 4 hours. Remove the springform, cut, and serve drizzled with white chocolate sauce and white and dark chocolate shavings for garnish.

White chocolate sauce:

- 1 cup heavy cream
- 4 ounces of white chocolate, chopped
- 1/2 tablespoon brandy
- 1 tablespoon sugar
- 1 tablespoon butter
- 1 egg yolk

Heat the cream in a saucepan over low heat until it is just warm Stir in the white chocolate. Continue stirring until it is completely melted. Stir in sugar until it completely dissolves. Add the brandy and the butter, stirring until it is completely incorporated into the sauce. Stir in the egg yolk and stir constantly until it is incorporated and cooked, about 5 minutes.

La Maison de Campagne, Lafayette, B&B

Joeann and Fred McLemore
825 Kidder Road
Carnecro, LA 70520
(318) 896-6529; (800) 895-0235;
FAX (318) 896-1494

All four of us kids stormed the house like gangbusters after the long bus ride from school. Mama often had the milk jug and glasses ready for us along with a hot syrup cake as an after-school snack. The aromic fragrance of spices and cane syrup filled the house, and our stomachs as well, as my brothers and I feasted on warm Cajun Syrup Cake. My uncles raised the cane, ground it, and boiled the green liquid for hours until it became thick and dark brown.

My kitchen often smells of cane syrup and spices too these days. No schoolchildren are here anymore, but lots of visitors catch the aroma before coming inside our B&B where they may also enjoy Mama's Cajun Syrup Cake.

Cajun Syrup Cake

1 cup cane syrup or molasses
2 tablespoons sugar
2 teaspoons vanilla
1/3 cup oil
1 1/2 cup flour
1 egg
1 teaspoon baking powder
1/4 teaspoon baking soda
1/2 cup milk

Beat egg and sugar until creamy, then add syrup. Add oil, then all remaining combined, dry ingredients. Beat 100 strokes, or 3 minutes with mixer. Add milk and vanilla. Do not overbeat! Pour into an 11x14 inch pan and bake at 375° for about 35 minutes, or use two 9 inch pans and bake at 375° approximately 25 minutes. Serve warm, plain, or with Praline Topping.

Praline Topping

1 cup dark corn syrup
1/4 cup cornstarch
2 tablespoons brown sugar
3/4 cup chopped pecans
1 teaspoon vanilla

Combine all but vanilla in small saucepan, cooking over medium heat until bubbly and thickened. Stir in vanilla. Serve warm over cheesecake or syrup cake.

Tea Time Gingerbread

1 cup softened butter
1 cup sugar
1 cup unsulfured molasses
3 large, room temperature eggs
3 cups sifted flour, spooned into cup
1/4 teaspoon salt
1/2 teaspoon ground cloves
2 teaspoons ground ginger
1 teaspoon cinnamon
1 1/2 teaspoons baking soda
1 cup sour cream

Sift the flour with the salt, spices, and baking soda. Cream the butter, sugar, molasses, and eggs for five minutes on medium speed of an electric mixer. Blend the sifted dry ingredients into the creamed mixture; beat 2 minutes at medium speed. Add the sour cream and blend well. Bake in a greased and floured 9x13 inch pan in a preheated 350° oven for 40 minutes, or until cake tests done. Cool on a wire rack 10 minutes, cut into squares and serve warm with whipped cream. Yields 18 servings.

Scarborough Inn: "An 1895 Bed and Breakfast"

Gus and Carol Bruno
720 Ocean Avenue
Ocean City, NJ 08226
(609) 399-1558; (800) 258-1558;
FAX (607) 399-4472

This is wonderful in the fall or at Christmas time! You can make it extra special by serving it with cinnamon ice cream.

1897 Victorian House Bed and Breakfast

Richard and Doris Johnson
306 South Clark Street
Forest City, IA 50436
(515) 582-3613

Gingerbread is a wonderful dessert to serve in the fall when the leaves on the trees start to turn gold and red. The smell of fall is in the air . . . our thoughts go to pumpkin pie, gingerbread and molasses cookies. Mmmm. This recipe also makes a wonderful and a little different way to top off a breakfast.

Our Famous Gingerbread

Whisk together:

- 2 1/4 cups sifted all-purpose flour
- 1/2 teaspoon baking soda
- 1/8 teaspoon salt
- 2 teaspoons ginger
- 1/2 teaspoon cinnamon
- 1/8 teaspoon cloves
- 1/8 teaspoon allspice

Set aside.

Pour 1 cup boiling water over:

- 1/2 cup shortening

Add:

- 3/4 cup white sugar
- 3/4 cup light molasses
- Beat 2 eggs and add to the above

Add the dry ingredients to the liquid and beat until smooth. Pour batter into a 11x7 inch pan which has been sprayed with a nonstick cooking spray.

Bake about 40 minutes in a 350° oven. Serve with Orange Sauce.

Orange Sauce

- 1 1/2 cups orange juice
- 1 cup granulated white sugar
- 4 teaspoons cornstarch
- 2 tablespoons butter or margarine
- 1 tablespoon lemon juice

Mix in a saucepan and bring to a boil, boil until clear, about one minute.

Blueberry Buckle

Mix thoroughly:
- 3/4 cup sugar
- 1/4 cup soft butter
- 1 egg

Stir in:
- 1/2 cup milk

Sift together and stir in:
- 1 3/4 cup sifted flour
- 2 teaspoons baking powder
- 1/2 teaspoon salt

Fold in:
- 3/4 cup to 1 cup fresh blueberries

Spread batter in greased and floured 9 inch square pan.

Sprinkle with topping:
- 1/2 cup sugar
- 1/3 cup flour
- 1/4 cup soft butter
- 1/2 teaspoon cinnamon

Bake at 375° for 45 minutes.

VanHorn House at Lions Ridge

Susan and John Laatsch
0318 Lions Ridge Road
Carbondale, CO 81623
(970) 963-3605; FAX (970) 963-1681

This is a recipe given to me by a co-worker more than 25 years ago. While there are many similar recipes (most of which I have tried), I keep coming back to this one. It is rich, moist, and absolutely delicious — especially when it is still warm from the oven. Our guests are never satisfied with one piece!

The Kitchen House (circa 1732)

Lois Evans
126 Tradd Street
Charleston, SC 29401
(803) 577-6362

Nestled in the heart of the historic district, The Kitchen House is a totally restored 18th-century dwelling. Southern hospitality, absolute privacy, fireplaces, and antiques. Private patio, Colonial herb garden, fishpond, and fountain. Full breakfast, plus concierge service. This pre-Revolutionary home was featured in Colonial Homes Magazine, *the* New York Times, *and* Best Places to Stay in the South.

Peach and Blueberry Crumbcake

Mix together and let stand for 10-15 minutes the following:

- 5 cups combination of blueberries and peaches (peeled and sliced)
- 1/2 cup sugar
- 2 tablespoons lemon juice
- 1/4 teaspoon ground cinnamon
- 3 tablespoons tapioca

Preheat oven to 425°. Mix together to form a crumbly mixture the following (best if done in food processor, turning on and off quickly):

- 1/2 cup cold butter (unsalted)
- 1/2 cup granulated sugar
- 1 1/2 cups all-purpose flour

Save 3/4 cup of this mixture for crumb topping. Press remaining mixture into 9 inch spring form pan. Will go up sides 1/2-1 inch. Spread fruit mixture evenly into crust. Bake at 425° for 20 minutes. Sprinkle on crumb topping and lower temperature to 375°. Bake for 30-35 minutes or until top is brown and fruit mixture bubbles appearing glazed. Remove from oven and cool.

Frozen fruit may be used but is nicest in South Carolina when peaches and blueberries are in season. May be served with vanilla ice cream or plain yogurt, or frozen vanilla yogurt.

Apple-Walnut Brunch Cake

- 2 cups all-purpose flour
- 2 teaspoons baking powder
- 2 teaspoons cinnamon
- 1/4 teaspoon salt
- 1 1/4 cups sugar
- 4 eggs
- 1/2 vegetable oil
- 1/2 cup raisins (if desired)
- 1 - 21 ounce can apple pie filling (not just sliced apples)
- 1 cup finely chopped walnuts

Heat oven to 350°. Grease 9x13x2 inch pan. Mix dry ingredients in large bowl. In a separate bowl, beat eggs and oil and combine with dry ingredients, mixing with wooden spoon until moistened. Fold in the pie filling (and raisins, if desired). Pour in pan. Sprinkle walnuts evenly over top. Bake 45 minutes at 350°. Cool completely before cutting.

The Inn at New Ipswich

Ginny and Steve Bankuti
11 Porter Hill Road, PO Box 208
New Ipswich, NH 03071
(603) 878-3711

This breakfast cake is excellent with a dollop of sour cream on top. It's great following a savory egg entree. I've made this coffee cake for more than 2 years, since I was a Cub Scout den mother. (One of my cub's moms gave me the recipe.) We still enjoy it, often, and our bed and breakfast guests do, too.

The Farm House

Mike and Pat Meierhenry
32617 Church Road
Murdock, NE 68407
(402) 867-2062

This is my grandmother's recipe, and the directions are just as she wrote them. I use a 9 inch square pan, so it gets higher, and serve it warm, as a coffee cake. I also use it as shortcake, and serve with strawberries. The ingredients are all items you would have on hand.

Crumb Cake

2 cups flour
1 1/2 cups sugar
3/4 cup butter
2 teaspoons baking powder
2 eggs
3/4 cup milk
1 teaspoon vanilla

Mix all together with hands into crumbs. Take out a small cupful and set aside. Break 2 eggs in remainder of crumbs, add milk, beat until it looks like cream. Flavor, and bake in long pan. Sprinkle cup of crumbs on before you bake. 350° oven, 35-40 minutes.

Coffee Cake

2 cans 10 count Hungry Jack Biscuits
1/4 cup peach preserves
1 tablespoon butter
1 stick melted butter
1 cup brown sugar
1/4 cup nuts
1 tablespoon cinnamon

Place peach preserves and cut-up butter in bottom of bundt pan. Melt butter. Dip each biscuit in butter and roll in the brown sugar, nuts, and cinnamon mixture. Stand biscuits around bundt pan like wheels. Pour remaining butter and sugar mixture over biscuits. Bake at 350° for 30 minutes or until done.

Miss Alice's Bed and Breakfast

Volene B. Barnes
8325 Highway 141 South
Hartsville, TN 37074
(615) 374-3015; (615) 444-4401

I place this coffee cake on a footed cake stand and use it as the table centerpiece. Serve this with gourmet coffee to complete the breakfast. This can also be served in the parlor as after-dinner dessert anytime.

Timberidge Bed and Breakfast

Donita Brookmyer
16801 State Route #4
Goshen, IN 45626
(219) 533-7133

The Austrian chalet, white pine log home is nestled in the beauty of the quiet woods, just two miles from Goshen and near many local points of interest. Our guests enjoy the privacy of a master suite. A path through the woods is frequented by birds, squirrels, and deer. Nearby are Amish farms where field work is done by horse-drawn equipment. Timberidge offers the best of city and country — close to town, yet removed to the majestic beauty of the woods that evokes a love of nature and a reverence for God's creation.

This is a very good moist cake. A 2x3 inch square brings raves from our guests.

Out - of-This-World Coffee Cake

1 cup brown sugar
3/4 cup white sugar
2 1/2 cups all-purpose flour
1/2 teaspoon cinnamon
1/8 teaspoon nutmeg
1/2 teaspoon salt
3/4 cup salad oil
1 cup buttermilk or sour milk
1 egg
2 teaspoons soda

Combine sugars, flour, spices, salad oil. Mix well to crumbs. Take out 1/3 cup crumbs. Add crushed nuts to make one cup, reserve for topping. Mix in the remaining ingredients. Mix well. Place in a greased 13x9 inch pan. Add topping. Bake at 350° for 30 minutes or until center is baked through.

Cinnamon Coffee Cake

- 1 - 15-19 ounce package yellow cake mix
- 1 - 5.1 ounce package vanilla instant pudding
- 3/4 cup oil
- 3/4 cup water
- 4 eggs
- 1 teaspoon vanilla extract
- 2 teaspoons butter
- 1/2 cup brown sugar
- 2 teaspoons cinnamon
- 2 cups chopped walnuts

In large mixing bowl, combine cake mix, pudding mix, oil, water, eggs, vanilla, and butter. Mix at high speed for 3 minutes. In a small bowl, combine brown sugar and cinnamon. Sprinkle chopped walnuts on bottom of greased 9x13 inch baking pan.

Over walnuts, layer half of brown sugar mixture, half of batter, remaining brown sugar mixture, and remaining batter. Using a knife, swirl ingredients in pan for a marble effect. Bake at 350° for 50-55 minutes.

Vanilla Frosting

- 1 cup powdered sugar
- 1 teaspoon vanilla extract
- 2 teaspoons butter
- cream or milk

To make frosting, combine powdered sugar, vanilla, butter and enough cream to achieve spreading consistency. Spread over cake while still warm, but not hot.

Trails End Bed and Breakfast

Richard and Bonnie Flood
641 Ten Mile Lake Drive
Chetek, WI 54728
(715) 924-2641

Peace and tranquillity await guests in this modern, spacious, log lodge, situated on our private island. The log home boasts antiques of every sort, with stories behind most every unique feature of the home from an 1887 jail door to a 300-pound, 7-foot wagon wheel and a huge stone fireplace. Each guest's bedroom is decorated for utmost comfort and relaxation.

I received this recipe from a very special neighbor, and it has turned out to be everyone's favorite. Moist and scrumptiously delicious.

Shiloh Bed and Breakfast

Ron and Joan Smith
3265 Triangle Park Road
Mariposa, CA 95338
(209) 742-7200

Being close to Yosemite National Park brings us guests with varied needs. Often a couple will want to leave early to do some hiking. Others want a more leisurely morning and plan to relax and enjoy our beautiful surroundings.

To accomodate everyone, I fix the Almond Paste Twirl a day ahead, then set it out the next morning in a glass covered dish with fruit, coffee and juice for the early risers. The more leisurely folks are served a sit-down breakfast on our sun porch, and the coffee cake still looks inviting and tastes delicious.

Almond Paste Twirl Coffee Cake

- 3-3 1/4 cups all-purpose flour
- 1 package active dry yeast
- 1 cup milk
- 6 tablespoons butter or margarine
- 1/3 cup granulated sugar
- 1/2 teaspoon salt
- 1 egg

Almond paste:

- 1/3 cup granulated sugar
- 2 tablespoons butter
- 1/4 cup ground almonds
- 1/2 teaspoon almond extract

Heat milk and butter to 115°-120° stirring constantly until butter almost melts. Add egg (beaten). Mix in flour, salt, sugar, and dry yeast. May be placed in a bread maker on dough setting, otherwise, knead on lightly floured suface until smooth, about 3-5 minutes. Shape into a ball and let rise in a greased bowl until double. After dough rises, punch it down and let set about 10 minutes. Roll into a 12x18 rectangle. Spread with almond paste. Roll up and place seam side down diagonally. Shape into ring on large greased baking sheet. Cut with kitchen shears every 1/2 inch to within 1/2 inch of bottom. Let rise in warm place until nearly double, about 45 minutes. Bake at 375° for 20-25 minutes.

A thin coating of orange or lemon glaze really adds a flair to this coffee cake. Use 1/2 cup of powdered sugar, 1 tablespoon fresh orange or lemon juice, and 1 teaspoon finely grated orange or lemon peel.

Homestead Apple Harvest Coffee Cake

4 cups diced apples
1 3/4 cups sugar
3 cups flour
2 teaspoons baking soda
1 teaspoon nutmeg
3/4 teaspoon cinnamon
2 eggs
1 cup cooking oil
1 teaspoon vanilla
Optional: 1/2 cup chopped walnuts or
  1 cup raisins

Mix apples and sugar. Let stand 1 hour. Sift flour, baking soda, and spices; beat eggs, then add oil and vanilla. Add apple mixture, and nuts and raisins if used. Add flour mixture and blend thoroughly. Bake in large greased cake pan at 350° for 1 hour. Cool in pan 15 minutes. This can be made a day ahead; but slices should be warmed when served at breakfast.

Homestead Inn Bed and Breakfast

Dan and Danielle Duffy
Short Sands Beach, Box 15
York Beach, ME 03910
(207) 363-8952

We keep our recipes to a New England flavor. Other recipes include cranberries, rhubarb, blueberries, maple (sap) syrup, etc. This recipe is served from September through October, in the fall. On cool evenings here in New England, we also serve it, complimented with spiced cider, to guests in the living room, before a warm fireplace glow.

Joan's Bed and Breakfast

Joan Hetherington
210R Lynn Street
Peabody, MA 01960
(508) 532-0191

Located 25 miles from Boston, 10 miles from historic Salem, and 25 miles from quaint Rockport. We have wonderful restaurants in the area, also two large shopping malls and a terrific summer theater. Guests also enjoy our in-ground pool!

All our meals and desserts are served on ruby red dishes. The afternoon tea is served on bone china.

One-Dish Apple-Raisin Coffee Cake

2/3 cup oil
1 teaspoon vanilla
2 eggs
2 cups flour
1 cup sugar
1 teaspoon salt
1 1/2 teaspoons soda
3/4 teaspoon cinnamon
dash nutmeg
1/2 cup raisins
1/2 cup nuts
1 can apple pie filling, unseasoned

Combine oil, vanilla, and eggs in large bowl. Mix all dry ingredients and add to egg mixture. Add apple filling and raisins, and nuts. Can be mixed by hand. Bake at 350° for 25-30 minutes in a 9x13 inch pan. Sprinkle with confectioners' sugar or make a confectioners' sugar glaze. Serves 15.

Overnight Coffee Cake

2 cups flour
1 teaspoon baking powder
1 teaspoon baking soda
1 teaspoon cinnamon
1/2 teaspoon salt
1 cup sugar
2/3 cup butter or margarine
1/2 cup brown sugar
2 eggs
1 cup buttermilk
1 cup chopped raw apple

Topping:
1/2 cup brown sugar
1/2 cup nuts, chopped
1 teaspoon cinnamon
1/4 teaspoon nutmeg

Mix all dry ingredients in a large mixing bowl. Add all remaining ingredients, except apple. Beat one minute. Stir in apple. Pour into a greased 9x13 inch pan. Mix the topping and sprinkle over the batter. Cover the pan and refrigerate overnight. The next day, preheat oven to 350°. Bake 45-50 minutes. Cut into squares and serve while warm.

Keystone Inn

Wilmer and Doris Martin
231 Hanover Street
Gettysburg, PA 17325
(717) 337-3888

This coffee cake sends a delightful aroma up the staircase and awakens guests to a wonderful morning! It is especially easy because you can mix it the night before.

The Inn on Golden Pond

Bonnie and Bill Webb
Route 3, PO Box 680
Holderness, NH 03245-0680
(603) 968-7269; FAX (603) 968-9226

From late spring to mid-summer, guests are treated to this recipe and many other rhubarb specialties made with rhubarb grown right in Bonnie and Bill's backyard. Bonnie's rhubarb jam is always on the breakfast table year-round, and her jam and breakfast specialties cookbook are available for purchase.

Rhubarb Coffee Cake

2 cups flour
1 1/4 cups sugar
1 teaspoon baking soda
1 teaspoon salt
1/4 teaspoon ground cloves
1 teaspoon cinnamon
1/4 teaspoon nutmeg
2 large eggs
1/4 cup vegetable oil
1/3 cup milk
2 cups chopped fresh rhubarb

Sift dry ingredients together in a bowl. Mix eggs and oil in another bowl and add to the dry ingredients. Blend in milk, then fold in rhubarb. Pour into a greased 9x13x2 inch pan. Spread topping over unbaked cake. Bake at 350° for 45-50 minutes. Yield: 10-12 servings.

Topping:

4 tablespoons butter
1/2 cup light brown sugar
2/3 cup flour
3/4 cup coconut
1/4 cup chopped walnuts

Cream butter and sugar together. Add rest of ingredients; mix well.

Sour Cream Coffee Cake

1 1/2 cups brown sugar
3/4 cup butter (softened)
3 eggs
1 1/2 teaspoons vanilla
3 cups flour
1 1/2 teaspoons baking powder
1 1/2 teaspoons baking soda
3/4 teaspoon salt
1 1/2 cups sour cream

Filling:

1/2 cup brown sugar
1/2 cup finely chopped nuts
2 teaspoons ground cinnamon
2 tablespoons butter
2 tablespoons flour

Glaze:

1/2 cup confectionery sugar
1/4 teaspoon vanilla
1-2 teaspoons milk

Heat oven to 350°. Grease tube pan. Prepare the brown sugar filling by mixing all 5 ingredients (reserve). Beat sugar, butter, eggs, and vanilla in large bowl. Beat for 2 minutes, scraping bowl often. Beat flour, baking powder, baking soda, and salt alternately with sour cream on low speed until completely mixed. Spread 1/3 of batter, about 2 cups, in pan. Sprinkle with 1/3 of filling. Repeat 2 times. Bake 45 minutes or until done. Cool slightly. Remove from pan. Cool 10 minutes. Drizzle with glaze. Makes 16 slices.

Pau-Lyn's Country Bed and Breakfast

Paul and Evelyn Landis
RT #3, Box 676
Milton, PA 17847

We serve a full country breakfast, most often a coffee cake, or other pastry at our bed and breakfast. They enjoy this particular one and I shared this recipe with several guests.

The Owl and Turtle Harbor View Guest Rooms

The Conrad Family
PO Box 1265, 8 Bay View
Camden, ME 04843
(207) 236-9014

This coffee cake cuts well after having been frozen. The recipe was given to us years ago by guests who came frequently until incapacitated. It's a wonderful standby. The number of servings depends upon the size of the slice.

Super Sour Cream Coffee Cake

3 cups flour
1/2 teaspoon salt
1 teaspoon baking soda
3 teaspoons baking powder
3/4 cup sugar
3 teaspoons almond extract
1/2 pound margarine
1 cup sugar
3 eggs
2 cups sour cream
1 teaspoon cinnamon
1 cup chopped nuts

Cream together softened margarine and sugar; add eggs. Blend in dry ingredients alternately with sour cream. Stir in almond extract. Pour 1/2 batter into greased 10 inch tube pan. Combine cinnamon and nuts and swirl half of mixture into batter; repeat.

Bake at 350° for 1 hour and 20 minutes, or until top is lightly browned. Remove from oven and let cool for 10 minutes before removing outside of tube. When well cooled, wrap in aluminum foil and freeze.

Sour Cream Coffee Cake

3/4 cup butter
1 1/2 cups sugar
3 eggs
1 1/2 teaspoons vanilla
3 cups flour
1 1/2 teaspoons baking soda
1 1/2 teaspoons baking powder
1/4 teaspoon salt
1 1/2 cups sour cream

Filling (mix together):
1/2 cup brown sugar (packed)
1/2 cup finely chopped nuts
1 1/2 teaspoons cinnamon

Preheat oven to 350°. Grease four 9x5x3 inch pans. Combine sugar, butter, eggs, and vanilla in large bowl. Beat vigorously. Mix in flour, baking powder, soda, and salt alternately with sour cream. Spread 1/2 of batter in each pan (about 1 1/2 cups). Sprinkle with 1/4 of filling (about 5 teaspoons). Repeat. Bake at 350° for 1 hour. Cool slightly in pans before removing.

Captain Dexter House of Vineyard Haven

Lori and Mike
100 Main Street, PO Box 2457
Vineyard Haven, MA 02568
(508) 693-6564; FAX (508) 693-8448

This recipe is a favorite of many of the guests that stay with us each year. They often ask when they arrive, "Are you going to make that wonderful coffee cake while we're here?" The cinnamon and brown sugar are a wonderful aroma to wake up to.

The coffee cake makes a nice centerpiece on the morning table. Allow it to cool slightly, making it easier to cut. Place the entire cake on a platter, cut about a third of it into slices and lay them out on the platter.

Yoder's Zimmer mit Fruhstuck Haus

Wilbur and Evelyn Yoder
PO Box 1396, 504 South Main
Middlebury, IN 46540
(219) 825-2378

I like to serve this coffee cake warm. It can be heated in the microwave. Sometimes I use half a can of two different pie fillings, therefore having more variety. This is a very delicious coffee cake, and one that is different from what most people expect of a coffee cake.

Fruit-Swirl Coffee Cake

1 1/2 cups sugar
1 cup butter or margarine, softened
1 1/2 tablespoons baking powder
1 teaspoon vanilla
1 teaspoon almond extract
4 eggs
3 cups all purpose flour
1 21 ounce can cherry, apricot, or blueberry pie filling

Glaze:
1 cup powdered sugar
1-2 tablespoons milk

Heat oven to 350°. Beat sugar, butter or margarine, baking powder, vanilla, almond extract, and eggs in large bowl on low speed until blended. Beat on high speed for 3 minutes. Stir in flour. Spread 2/3 of batter in greased jelly roll pan (15 1/2x10 1/2x1 inch). Spread pie filling over batter. Drop remaining batter by teaspoons over pie filling. Bake until light brown, about 45 minutes. Drizzle with glaze while warm.

Red Raspberry Coffee Cake

8 ounce cream cheese
1/2 cup butter
2 eggs
1 teaspoon baking powder
1/2 teaspoon vanilla
3/4 cup red raspberry preserves
1 cup sugar
1 3/4 cups flour
1/4 cup milk
1/2 teaspoon soda
1/4 teaspoon salt
powdered sugar

Cream cheese, butter, and sugar until fluffy. Combine all dry ingredients. Add 1/2 of dry ingredients to cheese mixture along with eggs, milk, and vanilla, beating on low speed until well blended. Add remaining flour, beating on low speed.

Spread into a 9x13x2 inch pan that's been greased and floured. Drop preserves in dollops on top, swirl with a knife. Bake at 350° for 35-40 minutes. When cool sprinkle with powdered sugar. Serves 24.

The Elegant Inn Bed and Breakfast

Martha and Ted Cline
215 North Walnut Street
Bryan, OH 43506
(419) 636-2873; (800) 577-2873

I've always liked to bake, so when I decided to open the Inn, I wanted something special to serve my guests for breakfast. As it turned out, much to my surprise, this coffee cake is one of my most requested recipes. Although the original recipe calls for red raspberry preserves, I sometimes use cherry, blueberry, or blackberry. Whatever the flavor, it never fails to receive a response from the guests.

The Inn on South Street

Jacques and Eva Downs
5 South Street, PO Box 478A
Kennebunkport, ME 04046
(207) 967-5151; (800) 963-5151;
FAX (207) 967-4639

Now approaching its 200th year, this stately Greek Revival house is in Kennebunkport's historic district. Located on a quiet street, the Inn is within walking distance of restaurants, shops, and the water. There are three beautifully decorated guest rooms and one luxury apartment/suite. Private baths, queen-size beds, fireplaces, a common room, afternoon refreshments, and early morning coffee. Breakfast is always special and is served in the large country kitchen with views of the river and ocean.

Zucchini-Apple Coffee Cake

3 cups flour
1 cup sugar
1 teaspoon baking powder
1 1/2 teaspoons baking soda
2 teaspoons cinnamon
1/2 teaspoon ground cloves
1/4 teaspoon nutmeg
1/2 teaspoon salt
3 eggs
3/4 cup oil
1/4 cup molasses
2 cups zucchini, grated
2 teaspoons vanilla
1 cup chopped nuts
2/3 cups raisins
1 cups chopped tart apple

Streusel:

1/4 cup butter
1/2 cup sugar
1/3 cup flour
1/2 teaspoon cinnamon
1/4 teaspoon nutmeg

Sift dry ingredients and set aside. Mix together next 5 ingredients. Combine eggs, oil, molasses, zucchini and vanilla with dry ingredients. Add nuts, raisins, and apples. Spread into well greased 9x13 inch baking dish. Blend all streusel ingredients with a pastry blender. Sprinkle cake batter with streusel and bake in 350° oven for 45 minutes or until done. Makes about 24 servings.

Pecan-Almond Cinnamon Coffee Cake

1/2 cup butter
1 cup sugar
2 eggs
1/2 cup heavy cream
1/2 cup sour cream
1/2 teaspoon baking soda
1 1/2 teaspoon baking powder
1 teaspoon vanilla
2 cups flour

Topping:
1/2 cup chopped pecans
1/2 cup sliced almonds
4 tablespoons brown sugar
2 teaspoons cinnamon

Preheat oven to 350°. Butter a 9 inch tube pan. Combine butter and sugar in a large bowl. Beat until light and fluffy. Add eggs, beating well. Beat in heavy cream, vanilla, and sour cream. Separately, mix together baking powder, baking soda, and flour. Sift flour mixture in a bit at a time to creamed mixture. Pour 1/2 of mixture into pan. Mix together pecans, almonds, brown sugar, and cinnamon. Sprinkle evenly over cake in pan. Spoon remaining batter mixture over nuts and cake mixture. Bake 50 minutes or until cake tester inserted in middle comes out clean. Cool in pan for 15 minutes. Remove from pan. Enjoy!

To make a lighter version, substitute condensed skim milk and plain yogurt for heavy cream and sour cream.

Cougar Creek Inn Bed and Breakfast

Mrs. Patricia Doucette
PO Box 1162
240 Grizzly Crescent
Canmore, Alberta
CANADA T0L 0M0
(403) 678-4751; FAX (403) 678-9529

Quiet, rustic, cedar chalet with mountain views in every direction. Grounds border on Cougar Creek and are surrounded by rugged mountain scenery which invites all types of outdoor activity. I have a strong love for the mountains and can assist guests with plans for local hiking, skiing, canoeing, mountain biking, backpacking, etc., as well as scenic drives. The bed and breakfast has a private entrance with sitting area, fireplace, games, TV, sauna, and numerous reading materials for guests' use. Breakfasts are hearty and wholesome with many home-baked items. I share this recipe which is always a breakfast favorite in the Canadian Rockies!

The Red House Country Inn

Joan Martin and Sandy Schmanke
4586 Picnic Area Road
Burdett, NY 14818-9716
(607) 546-8566; FAX (607) 546-4105, call first
Email: redshinn@aol.com

We are located in New York state's only national forest and have access to all kinds of wild berries and old fruit trees and love to make our own fillings (wild elderberries, black raspberries, choke cherries, etc.) But canned fillings work very well too. Our guests have enjoyed this breakfast cake for years and request it often. It offers 20 generous servings. Add nuts, currants, or raisins on top if you like.

Red House Coffee Cake Cobbler

4 cups Bisquick
1/2 cup sugar
1/4 cup melted butter
1/2 cup milk
1 teaspoon vanilla
3 eggs
1 can (21 ounce) fruit pie filling (any flavor)

Glaze:
1 cup powdered sugar
2 tablespoons orange juice or milk

Topping
1/2 cup sugar
1 teaspoon cinnamon
1/4 cup butter or margarine

Preheat oven to 350°. Grease jelly roll pan (15 1/2x10 1/2x1 inch). Mix all ingredients (except pie filling, glaze, and topping) together. Beat well for 30 seconds. Spread 2/3 of batter in pan. Spread pie filling over (may not cover completely.) Drop remaining batter by tablespoons onto pie filling. Mix topping with hands and sprinkle over cake. Bake 20-25 minutes until lightly browned. Mix glaze well and drizzle over coffee cake. Enjoy.

Low-fat Yogurt-Raisin Pie

1 9 inch baked pie shell
1 1/2 cups raisins
1 1/2 cups water
3/4 cup sugar
1/4 teaspoon salt
2 tablespoons flour
3 egg yolks
1/2 cup skim milk
1/2 cup low-fat vanilla yogurt
3 egg whites
6 tablespoons sugar

Simmer raisins and water until raisins are tender. Combine sugar, salt and flour. Beat egg yolks slightly with milk. Stir egg mixture into sugar mixture. Add to raisins, stirring constantly. Cook and stir over medium heat until mixture is very thick, 5-10 minutes. Remove from heat. Add low-fat vanilla yogurt, blending thoroughly. Pour into pie shell.

Meringue: Beat egg whites until soft peaks form. Gradually add sugar while beating. Pile evenly over filling. Bake in 400° oven until brown — about 5 minutes. Dip your cutting knife in water before cutting into pie each time.

Haverkamps Linn Street Homestay Bed and Breakfast

Clarence and Dorothy Haverkamp
619 N. Linn Street
Iowa City, IA 52245-4934
(319) 337-4363

We serve pie for dessert with our country breakfast. This pie is the most often chosen when they are asked the night before. Many have not had it before and then want the recipe to make it at home.

Calico Inn

Lill and Jim Katzbeck
757 Ranch Way
Sevierville, TN 37862
(423) 428-3833; (800) 235-1054

Our Pistachio Pie was always a favorite with our family. I made it every year around the holidays as with the green pistachio pudding and red cherries it looked very festive. Besides it being absolutely delicious, it is very light, so if you have a big turkey dinner there is always room for Pistachio Pie, and plenty of it.

We have four children and after our oldest daughter got married her husband loved the pie so much it became a tradition that each year for his birthday I would prepare this pie. Now that I have our bed and breakfast, I make it for our guests and they enjoy it too.

Last Christmas we had a couple get married and I served a candlelight dinner. She chose the Pistachio Pie for dessert which everyone enjoyed and raved about.

From Christmas to birthdays to weddings, it has been a special pie that everyone remembers for its flavor and special way it adds to each celebration.

Pistachio Pie

1 1/2 cups flour
1/4 cup walnuts, chopped
1 1/2 sticks margarine, softened
1 - 8 ounce softened cream cheese
1 teaspoon vanilla
1 cup powdered sugar
1 large tub Cool Whip
2 small boxes instant pistachio pudding
3 cups cold milk

For the first layer, mix flour, walnuts, and margarine. Spread in a 9x13 inch glass pan. Bake at 350° for 20-30 minutes. For second layer, mix cream cheese, vanilla, powdered sugar, and one cup Cool Whip. Beat well and spread over first layer. Put in refrigerator and let set for 1 hour. For the third layer, mix instant pudding with milk. Mix until dissolved, spread over second layer. Top with remaining Cool Whip, nuts and cherries.

You may substitute chocolate or lemon instant pudding (delicious) or any other of your choice.

Jefferson Davis Chocolate Chip Pie

3 cups sugar
3/4 butter
3 eggs
1 teaspoon vanilla
1 cup Pet milk
4 tablespoons flour
1 cup pecans (optional)
2 cups shredded coconut
1 cup chocolate chips

Cream sugar and butter together. Add in eggs, beaten, and vanilla. Alternately mix in milk and flour. Mix in pecans and coconut. Stir in chips with wooden spoon. Pour batter into two unbaked pie shells. Bake 15 minutes on 450° then 20-25 on 350° or until golden brown. Serve with real whipped cream.

Kane Springs Ranchstead

Charles and Lucy Nelson
1705 South Kane Springs Road
PO Box 940
Moab, UT 84532
(801) 259-7821

Just minutes away from Arches National Park; Canyonlands Air Field; Colorado River rafting, jet skiing, and kayaking; hiking; horseback riding; water slides; swimming; and bicycling. Singles: primative tent camping in canyon, along the rim of the Colorado River — an easy four miles from Moab. Also, accommodations for self-contained RVs among trees along the river near Native American pictoglyphs with ancient ladder used by inhabitants. Reserve you reservation in advance in order to experience this beautiful Red Rock Canyon — a bed outdoors.

Simple Pleasures

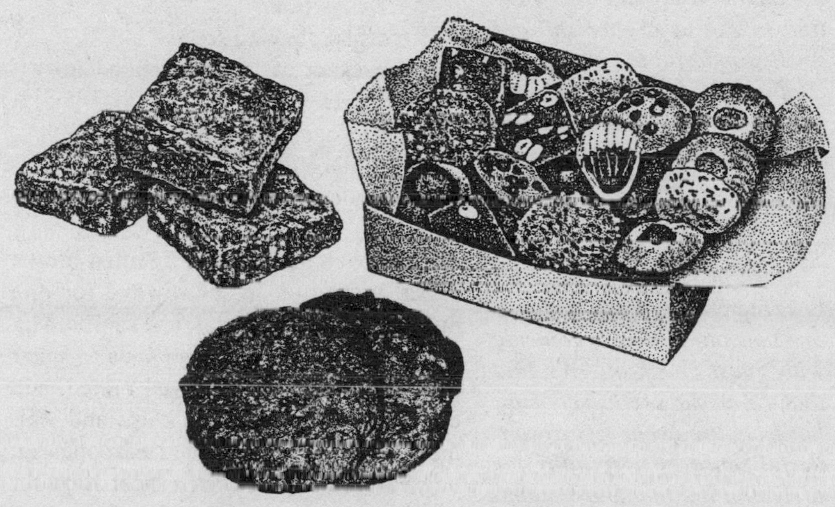

Cookies and Dessert Bars

"O taste and see that the Lord is good: blessed is the man that trusteth in him."

Psalm 34:8

Holden House—1902 Bed & Breakfast Inn

Sallie and Welling Clark
1102 W. Pikes Peak Avenue
Colorado Springs, CO 80904
(719) 471-3980 (voice and FAX)

Our garden grows many lovely flowers and herbs in the spring and summer. Lavender and mint flowers are beautiful to use as a garnish, and smell wonderful to compliment the food. We want each dish to look as good as it is to eat, and proper garnishing adds that special touch. Fresh fruit is used in winter months when flowers are difficult to come by.

Here at Holden House, we bake our cookies fresh each day and time our baking to coincide with guest check-ins. We find that the aroma of fresh cookies, hot from the oven, sets a wonderful sense of hospitality for arrival at the Inn. Our bottomless cookie jar is a big hit and our coffee/tea service is available to our guests 24 hours a day. Guests are also provided with a refrigerator to store their own drinks or leftovers from the many fine restaurants in Colorado Springs and the Pike Peak region.

Chocolate Chunk/White Chocolate Chip Cookies

3/4 cup brown sugar
3/4 cup butter or margarine
2 eggs
1 teaspoon vanilla
2 1/2 cups flour
1 teaspoon baking soda
1/2 package of 12 ounce chocolate chunks
1/2 package of 10 ounce Hershey's vanilla chips
1/4 cup chopped walnuts

Preheat oven to 375°-400°. Soften brown sugar and butter in microwave for one minute on high. Add eggs, and vanilla. Mix well. Add flour and baking soda to sugar and egg mixture. When well mixed, add chocolate chunks, vanilla chips and walnuts. Place, by well-rounded teaspoons, on ungreased, insulated cookie sheet. Bake for 10-12 minutes or until slightly brown on top. Makes approximately 2 dozen.

Foothill House Sweet Dream Cookies

- 1 cup (2 sticks) unsalted butter
- 1 1/2 cups firmly packed light brown sugar
- 1 egg, room temperature
- 1 teaspoon vanilla
- 2 1/2 cups unbleached all-purpose flour
- 1 teaspoon baking soda
- 1 teaspoon cinnamon
- 1 teaspoon ground ginger
- 1/2 teaspoon salt
- 1 - 12 ounce package semisweet chocolate chips
- 1 cup chopped walnuts
- 1 cup powdered sugar

Cream butter. Beat in brown sugar, egg, and vanilla. Combine flour, baking soda, cinnamon, ginger, and salt. Blend into butter mixture. Fold in chocolate chips and walnuts. Refrigerate until firm. (Can be prepared one day ahead.) Preheat oven to 375°. Lightly grease baking sheets. Break off small pieces of dough; roll between palms into 1 inch rounds. Dredge rounds in powdered sugar. Arrange round on prepared sheets, spacing at least 2 inches apart. Bake 10 minutes. Let cool 5 minutes on sheet. Transfer to racks and cool. Store in airtight container.

Foothill House Bed and Breakfast

Doris and Gus Beckert
3037 Foothill Boulevard
Calistoga, CA 94515
(707) 942-6933; (800) 942-6933;
FAX (701) 942-5692

Foothill House Bed and Breakfast has turndown service each evening. A jar of "Sweet Dream" cookies and Christian Bros. Cream Sherry are placed at the bedside table of each guest for a late night snack and beverage.

Tar Heel Inn

Shawna and Robert Hyde
508 Church Street, PO Box 176
Oriental, NC 28571
(919) 249-1078

We like to bake the cookies in the late afternoon, so when guests arrive for check-in the aroma is still in the house. We put a plate full of cookies in the living room for guests to enjoy upon arrival or when returning back to the Inn after their day's activities. We also have a cookie jar full in the guest pantry for late-night snacks.

Lindsay's Cookies

1/2 pound unsalted butter
1 cup each brown and white sugar
2 teaspoon vanilla extract
2 tablespoons milk
2 eggs
2 cups flour
1 teaspoon salt
1 teaspoon baking soda
1 teaspoon baking powder
2 1/2 cups old-fashioned oats
12 ounces (2 cups) semisweet chocolate chips
1 1/2 cups chopped pecans, or walnuts

Preheat oven to 350°. Cream together butter and sugars in a mixer or by hand. Add vanilla, milk, and eggs. Add flour, salt, baking soda, and baking powder to mixture and beat to combine. By hand, stir in oats, chips, and nuts. Drop onto greased cookie sheets 1 1/2 inches apart. Bake for 10-15 minutes. Let stand 1 minute, then remove to cooling racks. Makes about 4 dozen cookies.

Preacher Cookies

- 1/2 cup butter or margarine
- 2 cups sugar
- 1/2 cup milk
- 1/2 cup cocoa
- 2 cups regular oatmeal (old-fashioned), uncooked
- 1 teaspoon vanilla extract
- 1 cup nuts, pecans or walnuts
- 1 cup coconut

Combine butter, sugar, and milk in a medium saucepan; boil 3 minutes. Pour into mixing bowl. Stir in cocoa, oatmeal, vanilla, nuts, and coconut. Beat well, with wooden spoon; working quickly. Drop by spoonfuls onto waxed paper. Let cool completely. Yield: 3 dozen. Can be frozen in freezer bags.

The Breeden Inn and Carriage House

Wesley and Bonnie Park
404 East Main Street
Bennettsville, SC 29512
(803) 479-3665

Quick and easy, "Preacher Cookies" will win the hearts of chocolate lovers everytime, hands down. These make a delicious bedtime "sweet treat." Place two per person within a small Ziploc bag, and place on pillow.

Doublegate Inn Bed and Breakfast

Gary and Charlene Poston
26711 E. Welches Road
Welches, OR 97067
(503) 622-4859 (voice and FAX)

This is the recipe Grandma wished she had had. Mix the whole recipe and keep in the refrigerator, using as needed. We pack some up for our guests, and serve them hot on pretty plates with paper doilies — a great midnight snack! Makes the whole house smell wonderful!

Douglegate Inn Doublegood Cookies

3 cups brown sugar
3 cups butter
2 eggs
4 cups flour
2 tablespoons baking soda
1 tablespoon cinnamon
2 teaspoons ginger
1 teaspoon salt
2 cups nuts, chopped
3 cups chocolate chips
2 teaspoons vanilla
powdered sugar

Cream butter, brown sugar and eggs. Add combined flour, soda, salt, cinnamon, and ginger, blending well. Add nuts, chocolate chips and vanilla. Store covered in refrigerator, baking as needed. Form dough into 1 inch balls, roll in powdered sugar. Bake on greased cookie sheet at 375° for 10-12 minutes. Yields 12 dozen.

Mrs. King's Cookies

2 cups butter
2 cups brown sugar
2 cups white sugar
4 eggs
2 teaspoons vanilla
4 cups flour
2 teaspoons baking powder
2 teaspoons salt
2 teaspoons baking soda
2 cups white chocolate chips
2 cups chocolate chips
3 cups raisins
3 cups nuts
2 cups old-fashioned rolled oats
3 cups orange/almond granola mix

Blend butter, brown sugar and white sugar until creamy; add eggs and vanilla, beat until well mixed. Stir dry ingredients: flour, baking powder, salt and baking soda; then add to egg, butter, sugar mixture and beat well. Stir in remaining ingredients: chocolate chips, raisins, nuts, oats, granola mix. When well mixed, shape into golf ball size and bake on ungreased cookie sheet at 375° for 8-10 minutes or until barely golden. Best when slightly undercooked and warm from the oven. Makes lots for you, but they go fast from the tea cart here! Dough keeps well when refrigerated, and bake as needed.

Babbling Brook Inn

Helen King
1025 Laurel Street
Santa Cruz, CA 95060
(408) 427-2437; (800) 866-1131;
FAX (408) 427-2457

The foundations of the Inn date back to the 1790s when padres from the local mission built a grist mill to take advantage of the stream to grind corn. In the 19th century, a water wheel generated power for a tannery. Then a few years later, a rustic log cabin was built which remains as the heart of the inn. Most of the rooms are chalets in the garden, surrounded by pines and redwoods, cascading waterfalls, and gardens.

The English Inn

Nancy Borino
718 F Street
Port Townsend, WA 98368
(360) 385-5302; (800) 254-5302

Homemade cookies await guests' arrival! My father grew up on an apricot ranch. These are very popular with all our family and guests.

Built in 1885, this is one of the more gracious Victorian mansions in Port Townsend. A lovely garden, five sunny bedrooms, hot tub, lots of comfort, but, best of all, fresh scones for breakfast!

Oatmeal-Apricot Cookies

1/4 cup butter, softened
1/4 cup shortening
1/2 cup sugar
1/3 cup brown sugar, packed
1 egg
1/2 teaspoon vanilla
1 1/4 cups flour
1/2 teaspoon baking powder
1/2 teaspoon baking soda
1/2 teaspoon ground cinnamon
1/4 teaspoon salt
1 cup rolled oats
1/2 cup dried apricots, finely chopped
1/4 cup chopped walnuts

In a large bowl beat together butter, shortening, sugar and brown sugar. Beat in egg and vanilla. In another bowl, combine the flour, baking powder, baking soda, cinnamon and salt. Gradually add the dry ingredients to sugar mixture and beat until combined. Stir in the oats, chopped apricots and chopped walnuts. Cover the dough and chill 1 hour. Roll the dough into 1 inch balls, and place them on ungreased cookie sheets. Bake at 375° for 10-12 minutes. Cool cookies on wire rack. Makes 36 cookies.

English Toffee Cookie

1 cup butter
1 cup brown sugar (packed)
1 egg (separated)
2 cups flour
1/2 cup finely chopped pecans

Melt butter and mix in the brown sugar. Add one beaten egg yolk and mix well. Then add flour and mix; pat the mixture in a jelly roll pan. Beat the egg white and spread over the top. Sprinkle chopped pecans over beaten egg white. Bake at 350° for 30-35 minutes. Cut immediately into 48 squares.

Abriendo Inn

Kerrelyn Trent
300 W. Abriendo Avenue
Pueblo, CO 81004
(719) 544-2703; FAX (719) 542-6544

These cookies are a mainstay in the Abriendo Inn cookie jar. They are sinfully delicious and a wonderful accompaniment to a cup of tea or coffee. Best of all, they are so easy to make. This cookie keeps well if you can keep people from eating them. The recipe has been in the family for over thirty years.

Home Away From Home

E.M. Smith
122 Hillside Drive
Moab, UT 84532
(801) 259-6276

I love those who love me and those who seek me early and diligently shall find me." Proverbs 8:17. *The breakfast champions early morning prayer from the Amplified Bible.*

There are chairs, a swing, special places in the mini park backyard, to find and make a solitary place at our B&B.

The story is told of a man and his wife who after some years met in heaven. "My it is beautiful here," said the wife to her husband. "Yes," said he, and I would have been here much earlier if it hadn't been for you and those bran muffins."

Health Nut Cookies or Muffins

1 - 12 ounce can frozen apple juice (100% pure), thawed
1 cup old-fashioned oats
3 eggs
2 cups oat bran flour
1 teaspoon cinnamon
1/2 teaspoon nutmeg
1/2 teaspoon salt
1 teaspoon baking soda
1 cup chopped walnuts
1 cup sesame seeds (optional)
1/4 cup poppy seeds (optional)
1 cup diced dried fruit, fresh apples or raisins
If not sweet enough, add 1/2 cup brown sugar or honey

Cook oats 4 minutes in microwave oven with 1/2 the juice; let juice cool. Mix egg with remaining juice, rinse can with 1/4 cup water; stir, or whisk, into cooled oatmeal. Combine dry ingredients; mix well and add to oat mixture. Stir in nuts, seeds, and fruit. Bake at 350° (muffins bake for 25 minutes in greased muffin tin. Makes 18 muffins). Makes 3 dozen cookies, baked for 10 minutes on greased cookie sheet.

Crunchy Krisp Oatmeal Cookies

- 1 cup sugar
- 1 cup light brown sugar
- 1 cup butter
- 1 cup vegetable oil
- 1 teaspoon vanilla
- 1 egg
- 3 1/2 cups flour
- 1 teaspoon baking soda
- 1 teaspoon salt
- 1 teaspoon cream of tartar
- 1 1/2 cups Rice Krispies
- 1 1/2 cups oatmeal
- 1/2 cup chopped pecans

Cream the sugars, oil, and butter. Beat in egg and the vanilla. Sift dry ingredients (flour, soda, salt, and cream of tartar). Slowly add to creamed mixture. Fold in oatmeal, Rice Krispies, and pecans. Drop by teaspoonfuls onto a pan sprayed with vegetable coating spray. Bake at 350° for 12-15 minutes. Remove and cool.

Madelyn's in the Grove

Madelyn and John Hill
PO Box 298
1836 West Memorial Highway
Union Grove, NC 28689
(704) 539-4151; (800) 948-4473;
FAX (704) 539-4080
Email: mhill@i-america.net

These cookies have been family favorites for years. I serve them as snacks at night for our guests. Then as they leave they get a bag of cookies for their trip.

I sometimes add one cup butterscotch chips to the batter. Yummy!

Heritage Inn

James and Wanda Maupin
209 W. Main
Artesia, NM 88210
(505) 748-2552; (800) 594-7392;
FAX (505) 746-3407

New country/Victorian atmosphere will take you back in time and warm your heart and soul. Spacious rooms with private baths, room phones, color TV, continental breakfast, computer modem hookups for business travelers and outside patio and deck for relaxation. Very secure second floor, downtown location convenient to excellent restaurants.

Buffalo Chips

1 cup oleo
1 cup Crisco
2 cups brown sugar
2 cups white sugar
4 eggs
2 teaspoons vanilla
4 cups flour
2 teaspoons soda
2 teaspoons baking powder
2 cups quick oats
2 cups cornflake cereal
2 cups Hershey's milk chocolate chips
1 cup angel flake coconut
1 cup chopped pecans

Mix oleo and Crisco thoroughly. Cream with brown sugar, white sugar, eggs, and vanilla. Sift flour, soda, and baking powder, and add to mixture. Mix together oats, cereal, chips, coconut, and pecans, then add to mixture. Drop by large spoonfuls onto cookie sheet sprayed with PAM. Bake in 350° oven for 12 to 15 minutes.

Note: I usually make only half of this recipe, unless making for a very large crowd.

Mountain Almond Roca

- 1 pound butter
- 2 cups sugar
- 1 cup (heaping) almonds, slivered, unsalted, unblanched
- 1 pound high quality semisweet chocolate, melted at low temperature in double boiler
- 1 cup pecans, chopped

Cream butter and sugar then add almonds. Stirring constantly, cook to 290° on a candy thermometer. Watch closely to avoid cooking too long. Immediately spread out evenly on 11 1/2x17 1/2 cookie sheet. Blot any extra butter and then spread half of the pecans oven the chocolate while it is still warm so they will stick to the chocolate. When the candy is cooled and able to be turned over, spread the other side with the remaining chocolate and then remaining pecans. Cool completely and break into pieces. Makes 1 cookie sheet.

No, this is not one of our low-fat recipes! . . . but it's one of the reasons we make many of our other recipes low in fat.

Mt. Ashland Inn

Laurel and Chuck Biegert
550 Mt. Ashland Ski Road
Ashland, OR 97520
(541) 482-8707 (voice and FAX);
(800) 830-8707

This is a recipe my mother makes for the holidays every year. It is a very important part of our Christmas tradition, but you wouldn't mind eating it anytime!

Cedar Hill Farm

Russell and Gladys Swarr
305 Langenecker Road
Mount Joy, PA 17552
(717) 653-4655

This 1817 stone farmhouse overlooks a peaceful stream and was the birthplace of the host. Stroll the acreage or relax on the wicker rockers on the large front porch. Enjoy the singing of the birds and serene countryside. A winding staircase leads to the comfortable rooms, each with a private bath and centrally air-conditioned. A room for honeymooners offers a private balcony. Breakfast is served daily by a walk-in fireplace.

Cherry Crumb Squares

3/4 cup sugar
2 cups flour
1/2 teaspoon salt
1/2 cup butter or margarine
2 teaspoons baking powder
1 egg
1 can cherry pie filling

Mix sugar, flour, baking powder and salt. Cut in butter. Add egg and mix to make crumbs. Place half of crumbs in bottom of greased 13x9 pan. Pour cherries over crumbs. Top with remaining crumbs. Bake at 350° about 30 minutes. Cool slightly, cut into squares and serve warm on platter.

Holiday Raspberry-Chocolate Bars

2 1/2 cups flour
1 cup sugar
3/4 cup finely chopped pecans
1 cup butter, softened
1 egg
1 - 2 ounce jar seedless red raspberry jam
1 2/3 cups semisweet chocolate chips

Preheat oven to 350°. In a large bowl, combine flour, sugar, pecans, butter and egg; stir until crumbly. Set aside 1 1/2 cups of the pecan mixture. Press the remaining mixture into the bottom of a greased 13x9x2 inch baking pan. Spread the raspberry jam over all. Sprinkle with chocolate chips, then with the remaining crumb mixture. Bake for 40-45 minutes or until lightly browned. Cool completely in pan on wire rack; cut into bars. Makes 3 dozen bars.

Bed and Breakfast in the Pines

Reggie Ray
1940 Schneider Park Road
Lake City, MI 49651
(616) 839-4876

I like to receive my guests with warm hospitality, a cup of tea, and a treat, when they come in. The Holiday Raspberry-Chocolate Bars are served at Christmas. Other desserts are served with the seasons. A dish or raspberries is served in July. Homemade raspberry jam and apple butter are also served. Guests are welcome to pick raspberries and apples, and stroll through the garden.

Mottern's Bed and Breakfast

Jeffrey and Susan Mottern
28 East Main Street
Hummelstown, PA 17036
(Hershey area)
(717) 566-3840; FAX (717) 566-3780

These cakes are wonderful with Raspberry Tea or coffee, when served for breakfast or afternoon tea. Our guests come to visit "Chocolate USA," Hershey, PA, so the chocolate tie is obvious and they are a must for true Chocoholics! (PS: They can be made with the new lowfat baking chips, skim milk, and egg substitute, so they can be enjoyed be dieters as well.)

Chocolate-Raspberry Tea Cakes

1 1/2 cup flour
1/4 cup granulated sugar
2 teaspoons baking powder
1/2 cup (1 stick) butter or margarine, melted
1/2 cup milk
1 egg
1 cup Hershey's chocolate chips
1/3-1/2 cup seedless raspberry jam

Preheat oven to 350°. Line muffin tin with paper liners. Mix together dry ingredients. Combine wet ingredients. Stir together until just mixed. Add chocolate chips. Spoon batter into lined muffin cups until half full. Spoon in 1 teaspoon raspberry jam in each and top with remaining batter. Bake 20-25 minutes, until golden brown. Serve warm with additional jam. Serves 12.

Mor Munsen

- 2 cups butter or margarine, melted
- 4 eggs
- 2 cups sugar
- 1 teaspoon vanilla
- 2 cups flour
- 1/2 cup currants
- 1/2 cup sliced almonds

Put sugar in mixing bowl, add butter, mix well. Add eggs, mix well, then add vanilla. Lastly, add flour, mixing well. Pour into 9x13 inch greased baking pan. Sprinkle currants and almonds on top. Bake at 375° for about 1/2 hour, or until lightly brown. Cool and cut into squares. Makes about 24 squares.

The Siebeness Inn

Sue and Nils Andersen
3681 Mountain Road
Stowe, VT 05672
(802) 253-8942; (800) 426-9001;
FAX (802) 253-9232

This is a Norwegian recipe that we used to served during the holidays, until I found that guests enjoyed them for breakfast. Now it is one of the favorite items we serve in the morning with breakfast, or have out in the afternoon with lemonade or iced tea! It is a great brunch item, too.

Mistletoe Bough Bed and Breakfast

Carlice E. and Jean H. Payne
497 Hillabee Street
Alexander City, AL 35010
(205) 329-3717; FAX (205) 234-0094

Blitz Kuchen is a German cookie brought to America by Julia Hagedorn Herzfeld in 1875. Blitz Kuchens were made not only for family enjoyment, but were baked and taken to families with sickness and sorrow. The tradition has been passed down generation to generation and even today, granddaughters still bake and take Blitz Kuchens to families and special occasions just as "Grossmutter" did long ago.

Blitz Kuchen

4 eggs
1 cup butter, or margarine (2 sticks), softened
2 cups flour, sifted
1 tablespoon (or more) vanilla flavoring
1 cup sugar
1 teaspoon baking powder
2 cups pecans, finely chopped
granulated sugar and cinnamon
1 box - 10x powdered sugar

Cream softened butter and 1/4 cup sugar, beating well. Alternate adding eggs with remaining sugar. Add 1 cup flour, beating well. Mix second cup flour with baking powder, add to mixture, beating well. Add vanilla. Halve recipe, pour into 2 greased pans. Sprinkle with granulated sugar, cinnamon, and powdered sugar. Bake at 350° for 15-20 minutes, or until lightly browned. Cut into diamond shaped cookies while warm.

Apple/Plum/ Cherry Kuchen

Kuchen/Cake:

6 big apples, cut and peeled (for variation use cherry pie filling and do half of the cake as cherry streusel)
2 cups all-purpose flour
1/2 cup white sugar
1/4 pound unsalted/salted butter
2 eggs
2 teaspoons baking powder
1 teaspoon vanilla

Streusel topping:

1/4 pound unsalted/salted butter (room temperature)
1 cup all-purpose flour (approximately)
1/2 cup white sugar (approximately)

Note: depending on consistency of dough, add or take away approximate measures.

Beat butter, then eggs, then add sugar and vanilla. Slowly add flour and baking powder into your mixer. Towards the end mix by hand. Now put your dough in a large Teflon cookie sheet (grease only if not Teflon pan) and pat by hand. (Roll hands in flour if it's too sticky.) Then sprinkle your chosen fruit topping (apples, cherries, plums) on the dough. If apple topping, sprinkle with cinnamon; if plum topping sprinkle with white sugar. Now it's time to add the streusel topping. Bake at 350° for 25-35 minutes.

Wrays Lakeview Bed and Breakfast

Irma and Gord Wray
7368 L and A Road
Vernon, British Columbia
CANADA V1B 3S6
(250) 545-9821; (250) 545-9924

A dear friend gave us this recipe many years ago and we have made it in various ways for our guests and it has been well received. We serve it to our guests with tea or coffee on their arrival at our home, freshly baked.

Liberty Hill Farm

Bob and Beth Kennett
RR1, Box 158
Rochester, VT 05767
(802) 767-3926

At Liberty Hill Farm we attempt to use as much farm fresh produce as possible. Rhubarb is a welcomed sign of spring, and this is a frequently requested recipe by our guests.

Rhubarb Custard Kuchen

1 3/4 cups flour
1/2 teaspoon baking powder
1/8 teaspoon salt
3/4 cup shortening
2 eggs, beaten, divided
1 tablespoon milk
4 cups rhubarb, diced
1 1/4 cups sugar
2 tablespoons flour
1 teaspoon cinnamon
3/4 cup milk
1 teaspoon vanilla

Sift together 1 3/4 cup flour, baking powder, and salt. Cut in shortening and stir in 1 beaten egg and 1 tablespoon milk. Mix well and pat mixture into 13x9 inch pan. Place rhubarb on top of mixture. Combine sugar, 2 tablespoons flour, and cinnamon; sprinkle over rhubarb. Beat 1 egg, 3/4 cup milk and vanilla; pour oven rhubarb. Bake at 425° for 20 minutes. Reduce temperature to 375° and bake for 15 minutes more.

Gooey Lemon Piñon Bars

1 box lemon cake mix
1/2 cup butter or margarine (softened)
1 egg
1 cup toasted piñon nuts (or chopped pecans)
1 box powdered sugar
8 ounces cream cheese (softened)
2 eggs
2 teaspoons vanilla

Mix first 3 ingredients and pat into a greased and floured 9x13 inch pan. Pat up sides of pan a little and make sure corners are not too thick. Use the back of a wet spoon to smooth if needed. Sprinkle piñon nuts evenly over this. Mix together next 4 ingredients until very smooth. Pour this over crust and nuts already in pan. Bake at 350° for about 30-45 minutes. No icing needed — it's very rich. Bars will set upon cooking. Wait to cut until cool. 24 servings.

The Willows Inn

Janet and Doug Camp
NDCBU 6560 (Corner of Kit Carson Rd. and Dolan St.)
Taos, NM 87571-6223
(505) 758-2558; (800) 525-TAOS; FAX (505) 758-5445

The Willows Inn is a B&B located on a secluded acre lot just a short walk from the Taos Plaza. Listed on the National Historic Registry, the property was the home and studio of E. Martin Hennings. Hennings was a member of the revered Taos Society of Artists, the group that established Taos as an artists' colony in the 1920s. Scrumptious, full breakfasts are served family style in the dining rooms. Guests enjoy homemade snacks and beverages in the late afternoon on the flagstone courtyard in summer or by the fire in the cooler seasons. Each guest room has smooth adobe walls with kiva *fireplaces, open beam* (viga) *ceilings, and Douglas Fir floors with various decor themes which highlight cultures significant to the Taos area. The grounds and courtyards form a parklike oasis with flowers, fountains, and two of America's largest living willow trees.*

Bind It Together

Beverages and Preserves

"But my God shall supply all your need according to hls riches in glory by Christ Jesus."

Philippians 4:19

Palmer's Chart House

Don and Majean Palmer
PO Box 51
Deer Harbor, WA 98243
(360) 376-4231

Our home was the first B&B on Orcas Island (since 1975) and it boasts a magnificent water view. The 33-foot, private yacht Amante *is available to our guests for a minimal fee with skipper Don. Low-key, private, personal attention makes this B&B unique and attractive.*

Special Orange Juice

1 small can frozen orange juice
2 cans water
3 ice cubes
1/2 cup whole milk
1 tablespoon honey

Blend in blender. Serve.

Orange-Strawberry Frappé

4 cups orange juice
12-15 frozen strawberries

Blend on high speed in blender until frozen strawberries are completely chopped and juice appears frothy. Serve immediately while ice crystals are still present in the drink.

Oak Hill Manor Bed and Breakfast

Donna and Glen Rothe
401 E. Main Street
Albany, WI 53502
(608) 862-1400; FAX (608) 862-1404

Our guests step back into time in our 1908 manor home. Rich oak woodwork, gasoliers, and period furnishings are to be enjoyed. Spacious, sunny corner rooms are air-conditioned and include queen-size beds and cozy reading areas. Guests can choose a room with a fireplace, porch, or canopy bed. The garden gazebo and our spacious porch provide relaxation. Sumptuous breakfasts are served by fireside and candlelight.

Otter Creek Inn

Shelley and Randy Hansen
2536 Highway 12
Eau Claire, WI 54701
(715) 832-2945

On a brisk winter morning in snowy Wisconsin what could be more relaxing than staying snuggled deep under the covers and hearing a gentle knock announce that breakfast has been delivered to your room door?

Many guests request our homemade cocoa with their breakfast. Shelley tells how she drank this cocoa nearly every winter morning when she was a child, served with hot buttered toast for "dunking."

This is her mother's recipe with adaptations for today's kitchen.

Grandma's Hot Cocoa

1 tablespoon unsweetened powdered cocoa (not instant cocoa mix)
1/4 teaspoon vanilla extract
2 tablespoons sugar
1/8 teaspoon salt
1 cup milk
semi-sweet chocolate baking square, shaved

Place ingredients in a shaker type container with a secure lid. Shake until well combined. Place in a microwave-safe mug and microwave on high for 1 1/2 minutes. Stir well. Microwave again until hot. Top with a generous peak of whipped cream and sprinkle with shaved chocolate. For holiday flare, top with a mint leaf and cherry half!

Cranberry Juice

2 quarts boiling water
1 quart fresh cranberries
2-3 sticks of cinnamon
Juice of 2 lemons
Juice of 2 oranges
Honey, to taste

Pour cranberries into boiling water. Add cinnamon sticks and bring to boil. Simmer for 20 to 30 minutes (until berries are very mushy). Mash the berries, then cool to lukewarm. Strain juice and press the berry pulp to get out all the juice. Take out cinnamon sticks. Add the other fruit juices and honey to taste. Chill. Yield: 3 quarts.

Rhubarb Juice

2 1/2 pounds of rhubarb
2 quarts water
1 1/4 cup sugar
Juice of 2 lemons
Juice of 2 oranges
4 whole cloves

Cut rhubarb in 1 inch lengths and stew in simmering water. Strain through strainer cloth. Add sugar, lemon and orange juices, and cloves to rhubarb juice. Stir and refrigerate. Serve cold.

Bay View Farm

Helen Sawyer
337 Main Highway,
Route 132, Box 21
New Carlisle West, Quebec
CANADA G0C 1Z0
(418) 752-2725; (418) 752-6718

On the coastline of Quebec's picturesque Gaspe Peninsula, guests are welcomed into our comfortable home. Our country breakfast is complete with fresh farm, garden, and orchard produce.

George Fuller House Bed and Breakfast Inn

Cindy and Bob Cameron
148 Main Street
Essex, MA 01929
(508) 768-7766; (800) 477-0148;
FAX (508) 768-6178

Built in 1830, this handsome Federalist-style home retains much of its 19th-century charm, including Indian shutters and a captain's staircase. Three of the guest rooms have working fireplaces. Decorations include handmade quilts, braided rugs, and caned Boston rockers. A full breakfast might include such features as Cindy's French toast drizzled with brandy lemon butter. Gordon College and Gordon Conwell Seminary are close by.

Brandied Lemon Butter

1/2 cup unsalted butter
1 cup white sugar
1 tablespoon + 1 teaspoon lemon rind
2 lemons (juice of 2 lemons)
3 ounces brandy (or rum)

In a medium saucepan, melt the butter over medium heat. Blend in the sugar, stirring constantly. Stir in the grated lemon rind. Add the lemon juice and brandy. Stir until smooth. Serve with French toast. Serves 8.

Lemon-Pineapple Preserve

4 large lemons
2 1/2 quarts (2.25 l) water
1 cinnamon stick
2 cans (13 ounces) of crushed pineapple in juice
4 cups granulated or preserving sugar

Chop lemons roughly. Place them in a saucepan, adding the pips (seeds) with water and cinnamon stick. Bring to a boil, reduce the heat, and cover the pan. Simmer for 2 hours, or until the lemons are tender. Place the fruit in a fine nylon sieve (strainer) and press all the liquid out of it. Discard the pulp that remains.

Add the crushed pineapple in juice and granulated or preserving sugar; stir until the sugar have dissolved. Bring to a boil and boil hard until the preserve reaches setting point. Test for setting by putting a little of the preserve on a cold saucer. It should form a skin which wrinkles when pushed. Put preserves in sterilized jars and cover immediately with airtight lids.

Yields about four pounds.

Bay View Manor/ Manoir Bay View

Helen Sawyer
395, Route 132, Bonaventure East, PO Box 21
New Carlisle, Quebec,
CANADA G0C 1Z0
(418) 752-2725 or 6718

Comfortable, two-story, wood frame, home on the beautiful Gaspe Peninsula across the highway from the beach and beside an 18-hole golf course. The building was once a country store and rural post office. Stroll our quiet, natural beach; see nesting seabirds along the rocky cliffs; watch fishermen tend their nets and lobster traps; enjoy beautiful sunrises and sunsets; view the lighthouse beacon on the nearby point; and fall asleep to the sound of waves on the shore.

Parson's Place Bed and Breakfast

Robert and Margaret Bell
37 Leacock Road
Paradise, PA 17562
(717) 687-8529

We serve a lot of muffins and specialty breads at our B&B and are always looking for a good spread for these and to accompany our entree dishes. We have found it in this preserve, arrived at during a summer when we had cherry tomatoes by the boat load. The tang produced by the lemon and ginger "bite" is a good change from a sweeter spread and also works well with typical breakfast hot dishes and meats. Our guests say they have not had anything like it and it is relatively simple to make. I often give baby food jars of this as a take-home gift.

Cherry Tomato and Ginger Preserve

2 pounds cherry tomatoes
3 cup sugar
3 lemons
3 tablespoons crystallized ginger, cut in slivers

Wash tomatoes and place in a bowl. Cover with sugar and let stand overnight in the covered bowl. Drain off juice (I often halve the tomatoes to produce more juice). Boil this juice carefully, so as not to burn or stick, until juice will "sheet" as in making jelly. Wash and slice lemons in very thin slices. Discard seeds. Add these with ginger to the tomatoes and syrup. Cook, stirring until the mixture is thick and tomatoes are transparent. This takes about 40 minutes. Ladle into hot, sterilized jars and seal promptly.

Since this recipe produces only 6 half-pint jars, these will stay in the refrigerator until used. But if a longer storage period or a larger amount is planned, they should be processed in a boiling water bath for 10 minutes.

Taffy's Peach Chutney

- 8 large peaches, ripe but firm (to measure, 6 cups of chunks)
- 3/4 cup raisins
- 2 cups firmly packed, light brown sugar
- 3/4 cup cider vinegar
- 1/2 teaspoon salt
- 1 cup flaked coconut
- 1/2 cup chopped candied ginger
- 3/4 teaspoon Tabasco sauce
- 2 teaspoons mustard seed
- 2 small onions, chopped fine

Peel the peaches and cut into chunks. Combine with the remaining ingredients in a large saucepan. Cook over low heat, stirring frequently, until the peaches are tender and the mixture is thick, about 1 hour. Ladle the mixture into hot, sterilized jars and seal. Makes 3 pints.

1810 West Inn

Virginia White
254 N. Seymour Drive
Thomson, GA 30824
(706) 595-3156; (800) 515-1810

Virginia White has created a compound of historic buildings to house her ten-room bed and breakfast inn just thirty miles from Augusta. Georgia is known for its delicious peaches and they are plentiful in this area. So, when I was served Apple Chutney by a friend, I immediately thought of using peaches instead. The result was delicious! Guests at 1810 enjoy it on cream cheese with crackers as an appetizer, but it is equally tasty served with sliced pork or chicken. Put a spoonful on peach halves, bake until it is hot and bubbling and add to your dinner on a cool winter evening.

I make extra each summer and use for Christmas gifts.

Sincerely,

Taffy Moore

(Friend and helper at 1810)

The Country Porch Bed and Breakfast

Tom and Wendy Solomon
281 Moran Road
Hopkinton, NH 03229
(603) 746-6391

This recipe is an all-time favorite when served with popovers or rhubarb bread. Guests are impressed that the rhubarb came from our own patch and that we made the conserve — such a unique preserve.

Rhubarb Conserve

4 pounds rhubarb, cut into 1 inch pieces
2 oranges (grated rind and juice)
3/4 cup chopped walnuts
1/4 cup candied ginger, chopped
5 pounds white sugar (remove 1 cup; set aside)
1 package powdered pectin
1 pound raisins or currants

Combine rhubarb, raisins, grated rind, juice, walnuts, and ginger in a 12 quart, thick-bottomed pot. Combine the pectin with the cup of sugar. Add to the fruit. Add the remaining sugar. Mix all ingredients will. Let stand for 30 minutes. Bring to the boiling point, then simmer for 30 minutes. Pour into sterilized jars. Seal. (Optional: process in boiling water bath for 5 minutes.)

Index of Foods

A

B

INDEX OF FOODS

C

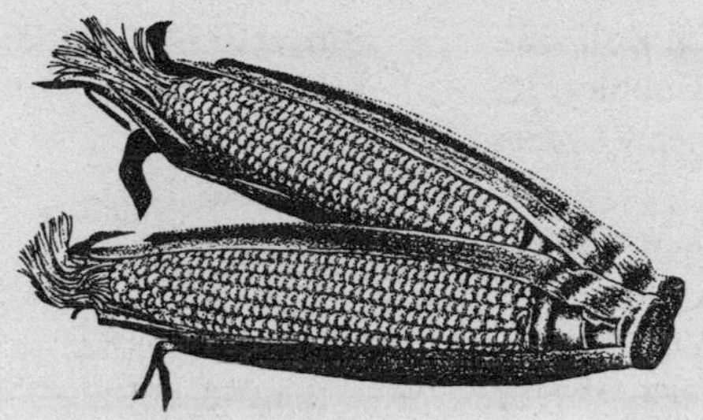

D

E

F

G

H

K

L

M

N

P

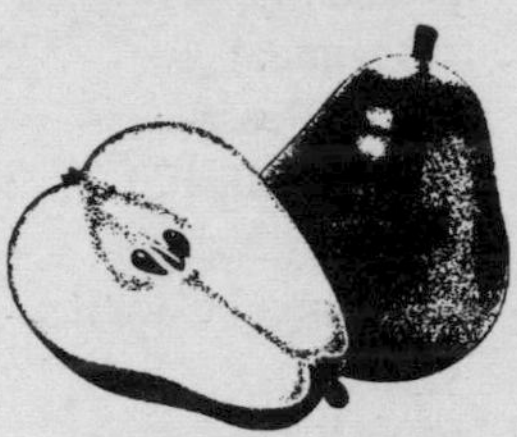

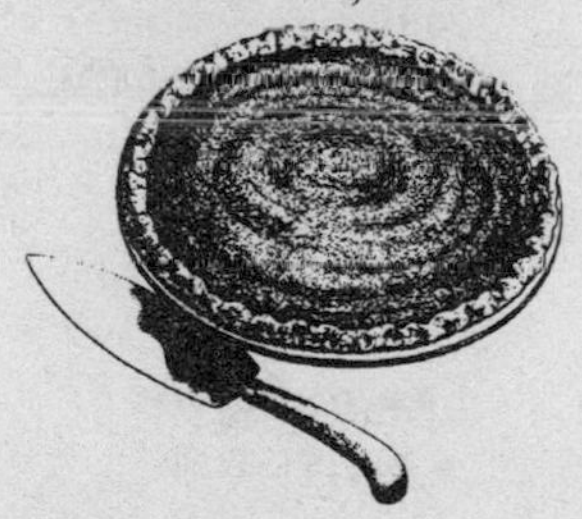

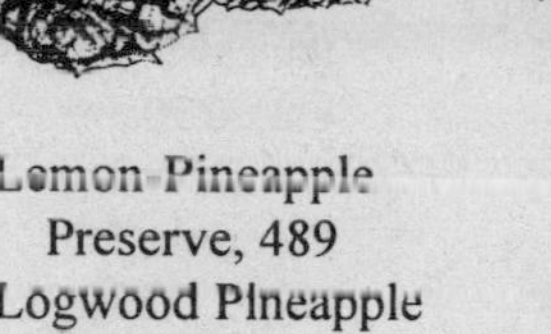

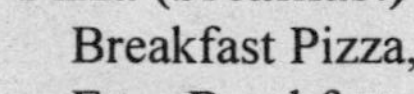

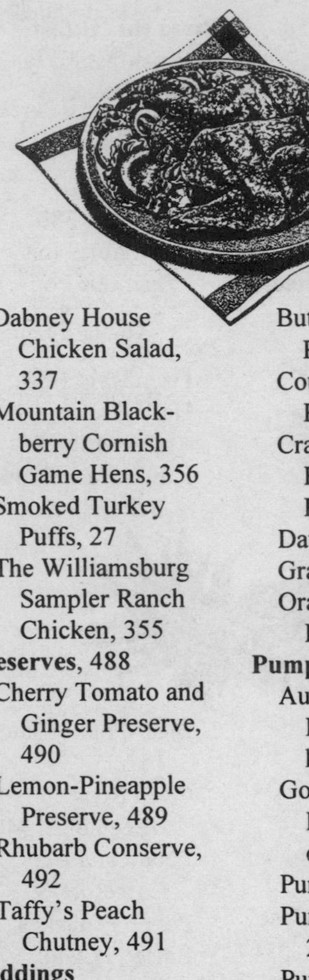

Q

R

S

V

W

Y

Z

Index
of Inns

United States

Yukon Don's B&B Inn of Wasilla, AK

The Gingerbread Mansion Inn
of Ferndale, CA

Briar Rose B&B of Boulder, CO

Timberidge B&B of Goshen, IN

The Colonial House Inn of Yarmouth Port, MA

Benson B&B of Oakland, NE

The Edge of Thyme, A B&B Inn
of Candor, NY

The 1890 Queen Anne B&B
of Sandusky, OH

Flowers & Thyme B&B of Lancaster, PA

The "B and J" B&B of Hot Springs, SD

Katy's Inn of LaConner, WA

Canada